J. B. Bury

History of the Eastern Roman Empire

e-artnow 2020

J. B. Bury

History of the Eastern Roman Empire

From the Fall of Irene to the Accession of Basil I.

e-artnow, 2020
Contact: info@e-artnow.org

ISBN 978-80-273-0650-3

Contents

Preface

The history of Byzantine civilization, in which social elements of the West and the East are so curiously blended and fused into a unique culture, will not be written for many years to come. It cannot be written until each successive epoch has been exhaustively studied and its distinguishing characteristics clearly ascertained. The fallacious assumption, once accepted as a truism, that the Byzantine spirit knew no change or shadow of turning, that the social atmosphere of the Eastern Rome was always immutably the same, has indeed been discredited; but even in recent sketches of this civilization by competent hands we can see unconscious survivals of that belief. The curve of the whole development has still to be accurately traced, and this can only be done by defining each section by means of the evidence which applies to that section alone. No other method will enable us to discriminate the series of gradual changes which transformed the Byzantium of Justinian into that-so different in a thousand ways-of the last Constantine.

This consideration has guided me in writing the present volume, which continues, but on a larger scale, my History of the Later Roman Empire from Arcadius to Irene, published more than twenty years ago, and covers a period of two generations, which may be called for the sake of convenience the Amorian epoch. I think there has been a tendency to regard this period, occurring, as it does, between the revival under the Isaurian and the territorial expansion under the Basilian sovrans, as no more than a passage from the one to the other; and I think there has been a certain failure to comprehend the significance of the Amorian dynasty. The period is not a mere epilogue, and it is much more than a prologue. It has its own distinct, coordinate place in the series of development; and I hope that this volume may help to bring into relief the fact that the Amorian age meant a new phase in Byzantine culture.

In recent years various and valuable additions have been made to the material available to the historian. Arabic and Syriac sources important for the Eastern wars have been printed and translated. Some new Greek documents, buried in MSS., have been published. Perhaps the most unexpected accessions to our knowledge concern Bulgaria, and are due to archaeological research. Pliska, the palace of the early princes, has been excavated, and a number of interesting and difficult inscriptions have come to light there and in other parts of the country. This material, published and illustrated by MM. Uspenski and Shkorpil, who conducted the Pliska diggings, has furnished new facts of great importance.

A further advance has been made, since the days when Finlay wrote, by the application of modern methods of criticism to the chronicles on which the history of this period principally depends. The pioneer work of Hirsch (Byzantinische Studien), published in 1876, is still an indispensable guide; but since then the obscure questions connected with the chronographies of George and Simeon have been more or less illuminated by the researches of various scholars, especially by de Boor's edition of George and Sreznevski's publication of the Slavonic version of Simeon. But though it is desirable to determine the mutual relations among the Simeon documents, the historian of Theophilus and Michael III is more concerned to discover the character of the sources which Simeon used. My own studies have led me to the conclusion that his narrative of those reigns is chiefly based on a lost chronicle which was written before the end of the century and was not unfavourable to the Amorian dynasty.

Much, too, has been done to elucidate perplexing historical questions by the researches of A. A. Vasiliev (to whose book on the Saracen wars of the Amorians I am greatly indebted), E. W. Brooks, the late J. Pargoire, C. de Boor, and many others. The example of a period not specially favoured may serve to illustrate the general progress of Byzantine studies during the last generation.

When he has submitted his material to the requisite critical analysis, and reconstructed a narrative accordingly, the historian has done all that he can, and his responsibility ends. When he has had before him a number of independent reports of the same events, he may hope to have elicited an approximation to the truth by a process of comparison. But how when he has only one? There are several narratives in this volume which are mainly derived from a single independent source. The usual practice in such cases is, having eliminated any errors and inconsistencies that we may have means of detecting, and having made allowances for bias, to accept the story as substantially true and accurate. The single account is assumed to be veracious when there is no counter-evidence. But is this assumption valid? Take the account of the murder of Michael III. which has come down to us. If each of the several persons who were in various ways concerned in that transaction had written down soon or even immediately afterwards a detailed report of what happened, each endeavouring honestly to describe the events accurately, it is virtually certain that there would have been endless divergencies and contradictions between these reports. Is there, then, a serious probability that the one account which happens to have been handed down, whether written by the pen or derived from the lips of a narrator of whose mentality we have no knowledge, —is there a serious probability that this story presents to our minds images at all resembling those which would appear to us if the scenes had been preserved by a cinematographic process? I have followed the usual practice-it is difficult to do otherwise; but I do not pretend to justify it. There are many portions of medieval and of ancient "recorded" history which will always remain more or less fables convenues, or for the accuracy of which, at least, no discreet person will be prepared to stand security even when scientific method has done for them all it can do.

It would not be just to the leading men who guided public affairs during this period, such as Theophilus and Bardas, to attempt to draw their portraits. The data are entirely insufficient. Even in the case of Photius, who has left a considerable literary legacy, while we can appreciate, perhaps duly, his historical significance, his personality is only half revealed; his character may be variously conceived; and the only safe course is to record his acts without presuming to know how far they were determined by personal motives.

J. B. BURY.

Rome, January 1912.

Chapter I
Nicephorus I., Stauracius, and Michael I
(A.D. 802-813)

§1. The Fall of Irene

The Isaurian or Syrian dynasty, which had not only discharged efficiently the task of defending the Roman Empire against the Saracens and Bulgarians, but had also infused new life into the administration and institutions, terminated ingloriously two years after the Imperial coronation of Charles the Great at Rome. Ambassadors of Charles were in Constantinople at the time of the revolution which hurled the Empress Irene from the throne. Their business at her court was to treat concerning a proposal of marriage from their master. It appears that the Empress entertained serious thoughts of an alliance which her advisers would hardly have suffered her to contract, and the danger may have precipitated a revolution which could not long be postponed. Few palace revolutions have been more completely justified by the exigencies of the common weal, and if personal ambitions had not sufficed to bring about the fall of Irene, public interest would have dictated the removal of a sovran whose incapacity must soon have led to public disaster.

The career of Irene of Athens had been unusually brilliant. An obscure provincial, she was elevated by a stroke of fortune to be the consort of the heir to the greatest throne in Europe. Her husband died after a short reign, and as their son was a mere child she was left in possession of the supreme power. She was thus enabled to lead the reaction against iconoclasm, and connect her name indissolubly with an Ecumenical Council. By this policy she covered herself with glory in the eyes of orthodox posterity; she received the eulogies of popes; and the monks, who basked in the light of her countenance, extolled her as a saint. We have no records that would enable us to draw a portrait of Irene's mind, but we know that she was the most worldly of women, and that love of power was a fundamental trait of her character. When her son Constantine was old enough to assume the reins of government, she was reluctant to retire into the background, and a struggle for power ensued, which ended ultimately in the victory of the mother. The son, deprived of his eyesight, was rendered incapable of reigning (a.d. 797), and Irene enjoyed for five years undivided sovran power, not as a regent, but in her own right.

Extreme measures of ambition which, if adopted by heretics, they would execrate as crimes, are easily pardoned or overlooked by monks In the case of a monarch who believes rightly; But even in the narrative of the prejudiced monk, who is our informant, we can see that he himself disapproved of the behavior of the "most pious" Irene, and, what is more important, that the public sympathy was with her son. Her conduct of the government did not secure her the respect which her previous actions had forfeited. She was under the alternating influence of two favorite eunuchs, whose intrigues against each other divided the court. After the death of Stauracius, his rival Aetius enjoyed the supreme control of the Empress and the Empire. He may have been a capable man; but his position was precarious, his power was resented by the other ministers of state, and, in such circumstances, the policy of the Empire could not be efficiently carried on. He united in his own hands the commands of two of the Asiatic Themes, the Opsikian and the Anatolic, and he made his brother Leo strategos of both Macedonia and Thrace. By the control of the troops of these provinces he hoped to compass his scheme of raising Leo to the Imperial throne.

We can hardly doubt that the political object of mitigating her unpopularity in the capital was the motive of certain measures of relief or favour which the Empress adopted in March 801. She remitted the "urban tribute", the principal tax paid by the inhabitants of Constantinople, but we are unable to say whether this indulgence was intended to be temporary or permanent. She lightened the custom dues which were collected in the Hellespont and the Bosphorus. We may question the need and suspect the wisdom of either of these measures; but a better case could probably be made out for the abolition of the duty on receipts. This tax, similar to the notorious Chrysargyron which Anastasius I did away with, was from the conditions of its collection especially liable to abuse, and it was difficult for the fisc to check the honesty of the excise officers who gathered it. We have a lurid picture of the hardships which it entailed. Tradesmen of every order were groaning under extravagant exactions. Sheep-dealers and pig-dealers, butchers, wine-merchants, weavers and shoemakers, fullers, bronzesmiths, goldsmiths, workers in wood, perfumers, architects are enumerated as sufferers. The high-roads and the sea-coasts were infested by fiscal officers demanding dues on the most insignificant articles. When a traveller came to some narrow defile, he would be startled by the sudden appearance of a tax-gatherer, sitting aloft like a thing uncanny. The fisherman who caught three fishes, barely enough to support him, was obliged to surrender one to the necessities of the treasury, or rather of its representative. Those who made their livelihood by catching or shooting birds were in the same predicament. It is needless to say that all the proceeds of these exactions did not flow into the fisc; there was unlimited opportunity for peculation and oppression on the part of the collectors.

We learn that Irene abolished this harsh and impolitic system from a congratulatory letter addressed to her on the occasion by Theodore, the abbot of Studion. We must remember that the writer was an ardent partisan of the Empress, whom he lauds in hyperbolic phrases, according to the manner of the age, and we may reasonably suspect that he has overdrawn the abuses which she remedied in order to exalt the merit of her reform.

The monks of Studion, driven from their cloister by her son, had been restored with high honor by Irene, and we may believe that they were the most devoted of her supporters. The letter which Theodore addressed to her on this occasion shows that in his eyes her offences against humanity counted as nothing, if set against her services to orthodoxy and canonical law. It is characteristic of medieval Christianity that one who made such high professions of respect for Christian ethics should extol the "virtue" of the woman who had blinded her son, and assert that her virtue has made her government popular and will preserve it unshaken.

Even if Irene's capacity for ruling had equalled her appetite for power, and if the reverence which the monks entertained for her had been universal, her sex was a weak point in her position. Other women had governed-Pulcheria, for instance-in the name of an Emperor; but Irene was the first who had reigned alone, not as a regent, but as sole and supreme autocrat. This was an innovation against which no constitutional objection seems to have been urged or recognized as valid at Constantinople; though in Western Europe it was said that the Roman Empire could not devolve upon a woman, and this principle was alleged as an argument justifying the coronation of Charles the Great. But in the army there was undoubtedly a feeling of dissatisfaction that the sovran was disqualified by her sex from leading her hosts in war; and as the spirit of iconoclasm was still prevalent in the army, especially in the powerful Asiatic Themes, there was no inclination to waive this objection in the case of the restorer of image-worship.

The power exercised by the eunuch Aetius was intolerable to many of the magnates who held high offices of state, and they had good reason to argue that in the interests of the Empire, placed as it was between two formidable foes, a stronger government than that of a favourite who wielded authority at the caprice of a woman was imperatively required. The negotiations of the Empress with Charles the Great, and the arrival of ambassadors from him and the Pope, to discuss a marriage between the two monarchs which should restore in Eastern and Western Europe the political unity of the Roman Empire once more, were equally distasteful and alarming to Aetius and to his opponents. The overtures of Charles may well have impressed the patricians of New Rome with the danger of the existing situation and with the urgent need that the Empire should have a strong sovran to maintain its rights and prestige against the pretensions of the Western barbarian who claimed to be a true Augustus. It might also be foreseen that Aetius would now move heaven and earth to secure the elevation of his brother to the throne as speedily as possible.

These circumstances may sufficiently explain the fact that the discontent of the leading officials with Irene's government culminated in October 802, while the Western ambassadors were still in Constantinople. The leader of the conspiracy was Nicephorus, who held the post of Logothete of the General Treasury, and he was recognized by his accomplices as the man who should succeed to the Imperial crown. His two chief supporters were Nicetas Triphyllios, the Domestic of the scholarian guards, and his brother Leo, who had formerly been strategos of Thrace. The cooperation of these men was highly important; for Aetius counted upon their loyalty, as Nicetas had espoused his part against his rival Stauracius. Leo, who held the high financial office of Sakellarios, and the quaestor Theoktistos joined in the plot, and several other patricians.

On the night of October 31 the conspirators appeared before the Brazen Gate (Chalkê) of the Palace, and induced the guard to admit them, by a story which certainly bore little appearance of likelihood. They said that Aetius had been attempting to force the Empress to elevate his brother to the rank of Augustus, and that she, in order to obviate his importunities, had dispatched the patricians at this late hour to proclaim Nicephorus as Emperor. The authority of such important men could hardly be resisted by the guardians of the gate, and in obedience to the supposed command of their sovran they joined in proclaiming the usurper. It was not yet midnight. Slaves and others were sent to all quarters of the city to spread the news, and the Palace of Eleutherios, in which the Augusta was then staying, was surrounded by soldiers. This Palace, which she had built herself, was probably situated to the north of the harbour of Eleutherios, somewhere in the vicinity of the Forum which was known as Bous. In the morning she was removed to the Great Palace and detained in custody, while the ceremony of coronation was performed for Nicephorus by the Patriarch Tarasius, in the presence of a large multitude, who beheld the spectacle with various emotions.

The writer from whom we learn these events was a monk, violently hostile to the new Emperor, and devoted to the orthodox Irene, who had testified so brilliantly to the "true faith". We must not forget his bias when we read that all the spectators were imprecating curses on the Patriarch, and on the Emperor and his well-wishers. Some, he says, marvelled how Providence could permit such an event and see the pious Empress deserted by those courtiers who had professed to be most attached to her, like the brothers Triphyllios. Others, unable to believe the evidence of their eyes, thought they were dreaming. Those who took in the situation were contrasting in prophetic fancy the days that were coming with the blessed condition of things which existed under Irene. This description represents the attitude of the monks and the large number of people who were under their influence. But we may well believe that the populace showed no enthusiasm at the revolution; Nicephorus can hardly have been a popular minister.

The new Emperor determined, as a matter of course, to send the deposed Empress into banishment, but she possessed a secret which it was important for him to discover. The economy of Leo III. and Constantine V. had accumulated a large treasure, which was stored away in some secret hiding-place, known only to the sovran, and not communicated to the Sakellarios, who was head of the treasury. Nicephorus knew of its existence, and on the day after his coronation he had an interview with Irene in the Palace, and by promises and blandishments persuaded her to reveal where the store was hidden. Irene on this occasion made a dignified speech, explaining her fall as a punishment of her sins, and asking to be allowed to live in her own house of Eleutherios. Nicephorus, however, banished her first to Prince's Island in the Propontis, and afterwards to more distant Lesbos, where she died within a year. We cannot accept unhesitatingly the assertion of the Greek chronographer that Nicephorus broke his faith. There is some evidence, adequate at least to make us suspicious, that he kept his promise, and that Irene was not banished until she or her partisans organized a conspiracy against his life.

§2. Nicephorus I.

According to Oriental historians, Nicephorus was descended from an Arabian king, Jaballah of Ghassan, who in the reign of Heraclius became a Mohammadan, but soon, dissatisfied with the principle of equality which marked the early period of the Caliphate, fled to Cappadocia and resumed the profession of Christianity along with allegiance to the Empire. Perhaps Jaballah or one of his descendants settled in Pisidia, for Nicephorus was born in Seleucia of that province. His fame has suffered, because he had neither a fair historian to do him justice, nor apologists to countervail the coloured statements of opponents. He is described as an unblushing hypocrite, avaricious, cruel, irreligious, unchaste, a perjured slave, a wicked revolutionary. His every act is painted as a crime or a weakness, or as prompted by a sinister motive. When we omit the adjectives and the comments and set down the facts, we come to a different conclusion. The history of his reign shows him a strong and masterful man, who was fully alive to the difficulties of the task of governing and was prepared to incur unpopularity in discharging his duty as guardian of the state. Like many other competent statesmen, he knew how to play upon the weaknesses of men and to conceal his own designs; he seems indeed to have been expert in dissimulation and the cognate arts of diplomacy. It was said that tears came with convenient readiness, enabling him to feign emotions which he was far from feeling and win a false reputation for having a good heart.

Most of the able Roman Emperors who were not born in the purple had been generals before they ascended the throne. Nicephorus, who had been a financial minister, was one of the most notable exceptions. It is probable that he had received a military training, for he led armies into the field. He was thoroughly in earnest about the defence of the Empire against its foes, whether beyond the Taurus or beyond the Haemus; but he had not the qualities of a skillful general and this deficiency led to the premature end of his reign. Yet his financial experience may have been of more solid value to the state than the military talent which might have achieved some brilliant successes. He was fully determined to be master in his own house. He intended that the Empire, the Church as well as the State, should be completely under his control, and would brook no rival authorities, whether in the court or in the cloister. He severely criticized his predecessors, asserting that they had no idea of the true methods of government. If a sovran, he used to say, wishes to rule efficiently, he must permit no one to be more powerful than himself,—a sound doctrine under the constitution of the Roman Empire. The principles of his ecclesiastical policy, which rendered him execrable in the eyes of many monks, were religious toleration and the supremacy of the State over the Church. Detested by the monks on this account, he has been represented by one of them, who is our principal informant, as a tyrannical oppressor who imposed intolerable burdens of taxation upon his subjects from purely avaricious motives. Some of his financial measures may have been severe, but our ignorance of the economic conditions of the time and our imperfect knowledge of the measures themselves render it difficult for us to criticize them.

In pursuance of his conception of the sovran's duty, to take an active part in the administration himself and keep its various departments under his own control, Nicephorus resolved to exercise more constantly and regularly the supreme judicial functions which belonged to the Emperor. His immediate predecessors had probably seldom attended in person the Imperial Court of Appeal, over which the Prefect of the City presided in the Emperor's absence; but hitherto it had been only in the case of appeals, or in those trials of high functionaries which were reserved for his Court, that the sovran intervened in the administration of justice. Nicephorus instituted a new court which sat in the Palace of Magnaura. Here he used to preside himself and judge cases which ordinarily came before the Prefect of the City or the Quaestor. It was his purpose, he alleged, to enable the poor to obtain justice speedily and easily. It is instructive to observe how this innovation was construed and censured by his enemies. It was said that his motive was to insult and oppress the official classes, or that the encouragement of lawsuits was designed to divert the attention of his subjects from Imperial "impieties". The malevolence of these insinuations is manifest. Nicephorus was solicitous to protect his subjects against official oppression, and all Emperors who took an active personal part in the administration of justice were highly respected and praised by the public.

Not long after Nicephorus ascended the throne he was menaced by a serious insurrection. He had appointed an able general, Bardanes Turcus, to an exceptionally extensive command, embracing the Anatolic, the Armeniac, and the three other Asiatic Themes. The appointment was evidently made with the object of prosecuting vigorously the war against the Saracens, in which Bardanes had distinguished himself, and won popularity with the soldiers by his scrupulously fair division of booty, in which he showed himself no respecter of persons. He was, as his name shows, an Armenian by descent, but we are not told whence he derived the surname of "Turk". The large powers which were entrusted to him stirred his ambitions to seize the crown, and the fiscal rigour of the new Emperor excited sufficient discontent to secure followers for a usurper. The Armeniac troops refused to support him, but the regiments of the other four Themes which were under his command proclaimed him Emperor on Wednesday, July 19, 803.

This revolt of Bardanes has a dramatic interest beyond the immediate circumstances. It was the first act in a long and curious drama which was worked out in the course of twenty years. We shall see the various stages of its development in due order. The contemporaries of the actors grasped the dramatic aspect, and the interest was heightened by the belief that the events had been prophetically foreshadowed from the beginning. In the staff of Bardanes were three young men who enjoyed his conspicuous favour. Leo was of Armenian origin, like the general himself, but had been reared at a small place called Pidra in the Anatolic Theme. Bardanes had selected him for his fierce look and brave temper to be a "spear-bearer and attendant" or, as we should say, an aide-de-camp. Michael, who was known as Traulos, on account of his lisp, was a native of Amorion. The third, Thomas, probably came of a Slavonic family settled in Pontus near Gaziura. All three were of humble origin, but Bardanes detected that they were marked out by nature for great things and advanced them at the very beginning of their careers. When he determined to raise the standard of rebellion against Nicephorus, he took these three chosen ones into his confidence, and they accompanied him when he rode one day to Philomelion for the purpose of consulting a hermit said to be endowed with the faculty of foreseeing things to come. Leaving his horse to the care of his squires, Bardanes entered the prophet's cell, where he received a discouraging oracle. He was bidden to abandon his designs, which would surely lead to the loss of his property and of his eyes. He left the hermit's dwelling moody and despondent, and he was mounting his horse when the holy man, who had followed to the door and espied his three companions, summoned him to return. Eagerly expecting a further communication Bardanes complied, and he heard a strange prophecy: "The first and the second of these men will possess the Empire, but thou shalt not. As for the third, he will be merely proclaimed, but will not prosper and will have a bad end". The disappointed aspirant to the throne rushed from the hut, uttering maledictions against the prophet who refused to flatter his hopes, and jeeringly communicated to Leo, Michael, and Thomas the things which were said to be in store for them. Thus, according to the story, the destinies of the two Emperors Leo V. and Michael II. and of the great tyrant Thomas were shadowed forth at Philomelion long before it could be guessed how such things were to come to pass.

The destiny of their patron Bardanes was to be decided far sooner. The insurgent army advanced along the road to Nicomedia, but it was soon discovered that the Emperor was prepared for the emergency and had forces at his disposition which rendered the cause of the tyrant hopeless. Thomas, the Slavonian, stood by his master; but Leo, the Armenian, and Michael, of Amorion, deserted to Nicephorus, who duly rewarded them. Michael was appointed a Count of the tent, Leo to be Count of the Federates, and each of them received the gift of a house in Constantinople. When Bardanes found it impracticable to establish on the Asiatic shore a basis of operations against the capital, of which the inhabitants showed no inclination to welcome him, he concluded that his wisest course would be to sue for grace while there was yet time, and he retired to Malagina. The Emperor readily sent him a written assurance of his personal safety, which was signed by the Patriarch Tarasius and all the patricians; and the promise was confirmed by the pledge of a little gold cross which the Emperor was in the habit of wearing. The tyranny had lasted about seven weeks, when Bardanes secretly left the camp at midnight (September 8) and travelling doubtless by the road which passes Nicaea and skirts the southern shores of Lake Ascanias, escaped to the monastery of Heraclius at Kios, the modern town of Geumlek. There he was tonsured and arrayed in the lowly garment of a monk. The Emperor's bark, which was in waiting at the shore, carried him to the island of Prote, where he had built a private monastery, which he was now permitted to select as his retreat. Under the name of Sabbas, he devoted himself to ascetic exercises. But Nicephorus, it would seem, did not yet feel assured that the ex-tyrant was innocuous; for we can hardly doubt the assertion of our sources that it was with the Emperor's knowledge that a band of Lycaonians landed on the island by night and deprived the exiled monk of his eyesight. Nicephorus, however, professed to be sorely distressed at the occurrence; he shed the tears which were always at his disposal, and did not leave the Imperial bedchamber for seven days. He even threatened to put to death some Lycaonian nobles; and the Senate and the Patriarch could hardly venture to doubt the sincerity of his indignation. As for the rebellious army, it was punished by receiving no pay; several officers and landed owners were banished; the property of the chief insurgent was confiscated. Such was the fate of Bardanes Turcus and his revolt.

In February 808 a plot was formed to dethrone Nicephorus by a large number of discontented senators and ecclesiastical dignitaries. It is significant that the man who was designated by the conspirators to be the new Emperor was on this occasion also an Armenian. The patrician Arsaber held the office of Quaestor; and the chronicler, who regarded with favour any antagonist of Nicephorus, describes him as pious. The plot was detected; Arsaber was punished by stripes, made a monk and banished to Bithynia; the accomplices, not excepting the bishops, were beaten and exiled.

Nicephorus had two children, a daughter and a son. Procopia had married Michael Rangabé, who was created Curopalates; and one of their sons, Nicetas (destined hereafter to occupy the Patriarchal throne), was appointed, as a child, to be the Domestic or commander of the Hikanatoi, a new corps of guards which his grandfather had instituted. Stauracius was doubtless younger than Procopia, and was crowned Augustus in December 803, a year after his father's succession. Theophanes, perhaps malevolently, describes him as "physically and intellectually unfit for the position". His father took pains to choose a suitable wife for him. On December 20, 807, a company of young girls from all parts of the Empire was assembled in the Palace, to select a consort for Stauracius. For a third time in the history of New Rome an Athenian lady was chosen to be the bride of a Roman Augustus. The choice of Nicephorus now fell on Theophano, even as Constantine V had selected Irene for his son Leo, and nearly four centuries before Pulcheria had discovered Athenais for her brother Theodosius. Theophano had two advantages: she was a kinswoman of the late Empress Irene; and she had already (report said) enjoyed the embraces of a man to whom she was betrothed. The second circumstance gave Nicephorus an opportunity of asserting the principle that the Emperor was not bound by the canonical laws which interdicted such a union.

If a statement of Theophanes is true, which we have no means of disproving and no reason to doubt, the beauty of the maidens who had presented themselves as possible brides for the son, tempted the desires of the father; and two, who were more lovely than the successful Athenian, were consoled for their disappointment by the gallantries of Nicephorus himself on the night of his son's marriage. The monk who records this scandal of the Imperial Palace makes no other comment than "the rascal was ridiculed by all".

The frontiers of the Empire were maintained intact in the reign of Nicephorus, but his campaigns were not crowned by military glory. The death of the Caliph Harun (809) delivered him from a persevering foe against whom he had been generally unsuccessful, and to whom he had been forced to make some humiliating concessions; but the Bulgarian war brought deeper disgrace upon Roman arms and was fatal to Nicephorus himself. In an expedition which, accompanied by his son and his son-in-law, he led across the Haemus, he suffered himself to be entrapped, and his life paid the penalty for his want of caution (July 26, a.d. 811).

§3. Stauracius

The young Emperor Stauracius had been severely wounded in the battle, but he succeeded in escaping to the shelter of Hadrianople. His sister's husband, Michael Rangabé, had come off unhurt; and two other high dignitaries, the magister Theoktistos, and Stephanos the Domestic of the Schools, reached the city of refuge along with the surviving Augustus. But although Stauracius was still living, it was a question whether he could live long. His spine had been seriously injured, and the nobles who stood at his bedside despaired of his life. They could hardly avoid considering the question whether it would be wise at such a crisis to leave the sole Imperial power in the hands of one who had never shown any marked ability and who was now incapacitated by a wound, seemingly at the door of death. On the other hand, it might be said that the unanimity and prompt action which the emergency demanded would be better secured by acknowledging the legitimate Emperor, however feeble he might be. So at least it seemed to the Domestic of the Schools, who lost no time in proclaiming Stauracius autocrator. Stauracius himself, notwithstanding his weak condition, appeared in the presence of the troops who had collected at Hadrianople after the disaster, and spoke to them. The soldiers had been disgusted by the unskillfulness of the late Emperor in the art of war, and it is said that the new Emperor sought to please them by indulging in criticisms on his father.

But the magister Theoktistos, although he was present on this occasion, would have preferred another in the place of Stauracius. And there was one who had a certain eventual claim to the crown, and might be supposed not unequal to its burdens, Michael Rangabé, the Curopalates and husband of the princess Procopia. It would not have been a violent measure if, in view of the precarious condition of her brother, Procopia's husband had been immediately invested with the insignia of empire. Such a course could have been abundantly justified by the necessity of having an Emperor capable of meeting the dangers to be apprehended from the triumphant Bulgarian foe. Theoktistos and others pressed Michael to assume the diadem, and if he had been willing Stauracius would not have reigned a week. But Michael declined at this juncture, and the orthodox historian, who admires and lauds him, attributes his refusal to a regard for his oath of allegiance "to Nicephorus and Stauracius".

The wounded Emperor was removed in a litter from Hadrianople to Byzantium. The description of the consequence of his hurt shows that he must have suffered much physical agony and the chances of his recovery were diminished by his mental anxieties. He had no children, and the question was, who was to succeed him. On the one hand, his sister Procopia held that the Imperial power rightly devolved upon her husband and her children. On the other hand, there was another lady, perhaps even more ambitious than Procopia, and dearer to Stauracius. The Athenian Theophano might hope to play the part of her kinswoman Irene, and reign as sole mistress of the Roman Empire.

Concerning the intrigues which were spun round the bedside of the young Emperor in the autumn months (August and September) of 811, our contemporary chronicle gives only a slight indication. The influence of Theophano caused her husband to show marked displeasure to the ministers Stephanos and Theoktistos, and to his brother-in-law Michael, and also to regard with aversion his sister Procopia, whom he suspected of conspiring against his life. As his condition grew worse and he saw that his days were numbered, he wavered between two alternative plans for the future of the Empire. One of these was to devolve the succession on his wife Theophano.

The other alternative conceived by Stauracius is so strange that we hardly know what to make of it. The idea comes to us as a surprise in the pages of a ninth-century chronicle. It appears that this Emperor, as he felt death approaching, formed the conception of changing the Imperial constitution into a democracy. It was the wild vision of a morbid brain, but we cannot help wondering how Stauracius would have proceeded in attempting to carry out such a scheme. Abstractly, indeed, so far as the constitutional aspect was concerned, it would have been simple enough. The Imperial constitution might be abolished and a democratic republic established, in theory, by a single measure. All that he had to do was to repeal a forgotten law, which had regulated the authority of the early Caesars, and thereby restore to the Roman people the powers which it had delegated to the Imperator more than seven hundred years before. Of the Lex de imperio Stauracius had probably never heard, nor is it likely that he had much knowledge of the early constitutional history of Rome. Perhaps it was from ancient Athens that he derived the political idea which, in the circumstances of his age, was a chimera; and to his wife, thirsty for power, he might have said, "Athens, your own city, has taught the world that democracy is the best and noblest form of government".

The intervention of the Patriarch Nicephorus at this juncture helped to determine and secure the progress of events. He was doubtless relieved at the death of his stark namesake, however much he may have been distressed at the calamity which brought it about; and we are told that, when Stauracius arrived at Constantinople, the Patriarch hastened to give him ghostly advice and exhort him to console those who had been pecuniarily wronged by his father, by making restitution. But like his sire, according to the partial chronicler, Stauracius was avaricious, and was unwilling to sacrifice more than three talents in this cause, although that sum was but a small fraction of the monies wrongfully appropriated by the late Emperor. The Patriarch failed in his errand at the bedside of the doomed monarch, but he hoped that a new Emperor, of no doubtful voice in matters of orthodoxy, would soon sit upon the throne. And it appeared that it would be necessary to take instant measures for securing the succession to this legitimate and desirable candidate. The strange designs of Stauracius and the ambition of Theophano alarmed Nicephorus, and he determined to prevent all danger of a democracy or a sovran Augusta by anticipating the death of the Emperor and placing Michael on the throne. At the end of September he associated himself, for this purpose, with Stephanos and Theoktistos. The Emperor was already contemplating the cruelty of depriving his brother-in-law of eyesight, and on the first day of October he summoned the Domestic of the Schools to his presence and proposed to blind Michael that very night. It is clear that at this time Stauracius placed his entire trust in Stephanos, the man who had proclaimed him at Hadrianople, and he knew not that this officer had since then veered round to the view of Theoktistos. Stephanos pointed out that it was too late, and took care to encourage his master in a feeling of security. The next day had been fixed by the conspirators for the elevation of the Curopalates, and throughout the night troops were filing into the Hippodrome to shout for the new Emperor. In the early morning the senators arrived; and the constitutional formalities of election preliminary to the coronation were complied with (Oct. 2, A.D. 811). Michael Rangabé was proclaimed "Emperor of the Romans" by the Senate and the residential troops-that remnant of them which had escaped from the field of blood beyond the Haemus. Meanwhile the Emperor, who had been less lucky on that fatal day, escaping only to die after some months of pain, was sleeping or tossing in the Imperial bedchamber, unconscious of the scene which was being enacted not many yards away. But the message was soon conveyed to his ears, and he hastened to assume the visible signs of abdication by which deposed Emperors were wont to disarm the fears or jealousy of their successors. A monk, named Simeon, and a kinsman of his own, tonsured him and arrayed him in monastic garb, and he prepared to spend the few days of life left to him in a lowlier place and a lowlier station. But before his removal from the Palace his sister Procopia, in company with her Imperial husband and the Patriarch Nicephorus, visited him. They endeavored to console him and to justify the step which had been taken; they repudiated the charge of a conspiracy, and explained their act as solely necessitated by his hopeless condition. Stauracius, notwithstanding their plausible arguments, felt bitter; he thought that the Patriarch had dealt doubly with him. "You will not find", he said to Nicephorus, "a better friend than me".

Nicephorus took the precaution of requiring from Michael, before he performed the ceremony of coronation, a written assurance of his orthodoxy and an undertaking to do no violence to ecclesiastics, secular or regular. The usual procession was formed; the Imperial train proceeded from the Palace to the Cathedral; and the act of coronation was duly accomplished in the presence of the people. The rejoicings, we are told, were universal, and we may believe that there was a widespread feeling of relief, that an Emperor sound in limb was again at the head of the state. The bounty of Michael gave cause, too, for satisfaction on the first day of his reign. He bestowed on the Patriarch, who had done so much in helping him to the throne, the sum of 50 lbs. of gold ($ 952.140), and to the clergy of St. Sophia he gave half that amount.

The unfortunate Stauracius lived on for more than three months, but towards the end of that time the corruption of his wound became so horrible that no one could approach him for the stench. On the 11th of January 812 he died, and was buried in the new monastery of Braka. This was a handsome building, given to Theophano by the generosity of Procopia when she resolved, like her husband, to retire to a cloister.

§4. Reign and Policy of Michael I.

It is worthwhile to note how old traditions or prejudices, surviving from the past history of the Roman Empire, gradually disappeared. We might illustrate the change that had come over the "Romans" since the age of Justinian, by the fact that in the second year of the ninth century a man of Semitic stock ascends the throne, and is only prevented by chance from founding a dynasty, descended from the Ghassanids. He bears a name, too, which, though Greek and common at the time, was borne by no Emperor before him. His son's name is Greek too, but unique on the Imperial list. A hundred years before men who had names which sounded strange in collocation with Basileus and Augustus (such as Artemius and Apsimar) adopted new names which had an Imperial ring (such as Anastasius and Tiberius). It was instinctively felt then that a Bardanes was no fit person to occupy the throne of the Caesars, and therefore he became Philippicus. But this instinct was becoming weak in a city where strange names, strange faces, and strange tongues were growing every year more familiar. The time had come when men of Armenian, Slavonic, or even Semitic origin might aspire to the highest positions in Church and State, to the Patriarchate and the Empire. The time had come at last when it was no longer deemed strange that a successor of Constantine should be a Michael.

The first Michael belonged to the Rangabé family, of which we now hear for the first time. He was in the prime of manhood when he came to the throne; his hair was black and curling, he wore a black beard, and his face was round. He seems to have been a mild and good-humoured man, but totally unfit for the position to which chance had raised him. As a general he was incapable; as an administrator he was injudicious; as a financier he was extravagant. Throughout his short reign he was subject to the will of a woman and the guidance of a priest. It may have been the ambition of Procopia that led him to undertake the duties of a sovran; and she shared largely in the administration. Ten days after her lord's coronation, Procopia-daughter and sister, now wife, of an Emperor-was crowned Augusta in the throne-room of Augusteus, in the Palace of Daphne, and she courted the favour of the Senators by bestowing on them many gifts. She distributed, moreover, five pounds of gold ($ 95000) among the widows of the soldiers who had fallen with her father in Bulgaria. Nor did she forget her sister-in-law, who, if things had fallen out otherwise, might have been her sovran lady. Theophano had decided to end her life as a nun. Her triumphant rival enriched her, and, as has been already mentioned, gave her a noble house, which was converted into a cloister. Nor were the poor kinsfolk of Theophano neglected by the new Augusta. It was said at least that in the days of Nicephorus they had lived in pitiable penury, as that parsimonious Emperor would not allow his daughter-in-law to expend money in assisting them; but this may be only an ill-natured invention.

The following Christmas day was the occasion of another coronation and distribution of presents. Theophylactus, the eldest son of Michael, was crowned in the ambo of the Great Church. On this auspicious day the Emperor placed in the Sanctuary of St. Sophia a rich offering of golden vessels, inlaid with gems, and antique curtains for the ciborium, woven of gold and purple and embroidered with pictures of sacred subjects. It was a day of great rejoicing in the city, and people surely thought that the new sovran was beginning his reign well; he had made up his mind to ask for his son the hand of a daughter of the great Charles, the rival Emperor.

The note of Michael's policy was reaction, both against the ecclesiastical policy of Nicephorus, as we shall see, and also against the parsimony and careful book-keeping which had rendered that monarch highly unpopular. Procopia and Michael hastened to diminish the sums which Nicephorus had hoarded, and much money was scattered abroad in alms. Churches and monasteries were enriched and endowed; hermits who spent useless lives in desert places were sought out to receive of the august bounty; religious hostelries and houses for the poor were not forgotten. The orphan and the widow had their wants supplied; and the fortunes of decayed gentle people were partially resuscitated. All this liberality made the new lord and lady highly popular; complimentary songs were composed by the demes and sung in public in their honor. The stinginess and avarice of Nicephorus were now blotted out, and amid the general jubilation few apprehended that the unpopular father-in-law was a far abler ruler than his bountiful successor.

It was naturally part of the reactionary policy to recall those whom Nicephorus had banished and reinstate those whom he had degraded. The most eminent of those who returned was Leo the Armenian, son of Bardas. We have met this man before. We saw how he took part in the revolt of Bardanes against Nicephorus, and then, along with his companion in arms, Michael the Amorian, left his rebellious commander in the lurch. We saw how Nicephorus rewarded him by making him Count of the Federates. He subsequently received a command in the Anatolic Theme, but for gross carelessness and neglect of his duties he was degraded from his post, whipped, and banished in disgrace. He was recalled by Michael, who appointed him General of the Anatolic Theme, with the dignity of Patrician-little guessing that he was arming one who would dethrone himself and deal ruthlessly with his children. Afterwards when the General of the Anatolics had become Emperor of the Romans, it was said that signs and predictions of the event were not wanting. Among the tales that were told was one of a little slave-girl of the Emperor, who was subject to visitations of "the spirit of Pytho". On one occasion when she was thus seized she went down from the Palace to the seashore below, near the harbour of Bucoleon, and cried with a loud voice, addressing the Emperor, "Come down, come down, resign what is not thine!". These words she repeated again and again. The attention of those in the Palace above was attracted; the Emperor heard the fatal cry, and attempted to discover what it meant. He bade his intimate friend Theodotos Kassiteras to see that when the damsel was next seized she should be confined within doors, and to investigate the meaning of her words. To whom did the Palace belong, if not to its present lord? Theodotos was too curious himself to fail to carry out his master's order, and the girl made an interesting communication. She told him the name and mark of the true Lord of the Palace, and urged him to visit the acropolis at a certain time, where he would meet two men, one of them riding on a mule. This man, she said, was destined to sit on the Imperial throne. The cunning spatharo-candidate took good care not to reveal his discovery to his master. Questioned by Michael, he pretended that he could make nothing of the ravings of the possessed girl. But he did not fail to watch in the prescribed place at the prescribed time for the man who was to come riding on a mule. It fell out as the damsel said; Leo the Armenian appeared on a mule; and the faithless Theodotos hastened to tell him the secret and secure his favour. This story, noised abroad at the time and remembered long afterwards, is highly characteristic of the epoch, and the behaviour of Theodotos is thoroughly in the character of a Byzantine palace official.

In matters that touched the Church the pliant Emperor was obedient to the counsels of the Patriarch. In matters that touched the State he seems also to have been under the influence of a counsellor, and one perhaps whose views were not always in harmony with those of the head of the Church. No single man had done more to compass the elevation of Michael than the Magister Theoktistos. This minister had helped in the deposition of Irene, and he was probably influential, though he played no prominent part, in the reign of Nicephorus. Nicephorus was not one who stood in need of counsellors, except in warfare; but in Michael's reign Theoktistos stood near the helm and was held responsible by his contemporaries for the mistakes of the helmsman. The admirers of the orthodox Emperor were forced to admit that, notwithstanding his piety and his clemency, he was a bad pilot for a state, and they threw the blame of the false course on Theoktistos among others. It was Theoktistos, we may suspect, who induced Michael to abandon the policy, advocated by the Patriarch, of putting to death the Paulician heretics.

But Michael's reign was destined to be brief. The struggle of the Empire with the powerful and ambitious Bulgarian kingdom was fatal to his throne, as it had been fatal to the throne of Nicephorus. In the spring of A.D. 813 Michael took the field at the head of a great army which included the Asiatic as well as the European troops. Michael was no general, but the overwhelming defeat which he experienced at Versinicia (June 22) was probably due to the treachery of the Anatolic regiments under the command of Leo the Armenian.

Michael himself escaped. Whether he understood the import of what had happened or not, it is impossible to decide; but one would think that he must have scented treachery. Certain it is that he committed the charge of the whole army to the man who had either played him false or been the unwitting cause of the false play. A contemporary author states that he chose Leo as "a pious and most valiant man". A chronicler writing at the beginning of Leo's reign might put it thus. But two explanations are possible: Michael may have been really blind, and believed his general's specious representations; or he may have understood the situation perfectly and consigned the power to Leo in order to save his own life. Of the alternatives the latter perhaps is the more likely. In any case, the Emperor soon foresaw what the end must be, and if he did not see it for himself, there was one to point it out to him when he reached Constantinople two days after the battle. A certain man, named John Hexabulios, to whom the care of the city wall had been committed, met Michael on his arrival, and commiserating with him, inquired whom he had left in charge of the army. On hearing the name of Leo, Hexabulios exclaimed at the imprudence of his master: Why did he give such an opportunity to such a dangerous man? The Emperor feigned to be secure, but he secretly resolved to abdicate the throne. The Empress Procopia was not so ready to resign the position of the greatest lady in the Empire to "Barca", as she sneeringly called the wife of Leo, and the ministers of Michael were not all prepared for a change of master. Theoktistos and Stephanos consoled him and urged him not to abdicate. Michael thought, or feigned to think, that the disaster was a divine punishment, and indeed this supposition was the only alternative to the theory of treachery. "The Christians have suffered this", said the weeping Emperor in council of his patricians, "on account of my sins. God hates the Empire of my father-in-law and his race. For we were more than the enemy, and yet none had heart, but all fled". The advice of the Patriarch Nicephorus did not coincide with the counsels of the patricians. He was inclined to approve Michael's first intention; he saw that the present reign could not last, and thought that, if Michael himself proposed a successor, that successor might deal mercifully with him and his children.

Meanwhile the soldiers were pressing Leo to assume the Imperial title without delay. The general of the Anatolics at first resisted, and pretended to be loyal to the Emperor at such a dangerous crisis, when the enemy were in the land. But when he saw that the Bulgarians intended to advance on Constantinople, he no longer hesitated to seize the prize which had been placed within his reach. He did not intend to enter the Imperial city in any other guise than as an Emperor accepted by the army; and the defence of Constantinople could not be left in the hands of Michael. It may be asked why Leo did not attempt to hinder Krum from advancing, by forcing him to fight another battle, in which there should be no feigned panic. The answer is that it was almost impossible to inveigle the Bulgarians into a pitched battle when they did not wish. Their prince could not fail to have perceived the true cause of his victory, and he was not likely to be willing to risk another combat.

July had already begun when Leo at length took the step of writing a letter to the Patriarch. In it he affirmed his own orthodoxy; he set forth his new hopes, and asked the blessing and consent of the head of the Church. Immediately after this he arrived at Hebdomon, and was proclaimed in the Tribunal legitimate Emperor of the Romans by the assembled army. On Monday, July 11, at midday, he entered by the Gate of Charisios and proceeded to the Palace; on Tuesday he was crowned in the ambo of St. Sophia by the Patriarch.

When the tidings came that Leo had been proclaimed, the fallen Emperor with his wife and children hastened to assume monastic garb and take refuge in the Church of the Virgin of the Pharos. Thus they might hope to avert the suspicions of him who was entering into their place; thus they might hope to secure at least their lives and an obscure retreat. The lives of all were spared; the father, the mother, and the daughters escaped without any bodily harm, but the sons were not so lucky. Leo anticipated the possibility of future conspiracies in favour of his predecessor's male children by mutilating them. In eunuchs he would have no rivals to fear. The mutilation which excluded from the most exalted position in the State did not debar, however, from the most exalted position in the Church; and Nicetas, who was just fourteen years old when he underwent the penalty of being an Emperor's son, will meet us again as the Patriarch Ignatius. Parents and children were not allowed to have the solace of living together; they were transported to different islands. Procopia was immured in the monastery dedicated to her namesake St. Procopia. Michael, under the name of Athanasius, eked out the remainder of his life in the rocky islet of Plate, making atonement for his sins, and the new Emperor provided him with a yearly allowance for his sustenance. By one of those strange coincidences, which in those days might seem to men something more than chance, the death of Michael occurred on an anniversary of the death of the rival whom he had deposed. The 11th day of January, which had relieved Stauracius from his sufferings, relieved Michael from the regrets of fallen greatness. He was buried on the right side of the altar in the church of the island where he died. Opposite, on the left, was placed, five years later, the body of the monk Eustratios, who had once been the Augustus Theophylactus. This, however, was not destined to be the final resting-place of Michael Rangabé. Many years after, the Patriarch Ignatius remembered the grave of his Imperial father, and having exhumed the remains, transferred them to a new monastery which he had himself erected and dedicated to the archangel Michael at Satyros, on the Bithynian mainland, opposite to the Prince's islands. This monastery of Satyros was also called by the name of Anatellon or the Riser, an epithet of the archangel. The story was that the Emperor Nicephorus was hunting in the neighborhood, where there was good cover for game, and a large stag was pulled down by the hounds. On this spot was found an old table, supported by a pillar, with an inscription on this wise: "This is the altar of the Arch-Captain (*αϱχιστϱατηγου*) Michael, the Rising Star, which the apostle Andrew set up".

§5. Ecclesiastical Policies of Nicephorus I. and Michael I.

The principle that the authority of the autocrat was supreme in ecclesiastical as well as secular administration had been fundamental in the Empire since the days of Constantine the Great, who took it for granted; and, in spite of sporadic attempts to assert the independence of the Church, it always prevailed at Byzantium. The affairs of the Church were virtually treated as a special department of the affairs of the State, and the Patriarch of Constantinople was the minister of religion and public worship. This theory of the State Church was expressed in the fact that it was the function of the Emperor both to convoke and to preside at Church Councils, which, in the order of proceedings, were modelled on the Roman Senate. It was expressed in the fact that the canons ordained by ecclesiastical assemblies were issued as laws by the Imperial legislator, and that he independently issued edicts relating to Church affairs. It is illustrated by those mixed synods which were often called to decide ecclesiastical questions and consisted of the dignitaries of the Court as well as the dignitaries of the Church.

The Seventh Ecumenical Council (a.d. 787) marks an epoch in the history of the relations between Church and State. On that occasion the right of presiding was transferred from the sovran to the Patriarch, but this concession to the Church was undoubtedly due to the fact that the Patriarch Tarasius had been a layman and Imperial minister, who had been elevated to the Patriarchal throne in defiance of the custom which had hitherto prevailed of preferring only monks to such high ecclesiastical posts. The significance of the epoch of the Seventh Council is that a new principle was signalized: the assertion of ecclesiastical independence in questions of dogma, and the assertion of the autocrat's will in all matters pertaining to ecclesiastical law and administration. This was the view which guided the policy of Tarasius, who represented what has been called "the third party", standing between the extreme theories of thoroughgoing absolutism, which had been exercised by such monarchs as Justinian, Leo III. and Constantine V., and of complete ecclesiastical independence, of which the leading advocate at this time was Theodore, the abbot of Studion. The doctrine of the third party was ultimately, but not without opposition and protest, victorious; and the ecclesiastical interest of the reign of Nicephorus centres in this question.

Tarasius, who had submitted by turns to the opposite policies of Constantine VI and Irene, was an ideal Patriarch in the eyes of Nicephorus. He died on February 25, A.D. 806, and the Emperor looked for a man of mild and complacent disposition to succeed him. The selection of a layman was suggested by the example of Tarasius; a layman would be more pliable than a priest or a monk, and more readily understand and fall in with the Emperor's views of ecclesiastical policy. His choice was judicious. He selected a learned man, who had recently retired from the post of First Secretary to a monastery which he had built on the Bosphorus, but had not yet taken monastic vows. He was a man of gentle disposition, and conformed to the Imperial idea of a model Patriarch.

The celebrated Theodore, abbot of the monastery of Studion, now appears again upon the scene. No man contributed more than he to reorganize monastic life and render monastic opinion a force in the Empire. Nicephorus, the Emperor, knew that he would have to reckon with the influence of Theodore and the Studite monks, and accordingly he sought to disarm their opposition by writing to him and his uncle Plato before the selection of a successor to Tarasius, and asking their advice on the matter. The letter in which Theodore replied to the Imperial communication is extant, and is highly instructive. It permits us to divine that the abbot would have been prepared to fill the Patriarchal chair himself. He begins by flattering Nicephorus, ascribing his elevation to God's care for the Church. He goes on to say that he knows of no man really worthy of the Patriarchate, and he names three conditions which a suitable candidate should fulfill: he should be able, with perfect heart, to seek out the judgments of God; he should have been raised by gradual steps from the lowest to higher ecclesiastical ranks; he should be experienced in the various phases of spiritual life and so able to help others. This was manifestly aimed at excluding the possible election of a layman. But Theodore goes further and actually suggests the election of an abbot or an anchoret, without mentioning a bishop. We cannot mistake the tendency of this epistle. It is probable that Plato proposed his nephew for the vacant dignity. But Theodore 's bigotry and extreme views of ecclesiastical independence rendered his appointment by an Emperor like Nicephorus absolutely out of the question.

Respect for Church tradition, with perhaps a touch of jealousy, made Theodore and his party indignant at the designation of Nicephorus, a layman, as Patriarch. They agitated against him, and their opposition seemed to the Emperor an intolerable insubordination to his own authority. Nor did their attitude meet with much sympathy outside their own immediate circle. A contemporary monk, who was no friend of the Emperor, dryly says that they tried to create a schism. The Emperor was fain to banish the abbot and his uncle, and break up the monastery; but it was represented to him that the elevation of the new Patriarch would be considered inauspicious if it were attended by the dissolution of such a famous cloister in which there were about seven hundred brethren. He was content to keep the two leaders in prison for twenty-four days, probably till after Nicephorus had been enthroned. The ceremony was solemnized on Easter day (April 12) in the presence of the two Augusti, and the Studites did not persist in their protest.

The Emperor Nicephorus now resolved to make an assertion of Imperial absolutism, in the sense that the Emperor was superior to canonical laws in the same way that he was superior to secular laws. His assertion of this principle was the more impressive, as it concerned a question which did not involve his own interests or actions.

It will be remembered that Tarasius had given his sanction to the divorce of Constantine VI from his first wife and to his marriage with Theodote (Sept. a.d. 795). After the fall of Constantine, Tarasius had been persuaded by Irene to declare that both the divorce and the second marriage were illegal, and Joseph, who had performed the marriage ceremony, was degraded from the priesthood and placed under the ban of excommunication. This ban had not been removed, and the circumstance furnished Nicephorus with a pretext for reopening a question which involved an important constitutional principle. It would have been inconvenient to ask Tarasius to broach again a matter on which his own conduct had been conspicuously inconsistent and opportunist; but soon after the succession of the new Patriarch, Nicephorus proceeded to procure a definite affirmation of the superiority of the Emperor to canonical laws. At his wish a synod was summoned to decide whether Joseph should be received again into communion and reinstated in the sacerdotal office. The assembly voted for his rehabilitation, and declared the marriage of Constantine and Theodote valid.

In this assembly of bishops and monks one dissentient voice was raised, that of Theodore the abbot of Studion. He and his uncle Plato had suffered under Constantine VI. the penalty of banishment from their monastery of Sakkudion, on account of their refusal to communicate with Joseph, who had transgressed the laws of the Church by uniting Constantine with Theodote. It has been thought that the firm attitude which they then assumed may have been in some measure due to the fact that Theodote was nearly related to them; that they may have determined to place themselves beyond all suspicion of condoning an offence against the canons in which the interests of a kinswoman were involved. Now, when the question was revived, they persisted in their attitude, though they resorted to no denunciations. Theodore wrote a respectful letter to the Patriarch, urging him to exclude Joseph from sacerdotal ministrations, and threatening that otherwise a schism would be the consequence. The Patriarch did not deign to reply to the abbot, and for two years the matter lay in abeyance, the Studites saying little, but declining to communicate with the Patriarch.

The scandal of this schism became more public when Joseph, a brother of Theodore, became archbishop of Thessalonica. He was asked by the Logothete of the Course, why he would not communicate with the Patriarch and the Emperor. On his alleging that he had nothing against them personally, but only against the priest who had celebrated the adulterous marriage, the Logothete declared, "Our pious Emperors have no need of you at Thessalonica or anywhere else". This occurrence (a.d. 808) roused to activity Theodore's facile pen. But his appeals to court-dignitaries or to ecclesiastics outside his own community seem to have produced little effect. He failed to stir up public opinion against the recent synod, and in their schism the Studites were isolated. But the attitude of this important monastery could no longer be ignored.

The mere question of the rehabilitation of a priest was, of course, a very minor matter. Nor was the legitimacy of Constantine's second marriage the question which really interested the Emperor. The question at issue was whether Emperors had power to override laws established by the Church, and whether Patriarchs and bishops might dispense from ecclesiastical canons. Theodore firmly maintained that "the laws of God bind all men", and the circumstance that Constantine wore the purple made no difference. The significance of Theodore's position is that in contending for the validity of canonical law as independent of the State and the Emperor, he was vindicating the independence of the Church. Although the Studites stood virtually alone-for if any sympathized with them they were afraid to express their opinions-the persistent opposition of such a large and influential institution could not be allowed to continue. A mixed synod of ecclesiastics and Imperial officials met in January a.d. 809, the legality of the marriage of Theodote was reaffirmed, and it was laid down that Emperors were above ecclesiastical laws and that bishops had the power of dispensing from canons. Moreover, sentence was passed on the aged Plato, the abbot Theodore, and his brother Joseph, who had been dragged before the assembly, and they were banished to the Prince's Islands, where they were placed in separate retreats. Then Nicephorus proceeded to deal with the seven hundred monks of Studion. He summoned them to his presence in the palace of Eleutherios, where he received them with impressive ceremonial. When he found it impossible to intimidate or cajole them into disloyalty to their abbot or submission to their sovran, he said: "Whoever will obey the Emperor and agree with the Patriarch and the clergy, let him stand on the right; let the disobedient move to the left, that we may see who consent and who are stubborn". But this device did not succeed, and they were all confined in various monasteries in the neighborhood of the city. Soon afterwards we hear that they were scattered far and wide throughout the Empire.

During his exile, Theodore maintained an active correspondence with the members of his dispersed flock, and in order to protect his communications against the curiosity of official supervision he used the twenty-four letters of the alphabet to designate the principal members of the Studite fraternity. In this cipher, for example, alpha represented Plato, beta Joseph, omega Theodore himself. Confident in the justice of his cause, he invoked the intervention of the Roman See, and urged the Pope to undo the work of the adulterous synods by a General Council. Leo wrote a paternal and consolatory letter, but he expressed no opinion on the merits of the question. We may take it as certain that he had other information derived from adherents of the Patriarch, who were active in influencing opinion at Rome, and that he considered Theodore's action ill-advised. In any case, he declined to commit himself.

The resolute protest of the Studites aroused, as we have seen, little enthusiasm, though it can hardly be doubted that many ecclesiastics did not approve of the Acts of the recent synod. But it was felt that the Patriarch had, in the circumstances, acted prudently and with a sage economy. In later times enthusiastic admirers of Theodore were ready to allow that Nicephorus had wisely consented lest the Emperor should do something worse. And after the Emperor's death he showed that his consent had been unwillingly given.

If the Emperor Nicephorus asserted his supreme authority in the Church, it could not be said that he was not formally orthodox, as he accepted and maintained the settlement of the Council of Nicaea and the victory of Picture-worship. But though his enemies did not accuse him of iconoclastic tendencies, he was not an enthusiastic image-worshipper. His policy was to permit freedom of opinion, and the orthodox considered such toleration equivalent to heresy. They were indignant when he sheltered by his patronage a monk named Nicolas who preached against images and had a following of disciples. The favour which he showed to the Paulicians gave his enemies a pretext for hinting that he was secretly inclined to that flagrant heresy, and the fact that he was born in Pisidia where Paulicianism flourished lent a colour to the charge. These heretics had been his useful supporters in the rebellion of Bardanes, and the superstitious believed that he had been victorious on that occasion by resorting to charms and sorceries which they were accustomed to employ. Others said that the Emperor had no religion at all. The truth may be that he was little interested in religious matters, except in relation to the State. He was, at all events, too crafty to commit himself openly to any heresy. But it is interesting to observe that in the policy of toleration Nicephorus was not unsupported, though his supporters may have been few. There existed in the capital a party of enlightened persons who held that it was wrong to sentence heretics to death, and they were strong enough in the next reign to hinder a general persecution of the Paulicians.

But for the most part the policy of Nicephorus was reversed under Michael, who proved himself not the master but the obedient son of the Church. The Patriarch knew the character of Michael, and had reason to believe that he would be submissive in all questions of faith and morals. But he was determined to assure himself that his expectations would be fulfilled, and he resorted to an expedient which has a considerable constitutional interest.

The coronations of the Emperors Marcian and Leo I. by the Patriarch, with the accompanying ecclesiastical ceremony, may be said to have definitely introduced the new constitutional principle that the profession of Christianity was a necessary qualification for holding the Imperial office. It also implied that the new Emperor had not only been elected by the Senate and the people, but was accepted by the Church. But what if the Patriarch declined to crown the Emperor-elect? Here, clearly, there was an opportunity for a Patriarch to do what it might be difficult for him to do when once the coronation was accomplished. The Emperor was the head of the ecclesiastical organization, and the influence which the Patriarch exerted depended upon the relative strengths of his own and the monarch's characters. But the Patriarch had it in his power to place limitations on the policy of a future Emperor by exacting from him certain definite and solemn promises before the ceremony of coronation was performed. It was not often that in the annals of the later Empire the Patriarch had the strength of will or a sufficient reason to impose such capitulations. The earliest known instance is the case of Anastasius I., who, before the Patriarch crowned him, was required to swear to a written undertaking that he would introduce no novelty into the Church.

Nicephorus obtained from Michael an autograph assurance-and the sign of the cross was doubtless affixed to the signature-in which he pledged himself to preserve the orthodox faith, not to stain his hands with the blood of Christians, and not to scourge ecclesiastics, whether priests or monks.

The Patriarch now showed that, if there had been no persecutions during his tenure of office, he at least would not have been lacking in zeal. At his instance the penalty of capital punishment was enacted against the Paulicians and the Athingani, who were regarded as no better than Manichaeans and altogether outside the pale of Christianity. The persecution began; not a few were decapitated; but influential men, to whose advice the Emperor could not close his ears, intervened, and the bloody work was stayed. The monk, to whom we owe most of our knowledge of the events of these years, deeply laments the successful interference of these evil counsellors. But the penalty of death was only commuted; the Athingani were condemned to confiscation and banishment.

The Emperor had more excuse for proceeding against the iconoclasts, who were still numerous in the army and the Imperial city. They were by no means contented at the rule of the orthodox Rangabé. Their discontent burst out after Michael's fruitless Bulgarian expedition in June, a.d. 812. We shall have to return to the dealings of Michael with the Bulgarians; here we have only to observe how this June expedition led to a conspiracy. When the iconoclasts saw Thrace and Macedonia at the mercy of the heathen of the north, they thought they had good grounds for grumbling at the iconodulic sovran. When the admirers of the great Leo and the great Constantine, who had ruled in the days of their fathers and grandfathers, saw the enemy harrying the land at will and possessing the cities of the Empire, they might bitterly remember how heavy the arm of Constantine had been on the Bulgarians and how well he had defended the frontier of Thrace; they might plausibly ascribe the difference in military success to the difference in religious doctrine. It was a good opportunity for the bold to conspire; the difficulty was to discover a successor to Michael, who would support iconoclasm and who had some show of legitimate claim to the throne. The choice of the conspirators fell on the blind sons of Constantine V, who still survived in Panormos, or as it was also, and is still, called Antigoni, one of the Prince's Islands. These princes had been prominent in the reign of Constantine VI and Irene, as repeatedly conspiring against their nephew and sister-in-law. The movement was easily suppressed, the revolutionaries escaped with a few stripes, and the blind princes were removed to the more distant island of Aphusia. But though the iconoclasts might be disaffected, they do not seem to have provoked persecution by openly showing flagrant disrespect to holy pictures in the reigns of Nicephorus and Michael. Michael, however, would not suffer the iconoclastic propaganda which his father-in-law had allowed. He edified the people of Constantinople by forcing the iconoclastic lecturer Nicolas to make a public recantation of his error.

The Emperor and the Patriarch lost no time in annulling the decisions of those assemblies which the Studite monks stigmatized as "synods of adulterers". The notorious Joseph, who had celebrated the "adulterous" marriage, was again suspended; the Studites were recalled from exile; and the schism was healed. It might now be alleged that Nicephorus had not been in sympathy with the late Emperor's policy, and had only cooperated with him from considerations of "economy". But the dissensions of the Studite monks, first with Tarasius and then with Nicephorus, were more than passing episodes. They were symptomatic of an opposition or discord between the hierarchy of the Church and a portion of the monastic world. The heads of the Church were more liberal and more practical in their views; they realized the importance of the State, on which the Church depended; and they deemed it bad policy, unless a fundamental principle were at stake, to oppose the supreme authority of the Emperor. The monks were no politicians; they regarded the world from a purely ecclesiastical point of view; they looked upon the Church as infinitely superior to the State; and they were prepared to take extreme measures for the sake of maintaining a canon. The "third party" and the monks were united, after the death of Michael I, in a common struggle against iconoclasm, but as soon as the enemy was routed, the disagreement between these two powers in the Church broke out, as we shall see, anew.

Chapter II
Leo V. (The Armenian) and the Revival of Iconoclasm (A.D. 813-820)

§1. Reign and Administration of Leo V.

Leo V. was not the first Armenian who occupied the Imperial throne. Among the Emperors who reigned briefly and in rapid succession after the decline of the Heraclian dynasty, the Armenian Bardanes who took the name of Philippicus, had been chiefly noted for luxury and delicate living. The distinctions of Leo were of a very different order. If he had sown his wild oats in earlier days, he proved an active and austere prince, and he presented a marked contrast to his immediate predecessor. Born in lowly station and poor circumstances, Leo had made his way up by his own ability to the loftiest pinnacle in the Empire; Michael enjoyed the advantages of rank and birth, and had won the throne through the accident of his marriage with an Emperor's daughter. Michael had no will of his own; Leo's temper was as firm as that of his namesake, the Isaurian. Michael was in the hands of the Patriarch; Leo was determined that the Patriarch should be in the hands of the Emperor. Even those who sympathized with the religious policy of Michael were compelled to confess that he was a feeble, incompetent ruler; while even those who hated Leo most bitterly could not refuse to own that in civil administration he was an able sovran. A short description of Leo's personal appearance has been preserved. He was of small stature and had curling hair; he wore a full beard; his hair was thick; his voice loud.

On the very day of his entry into Constantinople as an Augustus proclaimed by the army, an incident is related to have occurred which seemed an allegorical intimation as to the ultimate destiny of the new Emperor. It is one of those stories based perhaps upon some actual incident, but improved and embellished in the light of later events, so as to bear the appearance of a mysterious augury. It belongs to the general atmosphere of mystery that seemed to envelop the careers of the three young squires of Bardanes, whose destinies had been so closely interwoven. The prophecy of the hermit of Philomelion, the raving of the slave-girl of Michael Rangabé, and the incident now to be related, mark stages in the development of the drama.

Since Michael the Amorian had been rewarded by Nicephorus for his desertion of the rebel Bardanes, we lose sight of his career. He seems to have remained an officer in the Anatolic Theme, of which he had been appointed Count of the tent, and when Leo the Armenian became the strategos of that province the old comrades renewed their friendship. Leo acted as sponsor to Michael's son; and Michael played some part in bringing about Leo's elevation. The latter is said to have shrunk from taking the great step, as he was not sure that he would obtain simultaneous recognition in the camp and in the capital, and Michael the Lisper, threatening to slay him if he did not consent, undertook to make the necessary arrangements. When Leo entered the city he was met and welcomed by the whole Senate near the Church of St. John the Forerunner, which still stands, not far from the Golden Gate, and marks the site of the monastery of Studion. Accompanied by an acclaiming crowd, and closely attended by Michael his confidant, the new Augustus rode to the Palace. He halted in front of the Brazen Gate (Chalkê) to worship before the great image of Christ which surmounted the portal. The Fifth Leo, who was afterwards to be such an ardent emulator of the third Emperor of his name, now dismounted, and paid devotion to the figure restored by Irene in place of that which Leo the Isaurian had demolished. Perhaps the Armenian had not yet decided on pursuing an iconoclastic policy; in any case he recognized that it would be a false step to suggest by any omission the idea that he was not strictly orthodox. Halting and dismounting he consigned to the care of Michael the loose red military garment which he wore. This cloak, technically called an eagle and more popularly a kolobion, was worn without a belt. Michael is said to have put on the "eagle" which the Emperor had put off. It is not clear whether this was strictly according to etiquette or not, but the incident was supposed to be an omen that Michael would succeed Leo. Another still more ominous incident is said to have followed. The Emperor did not enter by the Brazen Gate, but, having performed his act of devotion, proceeded past the Baths of Zeuxippos, and passing through the Hippodrome reached the Palace at the entrance known as the Skyla. The Emperor walked rapidly through the gate, and Michael, hurrying to keep up with him, awkwardly trampled on the edge of his dress which touched the ground behind.

It was said that Leo himself recognized the omen, but it certainly did not influence him in his conduct; nor is there anything to suggest that at this time Michael was jealous of Leo, or Leo suspicious of Michael. The Emperor made him the Domestic or commander of the Excubitors, with rank of patrician, and treated him as a confidential adviser. Nor did he forget his other comrade, who had served with him under Bardanes, but cleaved more faithfully to his patron than had either the Amorian or the Armenian. Thomas the Slavonian returned from Saracen territory, where he had lived in exile, and was now made Turmarch of the Federates. Thus the three squires of Bardanes are brought into association again. Another appointment which Leo made redounds to his credit, as his opponents grudgingly admitted. He promoted Manuel the Protostrator, who had strongly opposed the resignation of Michael and his own elevation, to the rank of patrician and made him General of the Armeniacs. Manuel could hardly have looked for such favour; he probably expected that his fee would be exile. He was a bold, outspoken man, and when Leo said to him, "You ought not to have advised the late Emperor and Procopia against my interests", he replied, "Nor ought you to have raised a hand against your benefactor and fellow-father", referring to the circumstance that Leo had stood as sponsor for a child of Michael.

The revolution which established a new Emperor on the throne had been accomplished speedily and safely at a moment of great national peril. The defenses of the city had to be hastily set in order, and Krum, the Bulgarian victor, appeared before the walls within a week. Although the barbarians of the north had little chance of succeeding where the Saracen forces had more than once failed, and finally retired, the destruction which they wrought in the suburbs was a gloomy beginning for a new reign. The active hostilities of the Bulgarian prince claimed the solicitude of Leo for more than a year, when his death, as he was preparing to attack the capital again, led to the conclusion of a peace.

On the eastern frontier the internal troubles of the Caliphate relieved the Empire from anxiety during this reign, and, after the Bulgarian crisis had passed, Leo was able to devote his attention to domestic administration. But of his acts almost nothing has been recorded except of those connected with his revival of iconoclasm. His warfare against image-worship was the conspicuous feature of his rule, and, occupied with execrating his ecclesiastical policy, the chroniclers have told us little of his other works. Yet his most bitter adversaries were compelled unwillingly to confess that his activity in providing for the military defenses of the Empire and for securing the administration of justice was deserving of all commendation. This was the judgment of the Patriarch Nicephorus, who cannot be accused of partiality. He said after the death of Leo: "The Roman Empire has lost an impious but great guardian". He neglected no measure which seemed likely to prove advantageous to the State; and this is high praise from the mouths of adversaries. He was severe to criminals, and he endeavored, in appointing judges and governors, to secure men who were superior to bribes. No one could say that love of money was one of the Emperor's weak points. In illustration of his justice the following anecdote is told. One day as he was issuing from the Palace, a man accosted him and complained of a bitter wrong which had been done him by a certain senator. The lawless noble had carried off the poor man's attractive wife and had kept her in his own possession for a long time. The husband had complained to the Prefect of the City, but complained in vain. The guilty senator had influence, and the Prefect was a respecter of persons. The Emperor immediately commanded one of his attendants to bring the accused noble and the Prefect to his presence. The ravisher did not attempt to deny the charge, and the minister admitted that the matter had come before him. Leo enforced the penalties of the law, and stripped the unworthy Prefect of his office.

Our authorities tell us little enough about the administration of this sovran, and their praise is bestowed reluctantly. But it is easy to see that he was a strenuous ruler, of the usual Byzantine type, devoted to the duties of his post, and concerned to secure efficiency both in his military and civil officers. He transacted most of his State business in the long hall in the Palace which was called the Lausiakos. There his secretaries, who were noted for efficiency, worked under his directions. In undertakings of public utility his industry was unsparing. After the peace with Bulgaria he rebuilt and restored the cities of Thrace and Macedonia, and himself with a military retinue made a progress in those provinces, to forward and superintend the work. He personally supervised the drill and discipline of the army.

§2. Conspiracy of Michael and Murder of Leo

The reign of Leo closes with another act in the historical drama which opened with the revolt of Bardanes Turcus. We have seen how the Emperor Leo bestowed offices on his two companions, Michael and Thomas. But Michael was not to prove himself more loyal to his Armenian comrade who had outstripped him than he had formerly shown himself to his Armenian master who had trusted him. Thomas indeed had faithfully clung to the desperate cause of the rebel; but he was not to bear himself with equal faith to a more legitimate lord.

The treason of Thomas is not by any means as clear as the treason of Michael. But this at least seems to be certain, that towards the end of the year 820 he organized a revolt in the East; that the Emperor, forming a false conception of the danger, sent an inadequate force, perhaps under an incompetent commander, to quell the rising, and that this force was defeated by the rebel. But with Thomas we have no further concern now; our instant concern is with the commander of the Excubitors, who was more directly under the Imperial eye. It appears that Michael had fallen under the serious suspicion of the Emperor.

The evidence against him was so weighty that he had hardly succeeded in freeing himself from the charge of treason. He was a rough man, without education or breeding; and while he could not speak polite Greek, his tongue lisped insolently against the Emperor. Perhaps he imagined that Leo was afraid of him; for, coarse and untrained as he may have been, Michael proved himself afterwards to be a man of ability, and does not strike us as one who was likely to have been a reckless babbler. He spoke doubtless these treasonable things in the presence of select friends, but he must have known well how perilous words he uttered. The matter came to the ears of the Emperor, who, unwilling to resort to any extreme measure on hearsay, not only set eavesdroppers to watch the words and deeds of his disaffected officer, but took care that he should be privately admonished to control his tongue. These offices he specially entrusted to the Logothete of the Course, John Hexabulios, a discreet and experienced man, whom we met before on the occasion of the return of Michael Rangabé to the city after the defeat at Hadrianople. We may feel surprise that he who then reproved Michael I for his folly in leaving the army in Leo's hands, should now be the trusted minister of Leo himself. But we shall find him still holding office and enjoying influence in the reign of Leo's successor. The same man who has the confidence of the First Michael, and warns him against Leo, wins the confidence of Leo, and warns him against another Michael, then wins the confidence of the Second Michael, and advises him on his dealing with an unsuccessful rebel. Had the rebellion of Thomas prospered, Hexabulios would doubtless have been a trusted minister of Thomas too.

Michael was deaf to the warnings and rebukes of the Logothete of the Course; he was indifferent to the dangers in which his unruly talk seemed certain to involve him. The matter came to a crisis on Christmas Eve, a.d. 820. Hexabulios had gained information which pointed to a conspiracy organized by Michael and had laid it before the Emperor. The peril which threatened the throne could no longer be overlooked, and the wrath of Leo himself was furious. Michael was arrested, and the day before the feast of Christmas was spent in proving his guilt. The inquiry was held in the chamber of the State Secretaries, and the Emperor presided in person. The proofs of guilt were so clear and overwhelming that the prisoner himself was constrained to confess his treason. After such a long space of patience the wrath of the judge was all the more terrible, and he passed the unusual sentence that his old companion-in-arms should be fastened to a pole and cast into the furnace which heated the baths of the Palace. That the indignity might be greater, an ape was to be tied to the victim, in recollection perhaps of the old Roman punishment of parricides.

This sentence would have been carried out and the reign of Leo would not have come to an untimely end, if the Empress Theodosia had not intervened. Shocked at the news of the atrocious sentence, she rose from her couch, and, not even taking time to put on her slippers, rushed to the Emperor's presence, in order to prevent its execution. If she had merely exclaimed against the barbarity of the decree, she might not have compassed her wish, but the very day of the event helped her. It was Christmas Eve. How could the Emperor dare, with hands stained by such foul cruelty, to receive the holy Sacrament on the morrow? Must he not be ashamed that such an act should be associated with the feast of the Nativity? These arguments appealed to the pious Christian. But Theodosia had also an argument which might appeal to the prudent sovran: let the punishment be postponed; institute a stricter investigation, and discover the names of all those who have been implicated in the plot. The appeal of the Empress was not in vain. Her counsels and her entreaties affected the mind of her husband. But while he consented to defer his final decision, it would seem that he had misgivings, and that some dim feeling of danger entered into him. He is reported to have said: "Wife, you have released my soul from sin today; perhaps it will soon cost me my life too. You and our children will see what shall happen".

In those days men were ready to see fatal omens and foreshadowings in every chance event and random word. The Emperor lay awake long on the night following that Christmas Eve, tossing in his mind divers grave omens, which seemed to point to some mortal peril, and to signify Michael as the instrument. There was the unlucky chance that on the day of his coronation Michael had trodden on his cloak. But there were other signs more serious and more recent. From a book of oracles and symbolic pictures Leo had discovered the time of his death. A lion pierced in the throat with a sword was depicted between the letters Chi and Phi. These are the first letters of the Greek expressions which mean Christmas and Epiphany, and therefore the symbol was explained that the Imperial lion was to be slain between those two feasts. As the hours went on to Christmas morning the Lion might feel uneasy in his lair. And a strange dream, which he had dreamt a short time before, expressly signified that Michael would be the cause of his death. The Patriarch Tarasius had appeared to him with threatening words and gestures, and had called sternly upon one Michael to slay the sinner. It seemed to Leo that Michael obeyed the command, and that he himself was left half dead.

Tortured with such fears the Emperor bethought him to make further provisions for the safety of the prisoner whose punishment he had deferred. He summoned the keeper (papias) of the Palace and bade him keep Michael in one of the rooms which were assigned to the Palace-sweepers, and to fasten his feet in fetters. Leo, to make things doubly sure, kept the key of the fetters in the pocket of his under-garment. But still his fears would not let him slumber, and as the night wore on he resolved to convince himself with his own eyes that the prisoner was safe. Along the passages which led to the room which for the time had been turned into a dungeon, there were locked doors to pass. But they were not solid enough to shut out the Emperor, who was a strong man and easily smashed or unhinged them. He found the prisoner sleeping on the pallet or bench of the keeper, and the keeper himself sleeping on the floor. He saw none save these two, but unluckily there was another present who saw him. A little boy in the service of Michael, who had been allowed (doubtless irregularly) to bear his master company, heard the approaching steps and crept under the couch, from which hiding-place he observed the movements of Leo, whom he recognized as the Emperor by his red boots. Leo bent over Michael and laid his hand on his breast, to discover whether the beating of his heart pointed to anxiety or security. When there was no response to his touch, the Emperor marvelled much that his prisoner, enjoyed such a sound and careless sleep. But he was vexed at the circumstance that the keeper had resigned his couch to the criminal; such leniency seemed undue and suspicious. Perhaps he was vexed too that the guardian was himself asleep. In any case the lad under the bed observed him, as he was retiring from the cell, to shake his hand threateningly at both the guardian and the prisoner. The unseen spectator of Leo's visit reported the matter to his master, and when the keeper of the Palace saw that he too was in jeopardy they took common counsel to save their lives. The only chance was to effect a communication with the other conspirators, whose names had not yet been revealed. The Emperor had directed that, if Michael were moved to confess his sins and wished for ghostly consolation, the offices of a priest should not be withheld from him, and the matter was entrusted to a certain Theoktistos, who was a servant of Michael, perhaps one of the Excubitors. It certainly seems strange that

Leo, who took such anxious precautions in other ways, should have allowed the condemned to hold any converse with one of his own faithful dependants. The concession proved fatal. The keeper led Theoktistos to Michael's presence, and Theoktistos soon left the Palace, under the plea of fetching a minister of religion, but really in order to arrange a plan of rescue with the other conspirators. He assured the accomplices that, if they did not come to deliver the prisoner from death, Michael would not hesitate to reveal their names.

The plan of rescue which the conspirators imagined and carried out was simple enough; but its success depended on the circumstance that the season was winter and the mornings dark. It was the custom that the choristers who chanted the matins in the Palace Chapel of St. Stephen should enter by the Ivory Gate at daybreak, and as soon as they sang the morning hymn, the Emperor used to enter the church. The conspirators arrayed themselves in clerical robes, and having concealed daggers in the folds, mingled with the choristers who were waiting for admission at the Ivory Gate. Under the cover of the gloom easily escaping detection, they entered the Palace and hid themselves in a dark corner of the chapel. Leo, who was proud of his singing (according to one writer he sang execrably, but another, by no means well-disposed to him, states that he had an unusually melodious voice), arrived punctually to take part in the Christmas service, and harbouring no suspicion of the danger-which lurked so near. It was a chilly morning, and both the Emperor and the priest who led the service had protected themselves against the cold by wearing peaked felt caps. At a passage in the service which the Emperor used to sing with special unction, the signal was given and the conspirators leaped out from their hiding-place. The likeness in head-dress, and also a certain likeness in face and figure, between Leo and the chief of the officiating clergy, led at first to a blunder. The weapons of the rebels were directed against the priest, but he saved his life by uncovering his head and showing that he was bald. Leo, meanwhile, who saw his danger, had used the momentary respite to rush to the altar and seize some sacred object, whether the cross itself, or the chain of the censer, or a candelabrum, as a weapon of defense. When this was shattered by the swords of the foes who surrounded him and only a useless fragment remained in his hands, he turned to one of them who was distinguished above the others by immense stature and adjured him to spare his life. But the giant, who for his height was nicknamed "One-and-a-half", swore a great oath that the days of Leo were numbered, and with the word brought down his sword so heavily on the shoulder of his victim that not only was the arm cut from the body, but the implement which the hand still held was cleft and bounded to a distant spot of the building. The Imperial head was then cut off, and the work of murder and rescue was accomplished.

Thus perished the Armenian Leo more foully than any Roman Emperor since Maurice was slain by Phocas. He was, as even his enemies admitted (apart from his religious policy), an excellent ruler, and a rebellion against him, not caused by ecclesiastical discontent, was inexcusable. Michael afterwards declared, in palliation of the conspiracy, that Leo had shown himself to be unequal to coping with the rebellion of Thomas, and that this incompetence had caused discontent among the leading men of the State. But this plea cannot be admitted; for although Thomas defeated a small force which Leo, not fully realizing the danger, had sent against him, there is no reason to suppose that, when he was fully informed of the forces and numbers of the rebel, he would have shown himself less able or less energetic in suppressing the insurrection than Michael himself. Certainly his previous conduct of warfare was not likely to suggest to his ministers that he was incapable of dealing with a revolt. But in any case we have no sign, except Michael's own statement, that the rebellion of Thomas was already formidable. We must conclude that the conspiracy was entirely due to Michael's personal ambition, stimulated perhaps by the signs and omens and soothsayings of which the air was full. It does not appear that the religious question entered into the situation; for Michael was himself favourable to iconoclasm.

The body of the slain Emperor was cast by his murderers into some sewer or outhouse for the moment. It was afterwards dragged naked from the Palace by the Gate of Spoils to the Hippodrome, to be exposed to the spurns of the populace, which had so lately trembled in the presence of the form which they now insulted. From the Hippodrome the corpse was borne on the back of a horse or mule to a harbour and embarked in the same boat which was to convey the widow and the children of the Emperor to a lonely and lowly exile in the island of Prote. Here a new sorrow was in store for Theodosia: the body of the son who was called by her own name was to be laid by that of his father. The decree had gone forth that the four sons were to be made eunuchs, in order that they might never aspire to recover the throne from which their father had fallen. The same measure which Leo had meted to his predecessor's children was dealt out to his own offspring. Theodosius, who was probably the youngest of the brothers, did not survive the mutilation, and he was buried with Leo. There is a tale that one of the other brothers, but it is not quite clear whether it was Constantine or Basil, lost his power of speech from the same cause, but that by devout and continuous prayer to God and to St. Gregory, whose image had been set up in the island, his voice was restored to him. The third son, Gregory, lived to become in later years bishop of Syracuse. Both Basil and Gregory repented of their iconoclastic errors, and iconodule historians spoke of them in after days as "great in virtue".

But although Michael, with a view to his own security, dealt thus cruelly with the boys, he did not leave the family destitute. He gave them a portion of Leo's property for their support, but he assigned them habitations in different places. The sons were confined in Prote, while the wife and the mother of Leo were allowed to dwell "safely and at their own will" in a more verdant and charming island of the same group, Chalkites, which is now known as Halki.

§3. The Revival of Iconoclasm

The revival of image-worship by the Empress Irene and the authority of the Council of Nicaea had not extinguished the iconoclastic doctrine, which was still obstinately maintained by powerful parties both in the Court circles of Byzantium and in the army. It is not surprising that the struggle should have been, however unwisely, renewed. The first period of iconoclasm and persecution, which was initiated by Leo the Isaurian, lasted for more than fifty, the second, which was initiated by Leo the Armenian, for less than thirty years. The two periods are distinguished by the greater prominence of the dogmatic issues of the question in the later epoch, and by the circumstance that the persecution was less violent and more restricted in its range.

We have already seen that Leo, before he entered Constantinople to celebrate his coronation, wrote to assure the Patriarch of his orthodoxy. No hint is given that this letter was a reply to a previous communication from the Patriarch. We may suppose that Leo remembered how Nicephorus had exacted a written declaration of orthodoxy from Michael, and wished to anticipate such a demand. We know not in what terms the letter of Leo was couched, but it is possible that he gave Nicephorus reason to believe that he would be ready to sign a more formal document to the same effect after his coronation. The crowned Emperor, however, evaded the formality, which the uncrowned Emperor had perhaps promised or suggested; and thus when he afterwards repudiated the Acts of the Seventh Ecumenical Council he could not legally be said to have broken solemn engagements. But his adversaries were eager to represent him as having broken faith. According to one account, he actually signed a solemn undertaking to preserve inviolate the received doctrines of the Church; and this he flagrantly violated by his war against images. According to the other account, he definitely promised to sign such a document after his coronation, but, when it came to the point, refused. The first story seizes the fact of his reassuring letter to Nicephorus and represents it as a binding document; the second story seizes the fact that Leo after his coronation declined to bind himself, and represents this refusal as a breach of a definite promise.

The iconoclastic doctrine was still widely prevalent in the army, and was held by many among the higher classes in the capital. If it had not possessed a strong body of adherents, the Emperor could never have thought of reviving it. That he committed a mistake in policy can hardly be disputed in view of subsequent events. Nicephorus I., in preserving the settlement of the Council of Nicaea, while he allowed iconoclasts perfect freedom to propagate their opinions, had proved himself a competent statesman. For, considered in the interest of ecclesiastical tranquillity, the great superiority of image-worship to iconoclasm lay in the fact that it need not lead to persecution or oppression. The iconoclasts could not be compelled to worship pictures, they had only to endure the offence of seeing them and abstain from insulting them; whereas the adoption of an iconoclastic policy rendered persecution inevitable. The course pursued by Nicephorus seems to have been perfectly satisfactory and successful in securing peace of the Church.

All this, however, must have been as obvious to Leo the Armenian as it seems to us. He cannot have failed to realize the powerful opposition which a revival of iconoclasm would arouse; yet he resolved to disturb the tranquil condition of the ecclesiastical world and enter upon a dangerous and disagreeable conflict with the monks.

Most of the Eastern Emperors were theologians as well as statesmen, and it is highly probable that Leo's personal conviction of the wrongfulness of icon-worship, and the fact that this conviction was shared by many prominent people and widely diffused in the Asiatic Themes, would have been sufficient to induce him to revive an aggressive iconoclastic policy. But there was certainly another motive which influenced his decision. It was a patent fact that the iconoclastic Emperors had been conspicuously strong and successful rulers, whereas the succeeding period, during which the worship of images had been encouraged or permitted, was marked by weakness and some signal disasters. The day is not yet entirely past for men, with vague ideas of the nexus of cause and effect, to attribute the failures and successes of nations to the wrongness or soundness of their theological beliefs; and even now some who read the story of Leo's reign may sympathize with him in his reasoning that the iconoclastic doctrine was proved by events to be pleasing in the sight of Heaven. We are told that "he imitated the Isaurian Emperors Leo and Constantine, whose heresy he revived, wishing to live many years like them and to become illustrious".

To the ardent admirer of Leo the Isaurian, his own name seemed a good omen in days when men took such coincidences seriously; and to make the parallel between his own case and that of his model nearer still, he changed the Armenian name of his eldest son Symbatios and designated him Constantine. The new Constantine was crowned and proclaimed Augustus at the end of 813, when the Bulgarians were still devastating in Thrace or just after they had retreated, and it pleased Leo to hear the soldiers shouting the customary acclamations in honor of "Leo and Constantine". Propitious names inaugurated an Armenian dynasty which might rival the Isaurian.

Stories were told in later times, by orthodox fanatics who execrated his memory, of sinister influences which were brought to bear on Leo and determine his iconoclastic policy. And here, too, runs a thread of that drama in which he was one of the chief actors. The prophecy of the hermit of Philomelion had come to pass, and it is said that Leo, in grateful recognition, sent a messenger with costly presents to seek out the true prophet. But when the messenger arrived at Philomelion he found that the man was dead and that another monk named Sabbatios had taken possession of his hut. Sabbatios was a zealous opponent of image-worship, and he prophesied to the messenger in violent language. The Empress Irene he reviled as "Leopardess" and "Bacchant", he perverted the name of Tarasius to "Taraxios" (Disturber), and he foretold that God would overturn the throne of Leo if Leo did not overturn images and pictures.

The new prophecy from Philomelion is said to have alarmed the Emperor, and he consulted his friend Theodotos Kassiteras on the matter. We already met this Theodotos playing a part in the story of the possessed damsel who foretold Leo's elevation. Whatever basis of fact these stories may have, we can safely infer that Theodotos was an intimate adviser of the Emperor. On this occasion, according to the tale, he did not deal straightforwardly with his master. He advised Leo to consult a certain Antonius, a monk who resided in the capital; but in the meantime Theodotos himself secretly repaired to Antonius and primed him for the coming interview. It was arranged that Antonius should urge the Emperor to adopt the doctrine of Leo the Isaurian and should prophesy that he would reign till his seventy-second year. Leo, dressed as a private individual, visited the monk at night, and his faith was confirmed when Antonius recognized him. This story, which, of course, we cannot unreservedly believe, became current at the time, and was handed down to subsequent generations in a verse pasquinade composed by Theophanes Confessor.

The Emperor discovered a valuable assistant in a young man known as John the Grammarian, who had the distinction of earning as many and as bitter maledictions from the orthodox party of the time and from subsequent orthodox historians as were ever aimed at Manes or at Arius or at Leo III. He was one of the most learned men of his day, and, like most learned men who fell foul of the Church in the middle ages, he was accused of practising the black art. His accomplishments and scientific ability will appear more conspicuously when we meet him again some years hence as an illustrious figure in the reign of Theophilus. He was known by several names. We meet him as John the Reader, more usually as John the Grammarian; but those who detested him used the opprobrious titles of Hylilas, by which they understood a forerunner and coadjutor of the devil, or Lekanomantis, meaning that he conjured with a dish. His parentage, if the account is true, was characteristic. He was the son of one Pankratios, a hermit, who from childhood had been possessed with a demon. But all the statements of our authorities with respect to John are coloured by animosity because he was an iconoclast. Patriarchs and monks loved to drop a vowel of his name and call him "Jannes" after the celebrated magician, just as they loved to call the Emperor Leo "Chameleon".

The project of reviving iconoclasm was begun warily and silently; Leo had determined to make careful preparations before he declared himself. At Pentecost, 814, John the Grammarian, assisted by several colleagues, began to prepare an elaborate work against the worship of images. The Emperor provided him with full powers to obtain access to any libraries that he might wish to consult. Rare and ancient books were scattered about in monasteries and churches, and this notice suggests that it was not easy for private individuals to obtain permission to handle them. It is said that the zeal of the scholar was increased by a promise of Leo to appoint him Patriarch, in case it should be found necessary to remove Nicephorus. John and his colleagues collected many books and made an extensive investigation. Of course their opponents alleged that they found only what they sought, and sought only for passages which might seem to tell in favour of iconoclasm, while they ignored those which told against it. The Acts of the Synod of 753 gave them many references, and we are told how they placed marks in the books at the relevant passages.

It was desirable to have a bishop in the commission, and in July a suitable person was found in Antonius, the bishop of Syllaion in Pamphylia. He is said to have been originally a lawyer and a schoolmaster, and in consequence of some scandal to have found it advisable to enter a monastery. He became an abbot, and, although his behavior was loose and unseemly, "God somehow allowed him" to become bishop of Syllaion. His indecent behavior seems to have consisted in amusing the young monks with funny tales and practical jokes. He was originally orthodox and only adopted the heresy in order to curry favour at the Imperial Court. Such is the sketch of the man drawn by a writer who was violently prejudiced against him and all his party.

Private apartments in the Palace were assigned to the committee, and the bodily wants of the members were so well provided for that their opponents described them as living like pigs. In the tedious monotony of their work they were consoled by delicacies supplied from the Imperial kitchen, and while the learning and subtlety of John lightened the difficulties of the labour, the jests and buffoonery of the bishop might enliven the hours of relaxation. The work of research was carried on with scrupulous secrecy. Whenever any curious person asked the students what they were doing they said, "The Emperor commissioned us to consult these books, because someone told him that he has only a short time to reign; that is the object of our search".

In December the work of the commission was completed and the Emperor summoned Nicephorus to a private interview in the Palace. Leo advocated the iconoclastic policy on the ground that the worship of images was a scandal in the army. "Let us make a compromise", he said, "to please the soldiers, and remove the pictures which are hung low". But Nicephorus was not disposed to compromise; he knew that compromise in this matter would mean defeat. When Leo reminded him that image-worship was not ordained in the Gospels and laid down that the Gospels were the true standard of orthodoxy, Nicephorus asserted the inspiration of the Holy Spirit in successive ages. This interview probably did not last very long. The Patriarch was firm and the Emperor polite. Leo was not yet prepared to proceed to extremes, and Nicephorus still hoped for his conversion, even as we are told that Pope Gregory II had hoped for the conversion of his Isaurian namesake.

The policy of the orthodox party at this crisis was to refuse to argue the question at issue. The Church had already declared itself on the matter in an Ecumenical Council; and to doubt the decision of the Church was heretical. And so when Leo proposed that some learned bishops whom the Patriarch had sent to him should hold a disputation with some learned iconoclasts, the Emperor presiding, they emphatically declined, on the ground that the Council of Nicaea in a.d. 787 had settled the question of image-worship for ever.

Soon after these preliminary parleys, soldiers of the Tagmata or residential regiments showed their sympathies by attacking the Image of Christ over the Brazen Gate of the Palace. It was said that this riot was suggested and encouraged by Leo; and the inscription over the image, telling how Irene erected a new icon in the place of that which Leo III. destroyed, might stimulate the fury of those who revered the memory of the Isaurian Emperors. Mud and stones were hurled by the soldiers at the sacred figure, and then the Emperor innocently said, "Let us take it down, to save it from these insults". This was the first overt act in the new campaign, and the Patriarch thought it high time to summon a meeting of bishops and abbots to discuss the danger which was threatening the Church. The convocation was held in the Patriarch's palace. All those who were present swore to stand fast by the doctrine laid down at the Seventh Council, and they read over the passages which their opponents cited against them. When Christmas came, Nicephorus begged the Emperor to remove him from the pontifical chair if he (Nicephorus) were unpleasing in his eyes, but to make no innovations in the Church. To this Leo replied by disclaiming either intention.

These preliminary skirmishes occurred before Christmas (a.d. 814). On Christmas day it was noticed by curious and watchful eyes that Leo adored in public a cloth on which the birth of Christ was represented. But on the next great feast of the Church, the day of Epiphany, it was likewise observed that he did not adore, according to custom. Meanwhile, the iconoclastic party was being reinforced by proselytes, and the Emperor looked forward to a speedy settlement of the question in his own favour at a general synod. He issued a summons to the bishops of the various dioceses in the Empire to assemble in the capital, and perhaps stirred the prelates of Hellas to undertake the journey by a reminiscence flattering to their pride. He reminded them that men from Mycenae in Argolis, men from Carystos in Euboea, men from Corinth, and many other Greeks, joined the Megarians in founding that colony of the Bosphorus which had now grown to such great estate. According as they arrived, they were conducted straightway to the Emperor's presence, and were prohibited from first paying a visit to the Patriarch, as was the usual practice. The Emperor wished to act on their hopes or fears before they had been warned or confirmed in the faith by the words of their spiritual superior; and this policy was regarded as one of his worst acts of tyranny. Many of the bishops submitted to the arguments or to the veiled threats of their sovran, and those who dared to resist his influence were kept in confinement. The Patriarch in the meantime encouraged his own party to stand fast. He was supported by the powerful interest of the monks, and especially by Theodore, abbot of Studion, who had been his adversary a few years ago. A large assembly of the faithful was convoked in the Church of St. Sophia, and a service lasting the whole night was celebrated. Nicephorus prayed for the conversion of the Emperor, and confirmed his followers in their faith.

The Emperor was not well pleased when the news reached the Palace of the doings in the Church. About the time of cockcrow he sent a message of remonstrance to the Patriarch and summoned him to appear in the Palace at break of day, to explain his conduct. There ensued a second and more famous interview between the Emperor and the Patriarch, when they discussed at large the arguments for and against image-worship. Nicephorus doubtless related to his friends the substance of what was said, and the admirers of that saint afterwards wrote elaborate accounts of the dialogue, which they found a grateful subject for exhibiting learning, subtlety, and style. Ultimately Nicephorus proposed that the bishops and others who had accompanied him to the gate should be admitted to the Imperial presence, that his Majesty might become fully convinced of their unanimity on the question at issue. The audience was held in the Chrysotriklinos, and guards with conspicuous swords were present, to awe the churchmen into respect and obedience.

The Emperor bent his brows and spoke thus:

> "Ye, like all others, are well aware that God has appointed us to watch over the interests of this illustrious and reasonable flock; and that we are eager and solicitous to smoothe away and remove every thorn that grows in the Church. As some members of the fold are in doubt as to the adoration of images, and cite passages of Scripture which seem unfavourable to such practices, the necessity of resolving the question once for all is vital; more especially in order to compass our great end, which, as you know, is the unity of the whole Church. The questioners supply the premisses; we are constrained to draw the conclusion. We have already communicated our wishes to the High Pontiff, and now we charge you to resolve the problem speedily. If you are too slow you may end in saying nothing, and disobedience to our commands will not conduce to your profit".

The bishops and abbots, encouraged by the firmness of the Patriarch, did not flinch before the stern aspect of the Emperor, and several spoke out their thoughts, the others murmuring approval. Later writers edified their readers by composing orations which might have been delivered on such an occasion. In Theodore, the abbot of Studion, the Emperor recognized his most formidable opponent, and some words are ascribed to Theodore, which are doubtless genuine. He is reported to have denied the right of the Emperor to interfere in ecclesiastical affairs:

> "Leave the Church to its pastors and masters; attend to your own province, the State and the army. If you refuse to do this, and are bent on destroying our faith, know that though an angel came from heaven to pervert us we would not obey him, much less you"

The protest against Caesaropapism is characteristic of Theodore. The Emperor angrily dismissed the ecclesiastics, having assured Theodore that he had no intention of making a martyr of him or punishing him in any way, until the whole question had been further investigated.

Immediately after this conclave an edict was issued forbidding members of the Patriarch's party to hold meetings or assemble together in private houses. The iconodules were thus placed in the position of suspected conspirators, under the strict supervision of the Prefect of the City; and Nicephorus himself was practically a captive in his palace, under the custody of one Thomas, a patrician.

The Patriarch did not yet wholly despair of converting the Emperor, and he wrote letters to some persons who might exert an influence over him. He wrote to the Empress Theodosia, exhorting her to deter her lord from his "terrible enterprise". He also wrote to the General Logothete to the same effect, and in more threatening language to Eutychian, the First Secretary. Eutychian certainly gave no heedful ear to the admonitions of the pontiff. If the Empress saw good to intervene, or if the General Logothete ventured to remonstrate, these representations were vain. The Emperor forbade Nicephorus to exercise any longer the functions of his office.

Just at this time the Patriarch fell sick, and if the malady had proved fatal, Leo's path would have been smoothed. A successor of iconoclastic views could then have been appointed, without the odium of deposing such an illustrious prelate as Nicephorus. If Leo did not desire the death of his adversary, he decided at this time who was to be the next Patriarch. Hopes had been held out to John the Grammarian that he might aspire to the dignity, but on maturer reflexion it was agreed that he was too young and obscure. Theodotos Kassiteras, who seems to have been the most distinguished supporter of Leo throughout this ecclesiastical conflict, declared himself ready to be ordained and fill the Patriarchal chair.

But Nicephorus did not succumb to the disease. He recovered at the beginning of Lent when the Synod was about to meet. Theophanes, a brother of the Empress, was sent to invite Nicephorus to attend, but was not admitted to his presence. A clerical deputation, however, waited at the Patriarcheion, and the unwilling Patriarch was persuaded by Thomas the patrician, his custodian, to receive them. Nicephorus was in a prostrate condition, but his visitors could not persuade him to make any concessions. Their visit had somehow become known in the city and a riotous mob, chiefly consisting of soldiers, had gathered in front of the Patriarcheion. A rush into the building seemed so imminent that Thomas was obliged to close the gates, while the crowd of enthusiastic iconoclasts loaded with curses the obnoxious names of Tarasius and Nicephorus.

After this the Synod met and deposed Nicephorus. The enemies of Leo encouraged the belief that the idea of putting Nicephorus to death was seriously entertained, and it is stated that Nicephorus himself addressed a letter to the Emperor, begging him to depose him and do nothing more violent, for his own sake. But there is no good reason to suppose that Leo thought of taking the Patriarch's life. By such a course he would have gained nothing, and increased his unpopularity among certain sections of his subjects. It was sufficient to remove Nicephorus from Constantinople, especially as he had been himself willing to resign his chair. On the Bosphorus, not far north of the Imperial city, he had built himself a retreat, known as the monastery of Agathos. Thither he was first removed, but after a short time it was deemed expedient to increase the distance between the fallen Patriarch and the scene of his activity. For this purpose Bardas, a nephew of the Emperor, was sent to transport him to another but somewhat remoter monastery of his own building, that of the great Martyr Theodore, higher up the Bosphorus on the Asiatic side. The want of respect which the kinsman of the Emperor showed to his prisoner as they sailed to their destination made the pious shake their heads, and the tragic end of the young man four years later served as a welcome text for edifying sermons. Bardas as he sat on the deck summoned the Patriarch to his presence; the guards did not permit "the great hierarch" to seat himself; and their master irreverently maintained his sitting posture in the presence of grey hairs. Nicephorus, seeing the haughty and presumptuous heart of the young man, addressed him thus: "Fair Bardas, learn by the misfortunes of others to meet your own". The words were regarded as a prophecy of the misfortunes in store for Bardas.

On Easter day (April 1) Theodotos Kassiteras was tonsured and enthroned as Patriarch of Constantinople. The tone of the Patriarchal Palace notably altered when Theodotos took the place of Nicephorus. He is described by an opponent as a good-natured man who had a reputation for virtue, but was lacking in personal piety. It has been already observed that he was a relative of Constantine V., and as soon as he was consecrated he scandalized stricter brethren in a way which that monarch would have relished. A luncheon party was held in the Patriarcheion, and clerks and monks who had eaten no meat for years, were constrained by the kind compulsion of their host to partake unsparingly of the rich viands which were set before them. The dull solemnity of an archiepiscopal table was now enlivened by frivolous conversation, amusing stories, and ribald wit.

The first duty of Theodotos was to preside at the iconoclastic Council, for which all the preparations had been made. It met soon after his consecration, in St. Sophia, in the presence of the two Emperors. The decree of this Synod reflects a less violent spirit than that which had animated the Council assembled by Constantine V. With some abbreviations and omissions it ran as follows: —

> "The Emperors Constantine (V.) and Leo (IV.) considering the public safety to depend on orthodoxy, gathered a numerous synod of spiritual fathers and bishops, and condemned the unprofitable practice, unwarranted by tradition, of making and adoring icons, preferring worship in spirit and in truth.
>
> "On this account, the Church of God remained tranquil for not a few years, and the subjects enjoyed peace, till the government passed from men to a woman, and the Church was distressed by female simplicity. She followed the counsel of very ignorant bishops, she convoked an injudicious assembly, and laid down the doctrine of painting in a material medium the Son and Logos of God, and of representing the Mother of God and the Saints by dead figures, and enacted that these representations should be adored, heedlessly defying the proper doctrine of the Church. So she sullied our latreutic adoration, and declared that what is due only to God should be offered to lifeless icons; she foolishly said that they were full of divine grace, and admitted the lighting of candles and the burning of incense before them. Thus she caused the simple to err.
>
> "Hence we ostracize from the Catholic Church the unauthorized manufacture of pseudonymous icons; we reject the adoration defined by Tarasius; we annul the decrees of his synod, on the ground that they granted undue honor to pictures: and we condemn the lighting and candles and offering of incense.
>
> "But gladly accepting the holy Synod, which met at Blachernae in the temple of the unspotted Virgin in the reign of Constantine and Leo as firmly based on the doctrine of the Fathers, we decree that the manufacture of icons-we abstain from calling them idols, for there are degrees of evil-is neither worshipful nor serviceable".

The theological theory of image-worship must be left to divines. In its immediate aspect, the question might seem to have no reference to the abstract problems of metaphysical theology which had divided the Church in previous ages. But it was recognized by the theological champions of both parties that the adoration of images had a close theoretical connexion with the questions of. Christology which the Church professed to have settled at the Council of Chalcedon. The gravest charge which the leading exponents of image-worship brought against the iconoclastic doctrine was that it compromised or implicitly denied the Incarnation. It is to be observed that this inner and dogmatic import of the controversy, although it appears in the early stages, is far more conspicuous in the disputations which marked the later period of iconoclasm. To the two most prominent defenders of pictures, the Patriarch Nicephorus and the abbot of Studion, this is the crucial point. They both regard the iconoclasts as heretics who have lapsed into the errors of Arianism or Monophysitisin. The other aspects of the veneration of sacred pictures are treated as of secondary importance in the writings of Theodore of Studion; the particular question of pictures of Christ absorbs his interest, as the great point at issue, believing, as he did, that iconoclasm was an insidious attack on the orthodox doctrine of the Incarnation.

We must now glance at the acts of oppression and persecution of which Leo is said to have been guilty against those who refused to join his party and accept the guidance of the new Patriarch. Most eminent among the sufferers was Theodore, the abbot of Studion, who seemed fated to incur the displeasure of his sovrans. He had been persecuted in the reign of Constantine VI.; he had been persecuted in the reign of Nicephorus; he was now to be persecuted more sorely still by Leo the Armenian. He had probably spoken bolder words than any of his party, when the orthodox bishops and abbots appeared before the Emperor. He is reported to have said to Leo's face that it was useless and harmful to talk with a heretic; and if this be an exaggeration of his admiring biographer, he certainly told him that Church matters were outside an Emperor's province. When the edict went forth, through the mouth of the Prefect of the City, forbidding the iconodules to utter their opinions in public or to hold any communications one with another, Theodore said that silence was a crime. At this juncture he encouraged the Patriarch in his firmness, and when the Patriarch was dethroned, addressed to him a congratulatory letter, and on Palm Sunday (March 25), caused the monks of Studion to carry their holy icons round the monastery in solemn procession, singing hymns as they went. And when the second "pseudo-synod" (held after Easter) was approaching, he supplied his monks with a formula of refusal, in case they should be summoned to take part in it. By all these acts, which, coming from a man of his influence were doubly significant, he made himself so obnoxious to the author of the iconoclastic policy that at length he was thrown into prison. His correspondence then became known to the Emperor, and among his recent letters, one to Pope Paschal, describing the divisions of the Church, was conspicuous. Theodore was accompanied into exile by Nicolas, one of the Studite brethren. They were first sent to a fort named Metopa situated on the Mysian Lake of Artynia. The second prison was Bonita, and there the sufferings of the abbot of Studion are said to have been terrible. His biographer delights in describing the stripes which were inflicted on the saint and dwells on the sufferings which he underwent from the extremes of heat and cold as the seasons changed. The visitations of fleas and lice in the ill-kept prison are not omitted. In reading such accounts we must make a large allowance for the exaggeration of a bigoted partisan, and we must remember that in all ages the hardships of imprisonment endured for political and religious causes are seldom or never fairly stated by those who sympathize with the "martyrs". In the present instance, the harsh treatment is intelligible. If Theodore had only consented to hold his peace, without surrendering his opinions, he would have been allowed to live quietly in some monastic retreat at a distance from Constantinople. If he had behaved with the dignity of Nicephorus, whose example he might well have imitated, he would have avoided the pains of scourgings and the unpleasant experiences of an oriental prison-house. From Bonita he was transferred to the city of Smyrna, and thrown into a dungeon, where he languished until at the accession of Michael II he was released from prison. In Smyrna he came into contact with a kinsman of Leo, named Bardas, who resided there as Strategos of the Thrakesian Theme.

There can be little doubt that this Bardas was the same young man who showed scant courtesy to the fallen Patriarch Nicephorus, on his way to the monastery of St. Theodore. At Smyrna Bardas fell sick, and someone, who believed in the divine powers of the famous abbot of Studion, advised him to consult the prisoner. Theodore exhorted the nephew of Leo to abjure his uncle's heresy. The virtue of the saint proved efficacious; the young man recovered; but the repentance was hollow, he returned to his error; then retribution followed and he died. This is one of the numerous stories invented to glorify the abbot of Studion, the bulwark of image-worship.

One of the gravest offences of Theodore in the Emperor's eyes was doubtless his attempt to excite the Pope to intervene in the controversy. We have two letters which he, in conjunction with other image-worshippers, addressed to Pope Paschal I from Bonita. His secret couriers maintained communications with Rome, where some important members of the party had found a refuge, and Paschal was induced to send to Leo an argumentative letter in defence of images.

The rigour of the treatment dealt out to Theodore was exceptional. Many of the orthodox ecclesiastics who attended the Synod of April a.d. 815 submitted to the resolutions of that assembly. Those who held out were left at large till the end of the year, but early in a.d. 816 they were conducted to distant places of exile. This hardship, however, was intended only to render them more amenable to the gentler method of persuasion. After a few days, they were recalled to Constantinople, kept in mild confinement, and after Easter (April 20), they were handed over to John the Grammarian, who presided over the monastery of Saints Sergius and Bacchus. He undertook to convince the abbots of their theological error, and his efforts were crowned with success in the case of at least seven. Others resisted the arguments of the seducer, and among them were Hilarion, the Exarch of the Patriarchal monasteries, and Theophanes the Chronographer

Theophanes, whose chronicle was almost our only guide for the first twelve years of the ninth century, had lived a life unusually ascetic even in his own day, in the monastery of Agros, at Sigriane near Cyzicus. He had not been present at the Synod nor sent into exile, but in the spring of a.d. 816 the Emperor sent him a flattering message, couched in soft words, requesting him to come "to pray for us who are about to march against the Barbarians". Theophanes, who was suffering from an acute attack of kidney disease, obeyed the command, and was afterwards consigned to the custody of John. Proving obstinate he was confined in a cell in the Palace of Eleutherios for nearly two years, and when he was mortally ill of his malady, he was removed to the island of Samothrace where he expired (March 12, a.d. 818) about three weeks after his arrival.

When we find that Leo's oppressions have been exaggerated in particular cases, we shall be all the more inclined to allow for exaggeration in general descriptions of his persecutions. We read that "some were put to death by the sword, others tied in sacks and sunk like stones in water, and women were stripped naked in the presence of men and scourged". If such atrocities had been fluent, we should have heard much more about them. The severer punishments were probably inflicted for some display of fanatical insolence towards the Emperor personally. His chief object was to remove from the capital those men, whose influence would conflict with the accomplishment of his policy. But there may have been fanatical monks, who, stirred with an ambition to outstrip the boldness of Theodore of Studion, bearded the Emperor to his face, and to them may have been meted out extreme penalties. Again, it is quite possible that during the destruction of pictures in the city, which ensued on their condemnation by the Synod, serious riots occurred in the streets, and death penalties may have been awarded to persons who attempted to frustrate the execution of the imperial commands. We are told that "the sacred representations" were at the mercy of anyone who chose to work his wicked will upon them. Holy vestments, embroidered with sacred figures, were torn into shreds and cast ignominiously upon the ground; pictures and illuminated missals were cut up with axes and burnt in the public squares. Some of the baser sort insulted the icons by smearing them with cow-dung and foul-smelling ointments.

Chapter III
Michael II., The Amorian
(A.D. 820-829)

§1. The Accession of Michael (A.D. 820)
The Coronation and Marriage of Theophilus (A.D. 821)

While his accomplices were assassinating the Emperor, Michael lay in his cell, awaiting the issue of the enterprise which meant for him death or empire, according as it failed or prospered. The conspirators, as we have seen, did not bungle in their work, and when it was accomplished, they hastened to greet Michael as their new master, and to bear him in triumph to the Imperial throne. With his legs still encased in the iron fetters he sat on his august seat, and all the servants and officers of the palace congregated to fall at his feet. Time, perhaps, seemed to fly quickly in the surprise of his new position, and it was not till midday that the gyves which so vividly reminded him of the sudden change of his fortunes were struck off his limbs. The historians tell of a difficulty in finding the key of the fetters, and it was John Hexabulios, Logothete of the Course, who remembered that Leo had hidden it in his dress

About noon, without washing his hands or making any other seemly preparation, Michael, attended by his supporters, proceeded to the Great Church, there to receive the Imperial crown from the hands of the Patriarch, and to obtain recognition from the people. No hint is given as to the attitude of the Patriarch Theodotos to the conspiracy, but he seems to have made no difficulty in performing the ceremony of coronation for the successful conspirator. The Amorian soldier received the crown from the prelate's hands, and the crowd was ready to acclaim the new Augustus. Those who held to image worship did not regret the persecutor of their faith, but thought that he had perished justly; and perhaps to most in that superstitious populace the worst feature in the whole work seemed to be that his blood had stained a holy building. We have already seen how Michael dealt with the Empress Theodosia and her children.

The new Roman Emperor was a rude provincial, coarse in manners, ill-educated, and superstitious. But he was vigorous, ambitious, and prudent, and he had worked his way up in the army by his own energy and perseverance. Amorion, the city of his birth, in Upper Phrygia, was at this time an important place, as the capital of the Anatolic province. It was the goal of many a Saracen invasion. Its strong walls had defied the generals of the Caliphs in the days of the Isaurian Leo; but it was destined, soon after it had won the glory of giving a dynasty to the Empire, to be captured by the Unbelievers. This Phrygian town was a head-quarter for Jews, and for the heretics who were known as Athingani. It is said that Michael inherited from his parents Athingan views, but according to another account he was a Sabbatian. Whatever be the truth about this, he was inclined to tolerate heresies, of which he must have seen much at his native town in the days of his youth. He was also favorably disposed to the Jews; but the statement that his grandfather was a converted Jew does not rest on very good authority. It is certain that his parents were of humble rank, and that his youth, spent among heretics, Hebrews, and half-Hellenized Phrygians, was subject to influences which were very different from the Greek polish of the capital. One so trained must have felt himself strange among the men of old nobility, of Hellenic education, and ecclesiastical orthodoxy with whom he had to deal in Constantinople. He did not disguise his contempt for Hellenic culture, and he is handed down to history as an ignorant churl. Such a man was a good aim for the ridicule of witty Byzantines, and it is recorded that many lampoons were published on the crowned boor.

The low-born Phrygian who founded a new dynasty in the ninth century reminds us of the low-born Dardanian who founded a new dynasty exactly three hundred years before. The first Justin, like the second Michael, was ignorant of letters. It was told of Justin that he had a mechanical contrivance for making his signature, and of Michael it was popularly reported that another could read through a book more quickly than he could spell out the six letters of his name. They were both soldiers and had worked their way up in the service, and they both held the same post at the time of their elevation. Justin was the commander of the Excubitors when he was called upon to succeed Anastasius, even as Michael when he stepped into the place of Leo. But Michael could not say like Justin that his hands were pure of blood. The parallel may be carried still further. The soldier of Ulpiana, like the soldier of Amorion, reigned for about nine years, and each had a successor who was a remarkable contrast to himself. After the rude Justin, came his learned and intellectual nephew Justinian; after the rude Michael, his polished son Theophilus.

Michael shared the superstitions which were not confined to his own class. He was given to consulting soothsayers and diviners; and, if report spoke true, his career was directed by prophecies and omens. It is said that his first marriage was brought about through the utterances of a soothsayer. He had been an officer in the army of the Anatolic Theme, in days before he had entered the service of Bardanes. The general of that Theme, whose name is not recorded, was as ready as most of his contemporaries to believe in prognostication, and when one of the Athingan sect who professed to tell fortunes, declared to him that Michael and another officer of his staff were marked out for Imperial rank in the future, he lost no time in taking measures to unite them with his family. He prepared a feast, and chose them out of all the officers to be his guests, to their own astonishment. But a greater surprise awaited them, for when they were heated with wine, he offered them his daughters in marriage. At this unexpected condescension, the young men, of whom one at least was of humble birth, were stupefied and speechless. They drew back at first from an honour of which they deemed themselves unworthy; but the superstitious general overcame their scruples, and the marriages took place. Thus it came about that Michael won Thecla, who became the mother of the Emperor Theophilus. The other son-in-law, whoever he may have been, was not so fortunate; in his case the soothsayer was conspicuously at fault.

Theophilus, for whom Leo V. had probably stood sponsor, was adult when his father came to the throne, and on the following Whitsunday (May 12 A.D. 821) Michael, according to the usual practice, secured the succession by elevating him to the rank of Basileus and Augustus. The ceremony of his marriage was celebrated on the same occasion. Having received the Imperial crown from his father's hands in St. Sophia, he was wedded by the Patriarch, in the Church of St. Stephen in the Palace, to Theodora, a Paphlagonian lady, whose father and uncle were officers in the army. The ceremony was followed by her coronation as Augusta.

It is probable that the provincial Theodora, of an obscure but well-to-do family, was discovered by means of the bride-show custom which in the eighth and ninth centuries was habitually employed for the purpose of selecting brides for Imperial heirs. Messengers were sent into the provinces to search for maidens who seemed by their exceptional physical attractions and their mental qualities worthy of sharing the throne of an Emperor. They were guided in their selection by certain fixed standards; they rejected all candidates who did not conform, in stature and in the dimensions of their heads and feet, to prescribed measures of beauty. It was thus that Maria, discovered in a small town in Paphlagonia, came to be the consort of Constantine VI., and we saw how a bride-show was held for the wedding of Stauracius. In later times Michael III. and Leo VI. would win their brides in the same fashion; and it is not improbable that Irene of Athens owed her marriage with Leo IV. to this custom.

The bride-show of Theophilus has been embroidered with legendary details, and it has been misdated, but there is no reason for doubting that it was actually held. The story represents Theophilus as still unmarried when he became sole Emperor after his father's death. His stepmother Euphrosyne assembled the maidens, who had been gathered from all the provinces, in the Pearl-chamber in the Palace, and gave the Emperor a golden apple to bestow upon her who pleased him best. Theophilus halted before Kasia, a lady of striking beauty and literary attainments, and addressed to her a cynical remark, apparently couched in metrical form, to which she had a ready answer in the same style.

Theophilus:
A woman was the fount and source
Of all man's tribulation.

Kasia:
And from a woman sprang the course
Of man's regeneration.

The boldness of the retort did not please the Emperor, and he gave the golden apple to Theodora.

It was in the spring of A.D. 821, and not nine years later, that Theophilus made his choice, and it was his mother, Thecla, if she was still alive, and not Euphrosyne, who presided over the bride-show. Some may think that the golden apple, the motif of the judgment of Paris, must be rejected as a legendary trait in the story; yet it seems possible that the apple had been deliberately borrowed from the Greek myth as a symbol by which the Emperor intimated his choice and was a regular feature of the Byzantine bride-shows. Nor does there seem any reason to doubt that the poetess Kasia was one of the chosen maidens; and the passage between her and the Emperor is, if not true, happily invented so far as her extant epigrams reveal her character, Disappointed in her chance of empire, Kasia resolved to renounce the world, and a letter of Theodore, the abbot of Studion, is preserved in which he approves of her design, and compliments her on the learning and skill of some literary compositions which she had sent him.

The pleasing story of the bride-show of Theophilus, in which Kasia is the heroine, did not find favour with the monk who wrote an edifying biography of the sainted Theodora. He would not allow that she owed her elevation to the too ready tongue of her rival who had presumed to measure wits with the Emperor, and he invented a different story in which Kasia is ignored. According to this frigid fiction, Theophilus selected seven of the maidens, gave each of them an apple, and summoned them again on the morrow. He asked each of them for her apple, but the apples were not forthcoming. Theodora alone produced hers, and along with it offered a second to the Emperor. "This first apple, which I have kept safe" she said, "is the emblem of my maidenhood; the second, do not decline it, is the fee of the son which shall be born to us". When Theophilus, in amazement, asked her to explain this oracle, she told him that at Nicomedia, on her way to Constantinople, she had visited a holy man who lived in a tower, and that he had prophesied her elevation to the throne and had given her the apple.

§2. The Civil War (A.D. 821-823)

Of the three actors in the historical drama which was said to have been shadowed forth by the soothsayer of Philomelion, one has passed finally from the scene. The last act is to take the form of a conflict between the two survivors, Michael of Amorion and Thomas of Gaziura. This conflict is generally known as the rebellion of Thomas, but it assumed the dimensions and the dignity of a civil war. Two rivals fought for a crown, which one of them had seized, but could not yet be said to have firmly grasped. Michael had been regularly elected, acclaimed, and crowned in the capital, and he had the advantage of possessing the Imperial city. His adversary had the support of most of the Asiatic provinces; he was only a rebel because he failed.

We have seen how Thomas clung to his master and patron Bardanes whom others had deserted (A.D. 803). When the cause of Bardanes was lost, he probably saved himself by fleeing to Syria and taking up his abode among the Saracens, with whom he had lived before. For in the reign of Irene he had entered the service of a patrician, and, having been discovered in an attempt to commit adultery with his master's wife, he was constrained to seek a refuge in the dominions of the Caliph, where he seems to have lived for a considerable time. His second sojourn there lasted for about ten years (A.D. 803-813). We saw how he received a military command from his old fellow-officer, Leo the Armenian, and he rose in arms shortly before that Emperor's death.

If he was tempted to rise against Leo, much more was he tempted to dispute the crown with Michael, with whom he seems to have had a rivalry of old standing. Thomas was much the elder of the two; at the time of his rising he was an old man. One of his legs was maimed; but his age and lameness did not impair his activity. The lame man was personally more popular than the lisper; for, while Michael's manners were coarse and brusque, Thomas was courteous and urbane. His Slavonic origin hardly counted against him; men were by this time becoming familiar with Romanized Slavs.

But Thomas did not come forward as himself; and this is a strange feature of the rebellion which it is difficult to understand. He did not offer himself to the inhabitants of Asia Minor as Thomas of Gaziura, but he pretended that he was really one who was generally supposed to be dead, a crowned Augustus, no other than Constantine the Sixth, son of Irene. That unfortunate Emperor, blinded by the orders of his mother, had died, if not before her dethronement, at all events in the first years of Nicephorus. The operation of blinding had not been performed in public, and a pretender might construct a tale that another had been substituted, and that the true Constantine had escaped. But it is hard to see how the fraud could have been successful even for a time in the case of Thomas. He might easily enough have palmed himself off among barbarian neighbors as the deposed Emperor. Or if he had produced an obscure stranger and given out that this was Constantine who for more than twenty years had lurked in some safe hiding-place, we could understand that the fiction might have imposed on the Themes of Asia. But we cannot easily conceive how one who had been recently before the eye of the world as Thomas, Commander of the Federate and whose earlier career must have been more or less known by his contemporaries, could suddenly persuade people that all this time he was not himself. One almost suspects that some link in the chain of events is lost which might have explained the feasibility of the deceit. If Thomas had withdrawn for some years to Syria, he might have returned in the new character of an Augustus who was supposed to be dead. And indeed in one account of the rebellion it is implied that he started from Syria, perhaps with some Saracen support at his back.

The pretender was not content with being Constantine, son of Irene; he resolved, like Constantine the Great, to have a son named Constantius. Accordingly he adopted a man of mongrel race, whose true name is unknown, and called him Constantius. Our record describes this adopted son in terms of the utmost contempt,—as a base and ugly manikin. But he must have had some ability, for his "father" trusted him with the command of armies.

It is impossible to distinguish with certainty the early stages of the insurrection of Thomas, or to determine how far it had spread at the time of Michael's accession. He established his power by winning the district of Chaldia, in eastern Pontus. He also secured some strong places in the Armeniac Theme, in which Gaziura, his native town, was situated, but the soldiers of this Theme did not espouse his cause. It was to the eastern provinces that he chiefly looked for support at first, but his power presently extended to the west. The false Constantine and his son could soon reckon the greater part of Asia Minor, from the borders of Armenia to the shores of the Aegean, as their dominion. The Paulician heretics, who were persecuted by Leo, flocked to their standard. They intercepted the taxes which should have been conveyed to Constantinople and used the money for winning adherents to their cause. The cities which would not voluntarily have acknowledged them were constrained by fear. Soon they could boast that only two armies in Asia had not joined them, the Opsikian and the Armeniac. The patrician Katakylas, Count of Opsikion, was a nephew of Michael, and remained true to his uncle. Olbianos, strategos of the Armeniacs, espoused the same cause. But the meagre and disorderly accounts of the war which have reached us do not inform us what Olbianos and Katakylas did, or whether they did anything, to stem the torrent of rebellion. No dates are given, and even the order of events is obscure.

But if Michael and his supporters made no signal effort to oppose the progress of the danger, the attention of Thomas was diverted to another enemy. The civil war in the Empire was an opportunity for the Caliph, and the Saracens began to make excursions in the Roman lands which were left insufficiently protected, as the regular defenders had abandoned their posts to swell the army of Thomas. Perhaps the murmurs of his soldiers convinced Thomas that he must relinquish for a time his war against his countrymen to repel the common foe. But if he was yielding to the wishes of his followers, in taking measures to protect their homes, he made a skilful use of the danger and turned it completely to his own advantage. His long sojourns among the Moslems stood him in good stead now. His first movement was to invade Syria and display his immense forces to the astonished eyes of the Saracens. Perhaps such a large Roman army had seldom passed the Taurus since Syria had become a Saracen possession. But the object of this invasion was not to harry or harm the invaded lands, but rather to frighten the enemy into making a treaty with such a powerful commander. The design was crowned with success. The Caliph Mamun empowered persons in authority to meet the pretender, and a compact of alliance was arranged. Thomas or Constantine was recognized as Emperor of the Romans by the Commander of the Faithful, who undertook to help him to dethrone his rival. In return for this service, Thomas is said to have agreed not only to surrender certain border territories which are not specified, but to become a tributary of the Caliph.

After the conclusion of this treaty, which turned a foe into a friend, we expect to find the Emperor Constantine hastening back to recover the throne of the Isaurians. But before he left Syria he took a strange step. With the consent or at the instance of his new allies he proceeded to Antioch, in order to be crowned by the Patriarch Job as Basileus of the Romans. The coronation of a Roman Emperor in Antioch in the ninth century was a singular event. We cannot imagine that Thomas was accompanied thither by his army; but doubtless the Greek Christians of the place flocked to see the unaccustomed sight, and when the Patriarch Job placed the crown on the head of the Basileus they may have joined his attendants in acclaiming him. We have to go back to the fifth century for a like scene. It was in Syrian Antioch that Leontius, the tyrant who rose against Zeno, was crowned and proclaimed Augustus. The scale and gravity of the rebellion of the Isaurian Leontius render it not unfit to be compared with the rebellion of the later pretender, who also professed to be of Isaurian stock.

But when we consider the circumstances more closely the coronation assumes a puzzling aspect. If Thomas had been simply Thomas, we can understand that he might have grasped at a chance, which was rare for a rebel in his day, to be crowned by a Patriarch out of Constantinople, even though that Patriarch was not a Roman subject. But Thomas, according to the story, gave out that he was an Emperor already. He had borrowed the name and identity of the Emperor

Constantine VI.; he had therefore, according to his own claim, been crowned Augustus by the Patriarch of Constantinople forty years before. What then is the meaning of his coronation at Antioch? One would think that such a ceremony would weaken rather than strengthen his position. It might be interpreted as a tacit confession that there was some flaw in the title of the re-arisen Constantine. It would have been requisite for an Emperor who had been first crowned at Antioch to repeat the ceremony when he had established himself on the Bosphorus; but it is strange that one who had declared that he had been formally consecrated at Constantinople by the chief Patriarch should come to Antioch to receive an irregular consecration from a lesser prelate. It does not appear that the tyrant had abandoned his claim to be another than himself, and, having won his first followers by an imposture, now threw off the cloak and came forward as Thomas of Gaziura. It may be suggested that the coronation was not contrived by the wish of the pretender, but by the policy of Mamun. The reception of the emblem of sovranty at the hands of a Patriarch, who was the subject of the Caliph, may have been intended as a symbolical acknowledgment of the Caliph's overlordship and a pledge of his future submission as a tributary.

The prospect of the tyrants looked brighter than ever when they returned to the lands of the Empire. Men of all sorts and races and regions had flocked to their standards-Slavs, Persians, Armenians, Iberians, and many from the regions of the Caucasus and the eastern shores of the Euxine. The total number of the forces is estimated at eighty thousand. Reports meanwhile reached Constantinople of the gathering of this large host. But Michael took it for granted that rumour outran the truth, and deemed it enough to send into the field a small army, totally insufficient to cope with the foe. The thousands of Michael were swallowed up by the tens of thousands of Thomas. As no formidable resistance was offered to the tyrant's progress in Asia Minor, he prepared to attack the city itself. For this enterprise, in which so many had failed before him, it was judged indispensable to possess a fleet. The City of the Bosphorus had over and over again defied a joint attack by land and sea; it was naturally inferred that an attack by land alone would have no chances of success. The pretender therefore set himself to gather a fleet, and it would seem that he had no difficulty in seizing the fleets of the Aegean and the Kibyrrhaeot Themes, which together formed the Thematic or provincial navy. Thus all the warships stationed in the eastern parts of the Empire were in his hands, except the Imperial fleet itself, which lay at the Imperial city. In addition to these, he built new warships and new ships of transport. When all was ready, he caused his naval forces to assemble at Lesbos and await his orders, while he himself advanced to the Hellespont and secured Abydos. And now he met his first reverse. All had yielded to him as he swept on through the Asiatic Themes, except one place, whose name our historians do not mention. He did not think it worthwhile to delay himself, but he left a considerable part of his army under the command of Constantius, to reduce this stubborn fortress. It seems probable too that this dividing of his forces formed part of a further design. We may guess that while Constantine was to cross by the western gate of the Propontis and advance on the city from the west, Constantius was to approach the eastern strait and attack the city on the south. But if this was the plan of operations, Constantius was not destined to fulfill his part of it. Olbianos, the general of the Armeniac Theme, was biding his time and watching for an opportunity. His army was not large enough to try an issue with the united forces of the enemy, but his chance came when those forces were divided. He set an ambush to waylay the younger tyrant, who, as he advanced securely, supposing that the way was clear, allowed his men to march in disorder. Constantius was slain and his head was sent to Constantine. This was the first check in the triumphant course of the war, though the death of the "son" may have caused little grief to the "father".

The scene of operations now shifts from Asia to Europe. The Emperor, seeing that his adversary was preparing to cross the straits, had gone forth at the head of a small army and visited some of the cities of Thrace in order to confirm them against the violence or seductions of the tyrant and assure himself of their steadfast faith. But his care availed little. On a dark moonless night Thomas transported his troops to various spots on the Thracian shore, starting from an obscure haven named Horkosion. About the same time the fleet arrived from Lesbos and sailed into the waters of the Propontis. No resistance was offered by the inhabitants of Thrace when they saw the immense numbers of the invading host. Michael seems to have lingered, perhaps somewhere on the shores of the Propontis, to observe what effect the appearance of his foe would produce on the cities which had yesterday pledged themselves to stand true, and when he learned that they were cowed into yielding, he returned to the city and set about making it ready to withstand a siege. The garrison was recruited by loyal soldiers from the Asiatic Themes, now free from the presence of the pretender. The Imperial fleet, supplied with "Marine Fire", was stationed not in the Golden Horn, but in the three artificial harbours on the southern shore of the city,—the port of Hormisdas, which was probably already known by its later name of Bucoleon; the Sophian harbour, further to the west; and beyond it the harbour of Kaisarios. The entrance to the Golden Horn was blocked by the Iron Chain, which was stretched across the water from a point near the Gate of Eugenios to the Castle of Galata. In making these dispositions Michael was perhaps availing himself of the experience of previous sieges. When the Saracens attacked the city in the seventh century, Constantine IV. had disposed a portion of his naval forces in the harbour of Kaisarios. In the second attack of the same foe in the eighth century Leo III. had stretched the Iron Chain, but he seems to have stationed his own ships outside the Horn.

The host of Thomas had been increased by new adherents from the European provinces, and Slavs from Macedonia flocked to the standard of the Slavonian pretender. But he needed a new general and a new son. To succeed the unlucky leader, whom he had destined to be Constantius the Fourth, he chose a monk, already bearing an Imperial name, and worthy in the opinion of the tyrant to be Anastasius the Third; not worthy, however, of such an exalted place, in the opinion of our historians, who describe him as an ugly man, with a face like an Ethiopian's from excessive wine-drinking, and of insane mind. But the monk was not fitted to lead troops to battle, and for this office Thomas won the services of a banished general named Gregory, who had perhaps better cause than himself to hate the name of Michael. Gregory Pterotos was a nephew of Leo the Armenian, and, on the death of his uncle, whom he loved, fear had not held him back from entering the presence of his successor, where, instead of falling among those who grovelled at the Imperial feet, he overwhelmed him with reproaches for the murderous deed. The Emperor merely said, "I know the greatness of your sorrow and the ocean of your distress", but two days later he banished this fearless kinsman of his predecessor to the island of Skyros. Gregory was not unwilling to attach himself to the rival of him who had banished himself and dethroned his uncle, and he was speedily entrusted with the command of ten thousand men and sent on to open the assault on the Imperial city.

It was already winter, and the first year of Michael's reign was drawing to a close, when Gregory took up his station on the north-west of the city, in the suburbs outside Blachernae, while the fleet, under another unnamed commander, reached the same quarter by sailing up the inlet of the Golden Horn, having evidently unfastened the Iron Chain where it was attached to the Castle of Galata. On the banks of the Barbyses, a stream which flows into the Horn, the leaders of the sea forces and the land forces could concert their plans together. No action, however, was taken until Constantius and Anastasius arrived with their mighty host. The leaders seem to have imagined that when this vast array spread out before the walls of the city, and their ships filled the Golden Horn and threatened the harbours on the Propontis, the inhabitants would be so utterly dismayed by the sight of the overwhelming numbers that they would throw open their gates in despair. But it soon became clear that the city and its masters were resolved to withstand even such a vast force; they trusted in their impregnable walls. It was the first business of Thomas, when he saw that a siege was inevitable, to reduce the suburbs and villages which lay north of the city along the shores of the Bosphorus. These places could not resist. The inhabitants were doubtless glad to submit as speedily as possible to any one engaged in besieging the city, remembering too well how but a few years ago they had been harried by another and more terrible enemy, the Bulgarian Krum.

The siege began in the month of December. The course of events from this point to the end of the war may be conveniently divided into five stages.

1. December 821 to February or March 822.—Thomas spent some days in disposing his forces and preparing his engines. He pitched his own tent in the suburbs beyond Blachernae, not far from the noble building which rose towards heaven like a palace, the church of St. Cosmas and St. Damian, the physicians who take no fee for their services to men. Until the reign of Heraclius the northwestern corner of the city between the Palace of Blachernae and the Golden Horn must have been defended by a fortification of which no traces survive. Heraclius, whether before or after the siege of the Avars (A.D. 626), had connected the Palace with the seaward fortifications by a wall which is flanked by three admirably built hexagonal towers. But the assaults of the Bulgarians in A.D. 813 seem to have proved that this "Single Wall of Blachernae", as it was called, was an insufficient defense, and Leo V., in expectation of a second Bulgarian siege, constructed a second outer wall, parallel to that of Heraclius, and forming with it a sort of citadel which was known as the Brachionion .

The troops on whom it devolved to attack the long western walls of Theodosius, from the Palace of Blachernae to the Golden Gate, were assigned to the subordinate tyrant Anastasius, to whose dignity a high command was due, but others were at hand to keep the inexperienced monk from blundering. The main attack was to be directed against the quarter of Blachernae. Here were gathered all the resources of the engineer's art, rams and tortoises, catapults and city-takers; and over these operations Thomas presided himself.

In the city meanwhile the aid of Heaven and the inventions of men were summoned to defend the walls. On the lofty roof of the church of the Mother of God in Blachernae, the Emperor solemnly fixed the Roman standard, in the sight of the enemy, and prayed for succour against them. Presently the besiegers beheld the young Emperor Theophilus walking at the head of a priestly procession round the walls of the city, and bearing with him the life-giving fragments of the holy Cross, and raiment of the mother of Christ.

But, if he employed superstitious spells, Michael did not neglect human precautions. He too, like his opponent, called to his service all the resources of the art of the engineer, and the machines of the besieged proved in the end more effectual than those of the besieger. Simultaneous attacks by land and sea were frustrated, and on land at least the repulse of the assailants was wholly due to the superior machines of the assailed. The missiles which were shot from the city carried farther than those of Thomas, and great courage was required to venture near enough to scale or batter the walls. Ladders and battering-rams were easily foiled by the skillful handling of engines mounted on the battlements, and at last the attacking host retired from the volleys of well-aimed missiles within the shelter of their camp. At sea, too, the assailants were discomfited, but the discomfiture was perhaps chiefly caused by the rising of an adverse wind. The ships of Thomas were provided both with "liquid fire" and with four-legged city-takers, from whose lofty storeys flaming missiles might be hurled upon and over the sea-walls of the city. But the violent wind rendered it impossible to make an effective use of these contrivances, and it was soon clear that the attack on the seaside had failed.

Foiled at every point, Thomas was convinced that he had no chance of succeeding until the severity of winter had passed, and he retired from his position to await the coming of spring, whether in the cities of Thrace or on the opposite coasts of Asia.

2. Spring, 822 A.D.—At the coming of spring Thomas reassembled his land forces and his ships at Constantinople and prepared for another simultaneous attack on both elements. Michael meanwhile had made use of the respite from hostilities to reinforce his garrison considerably, and during this second siege he was able to do more than defend the walls: he could venture to sally out against the enemy. It was also probably during the lull in the war that some repairs were made in the Wall of Leo, recorded by inscriptions which are still preserved.

We are told that when the day dawned on which a grand assault was to be made on the walls of Blachernae, the Emperor ascended the wall himself and addressed the enemy, who were within hearing. He urged them to desert the rebel and seek pardon and safety in the city. His words were not received with favour, nor did he imagine that they would move those whom he addressed. But he achieved the effect which he desired, though not the effect at which his speech seemed to aim. The foe concluded that the besieged must needs be in great straits, when the Emperor held such parley from the walls. With confident spirits and in careless array they advanced to the assault, supposing that they would encounter but a weak resistance. Suddenly, to their amazement and consternation, many gates opened, and soldiers, rushing forth from the city, were upon them before they had time to apprehend what had happened. The men of Michael won a brilliant victory, and Thomas was forced to abandon the assault on Blachernae. A battle by sea seems to have been fought on the same day, and it also resulted in disaster for the besiegers. The details are not recorded, but the marines of Thomas, seized by some unaccountable panic, retreated to the shore and absolutely refused to fight.

Time wore on, and the taking of the city seemed no nearer. One of the generals in the leaguer concluded that there was little chance of success, and weary of the delay he determined to change sides. This was Gregory, the exile of Skyros, and nephew of Leo the Armenian. His resolve was doubtless quickened by the fact that his wife and children were in the power of Michael; he reckoned that their safety would be assured if he deserted Thomas. Accordingly, at the head of his regiment, he left the camp and entrusted a Studite monk with the task of bearing the news to the Emperor. But the approaches to the city were so strictly guarded by the blockaders that the messenger was unable to deliver his message, and Michael remained in ignorance of the new accession to his cause. As it turned out, however, the act of Gregory proved of little profit to anyone except, perhaps, to him, whom it was intended to injure. Thomas saw that the traitor must be crushed, immediately, for it would be a serious disadvantage to have an enemy in his rear. Accordingly, he marched against him with a band of chosen soldiers; his army being so large that he could easily divert a portion without raising the blockade. The followers of Gregory were defeated, we know not where nor how; and Gregory himself, a fugitive from the field, was pursued and slain. There is a certain propriety in the part which this soldier plays in the last act of the drama, in which Leo, Michael, and Thomas were the chief performers. Leo had passed away before that last act; but his nephew, as it were, takes his place, and oscillates between his rivals, is banished by Michael and slain by Thomas.

3. Summer and Autumn A.D. 822.—The false Constantine, if he still sustained that pretence, made the most of his easy victory over the renegade. He proclaimed that he had conquered by land and sea, and sent letters to Greece and the islands of the Aegean, bearing this false news. His purpose was to reinforce his navy, which hitherto had accomplished nothing worthy of its size, by fresh ships from these regions. Nor was he disappointed. It was clearly thought in Greece, where the population was devoted to image-worship, that the pretender was carrying all before him, that the capture or surrender of the city was merely a matter of days, or at most months, and that Michael's days were numbered. A large fleet was sent, with all good-will, to hasten the success of one who professed to be an image-worshipper. No less than three hundred and fifty ships (it is alleged) arrived in the Propontis. Under given topographical conditions, when the same object is in view, history is apt to repeat itself, and we find Thomas mooring these reinforcements in the harbour of Hebdomon and on the adjacent beach, exactly as the Saracens had disposed their fleet on the two occasions on which they had attempted to capture the city.

He had formed the project of a twofold attack by sea. On the northern side the city was to be assailed by his original fleet, which lay in the Golden Horn; while the new forces were to operate against the southern walls and harbours, on the side of the Propontis. But Michael foiled this plan by prompt action. Sending his fire-propelling vessels against the squadron at Hebdomon, he destroyed it, before it had effected anything. Some of the ships were entirely burnt, others scattered, but most were captured, and towed into the city harbours, which the Imperial navy held. Such was the fate of the navy which the Themes of Hellas and Peloponnesus had sent so gladly to the discomfiture of the Phrygian Emperor.

Oh the seaside the danger was diminished; but by land the siege was protracted with varying success until the end of the year. Frequent excursions were made from the city, and sometimes prospered, whether under the leadership of the elder Emperor or of his son Theophilus, with the General Olbianos or the Count Katakylas. But on the whole the besieged were no match in the field for their foes, who far outnumbered them. Both parties must have been weary enough as the blockade wore on through the winter. It was at length broken by the intervention of a foreign power.

4. Intervention of the Bulgarians, Spring, A.D. 823.—It was from the kingdom beyond Mount Haemus that Michael received an opportune aid which proved the turning-point in the civil war. The Bulgarians had been at peace with the Empire, since Leo and king Omurtag, not long after the death of Krum, had concluded a treaty for thirty years. Communications now passed between Constantinople and Pliska, but it is uncertain who took the first step, and what was the nature of the negotiations. The simplest and earliest chronicle of the siege represents Michael as requesting Omurtag to take the field against Thomas, and Omurtag readily responding to the request. But an entirely different version is adopted in records which are otherwise unfavourable to Michael. According to this account, the proposal of alliance came from the Bulgarian king, and the Emperor declined the' offer because he was reluctant to permit Christian blood to be shed by the swords of the heathen. He tendered his sincere thanks to Omurtag, but alleged that the presence of a Bulgarian army in Thrace, even though acting in his own cause, would be a virtual violation of the Thirty Years' Peace. Omurtag, however, took the matter into his own hands, and, unable to resist the opportunity of plunder and pillage, assisted Michael in Michael's own despite. It was obviously to the interest of the Emperor that this version should obtain credit, as it relieved him from the odium of inviting pagans to destroy Christians and exposing Roman territory to the devastation of barbarians. We must leave it undecided whether it was Michael who requested, or Omurtag who offered help, but we cannot seriously doubt that the help was accorded with the full knowledge and at the desire of the besieged Emperor. It may well be that he declined to conclude any formal alliance with the Bulgarians, but merely gave them assurances that, if they marched against Thomas and paid themselves by booty, he would hold them innocent of violating the peace. The negotiations must have been conducted with great secrecy, and the account which represented Michael as unreservedly rejecting the proffered succour gained wide credence, though his enemies assigned to his refusal a less honourable motive than the desire of sparing Christian blood, and suggested that his avarice withheld him from paying the Bulgarians the money which they demanded for their services.

Omurtag then descended from Mount Haemus and marched by the great high road, by Hadrianople and Arcadiopolis, to deliver Constantinople from the Roman leaguer, even as another Bulgarian monarch had come down, more than a hundred years before, in the days of Leo III., to deliver it from the Saracens. When Thomas learned that the weight of Bulgaria was thrown into the balance and that a formidable host was advancing against him, he decided to abandon the siege and confront the new foe. It was a joyful day for the siege-worn citizens and soldiers, when they saw the camp of the besiegers broken up and the great army marching away from their gates. Only the remnant of the rebel navy still lay in the Golden Horn, as Thomas did not require it for his immediate work. The Bulgarians had already passed Arcadiopolis and reached the plain of Keduktos, near the coast between Heraclea and Selymbria. Here they awaited the approach of Thomas, and in the battle which ensued defeated him utterly. The victors soon retired, laden with booty; having thus worked much profit both to themselves and to their ally, for whom the way was now smoothed to the goal of final victory. They had destroyed the greater part of the rebel army on the field of Keduktos, and Michael was equal to dealing with the remnant himself.

5. Siege of Arcadiopolis and end of the Civil War, 823 A.D.—When the Bulgarians retreated, Thomas, still hopeful, collected the scattered troops who had been routed on the day of Keduktos, and marching north-eastward pitched his camp in the marshy plain of Diabasis,

watered by the streams of the Melas and Athyras which discharge into the lagoon of Buyak Chekmejè, about twenty miles west of Constantinople. This district was well provided with pasturage for horses, and well situated for obtaining supplies; moreover, it was within such distance from the capital that Thomas could harry the neighbouring villages. The month of May, if it had not already begun, was near at hand, when Michael went forth to decide the issue of the long struggle. He was accompanied by his faithful generals Katakylas and Olbianos, each at the head of troops of his own Theme. It is not recorded whether the younger Emperor marched with his father or was left behind to guard the city. But the city might justly feel secure now; for the marines whom Thomas had left in the Golden Horn espoused the cause of Michael, as soon as they learned the news of Keduktos.

Thomas, who felt confident of success, decided to entrap his foes by the stratagem of a feigned flight. But his followers did not share his spirit. They were cast down by the recent defeat; they were thoroughly weary of an enterprise which had lasted so much longer than they had dreamt when they lightly enlisted under the flag of the pretender; their ardour for the cause of an ambitious leader had cooled; they were sick of shedding Christian blood; they longed to return to their wives and children. This spirit in the army of the rebels decided the battle of Diabasis. They advanced against their enemies as they were commanded; when the word was given they simulated flight; but, when they saw that the troops of the Emperor did not pursue in disorder, as Thomas had expected, but advanced in close array, they lost all heart for the work, and surrendered themselves to Michaels clemency.

The cause of Thomas was lost on the field of Diabasis. The throne of the Amorian Emperor was no longer in jeopardy. But there was still more work to be done and the civil war was not completely over until the end of the year. The tyrant himself was not yet captured, nor his adopted son, Anastasius. Thomas, with a few followers, fled to Arcadiopolis and closed the gates against his conqueror. The parts of the tyrant and the Emperor were now changed. It was now Michael's turn to besiege Thomas in the city of Arcadius, as Thomas had besieged Michael in the city of Constantine. But the second siege was of briefer duration. Arcadiopolis was not as Constantinople; and the garrison of Thomas was not as the garrison of Michael. Yet it lasted much longer than might have been expected; for it began in the middle of May, and the place held out till the middle of October.

Arcadiopolis was not the only Thracian town that sheltered followers of Thomas. The younger tyrant, Anastasius, had found refuge not far off, in Bizye. Another band of rebels seized Panion, and Heraclea on the Propontis remained devoted to the cause of the Pretender. These four towns, Heraclea, Panion, Arcadiopolis and Bizye formed a sort of line, cutting off Constantinople from Western Thrace. But the subjugation of the last refuges of the lost cause was merely a matter of months. It would not have been more than a matter of days, if certain considerations had not hindered the Emperor from using engines of siege against the towns which still defied him. But two lines of policy concurred in deciding him to choose the slower method of blockade.

In the first place he wished to spare, so far as possible, the lives of Christians, and, if the towns were taken by violence, bloodshed would be unavoidable. That this consideration really influenced Michael is owned by historians who were not well disposed towards him, but who in this respect bear out a statement which he made himself in his letter to Lewis the Pious. He informed that monarch that he retreated after the victory of Diabasis, in order to spare Christian blood. Such a motive does not imply that he was personally a humane man; other acts show that he could be stark and ruthless. His humanity in this case rather illustrates the general feeling that prevailed against the horrors of civil war. It was Michael's policy to affect a tender regard for the lives of his Christian subjects, and to contrast his own conduct with that of his rival, who had brought so many miseries on the Christian Empire. We have already seen how important this consideration was for the purpose of conciliating public opinion, in the pains which were taken to represent the Bulgarian intervention as a spontaneous act of Omurtag, undesired and deprecated by Michael.

But there was likewise another reason which conspired to decide Michael that it was wiser not to storm a city of Thrace. It was the interest and policy of a Roman Emperor to cherish in the minds of neighbouring peoples, especially of Bulgarians and Slavs, the wholesome idea that fortified Roman cities were impregnable. The failure of Krum's attack on Constantinople, the more recent failure of the vast force of Thomas, were calculated to do much to confirm such a belief. And Michael had no mind to weaken this impression by showing the barbarians that Roman cities might yield to the force of skillfully directed engines. In effect, Michael seized the occasion to show the Bulgarians that he regarded Arcadiopolis as too strong to be taken by assault.

In following these two principles of policy, Michael placed himself in the light of a patriot, in conspicuous contrast to his beaten rival, who had been the author of the Civil War, and had used all his efforts to teach barbarians how the Imperial city itself might be taken by an enemy. The garrison of Arcadiopolis held out for five months, but Thomas was obliged to send out of the town all the women and children, and the men who were incapable of bearing arms, in order to save his supplies. By the month of October, the garrison was reduced to such straits that they were obliged to feed on the putrid corpses of their horses which had perished of hunger. Part of the garrison now left the town, some with the knowledge of Thomas, others as deserters to Michael. The latter, desperate with hunger, let themselves down by ropes, or threw themselves from the walls at the risk of breaking their limbs. The messengers of Thomas stole out of the gates and escaped to Bizye, where the younger tyrant Anastasius had shut himself up, in order to concert with the "son" some plan for the rescue of the "father". Then Michael held a colloquy with the garrison that was left in Arcadiopolis, and promised to all a free pardon, if they would surrender their master into his hands. The followers who had been so long faithful to their leader thought that the time had come when they might set their lives before loyalty to a desperate cause. They accepted the Imperial clemency and delivered Thomas to the triumphant Emperor.

The punishment that awaited the great tyrant who was so near to winning the throne was not less terrible than that to which Michael himself had been sentenced by Leo, the Armenian. All the distress which the Emperor had undergone for the space of three years was now to be visited on his head. The pretender, who had reduced his conqueror to dire extremities and had wasted three years of his reign, could hope for no easy death. The quarrel between Michael and Thomas was an old one; it dated from the days when they had both been officers under the general Bardanes. The time had now come for settling accounts, and the reckoning against the debtor was heavy indeed. The long war had inflicted immeasurable injury on the lands of the Empire, and it would be hard to estimate how much Thrace alone had suffered. The private ambition of the old Slav of Gaziura, the impostor who had deceived his followers, for a time at least, that he was a legitimate Emperor, was answerable for all this ruin and misery. When he was led in chains to the presence of his hated rival, Michael, not disguising his joy, set his foot upon the neck of the prostrate foe, and pronounced his doom. His hands and feet were to be cut off, and his body was to be pierced on a stake. The miserable man when he was led to punishment, cried aloud for mercy: "Pity me, O thou who are the true Emperor!". Hope may have been awakened in his heart for a moment, hope at least of some alleviation of the doom, when his judge deigned to ask him a question. It was one of those dangerous questions which tempt a man in the desperate position of Thomas to bear false witness if he has no true facts to reveal. Michael asked whether any of his own officers or ministers had held treacherous dealings with the rebel. But if the rebel had any true or false revelations to make, he was not destined to utter them, and if he conceived hopes of life or of a milder death, they were speedily extinguished. At this juncture John Hexabulios, the Logothete of the Course, intervened and gave the Emperor wise counsel. The part played in history by this Patrician was that of a monitor. We saw him warning Michael Rangabé against Leo; we saw him taking counsel with Leo touching the designs of Michael the Lisper; and now we see him giving advice to Michael. His counsel was, not to hear Thomas, inasmuch as it was improper and absurd to believe the evidence of foes against friends.

The sentence was carried out, probably before the walls of Arcadiopolis, and doubtless in the Emperor's presence; and the great rebel perished in tortures, "like a beast". A like doom was in store for his adopted son. But Bizye caused the Emperor less trouble than Arcadiopolis, for when the followers of Anastasius heard the news of the fate of Thomas, they resolved to save their own lives by surrendering him to Michael. The monk, who in an evil hour had exchanged the cloister for the world, perished by the same death as Thomas. But even after the extinction of the two tyrants, there was still resistance offered to the rule of Michael. The inland cities, Bizye and Arcadiopolis, had surrendered; but the maritime cities, Heraclea and Panion, still held out. In these neighboring places there was a strong enthusiasm for image-worship, and Michael had given clear proofs that he did not purpose to permit the restoration of images. But the resistance of these cities was soon overcome. The wall of Panion was opportunely shattered by an earthquake, and thus the city was disabled from withstanding the Imperial army. Heraclea, though it was visited by the same disaster, suffered less, and did not yield at once; but an assault on the seaside was successful, and here, too, Michael had a bloodless victory.

The Emperor, having completely established his power in Thrace, returned to the city with his prisoners. If his dealing with the arch-rebels Thomas and Anastasius had been cruel, his dealing with all their followers was merciful and mild. Those who were most deeply implicated he punished by banishment. On the rest he inflicted only the light ignominy of being exhibited at a spectacle in the Hippodrome with their hands bound behind their backs.

But there was still some work to be done in Asia, before it could be said that the last traces of the rebellion of Thomas had been blotted out. Two adherents of the rebel still held two strong posts in Asia Minor, and plundered the surrounding country as brigands. Kaballs, in the Anatolic Theme, to the north-west of Iconium, was in the hands of Choereas, while Gazarenos of Kolonea held Saniana, an important fortress on the Halys. Michael sent a golden bull to these chiefs, announcing the death of Thomas and offering to give them a free pardon and to confer on them the rank of Magister, if they submitted. But they were wild folk, and they preferred the rewards of brigandage to honors at the Imperial Court. The messenger of Michael, however, accomplished by guile what he failed to accomplish openly. He seduced some of the garrisons of both towns, and persuaded them to close the gates upon their captains while they were abroad on their lawless raids. The work of tampering with the men of Choereas and Gazarenos demanded subtlety and caution, but the imperial messenger was equal to the emergency. The manner in which he won the ear of an oekonomos or steward of a church or monastery in Saniana, without arousing suspicion, is recorded. He found a peasant, by name Gyberion, who had a talent for music and used to spend his leisure hours in practising rustic songs. The envoy from the Court cultivated the friendship of this man and composed a song for him, which ran thus:

> Hearken, Sir Steward, to Gyberis!
> Give me but Saniana town,
> New-Caesarea shalt thou win
> And eke a bishop's gown.

When these lines had been repeatedly sung by the man within the hearing of the oekonomos or of his friends, the meaning of the words was grasped and the hint taken. Shut out of their "cloud-capped towns" the two rebels, Choereas and Gazarenos took the road for Syria, hoping to find a refuge there, like their dead leader Thomas. But before they could reach the frontier they were captured and hanged.

The drama is now over; all the prophecies of the soothsayer of Philomelion have come true. The star of the Armenian and the star of the Slavonian have paled and vanished before the more puissant star of the man of Amorion; both Leo and Thomas have been done to death by

Michael. He now wears the Imperial crown, without a rival; he has no more to fear or hope from unfulfilled soothsay.

We may now turn from the personal interest in the story to the more general aspects of this great civil war, which caused abundant misery and mischief. The historians describe how it filled the world with all manner of evils, and diminished the population; fathers armed themselves against their sons, brothers against the sons of their mothers, friends against their dearest friends. It was as if the cataracts of the Nile had burst, deluging the land not with water but with blood. The immediate author of these calamities was Thomas, and there is no doubt that his motive was simply personal ambition. The old man with the lame leg was not fighting for a principle, he was fighting for a diadem. But nevertheless he could not have done what he did if there had not been at work motives of a larger and more public scope, urging men to take up arms. It must not be forgotten that he originally revolted against Leo, and that his war with Michael was merely a continuation of that revolt. Now there were two classes of subjects in the Empire, who had good cause to be discontented with the policy of Leo, the image-worshippers and the Paulicians. The policy of Thomas, which he skillfully pursued, was to unite these discordant elements, orthodoxy and heresy, under a common standard. His pretence to be Constantine VI. may have won the confidence of some image- worshippers, but he was possibly more successful in conciliating Paulicians and other heretics.

It is more important to observe that the rebellion probably initiated or promoted considerable social changes in the Asiatic province. The system of immense estates owned by rich proprietors and cultivated by peasants in a condition of serfdom, which had prevailed in the age of Justinian, had been largely superseded by the opposite system of small holdings, which the policy of the Isaurian Emperors seems to have encouraged. But by the tenth century, vast properties and peasant serfs have reappeared, and the process by which this second transformation was accomplished must be attributed to the ninth. The civil war could not fail to ruin numberless small farmers who in prosperous times could barely pay their way, and the fiscal burdens rendered it impossible for them to recuperate their fortunes, unless they were aided by the State. But it was easier and more conducive to the immediate profit of the treasury to allow these insolvent lands to pass into the possession of rich neighbours, who in some cases might be monastic communities. It is probable that many farms and homesteads were abandoned by their masters. A modern historian, who had a quick eye for economic changes, judged that the rebellion of Thomas was no inconsiderable cause of the accumulation of property in immense estates, which began to depopulate the country and prepare it for the reception of a new race of inhabitants. If the government of Michael II. had been wise, it would have intervened, at all costs, to save the small proprietors. Future Emperors might thus have been spared a baffling economic problem and a grave political danger.

§3. The Ecclesiastical Policy of Michael

It was probably during or just after the war with Thomas that Thecla, the mother of Theophilus, died. At all events we find Michael soon after the end of the war making preparations for a second marriage, notwithstanding the deep grief which he had displayed at the death of his first wife. A second marriage of any kind was deprecated by the strictly orthodox, and some thought that at this juncture, when the Empire was involved in so many misfortunes, the Emperor showed little concern to appease an offended Deity. But the Senators were urgent with him that he should marry. "It is not possible", they said, "that an Emperor should live without a wife, and that our wives should lack a Lady and Empress". The writer who records this wishes to make his readers believe that the pressure of the Senate was exerted at the express desire of Michael himself. However this may be, it is interesting to observe the opinion that an Augusta was needed in the interests of Court society.

But those who carped at the idea of a second marriage were still more indignant when they heard who she was that the Emperor had selected to be Empress over them. It was not unfitting that the conqueror of the false Constantine should choose the daughter of the true Constantine for his wife. But Euphrosyne, daughter of Constantine VI., and grand-daughter of Irene, had long been a nun in a monastery on the island of Prinkipo, where she lived with her mother Maria. Here, indeed, was a scandal; here was an occasion for righteous indignation. Later historians at least made much of the crime of wedding a nun, but at the time perhaps it was more a pretext for spiteful gossip than a cause of genuine dissatisfaction. The Patriarch did not hesitate to dissolve Euphrosyne from her vows, that she might fill the high station for which her birth had fitted her. The new Amorian house might claim by this marriage to be linked with the old Isaurian dynasty.

The ecclesiastical leanings of Michael II. were not different from those of his predecessor, but he adopted a different policy. He decided to maintain the iconoclastic reform of Leo, which harmonized with his own personal convictions; but at the same time to desist from any further persecution of the image-worshippers. We can easily understand that the circumstances of his accession dictated a policy which should, so far as possible, disarm the opposition of a large and influential section of his subjects. Accordingly, he delivered from prison and allowed to return from exile, all those who had been punished by Leo for their defiance of his authority. The most eminent of the sufferers, Theodore of Studion, left his prison cell in Smyrna, hoping that the change of government would mean the restoration of icons and the reinstallation of Nicephorus as Patriarch. He wrote a grateful and congratulatory letter to the Emperor, exhorting him to bestow peace and unity on the Church by reconciliation with the see of Rome. At the same time, he attempted to bring Court influence to bear on Michael, and we possess his letters to several prominent ministers, whom he exhorts to work in the cause of image-worship, while he malignantly exults over the fate of Leo the Armeniann. Theodore had been joined by many members of his party on his journey to the neighborhood of Constantinople, and when he reached Chalcedon, he hastened to visit the ex-Patriarch who was living in his own monastery of St. Theodore, on the Asiatic shore of the Bosphorus. Here and in the monastery of Crescentius, where Theodore took up his abode somewhere oil the Asiatic shore of the Propontis, the image-worshippers deliberated how they should proceed.

Their first step seems to have been the composition of a letter which Nicephorus addressed to the Emperor, admonishing him of his religious duties, and holding up as a warning the fate of his impious predecessor. In this document the arguments in favour of images were once more rehearsed. But Michael was deaf to these appeals. His policy was to allow people to believe what they liked in private, but not to permit image-worship in public. When he received the letter of Nicephorus he is reputed to have expressed admiration of its ability and to have said to its bearers words to this effect: "Those who have gone before us will have to answer for their doctrines to God; but we intend to keep the Church in the same way in which we found her walking. Therefore we rule and confirm that no one shall venture to open his mouth either for or against images. But let the Synod of Tarasius be put out of mind and memory, and likewise that of Constantine the elder (the Fifth), and that which was lately held in Leo's reign; and let complete silence in regard to images be the order of the day. But as for him who is so zealous to speak and write on these matters, if he wishes to govern the Church on this basis, preserving silence concerning the existence and worship of images, bid him come here".

But this attempt to close the controversy was vain; the injunction of silence would not be obeyed, and its enforcement could only lead to a new persecution. The Emperor presently deemed it expedient to essay a reconciliation, by means of a conference between leading representatives of both parties, and he requested the ex-Patriarch and his friends to meet together and consider this proposal. The image-worshippers decided to decline to meet heretics for the purpose of discussion, and Theodore, who was empowered to reply to the Emperor on behalf of the bishops and abbots, wrote that, while in all other matters they were entirely at their sovran's disposition, they could not comply with this command, and suggested that the only solution of the difficulty was to appeal to Rome, the head of all the Churches.

It was apparently after this refusal that, through the intervention of one of his ministers, Michael received in audience Theodore and his friends. Having permitted them to expound their views on image-worship, he replied briefly and decisively: "Your words are good and excellent. But, as I have never yet till this hour worshipped an image in my life, I have determined to leave the Church as I found it. To you, however, I allow the liberty of adhering with impunity to what you allege to be the orthodox faith; live where you choose, only it must be outside the city, and you need not apprehend that any danger will befall you from my government".

It is probable that these negotiations were carried on while the Patriarchal chair was vacant. Theodotos died early in the year, and while the image-worshippers endeavored to procure the restoration of Nicephorus on their own terms, the Emperor hoped that the ex-Patriarch might be induced to yield. The audience convinced him that further attempts to come to an understanding would be useless, and he caused the vacant ecclesiastical throne to be filled by Antonius Kassymatas, bishop of Syllaion, who had been the coadjutor of Leo V. in his iconoclastic work. By this step those hopes which the Imperial leniency had raised in the minds of Theodore and his party were dissipated.

The negotiations, as they were conducted by Theodore, had raised a question which was probably of greater importance in the eyes of Michael than the place of pictures in religious worship. The Studite theory of the supremacy of the Roman See in the ecclesiastical affairs of Christendom had been asserted without any disguise; the Emperor had been admonished that the controversy could only be settled by the cooperation of the Pope. This doctrine cut at the root of the constitutional theory, which was held both by the Emperors and by the large majority of their subjects, that the Imperial autocracy was supreme in spiritual as well as in secular affairs. The Emperor, who must have been well aware that Theodore had been in constant communication with Rome during the years of persecution, doubtless regarded his Roman proclivities with deep suspicion, and he was not minded to brook the interference of the Pope. His suspicions were strengthened and his indignation aroused by the arrival of a message from Pope Paschal I. Methodius (who was afterwards to ascend the Patriarchal throne) had resided at Rome during the reign of Leo V. and worked there as an energetic agent in the interests of image-worship. He now returned to Constantinople, bearing a document in which Paschal defined the orthodox doctrine. He sought an audience of the Emperor, presented the Papal writing, and called upon the sovran to restore the true faith and the true Patriarch. Michael would undoubtedly have resented the dictation of the Pope if it had been conveyed by a Papal envoy; but it was intolerable that one of his own subjects should be the spokesman of Borne. Methodius was treated with rigour as a treasonable intriguer; he was scourged and then imprisoned in a tomb in the little island of St. Andrew, which lies off the north side of the promontory of Akritas (Tuzla-Burnu), in the Gulf of Nicomedia. His confinement lasted for more than eight years.

After the outbreak of the civil war Michael took the precaution of commanding Theodore and his faction to move into the city, fearing that they might support his opponent, who was said to favour images. The measure was unnecessary, for the iconolaters of the better class seem to have had no sympathy with the cause of Thomas, and the ecclesiastical question did not prove a serious factor in the struggle. On the termination of the war, the Emperor made a new effort to heal the division in the Church. He again proposed a conference between the leading exponents of the rival doctrines, but the proposal was again rejected, on the ground that the question could be settled only in one of two ways-either by an ecumenical council, which required the concurrence of the Pope and the four Patriarchs, or by a local council, which would only have legal authority if the legitimate Patriarch Nicephorus were first restored.

The Emperor was convinced that the obstinacy of the image-worshippers rested largely on their hopes that the Roman See would intervene, and that if he could induce the Pope to assume a cold attitude to their solicitations the opposition would soon expire. In order to influence the Pope he sought the assistance of the Western Emperor, Lewis, to whom he indited a long letter, which contains an interesting description of the abuses to which the veneration of images had led. Lights were set in front of them and incense was burned, and they were held in the same honor as the life-giving Cross. They were prayed to, and their aid was besought. Some used even to cover them with cloths and make them the baptismal sponsors for their children. Some priests scraped the paint from pictures and mixed it in the bread and wine which they give to communicants; others placed the body of the Lord in the hands of images, from which the communicants received it. The Emperors Leo V. and his son caused a local synod to be held, and such practices were condemned. It was ordained that pictures which were hung low in churches should be removed, that those which were high should be left for the instruction of persons who are unable to read, but that no candles should be lit or incense burned before them. Some rejected the council and fled to Old Rome, where they calumniated the Church. The Emperors proceed to profess their belief in the Six Ecumenical Councils, and to assure King Lewis that they venerate the glorious and holy relics of the Saints. They ask him to speed the envoys to the Pope, to whom they are bearers of a letter and gifts for the Church of St. Peter.

The four envoys who were sent on this mission met with a favorable reception from the Emperor Lewis at Rouen, and were sent on to Rome, where Eugenius had succeeded Paschal in St Peter's chair. It is not recorded how they fared at Rome, but Lewis lost no time in making an attempt to bring about a European settlement of the iconoclastic controversy. The Frankish Church did not agree with the extreme views of the Greek iconoclasts, nor yet with the doctrine of image-worship which had been formulated by the Council of Nicaea and approved by the Popes; and it appeared to Lewis a good opportunity to press for that intermediate solution of the question which had been approved at the Council of Frankfurt (A.D. 794). The sense of this solution was to forbid the veneration of images, but to allow them to be set up in churches as ornaments and memorials. The first step was to persuade the Pope, and for this purpose Lewis, who, like his father, was accustomed to summon councils on his own authority, respectfully asked Eugenius to permit him to convoke the Frankish bishops to collect the opinions of the Fathers on the question at issue. Eugenius could not refuse, and the synod met in Paris in November 825. The report of the bishops agreed with the decision of Frankfurt; they condemned the worship of images, tracing its history back to the Greek philosopher Epicurus; they censured Pope Hadrian for approving the doctrine of the Nicene Council; but, on the other hand, they condemned the iconoclasts for insisting on the banishment of images from churches. Lewis despatched two learned bishops to Rome, bearing extracts from the report of the synod, but the story of the negotiations comes here to a sudden end. We hear of no further direct communications between Rome and Constantinople, but we may reasonably suspect that a Papal embassy to Lewis (A.D. 826), and two embassies which passed between the Eastern and Western Emperors in the following years, were concerned with the question of religious pictures.

Till his death, from disease of the kidneys, in October A.D. 829, Michael adhered to his resolution not to pursue or imprison the leaders of the ecclesiastical opposition. The only case of harsh dealing recorded is the treatment of Methodius, and he, as we have seen, was punished not as a recalcitrant but as an intriguer.

Chapter IV
Theophilus
(A.D. 829-842)

§1. The Administration of Theophilus

For eight years Theophilus had been an exemplary co-regent. Though he was a man of energetic character and active brain, he appears never to have put himself forward, and if he exerted influence upon his father's policy, such influence was carefully hidden behind the throne. Perhaps Michael compelled him to remain in the background. In any case, his position, for a man of his stamp, was an education in politics; it afforded him facilities for observing weak points in an administration for which he was not responsible, and for studying the conditions of the Empire which he would one day have to govern. He had a strong sense of the obligations of the Imperial office, and he possessed the capacities which his subjects considered desirable in their monarch. He had the military training which enabled him to lead an army into the field; he had a passion for justice; he was well educated, and, like the typical Byzantine sovran, interested in theology. His private life was so exemplary that even the malevolence of the chroniclers, who detested him as a heretic, could only rake up one story against his morals. He kept a brilliant Court, and took care that his palace, to which he added new and splendid buildings, should not be outshone by the marvels of Baghdad.

We might expect to find the reign of Theophilus remembered in Byzantine chronicle as a dazzling passage in the history of the Empire, like the caliphate of Harun al-Rashid in the annals of Islam. But the writers who have recorded his acts convey the impression that he was an unlucky and ineffective monarch. In his eastern warfare against the Saracens his fortune was chequered, and he sustained one crushing humiliation; in the West, he was unable to check the Mohammadan advance. His ecclesiastical policy, which he inherited from his predecessors, and pursued with vigour and conviction, was undone after his death. But though he fought for a losing cause in religion, and wrought no great military exploits, and did not possess the highest gifts of statesmanship, it is certain that his reputation among his contemporaries was far higher than a superficial examination of the chronicles would lead the reader to suspect. He has fared like Leo V. He was execrated in later times as an unrelenting iconoclast, and a conspiracy of silence and depreciation has depressed his fame. But it was perhaps not so much his heresy as his offence in belonging to the Amorian dynasty that was fatal to his memory. Our records were compiled under the Basilian dynasty, which had established itself on the throne by murder; and misrepresentation of the Amorians is a distinctive propensity in these partial chronicles. Yet, if we read between the lines, we can easily detect that there was another tradition, and that Theophilus had impressed the popular imagination as a just and brilliant sovran, somewhat as Harun impressed the East. This tradition is reflected in anecdotes, of which it would be futile to appraise the proportions of truth and myth,—anecdotes which the Basilian historiographers found too interesting to omit, but told in a somewhat grudging way because they were supposed to be to the credit of the Emperor.

The motive of these stories is the Emperor's desire to administer justice rigorously without respect of persons. He used to ride once a week through the city to perform his devotions in the church of the Virgin at Blachernae, and on the way he was ready to listen to the petitions of any of his subjects who wished to claim his protection. One day he was accosted by a widow who complained that she was wronged by the brother of the Empress, Petronas, who held the post of Drungary of the Watch. It was illegal to build at Constantinople any structure which intercepted the view or the light of a neighbor's house; but Petronas was enlarging his own residence at Blachernae, with insolent disregard for the law, in such a way as to darken the house of the widow. Theophilus promptly sent Eustathios the quaestor, and other officers, to test the accuracy of her statement, and on their report that it was true, the Emperor caused his brother-in-law to be stripped and flogged in the public street. The obnoxious buildings were levelled to the ground, and the ruins, apparently, bestowed upon the complainant. Another time, on his weekly ride, he was surprised by a man who accosted him and said, "The horse on which your Majesty is riding belongs to me". Calling the Count of the Stable, who was in attendance, the Emperor inquired, "Whose is this horse?" "It was sent to your Majesty by the Count of Opsikion", was the reply. The Count of the Opsikian Theme, who happened to be in the city at the time, was summoned and confronted next day with the claimant, a soldier of his own army, who charged him with having appropriated the animal without giving any consideration either in money or military promotion. The lame excuses of the Count did not serve; he was chastised with stripes, and the horse offered to its rightful owner. This man, however, preferred to receive 2 pounds of gold and military promotion; he proved a coward and was slain in battle with his back to the enemy. Another anecdote is told of the Emperor's indignation on discovering that a great merchant vessel, which he descried with admiration sailing into the harbour of Bucoleon, was the property of Theodora, who had secretly engaged in mercantile speculation. "What!" he exclaimed, "my wife has made me, the Emperor, a merchant!" He commanded the ship and all its valuable cargo to be consigned to the flames.

These tales, whatever measure of truth may underlie them, redounded to the credit of Theophilus in the opinion of those who repeated them; they show that he was a popular figure in Constantinople, and that his memory, as of a just ruler, was revered by the next generation. We can accept without hesitation the tradition of his accessibility to his subjects in his weekly progresses to Blachernae, and it is said that he lingered on his way in the bazaars, systematically examining the wares, especially the food, and inquiring the prices. He was doubtless assiduous also in presiding at the Imperial court of appeal, which met in the Palace of Magnaura, here following the examples of Nicephorus and Leo the Armenian.

The desirability of such minute personal supervision of the administration may have been forced on Theophilus by his own observations during his father's reign, and he evidently attempted to cross, so far as seemed politic, those barriers which hedged the monarch from direct contact with the life of the people. As a rule, the Emperor was only visible to the ordinary mass of his subjects when he rode in solemn pomp through the city to the Holy Apostles or some other church, or when he appeared to watch the public games from his throne in the Hippodrome. The regular, unceremonial ride of Theophilus to Blachernae was an innovation, and if it did not afford him the opportunities of overhearing the gossip of the town which Harun al-Rashid is said by the story-tellers to have obtained by nocturnal expeditions in disguise, it may have helped a discerning eye to some useful information.

The political activity of Theophilus seems to have been directed to the efficient administration of the existing laws and the improvement of administrative details; his government was not distinguished by novel legislation or any radical reform. His laws have disappeared and left no visible traces-like almost all the Imperial legislation between the reigns of Leo III. and Basil I. Of one important enactment we are informed. The law did not allow marriage except between orthodox Christians. But there was a large influx, during his reign, of orientals who were in rebellion against the Caliph, and Theophilus, to encourage the movement, passed a law permitting alliance between Mohammadan Persians and Romans. This measure accorded with his reputation for being a friend of foreigners.

One of the first measures of the reign was an act of policy, performed in the name of justice. According to one account the people had gathered in the Hippodrome to witness horseraces, and at the end of the performance the Emperor assembled the Senate in the Kathisma, from which he witnessed the games, and ordered Leo Chamaidrakon, the Keeper of the Private Wardrobe, to produce the chandelier which had been broken when Leo V. was cut down by his murderers in the chapel of the Palace. Pointing to this, Theophilus asked, "What is the desert of him who enters the temple of the Lord and slays the Lord's anointed?". The Senate replied, "Death", and the Emperor immediately commanded the Prefect of the City to seize the men who had slain Leo and decapitate them in the Hippodrome before the assembled people. The astonished victims of such belated justice naturally exclaimed, "If we had not assisted your father, O Emperor, you would not now be on the throne". There are other versions of the circumstances, and it is possible that the assassins were condemned at a formal silention in the Magnaura. It would be useless to judge this punishment by any ethical standard. Michael II. had not only a guilty knowledge of the conspiracy, but had urged the conspirators to hasten their work. The passion of a doctrinaire for justice will not explain his son's act in calling his father's accomplices to a tardy account; nor is there the least probability in the motive which some image-worshippers assigned, that respect for the memory of Leo as a great iconoclast inspired him to wreak vengeance on the murderers. The truth, no doubt, is that both Michael II. and Theophilus were acutely conscious that the deed which had raised them to power cast an ugly shadow over their throne; and it is noteworthy that in the letter which they addressed to the Emperor Lewis they stigmatize the conspirators as wicked men. Michael, we may be assured, showed them no favour, but he could not bring himself to punish the men whom he had himself encouraged to commit the crime. The conscience of Theophilus was clear, and he could definitely dissociate the Amorian house from the murder by a public act of retribution. It may well be that (as one tradition affirms) Michael, when death was approaching, urged his son to this step. In any case, it seems certain that the purpose of Theophilus was to remedy a weakness in his political position, and that he was taking account of public opinion.

The Augusta Euphrosyne, last Imperial descendant of the Isaurian house, retired to a monastery soon after her stepson's accession to the supreme power. Michael is related to have bound the Senate by a pledge that they would defend the rights of his second wife and her children after his death. If this is true, it meant that if she had a son his position should be secured as co-regent of his stepbrother. She had no children, and found perhaps little attraction in the prospect of residing in the Palace and witnessing Court functions in which Theodora would now be the most important figure. There is no reason to suppose that she retired under compulsion.

The first five children born to Theophilus during his father's lifetime were daughters, but just before or soon after his accession Theodora gave birth to a son, who was named Constantine and crowned as Augustus. Constantine, however, did not survive infancy, and the Emperor had to take thought for making some provision for the succession. He selected as a son-in-law Alexios Musele, who belonged to the family of the Krenitai, of Armenian descent, and betrothed him to his eldest daughter, Maria (c. A.D. 831). Alexios (who had been created a patrician and distinguished by the new title of anthypatos, and then elevated to the higher rank of magister) received the dignity of Caesar, which gave him a presumptive expectation of a still higher title. The marriage was celebrated about A.D. 836, but Maria died soon afterwards, and, against the Emperor's wishes, his son-in-law insisted on retiring to a monastery. There was a story that the suspicions of Theophilus had been aroused by jealous tongues against the loyalty of Alexios, who had been sent to fight with the Saracens in Sicily. It is impossible to say how much truth may underlie this report, nor can we be sure whether the Caesar withdrew from the world before or after the birth of a son to Theophilus (in A.D. 839), an event which would in any case have disappointed his hopes of the succession.

While he was devoted to the serious business of ruling, and often had little time for the ceremonies and formal processions which occupied many hours in the lives of less active Emperors, Theophilus loved the pageantry of royal magnificence. On two occasions he celebrated a triumph over the Saracens, and we are so fortunate as to possess an official account of the triumphal ceremonies. When Theophilus (in A.D. 831) reached the Palace of Hieria, near Chalcedon, he was awaited by the Empress, the three ministers-the Praepositus, the chief Magister, and the urban Prefect-who were responsible for the safety of the city during his absence, and by all the resident members of the Senate. At a little distance from the Palace gates, the senators met him and did obeisance; Theodora stood within the rails of the hall which opened on the court, and when her lord dismounted she also did obeisance and kissed him. The train of captives had not yet arrived, and ten days elapsed before the triumphal entry could be held. Seven were spent at Hieria, the senators remaining in ceremonial attendance upon the Emperor, and their wives, who were summoned from the city, upon the Empress. On the seventh day the Court moved to the Palace of St. Mamas, and remained there for three days. On the tenth, Theophilus sailed up the Golden Horn, disembarked at Blachernae, and proceeded on horseback outside the walls to a pavilion which had been pitched in a meadow near the Golden Gate. Here he met the captives who had been conveyed across the Propontis from Chrysopolis.

Meanwhile, under the direction of the Prefect, the city had been set in festive array, decorated "like a bridal chamber", with variegated hangings and purple and silver ornaments. The long Middle Street, through which the triumphal train would pass, from the Golden Gate of victory to the place of the Augusteon, was strewn with flowers. The prisoners, the trophies and the spoils of war preceded the Emperor, who rode on a white horse caparisoned with jewelled harness; a tiara was on his head; he wore a sceptre in his hand, and a gold-embroidered tunic framed his breastplate. Beside him, on another white steed similarly equipped, rode the Caesar Alexios, wearing a corslet, sleeves, and gaiters of gold, a helmet and gold headband, and poising a golden spear. At a short distance from the triumphal gate the Emperor dismounted and made three obeisances to the east, and, when he crossed the threshold of the city, the Praepositus, the Magister, and the Prefect, now relieved of their extraordinary authority, presented him with a crown of gold, which he carried on his right arm. The demes then solemnly acclaimed him as victor, and the procession advanced. When it reached the milestone at the gates of the Augusteon, the senators dismounted, except those who, having taken part in the campaign, wore their armour, and, passing through the gates, walked in front of the sovran to the Well of St. Sophia. Here the Emperor himself dismounted, entered the church, and, after a brief devotion, crossed the Augusteon on foot to the Bronze Gate of the Palace, where a pulpit had been set, flanked by a throne of gold, and a golden organ which was known as the Prime Miracle. Between these stood a large cross of gold. When Theophilus had seated himself and made the sign of the cross, the demes cried, "There is one Holy". The city community then offered him a pair of golden armlets, and wearing these he acknowledged the gift by a speech, in which he described his military successes. Amid new acclamations he remounted his horse, and riding through the Passages of Achilles and past the Baths of Zeuxippus, entered the Hippodrome and reached the Palace at the door of the Skyla. On the next day, at a reception in the Palace, many honors and dignities were conferred, and horse-races were held in the Hippodrome, where the captives and the trophies were exhibited to the people.

§2. Buildings of Theophilus

The reign of Theophilus was an epoch in the history of the Great Palace. He enlarged it by a group of handsome and curious buildings, on which immense sums must have been expended, and we may be sure that this architectural enterprise was stimulated, if not suggested, by the reports which reached his ears of the magnificent palaces which the Caliphs had built for themselves at Baghdad. His own pride and the prestige of the Empire demanded that the residence of the Basileus should not be eclipsed by the splendour of the Caliph's abode.

At the beginning of the ninth century the Great Palace consisted of two groups of buildings-the original Palace, including the Daphne, which Constantine the Great had built adjacent to the Hippodrome and to the Augusteon, and at some distance to the south-east the Chrysotriklinos (with its dependencies), which had been erected by Justin II. and had superseded the Daphne as the centre of Court life and ceremonial. It is probable that the space between the older Palace and the Chrysotriklinos was open ground, free from buildings, perhaps laid out in gardens and terraced (for the ground falls southward). There was no architectural connexion between the two Palaces, but Justinian II at the end of the seventh century had connected the Chrysotriklinos with the Hippodrome by means of two long halls which opened into one another-the Lausiakos and the Triklinos called after his name. These halls were probably perpendicular to the Hippodrome, and formed a line of building which closed in the principal grounds of the Palace on the southern side.

It is probable that the residence of Constantine bore some resemblance in design and style to the house of Diocletian at Spalato and other mansions of the period. The descriptions of the octagonal Chrysotriklinos show that it was built under the influence of the new style of ecclesiastical architecture which was characteristic of the age of Justinian. The chief group of buildings which Theophilus added introduced a new style and marked a third epoch in the architectural history of the Great Palace. Our evidence makes it clear that they were situated between the Constantinian Palace on the northwest and the Chrysotriklinos on the south-east.

These edifices were grouped round the Trikonchos or Triple Shell, the most original in its design and probably that on which Theophilus prided himself most. It took its name from the shell-like apses, which projected on three sides, the larger on the east, supported on four porphyry pillars, the others (to south and north) on two. This triconch plan was long known at Constantinople, whither it had been imported from Syria; it was distinctively oriental. On the west side a silver door, flanked by two side doors of burnished bronze, opened into a hall which had the shape of a half moon and was hence called the Sigma. The roof rested on fifteen columns of many-tinted marble. But these halls were only the upper storeys of the Trikonchos and the Sigma. The ground-floor of the Trikonchos had, like the room above it, three apses, but differently oriented. The northern side of this hall was known as the Mysterion or Place of Whispers, because it had the acoustic property, that if you whispered in the eastern or in the western apse, your words were heard distinctly in the other. The lower storey of the Sigma, to which you descended by a spiral staircase, was a hall of nineteen columns which marked off a circular corridor. Marble incrustations in many colours formed the brilliant decoration of the walls of both these buildings. The roof of the Trikonchos was gilded.

The lower part of the Sigma, unscreened on the western side, opened upon a court which was known as the Mystic Phiale of the Trikonchos. In the midst of this court stood a bronze fountain phiale with silver margin, from the centre of which sprang a golden pine-cone. Two bronze lions, whose gaping mouths poured water into the semicircular area of the Sigma, stood near that building. The ceremony of the saximodeximon, at which the racehorses of the Hippodrome were reviewed by the Emperor, was held in this court; the Blues and Greens sat on tiers of steps of white Proconnesian marble, and a gold throne was placed for the monarch. On the occasion of this and other levies, and certain festivals, the fountain was filled with almonds and pistacchio nuts, while the cone offered spiced wine to those who wished.

Passing over some minor buildings, we must notice the hall of the Pearl, which stood to the north of the Trikonchos. Its roof rested on eight columns of rose-coloured marble, the floor was of white marble variegated with mosaics, and the walls were decorated with pictures of animals. The same building contained a bed-chamber, where Theophilus slept in summer; its porticoes faced east and south, and the walls and roof displayed the same kind of decoration as the Pearl. To the north of this whole group, and fronting the west, rose the Karianos, a house which the Emperor destined as a residence for his daughters, taking its name from a flight of steps of Carian marble, which seemed to flow down from the entrance like a broad white river.

In another quarter (perhaps to the south of the Lausiakos) the Emperor laid out gardens and constructed shelters or "sunneries", if this word may be permitted as a literal rendering of Mliaka. Here he built the Kamilas, an apartment whose roof glittered with gold, supported by six columns of the green marble of Thessaly. The walls were decorated with a dado of marble incrustation below, and above with mosaics representing on a gold ground people gathering fruit. On a lower floor was a chamber which the studious Emperor Constantine VII afterwards turned into a library, and a breakfast-room, with walls of splendid marble and floor adorned with mosaics. Near at hand two other houses, similar yet different, attested the taste of Theophilus for rich schemes of decoration. One of these was remarkable for the mosaic walls in which green trees stood out against a golden sky. The lower chamber of the other was called the Musikos, from the harmonious blending of the colours of the marble plaques with which the walls were covered-Egyptian porphyry, white Carian, and the green riverstone of Thessaly,—while the variegated floor produced the effect of a flowering meadow.

If the influence of the luxurious art of the East is apparent in these halls and pavilions which Theophilus added to his chief residence, a new palace which his architect Patrikes built on the Bithynian coast was avowedly modelled on the palaces of Baghdad. It was not far from the famous palace of Hieras built by Justinian. The Asiatic suburbs of Constantinople not only included Chrysopolis and Chalcedon, but extended south-eastward along the charming shore which looks to the Prince's Islands, as far as Kartalimen. Proceeding in this direction from Chalcedon, one came first to the peninsula of Hieria (Phanaráki), where Justinian had chosen the site of his suburban residence. Passing by Eufinianae (Jadi-Bostan), one reached Satyros, once noted for a temple, soon to be famous for a monastery. The spot chosen by Theophilus for his new palace was at Bryas, which lay between Satyros and Kartalimen (Kartal), and probably corresponds to the modern village of Mal-tépé. The palace of Bryas resembled those of Baghdad in shape and in the schemes of decoration. The only deviations from the plan of the original were additions required in the residence of a Christian ruler, a chapel of the Virgin adjoining the Imperial bedroom, and in the court a church of the triconch shape dedicated to Michael the archangel and two female saints. The buildings stood in a park irrigated by watercourses.

Arabian splendor in his material surroundings meant modernity for Theophilus, and his love of novel curiosities was shown in the mechanical contrivances which he installed in the audience chamber of the palace of Magnaura. A golden plane-tree overshadowed the throne; birds sat on its branches and on the throne itself. Golden griffins couched at the sides, golden lions at the foot; and there was a gold organ in the room. When a foreign ambassador was introduced to the Emperor's presence, he was amazed and perhaps alarmed at seeing the animals rise up and hearing the lions roar and the birds burst into melodious song. At the sound of the organ these noises ceased, but when the audience was over and the ambassador was withdrawing, the mechanism was again set in motion.

One of the most remarkable sights in the throne room of the Magnaura was the Pentapyrgion, or cabinet of Five Towers, a piece of furniture which was constructed by Theophilus. Four towers were grouped round a central and doubtless higher tower; each tower had several, probably four, storeys; and in the chambers, which were visible to the eye, were exhibited various precious objects, mostly of sacred interest. At the celebration of an Imperial marriage, it was the usage to deposit the nuptial wreaths in the Pentapyrgion. On special occasions, for instance at the Easter festival, it was removed from the Magnaura to adorn the Chrysotriklinos.

If the Emperor's love of magnificence and taste for art impelled him to spend immense sums on his palaces, he did not neglect works of public utility. One of the most important duties of the government was to maintain the fortifications of the city in repair. Theophilus did not add new defences, like Heraclius and Leo, but no Emperor did more than he to strengthen and improve the existing walls. The experiences of the siege conducted by Thomas seem to have shown that the sea-walls were not high enough to be impregnable. It was decided to raise them in height, and this work, though commenced by his father on the side of the Golden Horn, was mainly the work of Theophilus. Numerous inscriptions-of which many are still to be seen, many others have disappeared in recent times-recorded his name, which appears more frequently on the walls and towers than that of any other Emperor. The restoration of the seaward defences facing Chrysopolis may specially be noticed: at the ancient gate of St. Barbara (Top-kapussi, close to Seraglio Point), and on the walls and towers to the south, on either side of the gate of unknown name (now Deirmen-kapussi) near the Kynegion. Just north of this entrance is a long inscription, in six iambic trimeters, praying that the wall which Theophilus "raised on new foundations" may stand fast and unshaken for ever. It may possibly be a general dedication of all his new fortifications. But the work was not quite completed when Theophilus died. South of the Kynegion and close to the Mangana, a portion of the circuit remained in disrepair, and it was reserved for Bardas, the able minister of Michael III., to restore it some twenty years later.

§3. Iconoclasm

It was not perhaps in the nature of Theophilus to adopt the passive attitude of his father in the matter of image-worship, or to refrain from making a resolute attempt to terminate the schism which divided the Church. But he appears for some years (perhaps till A.D. 834) to have continued the tolerant policy of Michael, and there may be some reason for believing, as many believe, that the influence of his friend John the Grammarian, who became Patriarch in A.D. 832, was chiefly responsible for his resolution to suppress icons. He did not summon a new council, and perhaps he did not issue any new edict; but he endeavoured, by severe measures, to ensure the permanence of the iconoclastic principles which had been established under Leo the Armenian. The lack of contemporary evidence renders it difficult to determine the scope and extent of the persecution of Theophilus; but a careful examination of such evidence as exists shows that modern historians have exaggerated its compass, if not its severity. So far as we can see, his repressive measures were twofold. He endeavoured to check the propagation of the false doctrine by punishing some leading monks who were actively preaching it; and he sought to abolish religious pictures from Constantinople by forbidding them to be painted at all.

Of the cases of corporal chastisement inflicted on ecclesiastics for pertinacity in the cause of image-worship, the most famous and genuine is the punishment of the two Palestinian brothers, Theodore and Theophanes, who had already endured persecution under Leo V. On Leo's death they returned to Constantinople and did their utmost in the cause of pictures, Theodore by his books and Theophanes by his hymns. But Michael II treated them like other leaders of the cause; he did not permit them to remain in the city. Under Theophilus they were imprisoned and scourged, then exiled to Aphusia, one of the Proconnesian islands. Theophilus was anxious to win them over; the severe treatment which he dealt out to them proves the influence they exerted; they had, in fact, succeeded Theodore of Studion as the principal champions of icons. The Emperor hoped that after the experience of a protracted exile and imprisonment they would yield to his threats; their opposition seemed to him perhaps the chief obstacle to the unity of the Church. So they were brought to Constantinople and the story of their maltreatment may be told in their own words.

"The Imperial officer arrived at the isle of Aphusia and hurried us away to the City, affirming that he knew not the purpose of the command, only that he had been sent to execute it very urgently. We arrived in the City on the 8th of July. Our conductor reported our arrival to the Emperor, and was ordered to shut us up in the Praetorian prison. Six days later (on the 14th) we were summoned to the Imperial presence. Conducted by the Prefect of the City, we reached the door of the Chrysotriklinos, and saw the Emperor with a terribly stern countenance and a number of people standing round. It was the tenth hour. The Prefect retired and left us in the presence of the Emperor, who, when we had made obeisance, roughly ordered us to approach. He asked us 'Where were ye born?' We replied, 'In the land of Moab'. 'Why came ye here?' We did not answer, and he ordered our faces to be beaten. After many sore blows, we became dizzy and fell, and if I had not grasped the tunic of the man who smote me, I should have fallen on the Emperor's footstool. Holding by his dress I stood unmoved till the Emperor said 'Enough' and repeated his former question. When we still said nothing he addressed the Prefect [who appears to have returned] in great wrath, 'Take them and engrave on their faces these verses, and then hand them over to two Saracens to conduct them to their own country'. One stood near-his name was Christodulos-who held in his hand the iambic verses which he had composed. The Emperor bade him read them aloud, adding, 'If they are not good, never mind'. He said this because he knew how they would be ridiculed by us, since we are experts in poetical matters. The man who read them said, 'Sir, these fellows are not worthy that the verses should be better".

They were then taken back to the Praetorium, and then once more to the Palace, where they received a flogging in the Imperial presence. But another chance was granted to them. Four days later they were informed by the Prefect that if they would communicate once with the iconoclasts it would be sufficient to save them from punishment; 'I', he said, 'will accompany you to the Church'. When they refused, they were laid upon benches, and their faces were tattooed-it was a long process-with the vituperative verses. Some admiration is due to the dexterity and delicacy of touch of the tormentor who succeeded in branding twelve iambic lines on a human face. The other part of the sentence was not carried out. The brethren were not reconducted to their own country; they were imprisoned at Apamea in Bithynia, where Theodore died. Theophanes, the hymn writer, survived till the next reign and became bishop of Nicaea.

Of the acts of persecution ascribed to Theophilus, this is the most authentic. Now there is a circumstance about it which may help to explain the Emperor's exceptional severity, the fact that the two monks who had so vehemently agitated against his policy were strangers from Palestine. We can easily understand that the Emperor's resentment would have been especially aroused against interlopers who had come from abroad to make trouble in his dominion. And there are two other facts which are probably not unconnected. The oriental Patriarchs (of Alexandria, Antioch, and Jerusalem) had addressed to Theophilus a 'synodic letter' in favour of the worship of images, a manifesto which must have been highly displeasing to him and to the Patriarch John. Further, it is recorded, and there is no reason to doubt, that Theophilus imprisoned Michael, the synkellos of the Patriarch of Jerusalem, who had formerly been persecuted by Leo V. We may fairly suspect that the offence of the Palestinian brethren was seriously aggravated in his eyes by the fact that they were Palestinian. This suspicion is borne out by the tenor of the bad verses which were inscribed on their faces.

There was another case of cruelty which seems to be well attested. Euthymios, bishop of Sardis, who had been prominent among the orthodox opponents of Leo V., died in consequence of a severe scourging. But the greater number of image-worshippers, whose sufferings are specially recorded, suffered no more than banishment, and the Proconnesian island Aphusia is said to have been selected as the place of confinement for many notable champions of pictures.

The very different treatment which Theophilus accorded to Methodius is significant. In order to bend him to his will, he tried harsh measures, whipped him and shut him up in a subterranean prison. But he presently released him, and Methodius, who, though an inflexible image-worshipper, was no fanatic, lived in the Palace on good terms with the Emperor, who esteemed his learning, and showed him high honour.

Of the measures adopted by Theophilus for the suppression of icon-worship by cutting off the supply of pictures we know nothing on authority that can be accepted as good. It is stated that he forbade religious pictures to be painted, and that he cruelly tortured Lazarus, the most eminent painter of the time. There is probably some truth behind both statements, and the persecution of monks, with which he is charged, may be explained by his endeavours to suppress the painting of pictures. Theophilus did not penalize monks on account of their profession; for we know from other facts that he was not opposed to monasticism. But they were the religious artists of the age, and we may conjecture that many of those who incurred his displeasure were painters.

If we review the ecclesiastical policy of Theophilus in the light of the few facts which are certain and compare it with other persecutions to which Christians have at various times resorted to force their opinions upon differing souls, it is obviously absurd to describe it as extraordinarily severe. The list of cases of cruel maltreatment is short. That many obscure monks besides underwent distress and privation we cannot doubt; but such distress seems to have been due to a severer enforcement of the same rule which Michael II had applied to Theodore of Studion and his friends. Those who would not acquiesce in the synod of Leo V. and actively defied it were compelled to leave the city. The monastery of Phoberon, at the north end of the Bosphorus, seems to have been one of the chief refuges for the exiles. This brings us to the second characteristic of the persecution of Theophilus, its geographical limitation. Following in his father's traces, he insisted upon the suppression of pictures only in Constantinople itself and its immediate neighbourhood. Iconoclasm was the doctrine of the Emperor and the Patriarch, but they did not insist upon its consequences beyond the precincts of the capital. So far as we can see, throughout the second period of iconoclasm, in Greece and the islands and on the coasts of Asia Minor, image-worship flourished without let or hindrance, and the bishops and monks were unaffected by the decrees of Leo V. This salient fact has not been realised by historians, but it sets the persecution of Theophilus in a different light. He would not allow pictures in the churches of the capital; and he drove out all active picture-worshippers and painters, to indulge themselves in their heresy elsewhere. It was probably only in a few exceptional cases that he resorted to severe punishment.

The females of the Emperor's household were devoted to images, and the secret opinion of Theodora must have been well known to Theophilus. The situation occasioned anecdotes turning on the motive that the Empress and her mother Theodora kept a supply of icons, but kept them well out of sight. The Emperor had a misshapen fool and jester, named Denderis, whose appearance reminded the courtiers of the Homeric Thersites. Licensed to roam at large through the Palace, he burst one day into Theodora's bedchamber and found her kissing sacred images. When he curiously asked what they were, she said, "They are my pretty dolls, and I love them dearly". He then went to the Emperor, who was sitting at dinner. Theophilus asked him where he had been. "With nurse", said Denderis (so he used to call Theodora), "and I saw her taking such pretty dolls out of a cushion". The Emperor comprehended. In high wrath he rose at once from table, sought Theodora, and overwhelmed her with reproaches as an idolatress. But the lady met him with a ready lie. "It is not as you suppose", she said; "I and some of my maids were looking in the mirror, and Denderis took the reflexions for dolls and told you a foolish story". Theophilus, if not satisfied, had to accept the explanation, and Theodora carefully warned Denderis not to mention the dolls again. When Theophilus asked him one day whether nurse had again kissed the pretty dolls, Denderis, placing one hand on his lips and the other on his posterior parts, said, "Hush, Emperor, don't mention the dolls".

Another similar anecdote is told of the Emperor's mother-in-law, Theoktiste, who lived in a house of her own, where she was often visited by her youthful granddaughters. She sought to imbue them with a veneration for pictures and to counteract the noxious influence of their father's heresy. She would produce the sacred forms from the box in which she kept them, and press them to the faces and lips of the young girls. Their father, suspecting that they were being tainted with the idolatrous superstition, asked them one day, when they returned from a visit to their grandmother, what presents she had given them and how they had been amused. The older girls saw the trap and evaded his questions, but Pulcheria, who was a small child, truthfully described how her grandmother had taken a number of dolls from a box and pressed them upon the faces of herself and her sisters. Theophilus was furious, but it would have been odious to take any severe measure against the Empress's mother, who was highly respected for her piety. All he could do was to prevent his daughters from visiting her as frequently as before.

§4. Death of Theophilus and Restoration of Icon Worship

Theophilus died of dysentery on January 20, A.D. 842. His last illness was disturbed by the fear that his death would be followed by a revolution against the throne of his infant son. The man who seemed to be the likely leader of a movement to overthrow his dynasty was Theophobos, a somewhat mysterious general, who was said to be of Persian descent and had commanded the Persian troops in the Imperial service. Theophobos was an orthodox Christian, but he was one of the Emperor's right-hand men in the eastern wars, and had been honoured with the hand of his sister or sister-in-law. He had been implicated some years before in a revolt, but had been restored to favour and lived in the Palace. It is said that he was popular in Constantinople, and the Emperor may have had good reasons for thinking that he might aspire with success to the supreme power. From his deathbed he ordered Theophobos to be cast into a dungeon of the Bucoleon Palace, where he was secretly decapitated at night.

Exercising a constitutional right of his sovran authority, usually employed in such circumstances, the Emperor had appointed two regents to act as his son's guardians and assist the Empress, namely, her uncle Manuel, the chief Magister, and Theoktistos, the Logothete of the Course, who had proved himself a devoted servant of the Amorian house. It is possible that Theodora's brother Bardas was a third regent, but this cannot be regarded as probable. The position of Theodora closely resembled that of Irene during the minority of Constantine. The government was carried on in the joint names of the mother and the son, but the actual exercise of Imperial authority devolved upon the mother provisionally. Yet there was a difference in the two cases. Leo IV., so far as we know, had not appointed any regents or guardians of his son to act with Irene, so that legally she had the supreme power entirely in her hands; whereas Theodora was as unable to act without the concurrence of Manuel and Theoktistos as they were unable to act without her.

It has been commonly thought that Theophilus had hardly closed his eyes before his wife and her advisers made such pious haste to repair his ecclesiastical errors that a council was held and the worship of images restored, almost as a matter of course, a few weeks after his death. The truth is that more than a year elapsed before the triumph of orthodoxy was secured. The first and most pressing care of the regency was not to compose the ecclesiastical schism, but to secure the stability of the Amorian throne; and the question whether iconoclasm should be abandoned depended on the view adopted by the regents as to the effect of a change in religious policy on the fortunes of the dynasty. For the change was not a simple matter, nor one that could be lightly undertaken. Theodora, notwithstanding her personal convictions, hesitated to take the decisive step. It is a mistake to suppose that she initiated the measures which led to the restoration of pictures. She had a profound belief in her husband's political sagacity; she shrank from altering the system which he had successfully maintained; and there was the further consideration that, if iconoclasm were condemned by the Church as a heresy, her husband's name would be anathematized. Her scruples were overcome by the arguments of the regents, who persuaded her that the restoration of images would be the surest means to establish the safety of the throne. But when she yielded to these reasons, to the pressure of other members of her own family, and probably to the representations of Methodius, she made it a condition of her consent, that the council which she would have to summon should not brand the memory of Theophilus with the anathema of the Church.

Our ignorance of the comparative strength of the two parties in the capital and in the army renders it impossible for us to understand the political calculations which determined the Empress and her advisers to act in accordance with her religious convictions. But the sudden assassination of Theophobos by the command of the dying Emperor is a significant indication that a real danger menaced the throne, and that the image-worshippers, led by some ambitious insurgent, would have been ready and perhaps able to overthrow the dynasty. The event seems to corroborate the justice of their fears. For when they re-established the cult of pictures, iconoclasm died peacefully without any convulsions or rebellions. The case of Theoktistos may be adduced to illustrate the fact that many of those who held high office were not fanatical partisans. He had been perfectly contented with the iconoclastic policy, and was probably a professed iconoclast, but placed in a situation where iconoclasm appeared to be a peril to the throne, he was ready to throw it over for the sake of political expediency.

Our brief, vague, and contradictory records supply little certain information as to the manner in which the government conducted the preparations for the defeat of iconoclasm. It is evident that astute management was required; and a considerable time was demanded for the negotiations and intrigues needful to facilitate a smooth settlement. We may take it for granted that Theodora and her advisers had at once destined Methodius (who had lived for many years in the Palace on intimate terms with the late Emperor, and who, we may guess, had secretly acted as a spiritual adviser to the Imperial ladies) as successor to the Patriarchal chair. To him naturally fell the task of presiding at a commission, which met in the official apartments of Theoktistos and prepared the material for the coming Council.

Before the Council met, early in March (A.D. 843), the Patriarch John must have been officially informed by the Empress of her intention to convoke it, and summoned to attend. He was not untrue to the iconoclastic doctrine which he had actively defended for thirty years, and he declined to alter his convictions in order to remain in the Patriarchal chair. He was deposed by the Council, Methodius was elected in his stead, and the decrees of the Seventh Ecumenical Council were confirmed. The list of heretics who had been anathematized at that Council was augmented by the names of the prominent iconoclastic leaders who had since troubled the Church, but the name of the Emperor Theophilus was omitted. We can easily divine that to spare his memory was the most delicate and difficult part of the whole business. Methodius himself was in temper a man of the same cast as the Patriarchs Tarasius and Nicephorus; he understood the necessities of compromise, he appreciated the value of 'economy', and he was ready to fall in with the wishes of Theodora. We may suspect that it was largely through his management that the members of the Council agreed, apparently without dissent, to exclude the late Emperor from the black list; and it is evident that their promises to acquiesce in this course must have been secured before the Council met. According to a story which has little claim to credit, Theodora addressed the assembly and pleaded for her husband on the ground that he had repented of his errors on his death-bed, and that she herself had held an icon to his lips before he breathed his last. But it is not improbable that the suggestion of a death-bed repentance was circulated unofficially for the purpose of influencing the monks who execrated the memory of the last imperial iconoclast. It seems significant that the monks of Studion took no prominent part in the orthodox reform, though they afterwards sought to gain credit for having indirectly promoted it by instigating Manuel the Magister. We shall hardly do them wrong if we venture to read between the lines, and assume that, while they refrained from open opposition, they disapproved of the methods by which the welcome change was manoeuvred.

But the flagrant fact that the guilty iconoclast, who had destroyed icons and persecuted their votaries, was excepted from condemnation by the synod which abolished his heresy, stimulated the mythopoeic fancy of monks, who invented divers vain tales to account for this inexplicable leniency. The story of Theodora's personal assurances to the synod belongs to this class of invention. It was also related that she dreamed that her husband was led in chains before a great man who sat on a throne in front of an icon of Christ, and that this judge, when she fell weeping and praying at his feet, ordered Theophilus to be unbound by the angels who guarded him, for the sake of her faith. According to another myth, the divine pardon of the culprit was confirmed by a miracle. Methodius wrote down the names of all the Imperial heretics, including Theophilus, in a book which he deposited on an altar. Waking up from a dream in which an angel announced to him that pardon had been granted, he took the book from the holy table, and discovered that where the name of Theophilus had stood, there was a blank space.

Of one thing we may be certain: the Emperor did not repent. The suggestion of a death-bed repentance was a falsification of fact, probably circulated deliberately in order to save his memory, and readily believed because it was edifying. It helped to smooth the way in a difficult situation, by justifying in popular opinion the course of expediency or 'economy', which the Church adopted at the dictation of Theodora.

After the Council had completed its work, the triumph of orthodoxy was celebrated by a solemn festival service in St. Sophia, on the first Sunday in Lent (March 11, A.D. 843). The monks from all the surrounding monasteries, and perhaps even hermits from the cells of Athos, flocked into the city, and we may be sure that sacred icons were hastily hung in the places from which others had been torn in all the churches of the capital. A nocturnal thanksgiving was held in the church of the Virgin in Blachernae, and on Sunday morning the Empress, with the child Emperor, the Patriarch and clergy, and all the ministers and senators, bearing crosses and icons and candles in their hands, devoutly proceeded to St. Sophia. It was enacted that henceforward the restoration of icons should be commemorated on the same day, and the first Sunday of Lent is still the feast of Orthodoxy in the Greek Church.

All our evidence for this ecclesiastical revolution comes from the records of those who rejoiced in it; we are not informed of the tactics of the iconoclastic party, nor is it hinted that they made any serious effort to fight for a doomed cause. We can hardly believe that the Patriarch John was quiescent during the year preceding the Council, and silently awaited the event. But the only tradition of any counter-movement is the anecdote of a scandalous attempt to discredit Methodius after his elevation to the Patriarchate. The iconoclasts, it was said, bribed a young woman to allege publicly that the Patriarch had seduced her. An official inquiry was held, and Methodius proved his innocence, to the satisfaction of a curious and crowded assembly, by a cynical ocular demonstration that he was physically incapable of the offence with which he was charged. He explained that many years ago, during his sojourn at Rome, he had been tormented by the stings of carnal desire, and that in answer to his prayer St. Peter's miraculous touch had withered his body and freed him for ever from the assaults of passion. The woman was compelled to confess that she had been suborned, and the heretics who had invented the lie received the mild punishment of being compelled every year, at the feast of orthodoxy, to join the procession from Blachernae to St. Sophia with torches in their hands, and hear with their own ears anathema pronounced upon them. There was some kernel of truth in this edifying fiction, but it is impossible to disentangle it.

It would seem that the great majority of the iconoclastic bishops and clergy professed repentance of their error and were allowed to retain their ecclesiastical dignities. Here Methodius, who was a man of moderation and compromise, followed the precedent set by Tarasius at the time of the first restoration of image-worship. But the iconoclastic heresy was by no means immediately extinguished, though it never again caused more than administrative trouble. Some of those who repented lapsed into error, and new names were added, twenty-five years later, to the list of the heretics who were held up to public ignominy on the Sunday of Orthodoxy, and stigmatized as Jews or pagans.

The final installation of icons among the sanctities of the Christian faith, the authoritative addition of icon-worship to the superstitions of the Church, was a triumph for the religious spirit of the Greeks over the doctrine of Eastern heretics whose Christianity had a more Semitic flavour. The struggle had lasted for about a hundred and twenty years, and in its latest stage had been virtually confined to Constantinople. Here the populace seems to have oscillated between the two extreme views, and many of the educated inhabitants probably belonged to that moderate party which approved of images in Churches, but was opposed to their worship. Of the influence of the iconoclastic movement on Byzantine art something will be said in another chapter, but it must be noticed here that in one point it won an abiding victory. In the doctrine laid down by the Council no distinction was drawn between sculptured and painted representations; all icons were legitimized. But whereas, before the controversy began, religious art had expressed itself in both forms, after the Council of A.D. 843, sculpture was entirely discarded, and icons came to mean pictures and pictures only. This was a silent surrender, never explicitly avowed by the orthodox Church, to the damnable teaching of the iconoclasts; so that these heretics can claim to have so far influenced public opinion as to induce their victorious adversaries to abandon the cult of graven images. After all, the victory was a compromise.

Chapter V
Michael III
A.D. 842-867

§1. The Regency

Michael III reigned for a quarter of a century, but he never governed. During the greater part of his life he was too young; when he reached a riper age he had neither the capacity nor the desire. His reign falls into two portions. In his minority, the Empress Theodora held the reins, guided by the advice of Theoktistos, the Logothete of the Course, who proved as devoted to her as he had been to her husband. During the later years, when Michael nominally exercised the sovranty himself, the real power and the task of conducting the administration devolved upon her brother Bardas. In the first period, the government seems to have been competent, though we have not sufficient information to estimate it with much confidence; in the second period it was eminently efficient.

The Empress Theodora occupied the same constitutional position which the Empress Irene had occupied in the years following her husband's death. She was not officially the Autocrat, any more than her daughter Thecla, who was associated with her brother and mother in the Imperial dignity; she only acted provisionally as such on behalf of her son. The administration was conducted in their joint names; but she possessed no sovran authority in her own right or independently of him. Her actual authority was formally limited (unlike Irene's) by the two guardians or co-regents whom Theophilus had appointed. To find two men who would work in harmony and could be trusted not to seek power for themselves to the detriment of his son was difficult, and Theophilus seems to have made a judicious choice. But it was almost inevitable that one of the two should win the effective control of affairs and the chief place in the Empress's confidence. It may well be that superior talent and greater political experience rendered Theoktistos a more capable adviser than Manuel, her uncle, who had probably more knowledge of warfare than of administration. Theoktistos presently became the virtual prime minister, and Manuel found it convenient to withdraw from his rooms in the Palace and live in his house near the Cistern of Aspar, though he did not formally retire from his duties and regularly attended in the Palace for the transaction of business.

Her uncle's practical abdication of his right to a voice in the management of the Empire corresponds to the policy which Theodora pursued, under the influence of the Logothete, towards the other members of her own family. Her brother Petronas, who was a competent general and had done useful work for her husband, seems to have been entrusted with no important post and allowed no opportunity of winning distinction under her government; he proved his military capacity after her fall from power. Her more famous and brilliant brother Bardas was forced to be contented with an inactive life in his suburban house. Theodora had also three sisters, of whom one, Sophia, had married Constantine Babutzikos. Another, Calomaria, was the wife of Arsaber, a patrician, who was elevated to the higher rank of magister. On his death Calomaria lived in the Palace with her sister, and is said to have worn mean raiment and performed the charitable duty of paying monthly visits to the prisons and distributing blessings and alms to the prisoners.

Michael was in his seventeenth year when his mother decided to marry him. The customary bride-show was announced throughout the provinces by a proclamation inviting beautiful candidates for the throne to assemble on a certain day in the Imperial Palace. The choice of the Empress fell on Eudocia, the daughter of Dekapolites (A.D. 855). We know nothing of this lady or her family; she seems to have been a cipher, and her nullity may have recommended her to Theodora. But in any case the haste of the Empress and Theoktistos to provide Michael with a consort at such an early age was prompted by their desire to prevent his union with another lady. For Michael already had a love affair with Eudocia Ingerina, whom Theodora and her minister regarded as an unsuitable spouse. A chronicler tells us that they disliked her intensely "on account of her impudence"; which means that she was a woman of some spirit, and they feared her as a rival influence. The young sovran was obliged to yield and marry the wife who was not of his own choice, but if he was separated from the woman he loved, it was only for a short time. Eudocia Ingerina did not disdain to be his mistress, and his attachment to her seems to have lasted till his death.

But the power of Theodora and her favorite minister was doomed, and the blow was struck by a member of her own family (A.D. 856, January to March). Michael had reached an age when he began to chafe under the authority of his mother, whose discipline had probably been strict; and his uncle Bardas, who was ambitious and conscious of his own talents for government, divined that it would now be possible to undermine her position and win his nephew's confidence. The most difficult part of his enterprise was to remove Theoktistos, but he had. friends among the ministers who were in close attendance on the Emperor. The Parakoemomenos or chief chamberlain, Damianos (a man of Slavonic race), persuaded Michael to summon his uncle to the Palace, and their wily tongues convinced the boy that his mother intended to depose him, with the assistance of Theoktistos, or at all events-and this was no more than the truth-that he would have no power so long as Theodora and Theoktistos co-operated. Michael was brought to acquiesce in the view that it was necessary to suppress the too powerful minister, and violence was the only method. Theophanes, the chief of the private wardrobe, joined the conspiracy, and Bardas also won over his sister Calomaria. Some generals, who had been deposed from their commands and owed a grudge to Theoktistos, were engaged to lend active assistance. It was arranged that Bardas should station himself in the Lausiakos, and there attack the Logothete, whose duties frequently obliged him to pass through that hall in order to reach the apartments of the Empress. Calomaria concealed herself in an upper room, where, through a hole, perhaps constructed on purpose, she commanded a view of the Lausiakos, and could, by signalling from a window, inform the Emperor as soon as Bardas sprang upon his victim.

Theoktistos had obtained at the secretarial office the reports which he had to submit to the Empress, and as he passed through the Lausiakos he observed with displeasure Bardas seated at his ease, as if he had a full right to be there. Muttering that he would persuade Theodora to expel him from the Palace, he proceeded on his way, but in the Horologion, at the entrance of the Chrysotriklinos, he was stopped by the Emperor and Damianos. Michael, asserting his authority perhaps for the first time, angrily ordered him to read the reports to himself and not to his mother. As the Logothete was retracing his steps in a downcast mood, Bardas sprang forward and smote him. The ex-generals hastened to assist, and Theoktistos drew his sword. The Emperor, on receiving a signal from his aunt, hurried to the scene, and by his orders

Theoktistos was seized and dragged to the Skyla. It would seem that Bardas did not contemplate murder, but intended to remove the Logothete to a place of banishment. But the Emperor, advised by others, probably by Damianos, that nothing short of his death would serve, called upon the foreign Guards (the Hetairoi) to slay Theoktistos. Meanwhile the Empress had heard from the Papias of the Palace that the Logothete's life was in danger, and she instantly rushed to the scene to save her friend. But she was scared back to her apartments by one of the conspirators, a member of the family of Melissenos, who cried in a voice of thunder, "Go back, for this is the day of strikers". The Guards, who were stationed in the adjoining Hall of Justinian, rushed in; one of them dragged the victim from the chair under which he had crawled and stabbed him in the belly (A.D. 856).

Of the two offices which Theoktistos had held, the less onerous, that of Chartulary of the Kanikleion, was conferred on Bardas, while his son-in-law Symbatios-whose name shows his Armenian lineage-was appointed Logothete of the Course. The reign of Theodora was now over. She had held the reins of power for fourteen years, and she was unwilling to surrender them. She was not an unscrupulous woman like Irene, she did not aspire to be Autocrat in her own right or set aside her son; but well knowing her son's incapacity she had doubtless looked forward to keeping him in perpetual tutelage and retaining all the serious business of government in her own hands. The murder of Theoktistos cut her to the heart, and though the Emperor endeavoured to pacify and conciliate her, she remained unrelenting in her bitterness.

The Senate was convoked, and that body applauded the announcement that Michael would henceforward govern alone in his own name. Bardas was elevated to the rank of magister and was appointed Domestic of the Schools. It would appear that for nearly two years Theodora resided in the Palace, powerless but unforgiving, and perhaps waiting for a favourable opportunity to compass the downfall of her brother. It is said that her son plagued her, trying perhaps to drive her into voluntary retirement. At last, whether his mother's proximity became intolerable, or she involved herself in intrigues against Bardas, it was decided that she should not only be expelled from the Palace but consigned to a nunnery. The Patriarch Ignatius, who owed his appointment to her, was commanded to tonsure her along with her daughters, but he absolutely declined on the sufficient ground that they were unwilling to take the monastic vow. The hair of their heads was shorn by other hands, and they were all immured in the monastery of Karianos (autumn A.D. 858).

It was probably soon afterwards that the Empress, thirsting for revenge if she did not hope to regain power, entered into a plot against her brother's life. The Imperial Protostrator was the chief of the conspirators, who planned to kill Bardas as he was returning to the Palace from his suburban house on the Golden Horn. But the design was discovered, and the conspirators were beheaded in the Hippodrome.

§2. Bardas and Basil the Macedonian.

Bardas was soon raised to the high dignity of Curopalates, which was only occasionally conferred on a near relative of the Emperor and gave its recipient, in case the sovran died childless, a certain claim to the succession. His position was at the same time strengthened by the appointments of his two sons to important military posts. The Domesticate of the Schools, which he vacated, was given to Antigonus who was only a boy, while an elder son was invested with the command of several western Themes which were exceptionally united. But for Bardas the office of Curopalates was only a step to the higher dignity of Caesar, which designated him more clearly as the future colleague or successor of his nephew, whose marriage had been fruitless. He was created Caesar on the Sunday after Easter in April A.D. 862.

The government of the Empire was in the hands of Bardas for ten years, and the reluctant admissions of hostile chroniclers show that he was eminently fitted to occupy the throne. A brilliant success won (A.D. 863) against the Saracens, and the conversion of Bulgaria, enhanced the prestige of the Empire abroad; he committed the care of the Church to the most brilliant Patriarch who ever occupied the ecclesiastical throne of Constantinople; he followed the example of Theophilus in his personal attention to the administration of justice; and he devoted himself especially to the improvement of education and the advancement of learning. The military and diplomatic transactions of this fortunate decade, its importance for the ecclesiastical independence of the Eastern Empire, and its significance in the history of culture, are dealt with in other chapters.

Michael himself was content to leave the management of the state in his uncle's capable hands. He occasionally took part in military expeditions, more for the sake of occupation, we may suspect, than from a sense of duty. He was a man of pleasure, he only cared for amusement, he had neither the brains nor the taste for administration. His passion for horseraces reminds us of Nero and Commodus; he used himself to drive a chariot in the private hippodrome of the Palace of St. Mamas. His frivolity and extravagance, his impiety and scurrility, are held up to derision and execration by an imperial writer who was probably his own grandson but was bitterly hostile to his memory.

Little confidence can be placed in the anecdotes related by the Emperor Constantine Porphyrogennetos and his literary satellites, but there is no doubt that they exhibit, in however exaggerated a shape, the character and reputation of Michael. We may not be prepared, for instance, to believe that the fire-signals of Asia Minor were discontinued, because on one occasion he was interrupted in the hippodrome by an inopportune message; but the motive of the story reflects his genuine impatience of public business. The most famous or infamous performance of Michael was his travesty of the mysteries and ministers of the Church. One of his coarse boon-companions, a buffoon known as the "Pig", was arrayed as Patriarch, while the Emperor and eleven others dressed themselves in episcopal garments, as twelve prominent bishops. With citherns, which they hid in the folds of their robes and secretly sounded, they intoned the liturgy. They enacted the solemn offices of consecrating and deposing bishops, and it was even rumoured that they were not ashamed to profane the Eucharist, using mustard and vinegar instead of the holy elements. A story was current that one day the mock Patriarch riding on an ass, with his execrable cortege, came face to face with the true Patriarch Ignatius, who was conducting a religious procession to a suburban church. The profane satyrs raised their hoods, loudly struck their instruments, and with lewd songs disturbed the solemn hymns of the pious procession. But this was only a sensational anecdote, for we have reason to believe that Michael did not begin to practise these mummeries till after the deposition of Ignatius. Mocking at the ecclesiastical schism, he is said to have jested "Theophilus (the Pig) is my Patriarch, Photius is the Patriarch of the Caesar, Ignatius of the Christians". How far mummeries of this kind shocked public opinion in Constantinople it is difficult to conjecture.

The Imperial pleasures were costly, and Michael's criminal generosity to his worthless companions dissipated large treasures. He made it a practice to stand sponsor at the baptisms of children of his jockeys, and on such occasions he would bestow upon the father a present varying from £1296 to £2160, occasionally even as much as £4320—sums which then represented a considerably higher value than today. Not only was no saving effected during the eleven years in which he was master of the Empire, but he wasted the funds which had been saved by his father and by his mother, and towards the end of his reign he was in such straits for ready money that he laid hands upon some of the famous works of art with which Theophilus had adorned the Palace. The golden plane-tree, in which the mechanical birds twittered, the two golden lions, the two griffins hammered out of solid gold, and the organ of solid gold, all weighing not less than 200 pounds, were melted down; but before they were minted, Michael perished. It seems probable that it was in the last year or two of his reign that his extravagance became excessive and ruinous. For there is no sign that the Empire was in financial difficulties during the government of Bardas, who seems to have been able to restrain his nephew within certain bounds.

The weak point of the position of the Caesar lay in the circumstance that he had to share his influence over the Emperor with boon companions; for there was always the danger that a wily schemer, concealing ambition under the mask of frivolity, might successfully use the opportunities of intimate intercourse to discredit him and undermine his power. The fact that he retained for ten years the unshaken, almost childish confidence of his nephew is a striking proof of his talent and tact; and when at last he was overthrown, his supplanter was one of the two ablest men who arose in the Eastern Empire during the ninth century.

Basil the Macedonian, who now comes on the stage, is the typical adventurer who rises from the lowliest circumstances to the highest fortune. His career, wonderful in itself, was made still more wonderful by mythopoeic fancy, which converted the able and unscrupulous upstart into a hero guided by Heaven. He was born about A.D. 812, of poor Armenian parents, whose family had settled in the neighbourhood of Hadrianople. His Armenian descent is established beyond doubt, and the legend that he was a Slav has no better a foundation than the fiction which claimed Slavonic parentage for the Emperor Justinian. But his family was obscure; and the illustrious lineage which his descendants claimed, connecting him through his grandfather with the Arsacids and by his grandmother with Constantine the Great and Alexander, was an audacious and ingenious invention of the Patriarch Photius. In his babyhood he was carried into captivity, along with his parents, by the Bulgarian Krum, and he spent his youth in the region beyond the Danube which was known as "Macedonia".

We may conjecture that he derived his designation as Basil the Macedonian from his long sojourn in this district, for "Macedonian" can hardly refer to his birthplace, which was in Thrace. He was twenty-five years old when the captives succeeded (as is related in another Chapter) in escaping from the power of the Bulgarians and returning to their homes. Basil obtained some small post in the service of a strategos, but seeing no hope of rising in the provinces he decided to seek his fortune in Constantinople. His arrival in the city has been wrought by the storyteller into the typical form of romance. On a Sunday, near the hour of sunset, he reached the Golden Gate, a poor unknown adventurer, with staff and scrip, and he lay down to sleep in the vestibule of the adjacent church of St. Diomede. During the night, Nicolas, who was in charge of the church, was awakened by a mysterious voice, saying, "Arise and bring the Basileus into the sanctuary". He got up and looking out saw nothing but a poor man asleep. He lay down again, and the same thing was repeated. The third time, he was poked in the side by a sword and the voice said, "Go out and bring in the man you see lying outside the gate". He obeyed, and on the morrow he took Basil to the bath, gave him a change of garments, and adopted him as a brother. So much is probable that Basil found shelter in St. Diomede, and that through Nicolas he was enabled to place his foot on the first rung of the ladder of fortune. The monk had a brother who was a physician in the service of Theophilus Paidenomenos, or, as he was usually called, Theophilitzes, a rich courtier and a relative of the Empress Theodora. The physician, who saw Basil at St. Diomede, and admired his enormous physical strength, recommended him to his employer, who hired him as a groom. Basil gained the favour of Theophilitzes, who was struck by the unusual size of his head; and when his master was sent on a special mission to the Peloponnesus, Basil accompanied him. Here he met with a singular stroke of good fortune. At Patrae he attracted the attention of a rich lady, who owned immense estates in the neighbourhood. Her name was Danelis. When Theophilitzes had completed his business and prepared to return, Basil fell ill and remained behind his patron. On his recovery Danelis sent for him, and gave him gold, thirty slaves, and a rich supply of dresses and other things, on the condition of his becoming the "spiritual brother" of her son. The motive assigned for her action is the conviction, on the strength of a monk's prophecy, that he would one day ascend the throne; and Basil is said to have promised that, if it ever lay in his power, he would make her mistress of the whole land. But whatever her motive may have been, there is no doubt that she enriched Basil, and she lived to see him Emperor and to visit his Court.

It is said that the munificence of the Greek lady enabled Basil to buy estates in Thrace and to assist his family. But he remained in his master's service, till a chance brought him under the notice of the Emperor. Michael had received as a gift an untamed and spirited horse. His grooms were unable to manage it, and Michael was in despair, when his relative Theophilitzes suggested that his own groom, Basil, might be able to master it. Basil knew how to charm horses, and when he held its bridle with one hand and placed the other on its ear, the animal instantly became amenable. The Emperor, delighted with this achievement and admiring his physical strength, took him into his own service and assigned him a post under the Hetaeriarch or captain of the foreign guards of the Palace. His rise was rapid. He was invested with the dignity of a strator, and soon afterwards he received the important office of Protostrator, whose duties involved frequent attendance upon the Emperor (A.D. 858-859).

So far the wily Armenian adventurer, whose mental powers were little suspected, had owed his success to fortune and his physical prowess, but now he was in a position to observe the intrigues of the Court and to turn them to his own advantage. Damianos, the High Chamberlain, who had assisted Bardas in the palace revolution which had overthrown Theodora, became hostile to the Caesar, and attempted to discredit him with the Emperor. The crisis came when, as Bardas, arrayed in the Caesar's purple skaramangion and accompanied by the magnates of the Court, was passing in solemn procession through the Horologion, Damianos refrained from rising from his seat and paying the customary token of respect. Bardas, overwhelmed with wrath and chagrin at this insult, hurried into the Chrysotriklinos and complained to the Emperor, who immediately ordered Damianos to be arrested and tonsured. But the triumph of Bardas was to turn to his hurt. Basil was appointed to fill the confidential post of High Chamberlain (with the rank of patrician), though it was usually confined to eunuchs, and Basil the Armenian was to prove a more formidable adversary than Damianos the Slav.

The confidential intimacy which existed between Michael and his Chamberlain was shown by the curious matrimonial arrangement which the Emperor brought to pass. Basil was already married, but Michael caused him to divorce his wife, and married him to his own early love, Eudocia Ingerina. But this was only an official arrangement; Eudocia remained the Emperor's mistress. A mistress, however, was also provided for Basil, of distinguished rank though not of tender years. It appears that Theodora and her daughters had been permitted to leave their monastery and return to secular life, and Thecla, who seems to have been ill-qualified for the vows of a nun, consented to become the paramour of her brother's favourite. Thus three ladies, Eudocia Ingerina, Eudocia the Augusta, and Thecla the Augusta, fulfilled between them the four posts of wives and mistresses to the Emperor and his Chamberlain. Before Michael's death, Eudocia Ingerina bore two sons, and though Basil was obliged to acknowledge them, it was suspected or taken for granted that Michael was their father. The second son afterwards succeeded Basil on the Imperial throne, as Leo VI; and if Eudocia was faithful to Michael, the dynasty known as the Macedonian was really descended from the Amorians. The Macedonian Emperors took pains to conceal this blot or ambiguity in their origin; their animosity to the Amorian sovrans whose blood was perhaps in their veins, and their excessive cult of the memory of Basil, were alike due to the suspicion of the sinister accident in their lineage.

Such proofs of affection could not fail to arouse the suspicion and jealousy of Bardas, if he had, till then, never considered Basil as a possible rival. But he probably underestimated the craft of the man who had mounted so high chiefly by his physical qualities. Basil attempted to persuade the Emperor that Bardas was planning to depose him from the throne. But such insinuations had no effect. Michael, notwithstanding his frivolity, was not without common sense. He knew that the Empire must be governed, and believed that no one could govern it so well as his uncle, in whom he reposed entire confidence. Basil was the companion of his pleasures, and he declined to listen to his suggestions touching matters of state. Basil then resorted to a cunning device. He cultivated a close friendship with Symbatios-an Armenian like himself-the Logothete of the Course and son-in-law of Bardas. He excited this ambitious minister's hope of becoming Caesar in place of his father-in-law, and they concocted the story of a plot which Symbatios revealed to Michael. Such a disclosure coming from a minister, himself closely related to Bardas, was very different from the irresponsible gossip of the Chamberlain, and Michael, seriously alarmed, entered into a plan for destroying his uncle.

At this time-it was the spring of A.D. 866 —preparations were being made for an expedition against the Saracens of Crete, in which both the Emperor and the Caesar were to take part. Bardas was wide-awake. He was warned by friends or perhaps by a change in the Emperor's manner, and he declined to accompany the expedition. He must have openly expressed his fears to his nephew, and declared his suspicion of Basil's intentions; for they took a solemn oath in order to reassure him. On Lady Day (March 25) the festival of the Annunciation was celebrated by a Court procession to the church of the Virgin in Chalkoprateia; after the ceremonies, the Emperor, the Patriarch, the Caesar, and the High Chamberlain entered the Katechumena of the church; Photius held the blood of Jesus in his hands, and Michael and Basil subscribed with crosses, in this sacred ink, a declaration that the Caesar might accompany them without fear.

The expedition started after Easter, and troops from the various provinces assembled at a place called the Gardens (Kêpoi) in the Thrakesian Theme, on the banks of the Maeander. Here Basil and Symbatios, who had won others to their plot, determined to strike the blow. A plan was devised for drawing away Antigonus, the Domestic of the Schools, to witness a horse-race at a sufficient distance from the Imperial tent, so that he should not be at hand to come to his father's rescue. On the evening before the day which was fixed by the conspirators, John Neatokometes visited the Caesar's tent at sunset, and warned Procopius, the Keeper of his Wardrobe, "Your lord, the Caesar, will be cut in pieces tomorrow". Bardas pretended to laugh at the warning. "Tell Neatokometes", he said, "that he is raving. He wants to be made a patrician —a rank for which he is much too young; that is why he goes about sowing these tares". But he did not sleep. In the morning twilight he told his friends what he had heard. His friend Philotheos, the General Logothete, said, "Put your gold coloured cloak and appear to your foes, —they will flee before you". Bardas mounted his horse (April 21) and rode with a brilliant company to the Emperor's pavilion. Basil, in his capacity of High Chamberlain, came out, did obeisance to the Caesar, and led him by the hand to the Emperor's presence. Bardas, sitting down beside the Emperor, suggested that, as the troops were assembled and all was ready, they should immediately embark. Suddenly looking round, he saw Basil making threatening signs with his hand. Basil then lunged at him with his sword, and the other conspirators rushed in and hewed him in pieces. Their violent onrush frightened and endangered the Emperor, who mutely watched, but Constantine the Armenian protected him from injury.

The role of Constantine, who still held the post of Drungary of the Watch, is that of a preventer of mischief, when he appears on the stage at critical moments only to pass again into obscurity. He attempted to save Theoktistos from his murderers; and now after the second tragedy, it is through his efforts that the camp is not disordered by a sanguinary struggle between the partisans of Bardas and the homicides.

The Emperor immediately wrote a letter to the Patriarch Photius informing him that the Caesar had been convicted of high treason and done to death. We possess the Patriarch's reply. It is couched in the conventional style of adulation repulsive to our taste but then rigorously required by Court etiquette. Having congratulated the Emperor on his escape from the plots of the ambitious man who dared to raise his hand against his benefactor, Photius deplores that he was sent without time for repentence to the tribunal in another world. The Patriarch owed his position to Bardas, and if he knew his weaknesses, must have appreciated his merits. "We can detect in the phraseology of his epistle, and especially in one ambiguous sentence, the mixture of his feelings. The virtue and clemency of your Majesty forbid me to suspect that the letter was fabricated or that the circumstances of the fall of Bardas were otherwise than it alleges-circumstances by which he (Bardas) is crowned and others will suffer". These words intimate suspicion as clearly as it could decently be intimated in such a case. It was impossible not to accept the sovran's assurance of the Caesar's guilt, if it were indeed his own assurance, yet Photius allows it to be seen that he suspects that the Imperial letter was dictated by Basil and that there was foul play. But perhaps the most interesting passage in this composition of Photius-in which we can feel his deep agitation under the rhetorical figures of his style-is his brief characterization of the Caesar as one who was "to many a terror, to many a warning, to many a cause of pity, but to more a riddle".

Photius concluded his letter with an urgent prayer that the Emperor should instantly return to the capital, professing that this was the unanimous desire of the Senate and the citizens; and shortly afterwards he dispatched another brief but importunate request to the same effect. It is absurd to suppose that this solicitude was unreal, or dictated by motives of vulgar flattery. We cannot doubt the genuine concern of the Patriarch; but in our ignorance of the details of the situation we can only conjecture that he and his friends entertained the fear that Michael might share the fate of his uncle. The intrigues of Basil were, of course, known well to all who were initiated in Court affairs; and modern partisan writers of the Roman Church, who detest Photius and all his works, do not pause to consider, when they scornfully animadvert upon these "time-serving" letters, that to have addressed to Michael holy words of condemnation or reproof would have been to fling away every chance of rescuing him from the influence of his High Chamberlain. We know not whether the Emperor was influenced by the pressing messages of the Patriarch, but at all events the Cretan expedition was abandoned, and he returned with Basil to Constantinople.

§3. The Elevation of Basil and the Murder of Michael

The High Chamberlain promptly reaped the due reward of his craft and audacity. He was adopted as a son by the childless Emperor, and invested with the order of Magister. A few weeks later, Michael suddenly decided to elevate him to the throne. We can easily understand that this step seemed the easiest way out of his perplexities to the Emperor, who felt himself utterly lost when Bardas was removed from the helm. Basil, firm and self-confident, was a tower of strength, and at this moment he could exert unlimited influence over the weak mind of his master. The Court and the city were kept in the dark till the last moment. On the eve of Pentecost, the Chief of the Private Wardrobe waited on the Patriarch and informed him that on the morrow he would be required to take part in the inauguration of Basil as Basileus and Augustus.

On Whitsunday (May 26), it was observed with surprise that two Imperial seats were placed side by side in St. Sophia. In the procession from the Palace, Basil walked behind the Emperor, in the usual guise of the High Chamberlain; but Michael on entering the church did not remove the crown from his head as was usual. He ascended the ambo wearing the diadem, Basil stood on a lower step, and below him Leo Kastor, a secretary, with a document in his hand, while the Praepositus, the demarchs, and the demes stood around. Leo then read out an Imperial declaration: "The Caesar Bardas plotted against me to slay me, and for this reason induced me to leave the city. If I had not been informed of the plot by Symbatios and Basil, I should not have been alive now. The Caesar died through his own guilt. It is my will that Basil, the High Chamberlain, since he is faithful to me and protects my sovranty and delivered me from my enemy and has much affection for me, should be the guardian and manager of my Empire and should be proclaimed by all as Emperor". Then Michael gave his crown to the Patriarch, who placed it on the holy table and recited a prayer over it. Basil was arrayed by the eunuchs in the Imperial dress (the divetesion and the red boots),and knelt before the Emperor. The Patriarch then crowned Michael, and Michael crowned Basil.

On the following day (Whitmonday) Symbatios, the Logothete of the Course, deeply incensed at the trick that Basil had played on him and disappointed in his hopes of promotion to the rank of Caesar, requested Michael to confer upon him the post of a strategos. He was made Strategos of the Thrakesian Theme, and his friend George Peganes was appointed Count of the Opsikian Theme. These two conspired and marched through the provinces, ravaging the crops, declaring their allegiance to Michael and disowning Basil. The Emperors ordered the other strategoi to suppress them, and Nicephorus Maleinos, by distributing a flysheet, induced their soldiers to abandon them. When Peganes was caught, his eyes were put out and he was placed at the Milestone in the Augusteon, with a plate in his hand, into which the passers-by might fling alms—a form of public degradation which gave rise to the fable that the great general Belisarius ended his days as a beggar. A month later Symbatios, who had fled across Asia Minor, was caught in an inn in Keltyzne. His right hand was cut off and he was blinded of one eye, and placed outside the palace of Lausos in Middle Street, to beg like his comrade. At the end of three days, the two offenders were restored to their abodes, where they were kept under arrest.

The joint reign of Michael and Basil lasted for less than a year and a half. Michael continued to pursue his amusements, but we may suspect that in this latest period of his life his frivolous character underwent a change. He became more reckless in his extravagance, more immoderate in his cups, and cruel in his acts. The horror of his uncle's murder may have cast its shadow, and Basil, for whom he had not the same respect, was unable to exert the same kind of ascendency as Bardas. We cannot suppose that all the essential facts of the situation are disclosed to us in the meagre reports of our chronicles. The following incident can only have marked the beginning of the final stage of intensely strained relations.

Michael held a horse-race in the Palace of St Mamas. He drove himself as a Blue charioteer, Constantine the Armenian drove as a White, other courtiers as Green and Bed. The

Emperor won the race, and in the evening he dined with Basil and Eudocia Ingerina, and was complimented by the patrician Basiliskianos on his admirable driving. Michael, delighted by his flattery, ordered him to stand up, to take the red boots from his own feet and put them on. Basiliskianos hesitated and looked at Basil, who signed to him not to obey. The Emperor furiously commanded him to do as he was bidden, and turning on Basil cried with an oath, " The boots become him better than you. I made you Emperor, and have I not the power to create another Emperor if I will?" Eudocia in tears, remonstrated: "The Imperial dignity is great, and we, unworthy as we are, have been honoured with it. It is not right that it should be brought into contempt". Michael replied, "Do not fear; I am perfectly serious; I am ready to make Basiliskianos Emperor"." This incident seriously alarmed Basil. Some time later when Michael was hunting, a monk met him and gave him a paper which purposed to reveal a plot of Basil against his life. He then began to harbour designs against his colleague. He had small chance against such an antagonist.

Basil struck the blow on Sept. 24, A.D. 867. Michael had bidden him and Eudocia to dinner in the Palace of St. Mamas. When Michael had drunk deeply, Basil made an excuse to leave the room, and entering the Imperial bedchamber tampered with the bolts of the door so that it could not be locked. He then returned to the table, and when the Emperor became drunk as usual, he conducted him to his bed and kissing his hand went out. The Keeper of the Private Wardrobe, who was accustomed to sleep in the Emperor's room, was absent on a commission, and Basiliskianos had been commanded to take his place. Michael sank on his bed in the deep sleep of intoxication, and the chamberlain on duty, discovering that the door could not be bolted, divined the danger, but could not waken the Emperor.

Basil had engaged the help of eight friends, some of whom had taken part in his first crime, the murder of Bardas. Accompanied by these, Basil opened the door of the bed-chamber, and was confronted by the chamberlain, who opposed his entrance. One of the conspirators diving under Basil's arm rushed to the bed, but the chamberlain sprang after him and gripped him. Another then wounded Basiliskianos and hurled him on the floor, while a third, John Chaldos (who had been prominent among the slayers of Bardas), hewed at the sleeping Emperor with his sword, and cut off both his hands. Basil seems to have stood at the door, while the other accomplices kept guard outside. John Chaldos thought that he had done enough; he left the room, and the conspirators consulted whether their victim should be despatched outright. One of them took it upon himself to return to the bed where Michael was moaning out piteous imprecations against Basil, and ripped up his body.

Through the darkness of a stormy night the assassins rowed across the Golden Horn, landing near the house of a Persian named Eulogios, who joined them. By breaking through an enclosure they reached a gate of the Great Palace. Eulogios called out to his fellow-countryman Artavasdos, the Hetaeriarch, in the Persian tongue, "Open to the Emperor, for Michael has perished by the sword". Artavasdos rushed to the Papias, took the keys from him by force, and opened the gate.

In the morning, Eudocia Ingerina was conducted in state from St. Mamas to the Great Palace, to take, as reigning Augusta, the place of the other Eudocia, who was restored to her parents. A chamberlain was sent to provide for the burial of the late Emperor. He found the corpse rolled up in a horsecloth, and the Empress Theodora, with her daughters, weeping over her son. He was buried in a monastery at Chrysopolis, on the Asiatic shore.

Such is the recorded story of the final act which raised Basil the Macedonian to supreme power. It is probably correct in its main details, but it not only leaves out some of the subordinate elements in the situation, such as the attitude of Eudocia-was she in the secret? —but fails to make it clear whether Basil was driven to the assassination of his benefactor by what he conceived to be a political necessity, or was prompted merely by the vulgar motive of ambition. No plea could be set up for the murder of Bardas on the ground of the public good, but the murder of Michael is a different case. The actual government had devolved on Basil, who was equal to the task; but if the follies and caprices of Michael, who was the autocrat, thwarted his subordinate colleague, the situation might have become well-nigh impossible. If we could trust the partial narrative of Basil's Imperial grandson, who is concerned not only to exonerate his ancestor, but to make out a case to justify the revolution, Michael had become an intolerable tyrant. In his fits of drunkenness he issued atrocious orders for the execution and torture of innocent men, —orders which he had forgotten the next day. In order to raise money, he began to make depredations on churches and religious houses, and to confiscate the property of rich people. There was nothing for it but to kill him like a noxious snake. "Therefore the most reputable of the ministers and the wise section of the Senate took counsel together, and caused him to be slain by the Palace guard. Allowing for some exaggeration and bias in this picture of the situation, we may be right in believing that Michael had become unmanageable and mischievous, and that it was to the general advantage to suppress him". The vigorous reign of Basil proves that he was deeply interested in the efficiency of the government. It is not our business either to justify or to condemn the murder of Michael III.; we are only concerned to understand it.

Chapter VI
Photius and Ignatius

Under the rule of the iconoclasts, the differences which divided the "orthodox" had been suffered to slumber; but the defeat of the common enemy was the signal for the renewal of a conflict which had disturbed the peace of the Church under Irene and Nicephorus. The two parties, which had suspended their feud, now again stood face to face.

The fundamental principle of the State Church founded by Constantine was the supremacy of the Emperor; the Patriarch and the whole hierarchy were subject to him; he not only protected, he governed the Church. The smooth working of this system demanded from churchmen a spirit of compromise and "economy". It might often be difficult for a Patriarch to decide at what point his religious duty forbade him to comply with the Emperor's will; and it is evident that Patriarchs, like Tarasius and Nicephorus, who had served the State in secular posts, were more likely to work discreetly and harmoniously under the given conditions than men who had been brought up in cloisters. We saw how the monks of Studion organized an opposition to these Patriarchs, whom they denounced for sacrificing canonical rules to expediency. The abbot Theodore desired to subvert the established system. He held that the Emperor was merely the protector of the Church, and that the Church was independent. He affirmed, moreover, the supremacy of the roman See in terms which no Emperor and few, if any, Patriarchs would have endorsed. But by their theory, which they boldly put into practice, the Studites were undermining Patriarchal and episcopal authority. They asserted the right of monks to pass an independent judgment on the administration of their bishop, and, in case his actions did not meet with their approval, to refuse to communicate with him. A movement of independence or insubordination, which was likely to generate schisms, was initiated, and the activity and influence of Theodore must have disseminated his views far beyond the limits of his own community.

Thus there arose two antagonistic sections, of which one approved more or less the doctrines of Theodore of Studion, while the other upheld Patriarchal authority and regarded Nicephorus as an ideal Patriarch. One insisted on the strictest observation of ecclesiastical canons and denounced the sudden elevations of Nicephorus and Tarasius from the condition of laymen to the episcopal office; the other condoned such irregularities which special circumstances commended to the Imperial wisdom. One declined to allow any relaxation of canonical rules in favour of the Emperor; the other was prepared to permit him considerable limits of dispensation. There were, in fact, two opposite opinions as to the spirit and method of ecclesiastical administration, corresponding to two different types of ecclesiastic. Both sides included monks; and it would not be true to say that the monks generally rallied to the section of the Studites. There were many abbots and many hermits who disliked the Studite ideal of a rigorous, disciplinary regulation of monastic life, and many who, like Theophanes of Sigriane, were satisfied with the State Church and had no sympathy with the aggressive policy of Theodore and his fellows.

Methodius had always been an ecclesiastic, and the Studites could not reproach him for any irregularity in his consecration as bishop. He had been a martyr in the cause of image-worship, and he had effectively assisted in its triumph. But his promotion to the Patriarchate was not pleasing to the Studite monks. His sympathies were with the other party, and he was prepared to carry on the tradition of Tarasius and Nicephorus. We can well understand that his intimacy with the Emperor Theophilus, with whom he agreed to differ on the iconoclastic question, was far from commending him to the stricter brethren. The Studites were prepared to be critical, and from the very beginning his administration was the subject of adverse comment or censure. He desired to conciliate them, and the bones of their revered abbot Theodore were brought back for interment at Studion, with great solemnity. But the satisfaction of the monks at this public honour to their abbot was mitigated, if it was not cancelled, by the translation, at the same time, of the remains of Nicephorus to the Church of the Apostles They recalled his uncanonical consecration, they recalled his condonation of "adultery". But if he could not conciliate them, the Patriarch was determined to crush their rebellious spirit. He called upon them to anathematize all that Theodore had written against Tarasius and Nicephorus, and he urged that Theodore had himself practically revoked his own strong language, had been reconciled with Nicephorus, and in fact changed his opinion. But the Studites obstinately refused, and Methodius asserted his Patriarchal authority. "You are monks", he said, "and you have no right to question the conduct of your bishops; you must submit to them". He pronounced against the rebellious brethren not the simple anathema, but the curse, the katathema, of the Church. The struggle seems to have ended with concessions on the part of the Patriarch.

The difficulties which troubled the short administration of Methodius possess a significant bearing on the more serious ecclesiastical strife which marked the reign of his successor, and which led, indirectly, to the great schism between the Eastern and the Western Churches. The two opposing parties of Ignatius and Photius represent the same parties which distracted the Patriarchate of Methodius, and the struggle is thus a continuation of the same division which had vexed Tarasius and Nicephorus, although the immediate and superficial issues are different. When we apprehend this continuity, we are able to see that the particular question which determined the course of the conflict between Photius and Ignatius only rendered acute an antagonism which had existed for more than half a century.

Methodius seems to have availed himself of the most popular kind of literature, edifying biographies of holy men, for the purpose of his struggle with the Studites. Under his auspices, Ignatius the Deacon composed the Lives of Tarasius and Nicephorus, in which the troubles connected with the opposition of Studion are diligently ignored. The ecclesiastical conflicts of the period are, indeed, reflected, more by hints and reticences than direct statements, in the copious hagiographical productions of the ninth century, to which reference is frequently made in this volume.

On the death of Methodius, the Empress Theodora and her advisers chose his successor from among three monks of illustrious birth, each of whom, if fortune had been kind, might have worn the Imperial crown. Nicetas, a son of the Emperor Michael I., had been tonsured after his father's death, had taken the name of Ignatius, and had founded new monasteries in the Islands of the Princes, over which he presided as abbot. Here he and his family, who had not been despoiled of their wealth, afforded refuge to image-worshippers who were driven from the capital. The sons of the Emperor Leo V. to join the family of Ignatius owed its downfall, had been cast into a monastery in the island of Prote; they renounced the errors of their father, and won a high reputation for virtue and piety. When the Patriarchal throne became vacant, these monks of Imperial parentage, Basil and Gregory, the sons of Leo, and Ignatius, the son of Michael, were proposed for election. Ignatius was preferred, perhaps because it was felt that notwithstanding their own merits the shadow of their father's heresy rested upon the sons of Leo; and he was consecrated on July 4, A.D. 847.

Ignatius had spent his life in pious devotion and monastic organization. Tonsured at the age of thirteen or fourteen, he had made no progress in secular learning, which he distrusted and disliked. He was not a man of the world like Methodius; he had the rigid notions which were bred in cloistral life and were calculated to lead himself and the Church into difficulties when they were pursued in the Patriarchal palace. It is probable that he was too much engaged in his own work to have taken any part in the disputes which troubled Methodius, and Theodora may have hoped that he would succeed in conciliating the opposing parties. But he was by nature an anti-Methodian, and he showed this on the very day of his consecration.

Gregory Asbestas, the archbishop of Syracuse, happened to be in Constantinople at the time. A Sicilian, he was a friend of the Sicilian Methodius, on whom he composed a panegyric, and he was a man of some learning. There was a charge against him of some ecclesiastical irregularity, and it was probably in connexion with this that he had come to the capital. He had taken his place among the bishops who attended in St. Sophia, bearing tapers, to acclaim the Patriarch, and Ignatius ordered him to withdraw, on the ground that his episcopal status was in abeyance until the charge which lay against him had been decided. This public slight enraged Gregory, who dashed his candle to the ground and loudly declared that not a shepherd but a wolf had intruded into the Church. The new Patriarch certainly displayed neither the wisdom of a serpent nor the harmlessness of a dove, and his own adherents admit that he was generally blamed. He had thus at the very outset taken pains to offend an able and eminent prelate of the party which had supported Methodius, and the action was interpreted as a declaration of war. The result was a schism. Gregory had many sympathizers; some bishops had marked their disapprobation of the action of Ignatius by leaving the church in his company. A schismatic group was formed which refused to acknowledge the new Patriarch —a group which expressed the general tendencies of the Methodian party and avowed an unreserved admiration for Methodius. But it was only a small group. The hierarchy in general supported Ignatius, as it had supported Methodius; for Ignatius was supported by Theodora. Nevertheless the followers of Gregory, though comparatively few, were influential. They alleged against the Patriarch that he was a detractor from the merits and memory of his predecessor, and that he was unduly rigorous and narrow in his application of the canons. Ignatius summoned Gregory to answer the charge which still hung over his head; Gregory declined, and, along with others of his party, was condemned by a synod. He appealed against this judgment to Pope Leo IV., who asked the Patriarch to send him a copy of the Acts. Ignatius did not comply, and Leo's successor, Benedict III., declined to confirm the deposition of Gregory, and contented himself with suspending him until he had inspected the documents.

The schism of Gregory might be allowed to rest in the obscurity of ecclesiastical records if it had not won distinction and importance by the adhesion of the most remarkable man of the age. Photius was probably born about the beginning of the ninth century. His father, Sergius, was a brother of the Patriarch Tarasius, and through his mother he was connected with the family of the Empress Theodora. His parents suffered exile for their devotion to image-worship under the iconoclastic sovrans, and it was probably in the first years of Theodora's reign that Photius entered upon his career as a public teacher of philosophy. He had an attractive personality, he was a stimulating teacher, and he soon found a band of disciples who hung upon his words. His encyclopaedic learning, in which he not only excelled all the men of his own time but was unequalled by any Greek of the Middle Ages, will call for notice in another chapter. His family connexions as well as his talents opened a career in the Imperial service; and he was ultimately appointed to the high post of Protoasecretis, or First Secretary, with the rank of a protospathar. It was probably during his tenure of this important post that he was sent as ambassador to the East, perhaps to Baghdad itself, perhaps only to some of the provincial emirs. Whatever his services as an envoy may have been, he established personal relations of friendship with Mohammadan magnates.

Photius had a high respect for Gregory Asbestas, and identified himself closely with the group which opposed Ignatius. There was a natural antipathy between Photius, a man of learning and a man of the world, and Ignatius, who had neither tact nor secular erudition. It is probable that the Patriarch even displayed in some public way his dislike or disdain for profane learning. We can well understand that he was deeply vexed, by the opposition of a man whose talents and learning were unreservedly recognized by his contemporaries, and who exerted immense influence in the educated society of the city. The synod, which condemned Gregory, seems to have also condemned Photius, implicitly if not by name; and he was numbered among the schismatics.

In order to embarrass the Patriarch, and to prove that a training in logic and philosophy was indispensable for defending Christian doctrine and refuting false opinions, Photius conceived the idea of propounding a heresy. He promulgated the thesis that there are two souls in man, one liable to err, the other immune from error. Some took this seriously and were convinced by his ingenious arguments, to the everlasting peril of their souls. His friend, Constantine the Philosopher, who was afterwards to become famous as the Apostle of the Slavs, reproached Photius with propounding this dangerous proposition. "I had no idea", said Photius, "that it would do any harm. I only wanted to see how Ignatius would deal with it, without the aid of the philosophy which he rejects".

The Palace revolution which resulted in the fall of Theodora and placed the government in the hands of Bardas changed the ecclesiastical situation. Whatever difficulties beset Ignatius in a post which he was not well qualified to fill, whatever vexation might be caused to him through the active or passive resistance of his opponents, he was secure so long as the Empress was in power. But Bardas was a friend and admirer of Photius, and the Ignatian party must have felt his access to power as a severe blow. Bardas, however, was a sufficiently prudent statesman to have no desire wantonly to disturb the existing state of things, or to stir up a serious ecclesiastical controversy. If Ignatius had behaved with discretion and reconciled himself to a regime which personally he disliked, it is not probable that the sympathies of Bardas with the Photian party would have induced him to take any measure against the Patriarch.

Ignatius found in the private morals of the powerful minister a weak spot for attack. According to the rumour of the town, Bardas was in love with his daughter-in-law, and had for her sake abandoned his wife. Acting on this gossip, the Patriarch admonished Bardas, who declined to take any notice of his rebukes and exhortations. We may suspect that he refused to admit that the accusation was true-it would perhaps have been difficult to prove-and recommended Ignatius to mind his own business. But Ignatius was determined to show that he was the shepherd of his flock, and that he was no respecter of persons. On the feast of Epiphany (Jan. A.D. 858) he refused the communion to the sinner. It is said that Bardas, furious at this public insult, drew his sword; but he managed to control his anger and vowed vengeance on the bold priest.

The ecclesiastical historians speak with warm approbation of this action of the Patriarch. The same prelate, who adopted such a strong measure to punish the vices of Bardas, had no scruples, afterwards, in communicating with the Emperor Basil, who had ascended to power by two successive murders. And the ecclesiastical historians seem to regard the Patriarch's action, in ignoring Basil's crimes and virtually taking advantage of them to reascend the Patriarchal throne, as perfectly irreproachable. The historian who is not an ecclesiastic may be allowed to express his respectful interest in the ethical standards which are implied.

About eight months later the Emperor Michael decided to tonsure his mother and sisters and immure them in the monastery of Karianos. He requested the Patriarch to perform the ceremony of the tonsure, and we have already seen that Ignatius refused on the ground that the ladies themselves were unwilling. Bardas persuaded the Emperor that his disobedience, in conjunction with his unconcealed sympathy with the Empress, was a sign of treasonable purposes, and a pretended discovery was made that he was in collusion with an epileptic impostor, named Gebeon, who professed to be the son of the Empress Theodora by a former marriage. Gebeon had come from Dyrrhachium to Constantinople, where he seduced some foolish people; he was arrested and cruelly executed in one of the Princ's Islands. On the same day the Patriarch was seized as an accomplice, and removed, without a trial, to the island of Terebinthos (Nov. 23).

It is evident that there were no proofs against Ignatius, and that the charge of treason was merely a device of the government for the immediate purpose of removing him. For in the subsequent transactions this charge seems to have been silently dropped; and if there had been any plausible grounds, there would have been some sort of formal trial. Moreover, it would appear that before his arrest it was intimated to the Patriarch that he could avoid all trouble by abdication, and he would have been tempted to yield if his bishops had not assured him that they would loyally stand by him. Before his arrest he issued a solemn injunction that no service should be performed in St. Sophia without his consent. A modern ecclesiastical historian, who has no high opinion of Ignatius, cites this action as a proof that he was ready to prefer his own personal interests to the good of the Church.

In the place of his banishment Ignatius was visited repeatedly by bishops and Imperial ministers pressing on him the expediency of voluntary abdication. As he refused to listen to arguments, threats were tried, but with no result. The Emperor and Bardas therefore decided to procure the election of a new Patriarch, though the chair was not de iure vacant, inasmuch as Ignatius had neither resigned nor been canonically deposed. Such a procedure was not an innovation; there were several precedents. The choice of the government and the ecclesiastical party which was opposed to Ignatius fell upon Photius. He was not only a grata persona at Court; but his extraordinary gifts, his eminent reputation, along with his unimpeachable orthodoxy, were calculated to shed prestige on the Patriarchal chair, and to reconcile the public to a policy which seemed open to the reproaches of violence and injustice. Many of the bishops who had vowed to support the cause of Ignatius were won over by Bardas, and Photius accepted the high office, which, according to his enemies, had long been the goal of his ambition, and which, according to his own avowal, he would have been only too glad to decline. He was tonsured on December 20; on the four following days he was successively ordained lector, sub-deacon, deacon, and priest, and on Christmas Day consecrated bishop, by his friend Gregory Asbestas. For this rapid and irregular elevation to the highest dignity of the Church, which was one of the principal objections urged against Photius, the recent precedents of his uncle Tarasius and Nicephorus, as well as others, could be alleged. The ambiguous position of Gregory, who had been deposed by a synod and suspended by a Pope, furnished another handle against the new Patriarch. But all the bishops who were present in Constantinople, except five, acknowledged him, and the five dissentients were persuaded to acquiesce when he gave them a written undertaking that he would honour Ignatius as a father and act according to his wishes. But two months later he is said to have recovered the document on some pretext and torn it up into small pieces. Then those bishops who were really on the side of Ignatius, and had unwillingly consented to an impossible compromise, held a series of meetings in the church of St. Irene, and deposed and excommunicated Photius with his adherents. Such an irregular assembly could not claim the authority of a synod, but it was a declaration of war. Photius immediately retorted by holding a synod in the Holy Apostles. Ignatius, in his absence, was deposed and anathematized; and the opportunity was probably used to declare Gregory Asbestas absolved from those charges which had led to his condemnation by the ex-Patriarch (spring A.D. 859).

In the meantime Bardas persistently endeavoured to force Ignatius to an act of abdication. He was moved from place to place and treated with cruel rigour. His followers were barbarously punished. The writers of the Ignatian party accuse Photius of having prompted these acts of tyranny, but letters of Photius himself to Bardas, bitterly protesting against the cruelties, show that he did not approve this policy of violence, which indeed only served to increase his own unpopularity. The populace of the city seems to have been in favour of Ignatius, who had also sympathizers among the Imperial ministers, such as Constantine the Drungarios of the Watch. The monks, from whose rank he had risen, generally supported him; the Studites refused to communicate with the new Patriarch, and their abbot Nicolas left Constantinople. Photius, as is shown by his correspondence, took great pains to win the goodwill of individual monks and others by flattery and delicate attentions.

The announcement of the enthronement of a new Patriarch, which it was the custom to send to the other four Patriarchal Sees-Rome, Alexandria, Antioch, and Jerusalem-had been postponed, evidently in the hope that Ignatius would be induced to abdicate. When more than a year had passed and this hope was not fulfilled, the formal announcement could no longer be deferred. An inthronistic letter was addressed to the Eastern Patriarchs, and an embassy was sent to Rome bearing letters to the Pope from Michael and Photius. The chair of St. Peter was now filled by Nicolas I., who stands out among the Pontiffs between Gregory I. and Gregory VII. as having done more than any other to raise the Papal power to the place which it was to hold in the days of Innocent III. A man of deeds rather than of words, as one of his admirers says, he was inspired with the idea of the universal authority of the Roman See. The internal troubles in the Carolingian realm enabled him to assert successfully the Papal pretensions in the West; the schism at Constantinople gave him a welcome opportunity of pressing his claims upon the East. But in Photius he found an antagonist, not only incomparably more learned than himself, but equally determined, energetic, and resourceful.

The letter of Photius to the Pope was a masterpiece of diplomacy. He enlarged on his reluctance to undertake the burdens of the episcopal office, which was pressed upon him by the Emperor and the clergy with such insistency that he had no alternative but to accept it. He then-in accordance with the usual custom in such inthronistic letters-made a precise statement of the articles of his religion and declared his firm belief in the seven Ecumenical Councils. He concluded by asking the Pope, not for any support or assistance, but simply for his prayers. He abstained from saying anything against his predecessor. But the letter which was sent in the Emperor's name gave a garbled account of the vacation of the Patriarchal throne, and requested the Pope to send legates to attend a synod which should decide some questions relating to the iconoclastic heresy. Neither the Patriarch nor the Emperor invited the Pope even to express an opinion on recent events, but Nicolas resolved to seize the occasion and assert a jurisdiction which, if it had been accepted, would have annulled the independence of the Church of Constantinople. He despatched two bishops, with instructions to investigate the facts in connexion with the deposition of Ignatius, and to make a report He committed to them letters (dated September 25, 860) to the Emperor and to Photius. These letters have considerable interest as a specimen of Papal diplomacy. The communication to the Emperor opens with the assertion of the primacy of the Roman See and of the principle that no ecclesiastical difficulty should be decided in Christendom without the consent of the Roman Pontiff; it goes on to point out that this principle has been violated by the deposition of Ignatius, and that the office has been aggravated by the election of a layman-an election which "our holy Roman Church" has always prohibited. On these grounds the Pope announces that he cannot give his apostolic consent to the consecration of Photius until his messengers have reported the facts of the case and have examined Ignatius. He then proceeds to reply to that part of the Emperor's letter which concerned the question of image-worship. The document concludes with the suggestion that Michael should show his devotion to the interests of the Church by restoring to the Roman See the vicariate of Thessalonica and the patrimonies of Calabria and Sicily, which had been withdrawn from the jurisdiction of the Pope by Leo III. The short letter to Photius censures the temerity of his elevation and declines to acknowledge his consecration, unless the Papal messengers, when they return from Constantinople, report favourably on his actions and devotion to the Church.

The diplomatic intent of these letters could hardly be misapprehended by a novice. The innocent suggestion (put forward as if it had no connexion with the other matters under discussion) that Illyricum and Calabria should be transferred from the See of Constantinople to that of Rome would never have been made if Nicolas had not thought that there was a reasonable chance of securing this accession to the dominion and revenue of his chair. It is plain that he could not hope that the Emperor and the Patriarch would agree to such a large concession unless they received a due consideration; and it is equally obvious that the only consideration which the Pope could offer, was to consent to the consecration of Photius, and crush by the weight of his authority the schism which was so seriously distressing the church of Constantinople. Notwithstanding his severe animadversions on the uncanonical elevation of Photius, he intimated that this was not an insuperable difficulty; if his delegates brought back a satisfactory report, matters might be arranged. It is perfectly clear that Pope Nicolas proposed a bargain, in the interest of what he calls ecclesiastica utilitas.

It is impossible to say whether the Imperial government took into serious consideration the Pope's proposal. But there were at all events some, probably among the moderate section of the Photians, who thought that the best solution of the ecclesiastical difficulty would be to agree to the bargain, and Photius was so gravely alarmed that, in a letter to Bardas, he complains bitterly of the desire of persons who are not named to deprive him of half his jurisdiction. It would seem that there was a chance that the diplomacy of Nicolas might have been successful. But if Michael and Bardas entertained any idea of yielding, they were persuaded by Photius to relinquish it.

The two legates of the Pope were won over to the Photian party by cajolements and threats. A council assembled in May (A.D. 861), remarkable for the large number of bishops who attended. The Emperor was present, and Ignatius unwillingly appeared. Seventy-two witnesses, including both highly-placed ministers and men of humble rank, came forward to prove that

Ignatius had been appointed to the Patriarchate, not by free election, but by the personal act of Theodora. We are in the dark as to the precise circumstances of the elevation of Ignatius. There is no doubt that he was chosen by Theodora, but it is almost incredible that the usual form of election was not observed, and if it was observed, to condemn his elevation was to condemn the elevation of every Patriarch of Constantinople as uncanonical. For virtually every Patriarch was appointed by the Imperial will. In any case at this synod-if we can trust the accounts of the supporters of Ignatius-the government exercised considerable pressure. The assembly, including the representatives of Rome, whether they were convinced or not, confirmed the deposition of Ignatius, and declared him unworthy. The authority of Photius was thus established by the formal act of a large council, subscribed by the legates of the Roman see.

The legates had exceeded their instructions. When they returned to Rome in the autumn, their action was repudiated by the Pope, who asserted that they had only been directed to report on the whole matter to him, and had received no power to judge the question themselves. There is no doubt that they had betrayed the interests of their master and suffered themselves to be guided entirely by the court of Byzantium. An Imperial secretary soon arrived at Rome, bearing a copy of the Acts of the Council with letters from the Emperor and the Patriarch. The letter of Photius could hardly fail to cause deep displeasure to the Roman bishop. It was perfectly smooth, courteous, and conciliatory in tone, but it was the letter of an equal to an equal, and, although the question of Roman jurisdiction was not touched on, it was easy to read between the lines that the writer had the will and the courage to assert the independence of the see of Constantinople. As for the ecclesiastical provinces of Illyricum and Calabria, he hypocritically threw upon the government the entire responsibility for not restoring them to Rome, and implied that he himself would have been willing to sacrifice them.

The Imperial secretary remained in Rome for some months, hoping that Nicolas would be persuaded to sanction all that his legates had done in his name. But the Pope was now resolved to embrace the cause of Ignatius and to denounce Photius. He addressed an encyclical letter to the three Patriarchs of the East, informing them that Ignatius had been illegally deposed, and that a most wicked man (homo scelestissimus) had occupied his church; declaring that the Roman see will never consent to this injustice; and ordering them, by his apostolical authority, to work for the expulsion of Photius and the restoration of Ignatius. At the same time he indited epistles to the Emperor and to Photius, asserting with stronger emphasis than before the authority of Rome as head and mistress of the churches, and declining to condemn Ignatius or to recognize Photius.

The ambassadors of the Pope, during their visit to Constantinople, had heard only one side. The authorities had taken care to prevent them from communicating with Ignatius or any of the Ignatian party, and they also attempted to hinder any one from repairing to Rome in the interests of the Ignatian cause. Theognostos, however, who was an ardent partisan of the deposed Patriarch, succeeded in reaching Rome in disguise, and he carried with him a petition setting forth the history of the deposition of Ignatius and the sufferings which he endured, and imploring the Pope, who was humbly addressed as "the Patriarch of all the thrones", to take pity and arise as a powerful champion against injustice.

It was probably the influence of the representations of Theognostos and other Ignatians who had found their way to Rome, that moved Nicolas a year later (April A.D. 863), to hold a Synod in the Lateran. Neither the Emperor nor the Patriarch had vouchsafed any answer to his letter, and as it was evident that they had no intention of yielding to his dictation, he punished the Church of Constantinople by the only means which lay in his power. The synod deprived Photius of his ecclesiastical status, and excommunicated him unless he immediately resigned the see which he had usurped; it pronounced the same penalty upon all ecclesiastics who had been consecrated by Photius; and it restored Ignatius and all those bishops who had been deposed and exiled in his cause. A copy of the proceedings was sent to Constantinople.

It was impossible for Constantinople to ignore the formal condemnation pronounced by the Lateran Synod, and Photius was prepared to assert the independence of his see, by dealing out to the Pope the same measure which the Pope had dealt out to him. In August 865, Nicholas received a letter from the Emperor assuring him that all his efforts in behalf of Ignatius were useless, and requiring him to withdraw his judgment, with a threat that, if he refused, the Emperor would march to Rome and destroy the city. The document, which was evidently drafted under the direction of Photius, must have been couched in sufficiently provocative terms; but the threat was not seriously meant, and the writer did not expect that the Pope would yield. The real point of the letter was the repudiation of the papal claim to supreme jurisdiction, as the real point of the Pope's long reply was the assertion of the privileges of the chair of St. Peter. The Pope indeed makes what may be represented as a concession. He offers to revise his judgment at Rome, and demands that the two rivals shall appear personally before him, or if they cannot come, send plenipotentiaries. The concession was as nugatory as the Emperor's threat, and it assumed, in an aggravated form, the claims of the Papacy as a supreme court of appeal.

The quarrel between Rome and Constantinople was soon augmented by the contest between the two sees for the control of the infant church of Bulgaria, and Photius judged that the time was ripe for a decisive blow. He held a local synod for the condemnation of various heresies which Latin clergy had criminally introduced into Bulgaria. These "servants of Antichrist, worthy of a thousand deaths", permitted the use of milk and cheese in the Lenten fast; they sowed the seed of the Manichaean doctrine by their aversion to priests who are legally married; they had the audacity to pour anew the chrism of confirmation on persons who had already been anointed by priests, as if a priest were not as competent to confirm as to baptize. But above all they were guilty of teaching the blasphemous and atheistic doctrine that the Holy Ghost proceeds not only from the Father, but also from the Son.

The eloquent Patriarch can hardly find words adequate to characterize the enormity of these false doctrines, in the encyclical letter which he addressed to the three Eastern Patriarchs, inviting them to attend a general council at Constantinople, for the purpose of rooting out such abominable errors. Other questions too, Photius intimated, would come before the council. For he had received from Italy an official communication full of grave complaints of the tyranny exercised by the Roman bishop in the west.

The document to which Photius refers seems to have emanated from the archbishops of Koln and Trier, who were at this time leading an anti-papal movement. The occasion of this division in the western Church was the love of king Lothar II of Lotharingia for his mistress Waldrade. To marry her he had repudiated his queen, and his action was approved by a synod at Metz, guided by the influence of the two archbishops. But the Pope embraced the cause of the queen, and in a synod in the Lateran (October 863), annulled the acts of Metz, and deposed the archbishops of Koln and Trier. These prelates received at first support from the Emperor Lewis II., but that vacillating monarch soon made peace with the Pope, and the archbishops presumed to organize a general movement of metropolitan bishops against the claims of the Roman see. They distributed to the bishops of the west a circular Protest, denouncing the tyranny, arrogance, and cunning of Nicholas, who would "make himself the Emperor of the whole world". They sent a copy to the Patriarch of Constantinople, imploring him to come to their help and deliverance.

This movement in the western church was well calculated to confirm Photius and the Imperial government in the justice of their own cause, and it led the Patriarch to a far-reaching scheme which it required some time to mature. It is certain that during the years A.D. 865-867, there were secret negotiations between Constantinople and the Emperor Lewis. It is improbable that any formal embassies were interchanged. But by unofficial means-perhaps by communications between Photius and the Empress Engelberta-an understanding was reached that if the Pope were excommunicated by the eastern Patriarchs, Lewis might be induced to drive him from Rome as a heretical usurper, and that the court of Constantinople would officially recognize the Imperial dignity and title of the western Emperor.

Constantinople carried out her portion of the programme. The Council met in A.D. 867 (perhaps the late summer), and the Emperor Michael presided. The Pope was condemned and anathema pronounced against him for the heretical doctrines and practices which were admitted by the Roman Church, and for his illegitimate interference in the affairs of the Church of Constantinople. The acts of the Synod were afterwards burned, and we know of it only from the brief notices of the enemies of Photius. They insinuate that the signature of Michael had been appended when he was drunk; that the signature of his colleague Basil, had been forged; that the subscriptions of almost all those who were present, numbering about a thousand, were fabricated. These allegations are highly improbable, and the writers themselves are inconsistent in what they allege. It is obvious that if the Emperors had disapproved of the purpose of the Council, the Council could never have met; and it is equally clear that if the overwhelming majority of the Council, including the Emperors, had disapproved of the decrees, the decrees could not have been passed. But there seems to have been some chicanery. At the Eighth Ecumenical Council, the metropolitan bishops whose signatures appeared, were asked whether they had subscribed, and they said, "God forbid, we did not subscribe". Are we to suppose that they consented to the acts and afterwards refused to append their names?

The scandal about the legates of the Eastern Patriarchs is hardly less obscure. It is stated that Photius picked up in the streets three evil men whom he foisted upon the synod as the representatives of the Patriarchs. They pretended to be Peter, Basil, and Leontios. But the true Peter, Basil, and Leontios appeared at the Eighth Ecumenical Council, where they asserted that they had not been named as legates by the Patriarchs, that they knew nothing about the Synod, had not attended it, and had not signed its acts. It is impossible to discover the truth, nor has it much interest except for ecclesiastical historians, who, if they are members of the Latin Church, will readily credit Photius with a wholesale and barefaced scheme of deception, and if they belong to the Greek communion, may be prepared to maintain that at the Eighth Ecumenical Council mendacity was the order of the day. In either case, those who stand outside the Churches may find some entertainment in an edifying ecclesiastical scandal.

That the Emperors were acting in concert with Photius is, if there could be any doubt, definitely proved by the fact that Lewis was solemnly acclaimed as Basileus and Engelberta as Augusta. No Council, no Patriarch, could have dared to do what, done without the Imperial consent, or rather command, would have been an overt act of treason. The Patriarch sent a copy of the Acts of the Council to Engelberta, with a letter in which, comparing her to Pulcheria, he urged her to persuade her husband to drive from Rome a bishop who had been deposed by an Ecumenical Council.

The schism between Rome and Constantinople was now complete for the moment. The Pope had anathematized the Patriarch, and the Patriarch had hurled back his anathema at the Pope. But this rent in the veil of Christendom was thinly patched up in a few months, and the designs of Photius for the ruin of his antagonist came to nought. On the death of Michael, the situation was immediately reversed. When Basil gained the sovran power, one of his first acts was to depose Photius and restore Ignatius. It is probable that his feelings towards Photius, the friend and relative of Bardas, were not over friendly, but his action was doubtless determined not by personal or religious considerations, but by reasons of state. We cannot say whether he was already forming projects which rendered the alienation from Rome undesirable; but his principal and immediate purpose was assuredly to restore ecclesiastical peace and tranquillity in his own realm, and to inaugurate his reign by an act of piety and orthodoxy which would go far in the eyes of the inhabitants of Constantinople to atone for the questionable methods by which he had won the autocratic power.

Nothing proves more convincingly than Basil's prompt reversal of his predecessor's ecclesiastical policy, that this policy was generally unpopular. Unless he had been sure that the restitution of Ignatius would be welcomed by an important section of his subjects at Constantinople, it is incredible, in view of the circumstances of his accession, that it would have been his first important act. Photius had his band of devoted followers, but they seem to have been a small minority; and there are other indications that public opinion was not in his favour. The severe measures to which the government had resorted against Ignatius and his supporters would hardly have been adopted if the weight of public opinion had leaned decisively on the side of Photius. There was, however, some embarrassment for Basil, who only a few months before had cooperated in the council which excommunicated the Pope, and there was embarrassment for many others who shared the responsibility, in turning about and repudiating their acts. The natural instinct was to throw all the blame upon Photius; Basil's signature was officially declared to be spurious; and most of those, who had taken part willingly or unwillingly in the condemnation of the Pope, were eager to repudiate their consent to that audacious transaction.

The proceedings of the Eighth Council, which procured a temporary triumph for Rome, the second patriarchate of Photius, and his second dethronement, lie outside the limits of this volume. He died in exile, almost a centenarian. Immediately after his death he was recognized as a Father of the Church, and anathema was pronounced on all that Councils or Popes had uttered against him. The rift between Rome and Constantinople, which Photius had widened and deepened, was gradually enlarged, and after the final rent (in the middle of the eleventh century), which no subsequent attempts at union could repair, the reputation of Photius became brighter than ever, and his council of 861, which the Pope had stigmatized as a pirate synod, was boldly described by Balsamon as ecumenical. It was recognized that Photius was the first great champion of the independence of the see of Constantinople, and of the national development of the Greek Church, against the interference of Rome. He formulated the points of difference between the two Churches which were to furnish the pretext for the schism; he first brought into the foreground, as an essential point of doctrine, the mystery of the procession of the Holy Ghost.

The members of the Latin and the Greek Churches are compelled, at the risk of incurring the penalties of a damnable heresy, to affirm or to deny that the Holy Ghost proceeds from the Son as well as from the Father. The historian, who is not concerned, even if he were qualified, to examine the mutual relations which exist among the august persons of the Trinity, will yet note with some interest that on this question the Greeks adhered to the official doctrine of the Church so far as it had been expressed by the authority of Ecumenical Councils. The theologians of the Second Council at Constantinople (A.D. 381) had distinctly declared the procession from the Father, and against this pronouncement it could only be argued that they had not denied the procession from the Son. It was not till A.D. 589 that a council in Spain added the words "and the Son" to the creed of Nicaea, and this addition was quickly adopted in Gaul. It corresponded to the private opinions of most western theologians, including Augustine and Pope Leo I. But the Greek Fathers generally held another doctrine, which the layman may find it difficult to distinguish. They maintained that the Third person proceeded not from, but through the Second. In the ninth century, the Popes, though they repudiated the opposite dogma, hesitated to introduce the Spanish interpolation into the Creed, and perhaps it was not adopted till the beginning of the eleventh. The Reformed Churches have accepted the formula of the Creed, as it was revised in Spain, though they acknowledge only the authority of the first four Ecumenical Councils. It can hardly make much difference to the mass of believers; since we may venture to suspect that the majority of those who profess a firm belief in the double procession attach as little significance to the formula which they pronounce as if they declared their faith in a fourth dimension of space.

The beginnings of the antagonism and mutual dislike between the Greeks and Latins, which are so conspicuous at a later stage of history, may be detected in the Ignatian controversy. In the correspondence between Pope and Emperor, we can discern the Latin distrust of the Greeks, the Greek contempt for the Latins. The Emperor, probably prompted by Photius, describes Latin as a "barbarous and Scythian" language. He has quite forgotten that it was the tongue of Constantine and Justinian, and the Pope has to remind him that his own title is "Emperor of the Romans" and that in the ceremonies of his own court Latin words are daily pronounced. But this childish and ignorant attack on the language of Roman law shows how the wind was blowing, and it well illustrates how the Byzantines, in the intense conviction of the superiority of their own civilization-for which indeed they had many excellent reasons-already considered the Latin-speaking peoples as belonging to the barbarian world. It was not to be expected that the Greeks, animated by this spirit, would accept such claims of ecclesiastical supremacy as were put forward by Nicolas, or that the Church of Constantinople would permit or invite a Pope's interference, except as a temporary expedient. Photius aroused into consciousness the Greek feeling of nationality, which throughout the Middle Ages drew strength and nourishment from bitter antagonism to Roman Christianity, and the modern Hellenes have reason to regard him, as they do, with veneration as a champion of their nationality.

The Ignatian affair has another aspect as a conspicuous example of the Caesaropapism which was an essential feature in the system of the Byzantine state. Ignatius was removed, because he offended the Emperor, just as any minister might be deprived of his office. It may be said that the Ignatian party represented a feeling in the Church against such an exertion of the secular power; and it is doubtless true that the party included, among its active members, some who inherited the traditions of the opposition to the Patriarchs Tarasius and Nicephorus and considered the influence of the Emperors in ecclesiastical affairs excessive. But we may hesitate to believe that the party as a whole supposed that they were protesting on principle against the authority of the autocrat over the Church. It is more probable that they were guided by personal ties and considerations, by sympathy with Ignatius who seemed to have been most; unjustly treated, and by dislike of Photius. It is to be observed that the Emperor made his will prevail, and though the policy of Michael was reversed by Basil, this was simply a change in policy, it was not a change in principle. It was a concession to public opinion and to Rome, it was not a capitulation of the State to the Church. It was a new act of the autocrat as head of the ecclesiastical organization, it was not an abdication of the Caesar-pope.

It is hardly necessary to speak of the canonical irregularities of which so much was made in the indictment of the Pope and the Ignatian synods against Photius. In regard to the one fact which we know fully, the sudden elevation of a layman to the episcopal office, we may observe that the Pope's reply to the case, which Photius made out is unsatisfactory and imperfect. The instances of Tarasius and Nicephorus were sufficient for the purpose of vindication. In regard to Tarasius, it is urged by Nicolas that Pope Hadrian protested against his elevation, in a message addressed to the Seventh Ecumenical Council. But the Council had not hesitated to accept Tarasius, and it did not concern the Church of Constantinople, what the Bishop of Rome, apart from the Council, chose to think or say about the matter. In regard to Nicephorus, the Pope said nothing because he had nothing to say. Nicephorus was in communion with Rome; the Popes of his day raised no protest against his elevation. We have seen that if the first overtures of Nicolas to Constantinople had met with a different reception, the canonical molehills would never have been metamorphosed into mountains. The real value of the objections may be measured by the fact that when Photius reascended the patriarchal throne after the death of his rival, he was recognized by Pope John III. The death of Ignatius had indeed removed one obstacle, but nevertheless on the showing of Nicolas he was not a bishop at all. Pope John recognized him simply because it suited the papal policy at the moment.

In the stormy ecclesiastical history of our period the monks had played a conspicuous part, first as champions of the worship of icons and then of the cause of Ignatius, who was himself a typical monk. In the earlier controversies over the mystery of the incarnation, gangs of monks had been the authors of scandal in those turbulent assemblies at Ephesus, of which one is extolled as an Ecumenical Council and the other branded as a synod of brigands; at Constantinople, they led an insurrection which shook the throne of Anastasius. The Emperor Constantine V. recognized that the monks were his most influential and implacable opponents and declared war upon monasticism. But monasticism was an instinct too deeply rooted in Byzantine society to be suppressed or exterminated; the monastic order rested on as firm foundations, secured by public opinion, as the Church itself. The reaction under Irene revived and confirmed the power of the cloister; and at the same time the Studite movement of reform, under the guidance of Plato and Theodore, exerted a certain influence beyond the walls of Studion and tended to augment the prestige of the monastic life, though it was far from being generally accepted. The programme of the abbot Theodore to render the authority of the Church independent of the autocrat was a revolutionary project which had no body of public opinion behind it and led to no consequences. The iconoclastic Emperors did their will, and the restoration of image-worship, while it was a triumph for the monks, was not a victory of the Church over the State. But within the State-Church monasticism flourished with as little check as it could have done if the Church had been an independent institution, and produced its full crop of economic evils. Hundreds of monasteries, some indeed with but few tenants, existed in Constantinople and its immediate neighbourhood in the ninth century, and the number was being continually increased by new foundations. For it was a cherished ambition of ordinary men of means to found a monastery, and they had only to obtain the licence of a bishop, who consecrated the site by planting a cross, and to furnish the capital for the upkeep of the buildings and the maintenance of three monks. It was a regular custom for high dignitaries, who had spent their lives in the service of the State, to retire in old age to cloisters which they had built themselves. It is too little to say that this was an ideal of respectability; it was also probably for the Byzantine man a realization of happiness in the present, enhanced as it was by the prospect of bliss in the future. But the State paid heavily for the indulgence of its members in the life of the cloister and the cell.

Chapter VII
Financial Amed Military Administration

§1. Finance

The Imperial revenue in the Middle Ages proceeded from the same principal sources as in the earlier ages of the Empire: taxation and the profits on the Imperial estates. The machinery for collecting the revenue had perhaps been little altered, but the central ministries which controlled the machinery had been considerably changed. The various financial and cognate departments which had been subject to the authority of the two great financial ministers and the Praetorian Prefects, under the system introduced by Constantine, are now distributed among eight mutually independent ministries.

The Logothete or Accountant of the General Treasury, or, as lie was briefly called, the General Logothete, had inherited the most important duties of the Count of the Sacred Largesses. He ordered and controlled the collection of all the taxes. He was the head of the army of surveyors, controllers, and collectors of the land and hearth taxes, and of the host of commerciarii or officers of the customs.

The Military Logothete administered the treasury which defrayed the pay of the soldiers and other military expenses, which used to be furnished from the chests of the Praetorian Prefects. The Wardrobe and the Special Treasury were stores for all kinds of material used for military and naval purposes; on the occasion of a warlike expedition they supplied sails and ropes, hides, tin and lead, and innumerable things required for the equipment. The President of the Special Treasury controlled the public factories, and the Chartulary of the Wardrobe was also master of the mint.

The estates of the Crown, which were situated chiefly in the Asiatic provinces, were controlled by two central offices. The revenues were managed by the Chartulary of the Sakellion, the estates were administered by the Great Curator. The pastures in western Asia Minor, however, where horses and mules were reared for the military service, were under the stewardship of another minister, the Logothete of the Herds, while the military stables of Malagina were directed by an important and independent officer, the Count of the Stable. These latter offices had been in earlier times subordinated to the Count of the Private Estate.

The Sakellion was the central treasury of the State. We have no particular information concerning the methods of disbursement and allocation, or the relations between the various bureaux. But we may suppose that the General Logothete, who received the income arising from taxation, paid directly to other departments the various standing expenses which were defrayed from this revenue, and handed over the surplus to the Sakellion. This treasury, which received directly the net income furnished by the rents of the Private Estates, would thus have contained the specie available for the expenses of military expeditions, for buildings and public works, for the extravagances of the Court and all the private expenses of the Emperor. The annual savings, if savings were effected, seem to have passed into the personal custody of the sovran, so that Irene was able to conceal the treasure which she had accumulated.

The Sakellion itself was under the control of the chief financial minister, the Sakellarios, who acted as general comptroller. The special financial ministries were not subordinate to him, but he had the right and duty to inquire into their accounts, and was doubtless responsible for all disbursements from the Sakellion.

Bullion, furnished by the State mines, came to the General Logothete, who must have sent it to the Wardrobe to be coined, while other bullion might be deposited before mintage in the Special Treasury. From the Wardrobe the coins would pass to the Sakellion.

The two principal direct taxes, on which the Imperial finance rested, were the land-tax and the hearth-tax. These had always been the two pillars of the treasury, for the hearth-tax was only a modification of the old capitation, being levied, not on the free man and woman, but on the household. The population of cities, including the capital, did not pay the hearth-tax, at least in the eastern provinces. The leaseholders on the Imperial estates were not exempted from the land-tax, which all landed proprietors and tenants paid; and the householders of Constantinople and the other cities were burdened by an analogous charge on sites, which was known as the "urban tribute". The uniform hearth rate was probably combined in the same schedules with the other tax and collected by the same officials. Other sources of income were the toll on receipts (an income-tax of the most odious form, which Irene was praised for abolishing), death duties, judicial fines, and, above all, the duties levied on imports, which must have amounted to a substantial sum.

The unpopular fiscal measures of the Emperor Nicephorus, which are briefly recapitulated by a hostile monk, afford us a vague glimpse into the obscure financial conditions of the Empire. His official experience as General Logothete had enabled him to acquire an expert knowledge of financial details which few sovrans possessed, and he was convinced that the resources of the State were suffering and its strength endangered by the policy of laxity and indulgence which had been adopted by Irene. In the first year of his reign there was a severe taxation, which may have driven many to embrace the cause of the rebel Bardanes. We may probably conjecture that his severity consisted in restoring wholly or partly the taxes which his predecessor had recently abolished. We may be disposed to believe that he acquiesced in the disappearance of the tax on receipts, for if he had revived it, his enemies, who complained of all his financial measures, would hardly have failed to include in their indictment the revival of a burden so justly odious. But we may reasonably assume that he restored the custom duties, which were levied at the toll-houses of Abydos and Hieron, to their former figure, and that he imposed anew upon Constantinople the urban tribute, which Irene had inequitably remitted.

But seven years later, in A.D. 809, in view perhaps of the imminent struggle with the Bulgarians, he prepared a formidable array of new measures to replenish the sinking contents of the treasury.

I. In all cases where taxes had been reduced in amount, they were raised again to the original sum. It is possible that this applied to reductions which had been allowed during the preceding twenty years.

II. The kapnikon or hearth-tax, which had replaced the old capitation-tax, was a fixed annual charge of two miliarisia (2s.). But monastic and religious institutions, orphanages, hospitals, homes for the aged, although legally liable, had been exempted from payment for many years with the connivance of the government. We cannot hesitate to ascribe this inequitable favour to the policy of the pious Empress Irene. It was monstrous that the tenants on the monastic lands should be free from the burden which was imposed on all other farms and estates. Religious institutions multiplied rapidly; private persons were constantly founding new monasteries; and there was a prospect that every year the proceeds of the hearth-tax would suffer further diminution. Nicephorus was fully justified in insisting that this exemption, unauthorised by law, should cease, and in forcing the institutions which had not contributed their due share to the maintenance of the State to pay the arrears of the tax since the year of his own accession.

III. The land-tax, which continued to be the most important source of revenue, was the most troublesome to adjust and to control. Nicephorus ordered that a new survey should be made, and that the tax should be raised in amount by the charge of a shilling on the receipt which the tax-collector delivered. In the case of large estates there was no difficulty in collecting the duties; the whole property was liable for a fixed sum, and if some tenants were too poor to pay, it did not matter to the fisc. But great estates (which were to increase in number and extent in the course of the ninth and tenth centuries) seem at this time not to have been numerous; small proprietorship prevailed. The system which the government employed to secure the treasury against loss when a farmer failed or could not make his land yield the necessary margin of profit did not work satisfactorily. The farms of a commune were grouped together for this purpose, and if one farmer was insolvent, the amount for which he was liable was distributed as an extracharge (epibole) among the other members of the group. For poorer members this imposition was a considerable hardship, and the circumstance that Nicephorus deemed it expedient to modify the system seems to show that there were many cases of small proprietors reduced to penury. So far as we can interpret our brief record of his measure, he sought to devolve the responsibility for the taxes of the poor upon their richer neighbours. The fiscal debt of a defaulting farm no longer fell upon a whole group, but upon some neighbouring proprietor, and this liability was termed Allelengyon or Mutual Security.

But what was to happen to the indigent defaulter? Nicephorus enrolled him as a soldier, compelling the same more prosperous neighbour to provide for his military equipment by paying the sum of eighteen and a half nomismata. We are not told whether this sum was regarded as a price for the land, which ought to have been transferred to the possession of the neighbour who was held responsible for it, or even whether the proprietor was compelled to sell it.

The growth of monastic property was an economic evil which was justly regarded by Nicephorus with disquietude, and he adopted the heroic measure of incorporating in the Imperial domains the better lands of some rich monasteries. We cannot doubt that the transaction took the form of a compulsory sale, the price being fixed by the treasury; it is impossible to suppose that it was naked confiscation, which would have been alien to the methods of Roman policy. But the taxes which had been paid on the entire property continued to be exacted, according to our informant, from the diminished estates of the monks. We know too little of the conditions and provisions to enable us to pronounce whether this measure was unreasonably oppressive; but it is clear that Nicephorus was prepared to brave the odium which always descended upon the medieval statesman who set the economic interests of the State above those of its monastic parasites.

But if Nicephorus increased his domains at the expense of pious institutions, he also alienated portions of the Imperial estates, and the motives of this policy are obscure. It is recorded as a hardship that he sold Imperial land on the coasts of Asia Minor, at a fixed price, to unwilling purchasers, who, accustomed to sea-faring and trade, knew little or nothing about agriculture. Here again we must remember that the case is presented by an enemy, and that we are ignorant of all the circumstances of the alleged coercion.

IV. In his diligent quest of ways and means, the sudden acquisition of wealth, which we might now classify under the title of unearned increment, did not escape the notice of Nicephorus as a suitable object of taxation. He imposed heavy charges upon those who could be proved to have suddenly risen from poverty to affluence through no work or merit of their own. He treated them as treasure-finders, and thus brought them under the law of Justinian by which treasure-trove was confiscated. The worst of this measure was that it opened a fruitful field to the activity of informers.

V. Death duties were another source of revenue which claimed the Emperor's attention. The tax of 5 per cent on inheritances which had been instituted by the founder of the Empire seems to have been abolished by Justinian; but a duty of the same kind had been reimposed, and was extended to successions in the direct line, which had formerly been exempted. The lax government of Irene had allowed the tax to be evaded, by some at least of those who inherited property from their fathers or grandfathers; and when Nicephorus ordered that it should be exacted from all who had so inherited during the last twenty years, many poor men were in consternation.

VI. It is remarkable that a statesman possessing the financial experience of Nicephorus should have shared the ancient prejudice against usury so far as to forbid the lending of money at interest altogether. The deliverance of society from the evils attendant upon merciless usury was dearly purchased by the injury which was inflicted upon industry and trade. The enterprise of merchants who required capital was paralyzed, and Nicephorus was forced to come to their rescue. He aided them in a way which was highly advantageous to the treasury. He advanced loans of twelve pounds of gold about, exacting the high interest of 16,2/3 per cent. The government was not bound by the prohibition of private usury, which it is possible that the successor of Nicephorus prudently abolished.

VII. The custom duties, which were levied at Abydos and had been remitted by Irene in her unscrupulous desire to conciliate the favour of Constantinople, had been immediately re-enacted by her successor. Household slaves of a superior kind were among the most valuable chattels which reached the capital by the route of the Hellespont, and the treasury profited by the cooks and pages and dancers who were sold to minister to the comfort and elegance of the rich families of Byzantium. But there was also a demand for these articles of luxury among the inhabitants of the Aegean coasts and islands, who could purchase them without paying the heavy charges that were exacted in the custom-houses of Abydos. Nicephorus abolished this immunity by imposing a tax of two gold pieces a head on all such slaves who were sold to the west of the Hellespont.

The chronicler Theophanes, whose hostile pen has recorded these fiscal measures, completes his picture of the Emperor's oppressions by alleging that he used to pry into men's private affairs, employing spies to watch their domestic life and encouraging ill-disposed servants to slander or betray their masters. "His cruelties to the rich, the middle class, and the poor in the Imperial city were beyond description. In the last two years of his reign, he excited the murmurs of the inhabitants by a strict enforcement of the market dues on the sales of animals and vegetables, by quartering soldiers in monasteries and episcopal mansions, by selling for the public benefit gold and silver plate which had been dedicated in churches, by confiscating the property of wealthy patricians. He raised the taxes paid by churches and monasteries, and he commanded officials, who had long evaded the taxation to which they were liable as citizens, to discharge the arrears which they had failed to pay during his own reign. This last order, striking the high functionaries of the Court, seemed so dangerous to Theodosius Salibaras, a patrician who had considerable influence with the Emperor, that he ventured to remonstrate. "My lord", he said, "all are crying out at us, and in the hour of temptation all will rejoice at our fall". Nicephorus is said to have made the curious reply: "If God has hardened my heart like Pharaoh's, what good can my subjects look for? Do not expect from Nicephorus save only the things which thou seest".

The laxity and indulgence which had been permitted in the financial administration of the previous reign rendered the severity of Nicephorus particularly unwelcome and unpopular. The most influential classes were hit by his strict insistence on the claims of the treasury. The monks, who suspected him of heterodoxy and received no favours at his hands, cried out against him as an oppressor. Some of his measures may have been unwise or unduly oppressive-we have not the means of criticizing them; but in his general policy he was simply discharging his duty, an unpopular duty, to the State.

Throughout the succeeding reigns we obtain no such glimpse into the details or vicissitudes of Imperial finance. If there was a temporary reaction under Michael I against the severities of Nicephorus, the following Emperors must have drawn the reins of their financial administration sufficiently tight. After the civil war, indeed, Michael II rewarded the provinces which had been faithful to his cause by a temporary remission of half the hearth-tax. The facts seem to show that the Amorian rulers were remarkably capable and successful in their finance. On one hand, there was always an ample surplus in the treasury, until Michael III at the very end of his reign deplenished it by wanton wastefulness. On the other, no complaints are made of fiscal oppression during this period, notwithstanding the fact that the chroniclers would have rejoiced if they had had any pretext for bringing such a charge against heretics like Theophilus and his father.

If our knowledge of the ways and means by which the Imperial government raised its revenue is sadly incomplete and in many particulars conjectural, we have no information as to its amount in the ninth century, and the few definite figures which have been recorded by chance are insufficient to enable us to guess either at the income or the expenditure. It is a remarkable freak of fortune that we should possess relatively ample records of the contemporary finance of the Caliphate, and should be left entirely in the dark as to the budget of the Empire.

We have some figures bearing on the revenue in the twelfth century, and they supply a basis for a minimum estimate of the income in the ninth, when the State was stronger and richer. We learn that Constantinople alone furnished the treasury with 7,300,000 nomismata or £4,380,000, including the profits of taxation on commerce and the city markets. It has been supposed that the rest of the Empire contributed five times as much, so that the total revenue would be more than £26,280,000. At this period the greater part of Asia Minor was in the hands of the Seljuk Turks, while, on the other hand, the Empire possessed Bulgaria and Crete. It might therefore be argued that the Emperor Theophilus, who also held Calabria and received a certain yearly sum from Dalmatia, may have enjoyed a revenue of twenty-seven to thirty millions.

But the proportion of 1 to 5, on which this calculation rests, is such an arbitrary hypothesis that we must seek some other means of forming a rough evaluation. We are told that in the twelfth century the island of Corcyra yielded 1500 pounds of gold or £64,800 to the Imperial treasury. The total area of the Imperial territory in the reign of Theophilus (counting Sicily as lost, and not including Calabria, Dalmatia, Cyprus, or Cherson) was about 546,000 kilometres. The area of Corcyra is 770, so that if its contribution to the treasury was as large in the ninth as in the twelfth century, and was proportional to its size, the amount of the whole revenue would be about £46,000,000. But the population of the islands was undoubtedly denser than in most regions of the mainland, and it is probably an insufficient set-off to have left out of account Calabria and some other outlying Imperial possessions, and to have made no allowance for the vast amount contributed by Constantinople. Yet this line of calculation suggests at least that the Imperial revenue may have exceeded thirty millions and was nearly half as large again as the revenue of the Caliphs.

If we accept £25,000,000 as a minimum figure for the revenue arising from taxation of all kinds, we must add a considerable sum for the profits arising from the Imperial Estates in Asia Minor. Disregarding this source of income, which we have no data for estimating, we must remember that the weight of gold which if sent to the mint today would be coined into twenty-five million sovereigns represented at Byzantium a far higher purchasing power. It is now generally assumed that the value of money was five times as great, and this is probably not an exaggeration. On this hypothesis the Imperial revenue from taxation would correspond in real value to £125,000,000.

It is impossible to conjecture how the expenditure was apportioned. Probably a sum of more than £1.000.000 was annually spent on the maintenance of the military establishment, not including the cost of campaigns. The navy, the civil service in all its branches, religious foundations, doles to charitable institutions, liberal presents frequently given to foreign potentates for political purposes, represented large claims on the treasury, while the upkeep of a luxurious Court, and the obligatory gifts on stated occasions to crowds of officials, consumed no small portion of the Emperor's income. Theophilus must have laid out more than a million a year on his buildings. It is only for the army and navy that we possess some figures, but these, are too uncertain and partial to enable us to reconstruct a military budget.

Perhaps the most striking evidence of the financial prosperity of the Empire is the international circulation of its gold currency. "In the period of 800 years from Diocletian to Alexius Comnenus the Roman government never found itself compelled to declare bankruptcy or stop payments. Neither the ancient nor the modern world can offer a complete parallel to this phenomenon. This prodigious stability of Roman financial policy therefore secured the "byzant" its universal currency. On account of its full weight it passed with all the neighbouring nations as a valid medium of exchange. By her money Byzantium controlled both the civilised and the barbarian worlds."

§2.Military and Naval Organization

I. Under the Amorian dynasty considerable administrative changes were made in the organization of the military provinces into which the Empire was divided, in order to meet new conditions. In the Isaurian period there were five great Themes in Asia Minor, governed by strategoi, in the following order of dignity and importance: the Anatolic, the Armeniac, the Thrakesian, the Opsikian, and the Bukellarian. This system of "the Five Themes", as they were called, lasted till the reign of Michael II, if not till that of Theophilus. But it is probable that before that time the penetration of the Moslems in the frontier regions had rendered it necessary to delimit from the Anatolic and Armeniac provinces districts which were known as kleisurarchies, and were under minor commanders, kleisurarchs, who could take measures for defending the country independently of the strategoi. In this way the kleisurarchy of Seleucia, west of Cilicia, was cut off from the Anatolic Theme, and that of Charsianon from the Armeniac. Southern Cappadocia, which was constantly exposed to Saracen invasion through the Cilician gates, was also formed into a frontier province. We have no record of the times at which these changes were made, but we may suspect that they were of older date than the reign of Theophilus.

This energetic Emperor made considerable innovations in the thematic system throughout the Empire, and this side of his administration has not been observed or appreciated. In Asia Minor he created two new Themes, Paphlagonia and Chaldia. Paphlagonia seems to have been cut off from the Bukellarian province; probably it had a separate existence already, as a "katepanate", for the governor of the new Theme, while he was a strategos, bore the special title of katepano, which looks like the continuation of an older arrangement. The rise of Paphlagonia in importance may connected with the active Pontic policy of Theophilus. It is not without significance that Paphlagonian ships played a part in the expedition which he sent to Cherson, and we may conjecture with probability that the creation of the Theme of the Klimata on the north of the Euxine and that of Paphlagonia on the south were not isolated acts, but were part of the same general plan. The institution of the Theme of Chaldia, which was cut off from the Armeniac Theme (probably A.D. 837), may also be considered as part of the general policy of strengthening Imperial control over the Black Sea and its coastlands, here threatened by the imminence of the Moslem power in Armenia. To the south of Chaldia was the duchy of Koloneia, also part of the Armeniac circumscription. In the following reign (before A.D. 863) both Koloneia and Cappadocia were elevated to the rank of Themes.

The Themes of Europe, which formed a class apart from those of Asia, seem at the end of the eighth century to have been four in number-Thrace, Macedonia, Hellas, and Sicily. There were also a number of provinces of inferior rank-Calabria, under its Dux; Dalmatia and Crete, under governors who had the title of archon; while Thessalonica with the adjacent region was still subject to the ancient Praetorian Prefect of Illyricum, an anomalous survival from the old system of Constantine. It was doubtless the Slavonic revolt in the reign of Nicephorus I that led to the reorganization of the Helladic province, and the constitution of the Peloponnesus as a distinct Theme, so that Hellas henceforward meant Northern Greece. The Mohammadan descent upon Crete doubtless led to the appointment of a strategos instead of an archon of Crete, and the Bulgarian wars to the suppression of the Praetorian prefect by a strategos of Thessalonica. The Theme of Kephalonia (with the Ionian Islands) seems to have existed at the beginning of the ninth century; but the Saracen menace to the Hadriatic and the western coasts of Greece may account for the foundation of the Theme of Dyrrhachium, a city which probably enjoyed, like the communities of the Dalmatian coast, a certain degree of local independence. If so, we may compare the policy of Theophilus in instituting the strategos of the Klimata with control over the magistrates of Cherson.

It is to be noted that the Theme of Thrace did not include the region in the immediate neighbourhood of Constantinople, cut off by the Long Wall of Anastasius, who had made special provisions for the government of this region. In the ninth century it was still a separate circumscription, probably under the military command of the Count of the Walls, and Arabic writers designate it by the curious name Talaya or Tafia.

A table will exhibit the general result of all these changes:

Asiatic Themes

Stratégiai .	1. Anatolic. 2. Armeniac. 3. Thrakesian. 4. Opsikian. 5. Bukellarian. 6. Cappadocia. 7. Paphlagonia. 8. Chaldia. 9. Koloneia.
Kleisurarchiai —	10. Charsianon. 11. Seleucia.

Naval Themes

1. Kibyrrhaiot. 2. Aigaion Pelagos.

European (and other) Themes

Stratégiai .	1. Macedonia. 2. Thrace. 3. Hellas. 4. Peloponnesus. 5. Thessalonica. 6. Dyrrhachium. 7. Kephalonia. 8. Sicily. 9. Klimata.
Ducate .	. 10. Calabria.
Archontates	. 11. Dalmatia. 12. Cyprus.

II. There were considerable differences in the ranks and salaries of the strategoi. In the first place, it is to be noticed that the governors of the Asiatic provinces, the admirals of the naval Themes, and the strategoi of Thrace and Macedonia were paid by the treasury, while the governors of the European Themes paid themselves a fixed amount from the custom dues levied in their own provinces. Hence for administrative purposes Thrace and Macedonia are generally included among the Asiatic Themes. The rank of patrician was bestowed as a rule upon the Anatolic, Armeniac, and Thrakesian strategoi, and these three received a salary of 40 lbs. of gold. The pay of the other strategoi and kleisurarchs ranged from 36 to 12 lbs, but their stipends were somewhat reduced in the course of the ninth century. We can easily calculate that the total cost of paying the governors of the eastern provinces (including Macedonia and Thrace) did not fall short of £15,000.

In these provinces there is reason to suppose that the number of troops, who were chiefly cavalry, was about 80,000. They were largely settled on military lands, and their pay was small. The recruit, who began service at a very early age, received one nomisma in his first year, two in his second, and so on, till the maximum of twelve, or in some cases of eighteen, was reached.

The army of the Theme was divided generally into two, sometimes three, turms or brigades; the turm into drungoi or battalions; and the battalion into banda or companies. The corresponding commanders were entitled turmarchs, drungaries, and counts. The number of men in the company, the sizes of the battalion and the brigade, varied widely in the different Themes. The original norm seems to have been a bandon of 200 men and a drungos of 5 banda. It is very doubtful whether this uniform scheme still prevailed in the reign of Theophilus. It is certain that at a somewhat later period the bandon varied in size up to the maximum of 400, and the drungos oscillated between the limits of 1000 and 3000 men. Originally the turm was composed of 5 drungoi (5000 men), but this rule was also changed. The number of drungoi in the turm was reduced to three, so that the brigade which the turmarch commanded ranged from 3000 upwards.

The pay of the officers, according to one account, ranged from 3 lbs. to 1 lb., and perhaps the subalterns in the company (the kentarchs and pentekontarchs) are included; but the turmarchs in the larger themes probably received a higher salary than 3 lbs. If we assume that the average bandon was composed of 300 men and the average drungos of 1500, and further that the pay of the drungary was 3 lbs., that of the count 2 lbs. and that of the kentarch 1 lb., the total sum expended on these officers would have amounted to about £64,000. But these assumptions are highly uncertain. Our data for the pay of the common soldiers form a still vaguer basis for calculation; but we may conjecture, with every reserve, that the salaries of the armies of the Eastern Themes, including generals and officers, amounted to not less than £500,000.

The armies of the Themes formed only one branch of the military establishment. There were four other privileged and differently organized cavalry regiments known as the Tagmata: the Schools, (2) the Excubitors, (3) the Arithmos or Vigla, and (4) the Hikanatoi. The first three were of ancient foundation; the fourth was a new institution of Nicephorus I., who created a child, his grandson Nicetas (afterwards the Patriarch Ignatius), its first commander. The commanders of these troops were entitled Domestics, except that of the Arithmos, who was known as the Drungary of the Vigla or Watch. Some companies of these Tagmatic troops may have been stationed at Constantinople, where the Domestics usually resided, but the greater part of them were quartered in Thrace, Macedonia, and Bitynia. The question of their numbers is perplexing. We are variously told that in the ninth century they were each 6000 or 4000 strong, but in the tenth the numbers seem to have been considerably less, the strength of the principal Tagma, the Scholarians, amounting to no more than 1500 men. If we accept one of the larger figures for the reign of Theophilus, we must suppose that under one of his successors these troops were reduced in number.

The Domestic of the Schools preceded in rank all other military commanders except the strategos of the Anatolic Theme, and the importance of the post is shown by the circumstance that it was filled by such men as Manuel and Bardas. In later times it became still more important; in the tenth century, when a military expedition against the Saracens was not led by the Emperor in person, the Domestic of the Schools was ex officio the Commander-in-Chief. The Drungary of the Watch and his troops were distinguished from the other Tagmata by the duties they performed as sentinels in campaigns which were led by the Emperor in person. The Drungary was responsible for the safety of the camp, and carried the orders of the Emperor to the generals.

Besides the Thematic and the Tagmatic troops, there were the Numeri, a regiment of infantry commanded by a Domestic; and the forces which were under the charge of the Count or Domestic of the Walls, whose duty seems to have been the defence of the Long Wall of Anastasius.These troops played little part in history. More important was the Imperial Guard or Hetaireia, which, recruited from barbarians, formed the garrison of the Palace, and attended the Emperor on campaigns.

The care which was spent on providing for the health and comfort of the soldiers is illustrated by the baths at Dorylaion, the first of the great military stations in Asia Minor. This bathing establishment impressed the imagination of oriental visitors, and it is thus described by an Arabic writer:

> "Dorylaion possesses warm springs of fresh water, over which the Emperors have constructed vaulted buildings for bathing. There are seven basins, each of which can accommodate a thousand men. The water reaches the breast of a man of average height, and the overflow is discharged into a small lake".

In military campaigns, careful provision was made for the wounded. There was a special corps of officers called deputatoi, whose duty was to rescue wounded soldiers and take them to the rear, to be tended by the medical staff. They carried flasks of water, and had two ladders attached to the saddles of their horses on the left side, so that, having mounted a fallen soldier with the help of one ladder, the deputatos could himself mount instantly by the other and ride off.

It is interesting to observe that not only did the generals and superior officers make speeches to the soldiers, in old Hellenic fashion, before a battle, but there was a band of professional orators, called cantatores, whose duty was to stimulate the men by their eloquence during the action. Some of the combatants themselves, if they had the capacity, might be chosen for this purpose. A writer on the art of war suggests the appropriate chords which the cantatores might touch, and if we may infer their actual practice, the leading note was religious. "We are fighting in God's cause; the issue lies with him, and he will not favour the enemy because of their unbelief".

III. Naval necessities imposed an increase of expenditure for the defence of the Empire in the ninth century. The navy, which had been efficiently organized under the Heraclian dynasty and had performed memorable services against the attacks of the Omayyad Caliphs, had been degraded in importance and suffered to decline by the policy of the Isaurian monarchs. We may criticize their neglect of the naval arm, but we must remember that it was justified by immediate impunity, for it was correlated with the simultaneous decline in the naval power of the Saracens. The Abbasids who transferred the centre of the Caliphate from Syria to Mesopotamia undertook no serious maritime enterprises. The dangers of the future lay in the west and not in the east,— in the ambitions of the Mohammadan rulers of Africa and Spain, whose only way of aggression was by sea. Sicily was in peril throughout the eighth century, and Constantine V. was forced to reorganize her fleet; accidents and internal divisions among the Saracens helped to save her till the reign of Michael II. We shall see in another chapter how the Mohammadans then obtained a permanent footing in the island, the beginning of its complete conquest, and how they occupied Crete. These events necessitated a new maritime policy. To save Sicily, to recover Crete, were not the only problems. The Imperial possessions in South Italy were endangered; Dalmatia, the Ionian islands, and the coasts of Greece were exposed to the African fleets. It was a matter of the first importance to preserve the control of the Hadriatic. The reorganization of the marine establishment was begun by the Amorian dynasty, though its effects were not fully realized till a later period.

The naval forces of the Empire consisted of the Imperial fleet, which was stationed at Constantinople and commanded by the Drungary of the Navy, and the Provincial fleets of the Kibyrrhaeot Theme, the Aegean, Hellas, Peloponnesus, and Kephalonia. The Imperial fleet must now have been increased in strength, and the most prominent admiral of the age, Doryphas, may have done much to reorganize it. An armament of three hundred warships was sent against Egypt in A.D. 853, and the size of this force may be held to mark the progress which had been made. Not long after the death of Michael III four hundred vessels were operating off the coast of Apulia.

We have some figures which may give us a general idea of the cost of these naval expeditions. Attempts were made to recover Crete from the Saracens in A.D. 902 and in A.D. 949, and the pay of officers and men for each of these expeditions, which were not on a large scale, amounted to over £140,000. This may enable us to form a rough estimate of the expenditure incurred in sending armaments oversea in the ninth century. We may surmise, for instance, that not less than a quarter of a million (pounds sterling), equivalent in present value to a million and a quarter, was spent on the Egyptian expedition in the reign of Michael III.

Chapter VIII
The Saracen Wars

§1. The Empire of the Abbasids

In the days of Nicephorus and Charles the Great, the Caliphate was at the height of its power and grandeur; a quarter of a century later the decline of Abbasid rule, a process which was eked out through several centuries, had already begun. An accomplished student of Mohammadan history has found, even in the reigns of Harun and his son Mamun, the last great Caliphs, signs and premonitions of decay; in their characters and tempers he discovers traits of the degeneracy which was to be fully revealed in their weak and corrupt successors. Without presuming to decide whether Harun should be called a degenerate because to a nature unscrupulously cruel he united susceptibility so sensitive to music and so prone to melancholy that he burst into tears on hearing the strains of a boatman's song wafted over the waters of the Tigris, we can see in his reign and that of his son the immense difficulties of government which confronted the rulers of the Mohammadan world, the strength of the elements of division and disruption, and the need of sovrans of singular ability and strenuous life, if the fabric of the Empire was to be held together.

The realm of the Abbasids, in its early period, presents some interesting points of comparison with the contemporary Roman Empire. The victory of the Abbasids and their establishment on the throne of the Caliphs had been mainly due to Persian support; the change of dynasty marked the triumph of Persian over Arabian influence. We may fairly compare this change with that which attended the elevation of the Isaurian dynasty to the throne of the Caesars. The balance was shifted in favour of the eastern regions of the Empire, and influences emanating from the mountains of Asia Minor strove to gain the upper hand over the prevailing influence of the Greeks. If the struggle between the two spirits expressed itself here in the form of the iconoclastic controversy, the anti-Arabian reaction in the Caliphate was similarly marked by a religious movement, which is called heretical because it was unsuccessful, and has a certain resemblance to iconoclasm in so far as it was an attempt of reason to assert itself, within certain limits, against authority and tradition. While the Omayyad Caliphs were still ruling in Damascus, there were some thoughtful Mohammadans who were not prepared to accept without reflexion the doctrines which orthodoxy imposed; and it is not improbable that such men were stimulated in theological speculation by friendly disputes and discussions with their Christian fellow-subjects. The sect of the Mutazalites proclaimed the freedom of the will, which the orthodox Mohammadan regards as inconsistent with the omnipotence of Allah, and they adopted the dangerous method of allegorical interpretation of the Koran. Their doctrines were largely accepted by the Shiites, and they had to endure some persecution under the Caliphs of Damascus. The first Abbasid rulers secretly sympathized with the Mutazalites, but orthodoxy was still too strong to enable them to do more than tolerate it. Mamun was the first who ventured to profess the heresy, and in A.D. 827 he issued an edict proclaiming that the Koran was created. This was the cardinal point at issue. The Mutazalites pointed out that if, as the orthodox maintained, the Koran existed from all eternity, it followed that there were two co-existing and equally eternal Beings, Allah and the Koran. The doctrine of the eternal existence of the Koran corresponds to the Christian doctrine of the inspiration of the Bible, and in denying it the Caliph and his fellow-heretics seemed to undermine the authority of the Sacred Book. There were some who had even the good sense to assert that a better book than the Koran might conceivably be written. The intellectual attitude of the Mutazalites is also apparent in their rejection of the doctrine, which the orthodox cherished, that in the next world God would reveal himself to the faithful in a visible shape. Mamun may have hoped to bring about a general reform of Islam, but his enlightened views, which his two successors,

Mutasim and Wathik, also professed and endeavoured to enforce, probably made few converts. These Caliphs, like the iconoclastic Emperors, resorted to persecution, the logical consequence of a system in which theological doctrine can be defined by a sovran's edict. When Wathik died, in consequence of his dissolute life, in A.D. 847, his successor Mutawakkil inaugurated a return to the orthodox creed, and executed those who persisted in denying the eternity of the Koran.

The genuine interest evinced by the Caliphs of this period in poetry and music, in literature and science, was the most pleasing feature of their rule. It was a coincidence that the brilliant period of Arabic literature, developing under Persian influence, was contemporary with the revival of learning and science at Constantinople, of which something will be said in another chapter. The debt which Arabic learning owed to the Greeks was due directly to the intermediate literature of Syria; but we must not ignore the general effect of influences of culture which flowed reciprocally and continually between the Empire and the Caliphate. Intercourse other than warlike between neighboring realms is usually unnoticed in medieval chronicles, and the more frequent it is, the more likely it is to be ignored. But various circumstances permit us to infer that the two civilizations exerted a mutual influence on each other; and the historians record anecdotes which, though we hesitate to accept them as literal facts, are yet, like the anecdotes of Herodotus, good evidence for the social or historical conditions which they presuppose. It must not be thought that the religious bigotry of the Moslems or the chronic state of war between the two powers were barriers or obstacles. At that time the Mohammadan society of the middle classes, especially in the towns, seems to have been permeated by a current of intellectual freedom: they were not afraid to think, they were broad-minded and humane. On the other hand, while the continuous hostilities on the frontiers do not appear to have seriously interrupted the commercial traffic between Europe and Asia, the war directly contributed to mutual knowledge. In the annual raids and invasions by which the Romans and Saracens harried each other's territories, hundreds of captives were secured; and there was a recognized system of exchanging or redeeming them at intervals of a few years. The treatment of these prisoners does not seem to have been very severe; distinguished Saracens who were detained in the State prison at Constantinople were entertained at banquets in the Imperial palace. Prisoners of the better classes, spending usually perhaps five or six years, often much longer terms, in captivity, were a channel of mutual influence between Greek and Saracen civilization. On the occasion of an exchange of captives in A.D. 845, Al-Garmi, a highly orthodox Mohammadan, was one of those who was redeemed. During a long period of detention, he had made himself acquainted with the general outline of Imperial history, with the government, the geography, and the highroads of the Empire, and had obtained information touching the neighbouring lands of the Slavs and the Bulgarians. He committed the results of his curiosity to writing, and the descriptive work of Ibn Khurdadhbah, which has come down to us, owed much to the compositions of the captive Al-Garmi.

In its political constitution, the most striking feature of the Caliphate, as contrasted with the Roman Empire, was the looseness of the ties which bound its heterogeneous territories together under the central government. There was no great administrative organization like that which was instituted by Diocletian and Constantine, and survived, however changed and modified, throughout the ages. At Constantinople the great chiefs of departments held in their hands the strings to all the administration in the provinces, and the local affairs of the inhabitants were strictly controlled by the governors and Imperial officials. In the Caliphate, on the other hand, the provincials enjoyed a large measure of autonomy, and there was no administrative centralisation. For keeping their subjects in hand, the Caliphs seem to have depended on secret police and an organized system of espionage. An exception to the principle of abstaining from State interference was made in favour of agriculture: the government considered itself responsible for irrigation; and the expenses of maintaining in repair the sluices of the Tigris and Euphrates, indispensable for the fertility of Mesopotamia, were defrayed entirely by the public treasury.

The small number of the ministries or divans in Baghdad is significant of the administrative simplicity of the Saracen State. The most important minister presided over the office of the ground-tax, and next to him was the grand Vezir. The duty of the Postmaster was to exercise some general control over the administration; and his title, though he was not responsible for the management of the State Post, suggests the methods by which such control was exerted. The chief purpose of the Post, which, like that of the Roman Empire, was exclusively used by officials, was to transmit reports from the provinces to the capital. It was carefully organized. The names of the postal stations, and their distances, were entered in an official book at Baghdad, and the oldest geographical works of the Arabs were based on these official itineraries. The institution served a huge system of espionage, and the local postmasters were the informers, sending reports on the conduct of governors and tax-collectors, as well as on the condition of agriculture, to headquarters.

We possess far fuller information on the budget of the Caliphate under the early Abbasids than on the finances of the later Empire at any period. We can compare the total revenues of the State at various periods in the eighth and ninth centuries, and we know the amount which each province contributed. Under Harun ar-Rashid the whole revenue amounted to more than 530 millions of dirhams (about £21,000,000), in addition to large contributions in kind, whose value in money it is impossible to estimate. In the reign of Mamun (A.D. 819-820) it was reduced perhaps by 200 millions, and about forty years later the sources point to a still lower figure. In the following century (A.D. 915-916), it is recorded that the income of the State, from the taxes which were paid in gold and silver, amounted to no more than 24 millions of dirhams.The sources of the revenue were the taxes on land and property, ships and mines, mills and factories, the duties on luxuries, on salt, and many other things. The falling off during the ninth century may be easily accounted for by such general causes as internal troubles and rebellions, constant wars, the dishonesty of provincial governors, and the lavish luxury of the Court. The Caliph Mamun is said to have spent on the maintenance of his Court six thousand dinars daily, which is equivalent nearly to £1,000,000 a year.

The circumstances of the elevation of the Abbasid house entailed, as a natural consequence, that the Persians should form an important element in the military establishments. Under the Omayyads the chief recruiting grounds were Basrah and Kufah, and the host consisted mainly of Arabians. In the army of Mansur there were three chief divisions-the northern Arabs, the southern Arabs, and, thirdly, the men of Khurasan, a geographical term which then embraced the mountainous districts of Persia. The third division were the privileged troops who, to use the technical Roman term, were in praesenti and furnished the guards of the Caliph. But in the reign of Mutasim, who ascended the throne in A.D. 833, the Persians were dislodged from their place of favour by foreigners. The Turkish bodyguard was formed by slaves imported from the lands beyond the Oxus, and so many came from Farghana that they were all alike known as Farghanese. We may suspect that many of these soldiers entered the Caliph's service voluntarily, and it is remarkable that much about the same time as the formation of the Turkish bodyguard of the Caliph we meet the earliest mention of Farghanese in the service of the Roman Empire. The unpopularity of the insolent Turkish guards among the inhabitants of Baghdad drove Mutasim into leaving the capital, and during the secession to Samarra, which lasted for sixty years, they tyrannized over their masters, like the Praetorians of past and the Janissaries of future history. Yet a fifth class of troops was added about the same time to the military forces of the Caliphate; it consisted of Egyptian Beduins, Berbers, and negroes, and was known as the African corps. The Saracens adopted the tactical divisions of the Roman army. The regiment of 1000 men, commanded by a kaid, was subdivided into hundreds and tens, and there were normally ten such regiments under the emir, who corresponded to the strategos of a Theme.

§2. Baghdad

The capital city of the Abbasids, from which they governed or misgoverned Western Asia, was the second city in the world. In size and splendour, Baghdad was surpassed only by Constantinople. There is a certain resemblance between the circumstances in which these two great centres of power were founded. Saffah, the first sovran of the new dynasty, had seen the necessity of translating the seat of government from Syria to Mesopotamia. A capital on the navigable waters of the Tigris or the Euphrates would be most favourably situated for ocean commerce with the far East; it would be at a safe distance from Syria, where the numerous adherents of the fallen house of the Omayyads were a source of danger; it would be near Persia, on whose support the risen house of the Abbasids especially depended. Perhaps, too, it may have been thought that Damascus was perilously near the frontier of the Roman Empire, whose strength and vigour had revived under its warlike Isaurian rulers. It was impossible to choose Kufah on the Euphrates, with its turbulent and fanatical population, and Saffah built himself a palace near the old Persian town of Anbar, a hundred miles further up the river. But his successor Mansur, having just essayed a new residence on the same stream, discerned the advantages of a situation on the Tigris. For the Tigris flows through fruitful country, whereas the desert approaches the western banks of the Euphrates; and in the eighth century it flowed alone into the Persian Gulf, while the Euphrates lost itself in a great swamp, instead of uniting with its companion river, as at the present day. Mansur did not choose the place of his new capital in haste. He explored the banks of the Tigris far to the north, and thought that he had discovered a suitable site not far from Mosul. But finally he fixed his choice on the village of Baghdad. Bricks bearing the name of Nebuchadnezzar show that the spot was inhabited in the days of the Assyrian monarchy; when Mansur inspected it, he found it occupied by monasteries of Nestorian Christians, who extolled the coolness of the place and its freedom from gnats. The wisdom of the Caliph's decision may be justified by the fact that Baghdad has remained unchallenged, till this day, the principal city of Mesopotamia. The experiments preliminary to its foundation remind us of the prologue to the foundation of Constantinople. When Diocletian determined to reside himself in the East, he chose Nicomedia, and Nicomedia corresponds to the tentative establishments of Saffah and Mansur on the Euphrates. When Constantine decided that Nicomedia would not suit the requirements of a new Rome, he was no less at a loss than Mansur, and we are told that various sites competed for his choice before he discovered Byzantium.

But the tasks which confronted the two founders were widely different. Constantine had to renew and extend an ancient city; and his plans were conditioned by the hilly nature of the ground. The architectural inventiveness of Mansur and his engineers was hampered by no pre-existing town; when they had cleared away a miserable hamlet and the abodes of infidel monks, they had a tabula rasa, level and unencumbered, oil which they could work their will, confined only by the Isa canal and the Tigris itself. The architects used the opportunity and built a wonderful city of a new type. It was in the form of a perfect circle, four miles in circumference, surrounded by three concentric walls constructed of huge sun-dried bricks. In the centre stood the Palace of Mansur, known as the Golden Gate, and close to it the Great Mosque. The whole surrounding area, enclosed by the inmost wall, was reserved for the offices of government, the palaces of the Caliph's children, and the dwellings of his servants. No one except the Caliph himself was permitted to pass into these sacred precincts on horseback. The ring between the inner and the middle wall was occupied by houses and booths. The middle wall was the principal defence of the town, exceeding the other two in height and thickness. Through its iron gates, so heavy that a company was required to open them, a rider could enter without lowering his lance; and at each gatehouse a-gangway was contrived by which a man on horseback could reach the top of the wall. From this massive fortification a vacant space divided the outmost wall, which was encompassed by a water-moat. This system of walls was pierced by four series of equidistant gates-the gates of Syria (N.W.), Khurasan (N.E.), Basrah (S.E.), and Kufah (S.W.). The imposing gatehouses of the middle circle were surmounted by domes. Such was the general plan of the round city of Mansur, to which he gave the name of Madinat as-Salam, the City of Peace. But if the name was used officially, it has been as utterly forgotten by the world as Aelia Capitolina and Theupolis, which once aspired to replace Jerusalem and Antioch.

The building of the city occupied four years (A.D. 762-766). Mansur also built himself another house, the Kasr-al-Khuld or Palace of Eternity, outside the walls, between the Khurasan Gate and the river. It was here that Harun ar-Rashid generally lived. South of the city stretched the great commercial suburb of Karkh, and the numerous canals which intersected it must have given it the appearance of a modern Dutch town. Here were the merchants and their stores, as carefully supervised by the government as the traders and dealers of Constantinople. The craftsmen and tradesmen did not live scattered promiscuously in the same street, as in our cities of today; every craft and every branch of commerce had its own allotted quarter. It is said that Mansur, in laying out the town of Karkh, which was not included in his original plan, was inspired by the advice of an envoy of the Roman Emperor, who was then Constantine V. When the patrician had been taken to see all the wonders of the new city, the Caliph asked him what he thought of it. "I have seen splendid buildings", he replied, "but I have also seen, 0 Caliph, that thine enemies are with thee, within thy city". He explained this oracular saying by observing that the foreign merchants in the markets within the walls would have opportunities of acting as spies or even as traitors. Mansur reflected on the warning, and removed the market to the suburbs.

This is not the only anecdote connecting Byzantine envoys with the foundation of Baghdad. We may not give these stories credence, but they have a certain value for the history of culture, because they would not have been invented if the Saracens had not been receptive of Byzantine influences. It was said that a Greek patrician advised Mansur on the choice of his site; and a visitor who walked through the western suburb and was shown the great "water-mill of the patrician" might feel convinced that here was an undoubted proof of the alleged debt to Byzantine civilization. His guide would have told him that the name of the builder of the mills was Tarath, who had come on behalf of the Roman Emperor to congratulate the Caliph Mahdi on his accession to the throne (A.D. 775). Tarath, who was himself fifth in descent from the Emperor Maruk, offered to build a mill on one of the canals. Five hundred thousand dirhams (about £20,000) were supplied for the cost, and the patrician guaranteed that the yearly rents would amount to this sum. When the forecast was fulfilled, Mahdi gratefully ordered that the rents should be bestowed on the patrician, and until his death the amount was transmitted to him year by year to Constantinople. The story sounds like a pleasing invention, called forth by the need of explaining the name of the mill; and it has been suggested that the name itself was originally derived, not from "Patrician", but from "Patriarch", and that the mills, older than the foundation of the city, were called after the Patriarch of the Nestorians. The name Tarath, however, is evidently Tarasius, while in his Imperial ancestor Maruk it is easy to recognize the Emperor Maurice; and it is to be observed that the age of the fifth generation from Maurice (who died in A.D. 602) corresponds to the reign of Mansur.

The traffic of Baghdad was not confined to Karkh; there were extensive market-places also in the region outside the western wall, and in the north-western suburb of Harbiyah, beyond the Syrian Gate. The quarters in all these suburbs which encompassed the city were distinguished for the most part by the names of followers of Mansur, to whom he assigned them as fiefs.

Although Baghdad was to live for ever, the Round City of the founder was destined soon to disappear. The Palace of the Golden Gate was little used after the death of Mansur himself, and four generations later the rest of the court and government was permanently established on the other side of the Tigris. At the very beginning, three important suburbs grew up on the opposite bank of the river, which was spanned by three bridges of boats. This region has aptly been described as a fan-shaped area, the point of radiation being the extremity of the Main Bridge, which led to the gate of Khurasan, and the curve of the fan sweeping round from the Upper Bridge to the Lower Bridge. But these quarters of Rusafah, Sham-masiyah, and Mukharrim were not destined to be the later city of the Abbasids; their interest is entirely connected with the events of the earlier period. Mansur built a palace in Rusafah for his son Malidi, in whose reign this quarter, inhabited by himself and his courtiers, became the most fashionable part of the capital. More famous was the palace of Jafar the Barmecide in the quarter of Mukharrim. It was given by its builder as a free gift to prince Mamun, who enlarged it, built a hippodrome, and laid out a wild beast park. When Mamun came to the throne, he generally lived here, whenever he was in Baghdad, and from this time we may date the upward rise of Eastern Baghdad. For the decline and destruction of the Bound City of Mansur had been initiated in the struggle between Mamun and his brother Amin, when its walls and houses were ruined in a siege which lasted for a year. Mamun rebuilt it, but neither he nor his successors cared to live in it, and the neglect of the Caliphs led to its ultimate ruin and decay. For a time indeed it seemed that Baghdad itself might permanently be abandoned for a new residence. The Caliph Mutasim, who had built himself a new palace in Mukharrim, was forced by the mutinies of the Turkish Guards to leave Baghdad, and Samarra, higher up the river, was the seat of the court and government of the Commander of the Faithful for about sixty years (A.D. 836-94). Once indeed, during this period, a caliph took up his quarters for a year in Baghdad. It was Mustain, who fled from Samarra, unable to endure his subjection to the Turkish praetorians (A.D. 865). But he came not to the city of Mansur, but to the quarter of Rusafah, which he surrounded with a wall to stand the siege of the rival whom the Turks had set up. This siege was as fatal to the old quarters of Eastern Baghdad as the earlier siege was to the Round City and its suburbs. When the Court finally returned from Samarra, thirty years later, new palaces and a new Eastern Baghdad arose farther to the south, on ground which was wholly beyond the limits of the suburbs of Mansur's city.

§3. The Frontier Defences of the Empire and the Caliphate

The sway of the Caliph extended from the northern shores of Africa to the frontiers of India, but after the year 800 his lordship over northern Africa was merely nominal, and the western limits of his realm were virtually marked by Cyprus and Egypt. For Ibrahim, son of Aghlab, who was appointed governor of Tunis, announced to the Caliph Harun that he was prepared to pay a yearly tribute but was determined to keep the province as a perpetual fief for himself and his descendants. Harun, who was at the moment beset by war and revolts elsewhere, was compelled to acquiesce, and the Aghlabid dynasty was thus founded in Africa. The whole Caliphate was divided into some fifteen administrative provinces, and the Asiatic provinces alone formed a far larger realm than the contemporary Roman Empire.

The circumscriptions of Syria and Armenia were separated from Roman territory by frontier districts, which were occupied by forts and standing camps. The standing camp, or fustat, was an institution which had been developed under the Omayyads, and was continued under the early Abbasids. The ancient towns of Tarsus, Adana, and Mopsuestia were little more than military establishments of this kind. If we survey the line of defences along the Taurus range from the Euphrates to the frontier of Cilicia, our eye falls first on Melitene (Malatia) which lies at the meeting of the great highroads leading from Sebastea (Sivas) and Caesarea to Armenia and northern Mesopotamia, not far from the loop which the river describes below the point at which its parent streams unite their waters. The road from Melitene to Germanicia, across the Taurus, was marked by the fastnesses of Zapetra (at Viran-shahr) and Hadath or Adata, both of which were frequently attacked by the Romans. Germanicia and Anazarbos were strongly fortified by the Caliph Harun, and between these main positions, in the hilly regions of the upper Pyramus, were the forts of Kanisah and Haruniyah. This line, from Melitene (which gave his title to the Emir of the district) to Anazarbos, formed the defence against invasion of Mesopotamia. The province of Syria was secured by another line, in which the chief points were Mopsuestia (Massisah), Adana and Tarsus. When the coast road, emerging from the Syrian Gates, had swept round the bay of Issus, it turned inland to Mopsuestia, and thence ran due westward to Tarsus, passing Adana, which it entered by the old bridge of Justinian across the Sarus. Under Harun, Tarsus was garrisoned by eight thousand soldiers, and it was fortified by double walls surrounded by a moat.

Of the Taurus mountain passes, through which the Christians and Moslems raided each other's lands, the two chief were (1) the defiles, known from ancient times as the Cilician Gates, through which the Saracens, when Tarsus was their base, carried the Holy War into the central regions of Asia Minor, and (2) the pass which connected Germanicia with Arabissos.

The pass of the Cilician Gates, famous in ancient as well as in medieval history, is about seventy miles in length from the point where the ascent from the central plateau of Asia Minor begins, south of Tyana, to the point where the southern foothills of Taurus merge in the Cilician plain. Near the northern extremity of the pass, a lofty isolated peak rises to the height of about a thousand feet, commanding a wide view both of the southern plains of Cappadocia and of the northern slopes of Taurus. On this impregnable height stood the fortress of Lulon, which, though it could defy armed assault, yet, whether by treachery or long blockades, passed frequently backwards and forwards from the Saracens to the Romans. It was the key of the Cilician pass. While it was in the hands of the Romans, it was difficult for a Saracen army to invade Cappadocia; while the Saracens held it, an Imperial army could not venture to enter the defiles. The northern road to Tyana and the western road to Heraclea meet close to Lulon at the foot of the pass, so that the fort commanded both these ways.

The road winding first eastward and then turning south ascends to the oval vale of Podandos, called the "Camp of Cyrus", because the younger Cyrus encamped here on his march against his brother. The path rises from Podandos through steep and narrow glens to the summit of the pass; and on the east side, high up on the mountain, it was commanded by a stronghold, built of black stone, known as the Fortress of the Slavs. From the summit, marked by a little plateau which is now called Tekir, a descent of about three miles leads to the rocky defile which was known as the Cilician Gates and gave its name to the whole pass. It is a passage, about a hundred yards long and a few yards wide, between rock walls rising perpendicular on either side, and capable of being held against a large force by a few resolute men. Above, on the western summit, are the remains of an old castle which probably dates from the times when Greeks and Saracens strove for the possession of the mountain frontier.

In the period with which we are concerned Podandos and the pass itself seem to have been durably held by the Saracens. Lulon frequently changed hands. When the Romans were in possession, it served as the extreme station of the line of beacons, which could flash to Constantinople, across the highlands and plains of Asia Minor, the tidings of an impending invasion. The light which blazed from the lofty hill of Lulon was seen by the watchers on the peak of Mount Argaios-not the Argaios which looks down on Caesarea, but another mountain, south-east of Lake Tatta. It travelled in its north-westward course across the waters of the lake, to be renewed on the hill of Isamos, and the signal was taken up on the far-off height of Aigilos. The beacon of Aigilos, visible to the great military station of Dorylaion which lies on the river Tembris some thirty miles to the north-west, signalled to Mamas, a hill in the south-eastern skirts of Mount Olympus, and another fire passed on the news to Mokilos. The light of Mokilos crossed the Bithynian Gulf, and the last beacon on the mountain of St. Auxentios transmitted the message to those who were set to watch for it in the Pharos of the Great Palace.

Such telegraphic communication had been devised in remote antiquity, and had been employed by the Romans elsewhere. But the mere kindling of beacons could only convey a single message, and if the line of fires in Asia Minor was established as early as the eighth century, they were probably lit solely to transmit the news that a Saracen incursion was imminent. But a simple plan for using the beacons to send as many as twelve different messages is said to have been contrived by Leo the mathematician and adopted by the Emperor Theophilus. Two clocks were constructed which kept exactly the same time and were set together; one was placed in the palace, the other in the fortress nearest to the Cilician frontier. Twelve occurrences, which were likely to happen and which it was important to know, were selected; one of the twelve hours was assigned to each; and they were written on the faces of both clocks. If at four o'clock the commander of Lulon became aware that the enemy were about to cross the frontier, he waited till the hour of one and then lit his beacon; and the watchers in the Palace, seeing the light on Mount Auxentios, knew at what hour the first fire was kindled and therefore what the signal meant. A signal made at two o'clock announced that hostilities had begun, and a three o'clock despatch signified a conflagration.

In expeditions to Commagene and Mesopotamia, the Imperial armies generally followed the road from Arabissos (Yarpuz) which, crossing the Taurus, descends to Germanicia. The troops of the Eastern Asiatic Themes met those which came from the west at Caesarea, and a road crossing the Antitaurus range by the Kuru-Chai pass took them to Sirica and Arabissos. But at Sirica (perhaps Kemer) they had an alternative route which was sometimes adopted. They could proceed southward by Kokusos (Geuksun) and reach Germanicia by the Ayer-Bel pass.

At the beginning of the ninth century, a great part of Cappadocia east and south-east of the upper Halys had become a frontier land, in which the Saracens, although they did not occupy the country, had won possession of important strongholds, almost to the very gates of Caesarea. If they did not hold already, they were soon to gain the forts in the Antitaurus region which commanded the roads to Sis, and Kokusos which lay on one of the routes to Germanicia. To the north, they seem to have dominated the country as far west as the road from Sebastea to Arabissos. And, south of the Antitaurus range, Arabissos was the only important place of which the Empire retained possession. The fact that the Charsian province was designated as a Kleisurarchy is a significant indication of the line of the eastern frontier. It was the business of the Charsian commander to defend the kleisurai or passes of the Antitaurus hills.

§4. The Warfare in the Reigns of Harun and Mamun (A.D. 802-833)

Till the middle of the tenth century when the Emperor Nicephorus Phocas made a serious effort to drive the Moslems from Syria, the wars between the Empire and Caliphate are little more than a chronicle of reciprocal incursions which seldom penetrated very far into the enemy's country. The chief events were the capture and recapture of the fortresses in the Taurus and Antitaurus highlands; occasionally an expedition on a larger scale succeeded in destroying some important town. The record of this monotonous warfare is preserved more fully in the Arabic than in the Greek chronicles. It would be as useless as it were tedious to reproduce here the details of these annual campaigns. It will be enough to notice the chief vicissitudes, and the more important incidents, in a struggle whose results, when the Amorian dynasty fell, showed a balance in favour of the Saracens.

During the last few years of the reign of Irene, the warfare slumbered; it would seem that she purchased immunity from invasion by paying a yearly sum to the Caliph. One of the first decisions of Nicephorus was to refuse to continue this humiliating tribute, and the Arab historians quote letters which they allege to have passed between the Emperor and the Caliph on this occasion. Nicephorus demanded back the money which had been paid through "female weakness". The epistle, if it is authentic, was simply a declaration of war. Harun was so incensed with fury that no one could look at him; he called for an inkpot and wrote his answer on the back of the Imperial letter:

> "Harun, Commander of the Faithful, to the Greek dog. I have read thy letter, son of an unbelieving mother. Thou shalt not only hear my answer but see it with thine eyes".

The Caliph marched immediately to chastise the insolent Roman, but Nicephorus, who, occupied with the revolt of Bardanes, was not prepared to meet him, offered to pay tribute, if the army, which had advanced from the Cilician Gates to Heraclea, would retire. Harun, satisfied with the booty he had collected and the damage he had inflicted, agreed to the proposal; but when he had reached the Euphrates, the news arrived that the Emperor had broken the compact, and notwithstanding the severe cold, for it was already winter, he retraced his steps and raided the lands of his enemy again.

Each succeeding year during the reign of Harun, and under his successor till A.D. 813, witnessed the regular incursions of the Moslem commanders of the frontier. We may notice particularly an expedition led by the Caliph himself, who wore a pointed cap inscribed "Raider and pilgrim", in the summer of A.D. 806. His army numbered 135,000 regular soldiers, with many volunteers, and besides capturing a number of important forts he took Heraclea and its subterranean grain stores. He seized Tyana, which lies north of Lulon on the road to Caesarea, and converted it into a permanent post of occupation, building a mosque, which the Greek chronicler designates as "the house of his blasphemy". The Emperor, who seems to have been unable to send a sufficient force to take the field against the invader, at length induced him to withdraw for the sum of 50,000 dinars.

During the last two years of Harun's reign (A.D. 808-9) insurrections in his eastern dominions prevented him from prosecuting the war against Romania with the same energy, and after his death the struggle of his sons for the throne was the signal for new rebellions, and secured the Empire for some years against any dangerous attack. Harun had obliged his three sons to sign a document, by which the government of the realm was divided among them, but Amin succeeded to the supreme position of Caliph and Mamun was designated as next in succession. Amin was younger than Mamun, but he was the son of the Princess Zubaidah who had Mansur's blood in her veins, while Mamun's mother was a slave. Civil war broke out when Amin attempted to violate the paternal will by designating his own son as heir apparent to the throne. It was decided by the long siege of Baghdad and the execution of Amin (A.D. 813).

The twenty years of Mamun's reign were marked by internal rebellions and disaffection so grave that all the military forces which he commanded were required to cope with these domestic dangers. The governors of Egypt were already aspiring to an independence which they were afterwards to achieve, and Babek, an unconquerable leader, who belonged to the communistic sect of the Hurramites, defied the Caliph's power in Adarbiyan and Armenia. The army of Mamun was annihilated by this rebel in A.D. 829-30, and the task of subduing him was bequeathed to the Caliph's successor. These circumstances explain the virtual cessation of war between the Empire and the Caliphate for a space of sixteen years (A.D. 814-829). There was no truce or treaty; the two powers remained at war; there were some hostilities; but the Saracens seem to have desisted from their yearly invasions, and the Emperors Leo and Michael were less eager to take advantage of Mamun's difficulties by aggressions on their side than glad to enjoy a respite from the eastern war. This long suspension of the Holy War was chequered, indeed, by Mamun's actions during the rebellion of Thomas, which showed that he cherished designs upon the Empire which only necessity held in abeyance. We saw how the Saracens took advantage of that crisis, first invading the Empire, and then supporting Thomas the Slavonian. The Caliph, whether he had made secret conditions with the pretender or not, undoubtedly hoped to augment his territory in Asia Minor.

If the Caliph had espoused the cause of Thomas, the Emperor had an opportunity of retaliating by supporting the rebel Babek. And as a matter of fact, the renewal of the war seems to have been caused by the opening of negotiations between Babek and the Emperor Theophilus. It must have been immediately after Theophilus ascended the throne that a considerable number of Hurramite insurgents passed into Roman territory and offered to serve in the Roman armies. It is probable that the negotiations with Babek were arranged with the help of a notable officer, of Persian origin, who had been brought up at Constantinople and bore a Greek name-Theophobos. Theophilus appointed him commander of the army of eastern fugitives, to whom his descent and knowledge of their language naturally recommended him. But the attachment of the soldiers to Theophobos was possibly based on a higher and transcendent claim.

The Hurramites cherished the firm belief that a Mahdi or Guide of their own race would appear who would guide them to faith in himself, would transmit his Empire to another, to be followed by a perpetual line of successors. Such a divine leader had recently arisen amongst them, but he was caught and executed. If Theophobos was recognised as his successor, we should understand both the ascendency which he exercised over them, and the motive of the legends which grew up about his origin. But the fact which suggests this explanation is the belief current among the "Persians" in later generations that Theophobos had never tasted death.

The foreigners had come to Sinope, having evidently followed the coast road by Trapezus, as they could not pass through the Saracen province of Melitene. Quarters were assigned to them here and at Amastris, but some years later they seized their commander and proclaimed him Emperor against his will (A.D. 837). Theophobos, whose services had been rewarded by the rank of patrician and the hand of a lady who was sister either to Theophilus himself or to Theodora, was a loyal subject, and he managed to send a secret message to the Emperor. Theophilus pardoned the troops, but took the precaution of distributing them among the armies of various Themes, in regiments of 2000, which were known as "the Persian turms".

We may pass briefly over the meagre details of the warfare during the next three years, noticing only the sack of Zapetra by Theophilus (A.D. 830), his victory in Cilicia (A.D. 831) which he celebrated by a triumphal entry into Constantinople, and the Saracen capture of the important fortress of Lulon. But we may linger longer over the overtures for peace which Theophilus addressed to the Caliph.

Defeated in a battle, in the autumn of 831, the Emperor wished for peace and from his camp he sent an ecclesiastic with a letter to Mamun. The Caliph received him in his camp, but on observing the superscription of the letter, he returned it to the envoy saying "I will not read his letter, which he begins with his own name". The ambassador retraced his steps, and Theophilus was compelled to rewrite his epistle and place the name of the Caliph before his own. The story may be an insolent invention of the Saracens, but it is certain that Mamun rejected the offers of Theophilus who proposed to give him 100,000 dinars and 7000 captives, if he would restore the fortresses which he had conquered and conclude a peace for five years. The time of the summer campaign, however, had drawn to a close, and Mamun retired into his own territories (September).

The capture of Lulon after a long siege was an important success for the arms of Mamun. The value of this fortress, the key to the northern entrance of the Cilician Gates, has already been explained. After its surrender. Theophilus addressed a letter to the Caliph, which according to an Arabic historian, was couched in the following phrases:

> "Of a truth, it is more reasonable for two antagonists, striving each for his own welfare, to agree than to cause injury to each other. Assuredly, you will not consent to renounce your own welfare for the sake of another's. You are sufficiently intelligent to understand this without a lesson from me. I wrote to you to propose the conclusion of peace, as I earnestly desire complete peace, and relief from the burden of war. We will be comrades and allies; our revenues will increase steadily, our trade will be facilitated, our captives liberated, our roads and uninhabited districts will be safe. If you refuse, then-for I will not dissimulate or flatter you with words —I will go forth against you, I will take your border lands from you, I will destroy your horsemen and your footmen. And if I do this, it will be after I have raised a flag of parleys between us. Farewell".

To this epistle the Caliph disdainfully replied in terms like these:

> "I have received your letter in which you ask for peace, and in mingled tones of softness and severity try to bend me by referring to commercial advantages, steady augmentation of revenues, liberation of captives, and the termination of war. Were I not cautious and deliberate before deciding to act, I would have answered your letter by a squadron of valiant and seasoned horsemen, who would attempt to tear you from your household, and in the cause of God would count as nought the pain which your valour might cause them. And then I would have given them reinforcements and supplies of arms. And they would rush to drink the draughts of death with more zest than you would flee to find a refuge from their insults. For they are promised one of two supreme blessings-victory here or the glorious future of paradise. But I have deemed it right to invite you and yours to acknowledge the One God and to adopt monotheism and Islam. If you refuse, then there shall be a truce for the exchange of captives; but if you also decline this proposition, you will have such personal acquaintance with our qualities as shall render further eloquence on my part needless. He is safe who follows the right path".

If these letters represent the tenor of the communications which actually passed it is clear that Mamun, encouraged by the successes of the three past years, would no bring war to a close. He looked forward, perhaps, to the entire subjugation of the Empire. But his days were numbered. In the following summer he crossed the frontier, took some fortresses, and returned to Podandos, where he was stricken down by a fatal fever. He died on August 7, A.D. 833, and was buried at Tarsus.

§5. The Embassy of John the Grammarian and the Flight of Manuel

It was probably in the first months of his reign that the Emperor sent to the Caliph an embassy which made such an impression on popular imagination that it has assumed a more or less legendary character. The fact seems to be, so far as can be made out from the perplexing evidence, that John the Synkellos, commonly known as the Grammarian, a savant who, it may well be, was acquainted with Arabic, was sent to Baghdad, to announce the accession of Theophilus. He carried costly presents for the Caliph, and large sums of money for the purpose of impressing the Saracens by ostentatious liberality. The imagination of the Greeks dwelt complacently on the picture of an Imperial ambassador astonishing the Eastern world by his luxury and magnificence, and all kinds of anecdotes concerning John's doings at Baghdad were invented. It was said that he scattered gold like the sand of the sea, and bestowed rich gifts on anyone who on any pretext visited him in his hostel.

An additional interest was attached to the embassy of John the grammarian by the link, whether actual or fictitious, which connected it with the adventures of a famous general of the time, and this connection led Greek tradition to misdate the embassy to a later period in the reign. Manuel, who under Leo V had been strategos of the Armeniac Theme, was distinguished for his personal prowess, and under Michael II he had apparently again acted as strategos, perhaps of the same Theme. He was of Armenian descent, and the Empress Theodora was his brother's daughter. In the Saracen war his boldness and determination saved the Emperor's life. It was related that Theophilus, in a battle which he fought and lost (A.D. 830) against the forces of Mamun, was hard pressed and sought safety among the Persian troops who formed the intention of handing over his person to the enemy and making terms for themselves. Manuel, who knew their language, became aware of the contemplated treachery, rushed through their ranks, and seizing the bridle of Theophilus dragged him, angry and reluctant, from the danger which he did not suspect. The Emperor rewarded his saviour with such lavish marks of favour that the jealousy of Petronas, the brother of the Empress, was aroused. Theophilus was informed that Manuel was aspiring to the throne, and he believed the accusation, based perhaps on some unguarded words. Made aware of his danger, Manuel crossed over to Pylae, and making use of the Imperial post reached the Cilician frontier. He was joyfully welcomed by the Saracens, and the Caliph, who was wintering in Syria, gladly accepted the services of his enemy's ablest general. The countrymen of Manuel, who were vainer of his reputation for warlike prowess than they were indignant at his desertion to the Unbelievers, relate with complacency that he performed great services for the Caliph against the sectaries of Babek and the rebellious population of Khurasan.

But in the meantime it had been proved to the Emperor that the charges against his general were untrue, and he was desirous to procure the return of one whose military talent he could ill afford to lose. It is said that John the Grammarian undertook to obtain a secret interview with Manuel and convey to him the Emperor's assurance of pardon, safety, and honour, if he would return to Constantinople. The ambassador executed this delicate mission successfully; he carried an Imperial letter with the golden seal, and the cross which Theophilus wore on his breast; and Manuel, reassured by these pledges, promised, at the first opportunity, to return to his own country. He accompanied the Caliph's son to invade the Empire, and succeeded in escaping somewhere near the frontier. Theophilus immediately conferred on him the post of Domestic of the Schools, and raised him from the rank of a Patrician to that of a Magister.

The whole story has a basis in fact. There is no doubt that Manuel fled to the Saracens, and afterwards returned. And it is not improbable that John the Grammarian was instrumental in communicating to him the assurances which led to his return. But if we accept the story, as it is told by the Greek writers, we have to suppose that Manuel deserted from the Caliph in A.D. 830, and returned in A.D. 832, and therefore to date the embassy of John to the winter of A.D. 831-2. Such a conclusion involves us in several difficulties; and the most probable solution of the problem appears to be that Manuel fled from the Court not of Theophilus, but of his father, and returned to Constantinople in A.D. 830. Both John's embassy and Manuel's adventures interested popular imagination, and in the versions which have come down to us the details have been variously embroidered by mythopoeic fancy. Even the incident of the rescue of Theophilus by Manuel may be said to be open to some suspicion, inasmuch as a similar anecdote is recorded of a battle thirty years later, in which Michael III. plays the part of his father.

§6. The Campaigns of A.D. 837 and 838

During the first years of Mamun's brother and successor, Mutasim, there was a suspension of hostilities, for the forces of the new Caliph were needed to protect his throne against internal rebellions, and he was bent on finally quelling the still unconquered Babek. The desire of Theophilus for peace was manifest throughout the war with Mamun; it was probably due to the need of liberating all the strength of his resources for the task of driving the Saracens from Sicily. But at the end of four years he was induced to renew the war, and Babek again was the cause. Pressed hard, and seeing that his only chance of safety lay in diverting the Caliph's forces, the rebel leader opened communications with Theophilus and promised to become a Christian. The movement of Babek was so useful to the Empire, as a constant claim on the Caliph's forces, that it was obviously to the interest of Theophilus to make an effort to support it, when it seemed likely to be crushed. On grounds of policy, it must be admitted that he was justified in reopening hostilities in A.D. 837. In choosing the direction of his attack he was probably influenced by the hope of coming into touch with the insurgents of Armenia and Adarbiyan. He invaded the regions of the Upper Euphrates with a large army. He captured and burned the fortress of Zapetra, putting to death the male population and carrying off the women and children. He appeared before Melitene, threatening it with the fate of Zapetra if it did not surrender. The chief men of the place, however, induced him to spare it; they came forth, offered him gifts, and restored to liberty Roman prisoners who were in the town. He crossed the Euphrates, and besieged and burned Arsamosata. But of all his achievements, the conquest of Zapetra was regarded by both the Moslems and the Christians as the principal result of the campaign.

The expedition of Theophilus into western Armenia deserves particular notice, for, though the Greek writers betray no consciousness of this side of his policy, there is some evidence that the situation in the Armenian highlands and the Caucasian region constantly engaged his attention and that his endeavours to strengthen the Empire on its north-eastern frontier met with considerable success. In A.D. 830 he had sent an expedition under Theophobos and Bardas against Abasgia, which had proclaimed itself independent of the Empire, but this enterprise ended in failure. He was more fortunate elsewhere. We may surmise that it is to the campaign of A.D. 837 that an Armenian historian refers who narrates that Theophilus went to Pontic Chaldea, captured many Armenian prisoners, took tribute from Theodosiopolis, and conferred the proconsular patriciate on Ashot, its ruler. It was probably in connexion with this expedition that the Emperor separated eastern Pontus from the Armeniac province, and constituted it an independent Theme, under a strategos who resided at Trapezus. The Theme of Chaldia reached southward to the Euphrates, included Keltzene and part of Little Sophene, while to the north-east, on the Boas (Chorok-Su), it embraced the district of Sper. It is at least evident that the Imperial conquests of A.D. 837 in Little Armenia would have furnished a motive for the creation of a new military province.

The triumph with which Theophilus celebrated the devastation which he had wrought within the borders of his foe was a repetition of the pageants and ceremonial which had attended his return, six years before, from the achievement of similar though less destructive victories. Troops of children with garlands of flowers went out to meet the Emperor as he entered the capital. In the Hippodrome he competed himself in the first race, driving a white chariot and in the costume of a Blue charioteer; and when he was crowned as winner, the spectators greeted him with the allusive cry, "Welcome, incomparable champion!"

In the autumn of the same year, Babek was at last captured and executed, and the Caliph Mutasim was free to prepare a scheme of revenge for the destruction of Zapetra and the barbarities which had been committed. He resolved to deal a crushing blow which would appear as a special insult and injury to the present wearer of the Imperial crown. Amorion was the original home of the family of Theophilus, and he resolved that it should be blotted out from the number of inhabited cities. But apart from this consideration, which may have stimulated his purpose, the choice of Amorion was natural on account of its importance. The Saracens considered its capture the great step to an advance on Constantinople. In the seventh century they took it, but only for a moment; in the eighth they attempted it three times in vain. In the year of his death, Mamun is said to have intended to besiege it. An Arabic chronicler describes it as the eye of Christendom, and a Greek contemporary writer ranks it next to the capital.

Mutasim left his palace at Samarra in April (A.D. 838), and the banners of his immense army were inscribed with the name of Amorion. The Caliph was a warrior of indisputable bravery, but we know not whether it was he or his generals who designed the strategical plan of the invasion. The two most eminent generals who served in this campaign were Ashnas and Afshin. The former was a Turk, and his prominence is significant of the confidence which Mutasim reposed in his new corps of Turkish guards. Afshin had distinguished himself by suppressing rebellion in Egypt, and he had done much to terminate the war against Babek which had been so long drawn out.

The city of Ancyra was fixed upon as the first objective of the invasion. An army of the east, under the command of Afshin, advanced by way of Germanicia, and crossed the frontier by the Pass of Hadath on a day which was so fixed as to allow him time to meet the army of the west in the plains of Ancyra.

The purposes of the Caliph were not kept secret. The dispositions of the Emperor show that he was aware of the designs on Ancyra and Amorion. He left Constantinople probably in May; and from Dorylaion, the first great military station on the road to the Saracen frontier, he made provisions for the strengthening of the walls and the garrison of Amorion. The duty of defending the city naturally devolved upon Aetius, the strategos of the Anatolic Theme, for Amorion was his official residence. The plan of the Emperor was to attack the forces of the enemy on their northward march to Ancyra. Knowing nothing of the eastern army under Afshin, he crossed the Halys and encamped with his army not far from the river's bank in the extreme south of the Charsian district, probably near Zoropassos, where there was a bridge. He calculated that the enemy would march from the Cilician Gates to Ancyra by the most direct road, which from Soandos to Parnassos followed the course of the river, and he hoped to attack them on the flank. The Caliph's western army advanced northward from Tyana in two divisions, and Ashnas, who was in front, was already near the Halys before the Emperor's proximity was suspected. The Caliph ordered a halt till the position and movements of the Romans should be discovered. But in the meantime Theophilus had been informed of the advance of the eastern army, and the news disconcerted his plans. He was now obliged to divide his forces. Taking, probably, the greater portion with him, he marched himself to oppose Afshin, and left the rest, under the command of a kinsman, to check or harass the progress of the Caliph. Afshin had already passed Sebastea (Sivas), and was in the district of Dazimon, when he was forced to give battle to the Emperor. Dazimon, the modern Tokat, commands the great eastern road from Constantinople to Sebastea, at the point where another road runs northward to Neo-Caesarea. The town lies at the foot of a hill, at one extremity of which the ruins of the ancient fortress are still to be seen. Situated near the southern bank of the Iris, it marks the eastern end of a fertile plain stretching to Gaziura (now Turkhal), which in the ancient and middle ages was known as Dazimonitis; the Turks call it Kaz-Ova. It was probably in this plain that the Saracens encamped. The Emperor, who may have arrived on the scene by way of Zela and Gaziura, halted near Anzen, a high hill, from whose summit the position of the enemy could be seen. This hill has not been identified; we may perhaps guess, provisionally, that it will be discovered to the south of the plain of Dazimonitis. The fortune of the ensuing battle at first went well for the Greeks, who defeated the enemy, on one wing at least, with great loss; but a heavy shower of rain descended, and the sudden disappearance of the Emperor, who at the head of 2000 men had ridden round to reinforce the other wing of his army, gave rise, in the overhanging gloom, to the rumour that he was slain. The Romans, in consternation, turned and fled, and, when the sun emerged from the darkness, the Emperor with his band was surrounded by the troops of Afshin. They held the enemy at bay, until the Saracen general brought up siege-catapults to bombard them with stones; then they fought their way, desperately but successfully, through the hostile ring.

The Emperor, with his handful of followers, fled northwestward to Chiliokomon, "the plain of a thousand villages" (now Sulu-Ova), and then, returning to his camp on the Halys, found to his dismay that his kinsman had allowed, or been unable to forbid, many of the troops to disperse to their various stations. Having punished the commander for his weakness, and sent orders that the soldiers who had left the camp should be beaten with stripes, he dispatched a eunuch to Ancyra, to provide, if there were still time, for the defence of that city. But it was too late; for the western army of the invaders was already there. Ancyra ought to have offered resistance to a foe. Its fortifications were probably strengthened by Nicephorus I. But the inhabitants, thoroughly alarmed by the tidings of the victory of Afshin, deserted the city and fled into the mountains, where they were sought out by Ashnas and easily defeated. Thus the town fell without a blow into the hands of the destroyer. The Emperor, at this crisis, did not disdain to humble himself before the Caliph. He sent an embassy, imploring peace, and offering to rebuild the fortress of Zapetra, to release all the captives who were in his hands, and to surrender those men who had committed cruel outrages in the Zapetra campaign. The overtures were rejected, with contempt and taunts, by the Caliph, and Theophilus betook himself to Dorylaion to await the fate of Amorion, for the safety of which he believed that he had done all that could be done.

The army of the Saracens advanced westwards from Ancyra in three columns, Ashnas in front, the Caliph in the centre, and Afshin behind, at distances of two parasangs. Ravaging and burning as they went, they reached Amorion in seven days. The siege began on the first of August. The city was strong; its high wall was fortified by forty-four bastions and surrounded by a wide moat; its defence had been entrusted by Theophilus to Aetius, strategos of the Anatolic Theme; and reinforcements had been added to its garrison, under Constantine Babutzikos, who had married a sister of the Empress Theodora and was Drungary of the Watch, and the eunuch Theodore Krateros and others. But there was a weak spot in the fortification. Sometime before, the Emperor, riding round the city, had observed that in one place the wall was dilapidated, and had ordered the commander of the garrison to see that it was repaired. The officer delayed the execution of the command, until, hearing that Theophilus was marching from Constantinople to take the field against the Saracens, he hastily filled up the breach with stones and made the place, to outward view, indistinguishable from the rest of the wall. This specious spot, well known to the inhabitants, was revealed to the enemy by a traitor who is said to have been a Mohammadan captive converted to Christianity. The Caliph directed his engines against the place, and after a bombardment of two days the wall gave way and a breach was made. Aetius immediately dispatched a letter to the Emperor, communicating to him what had befallen, explaining the hopelessness of further defence, and announcing that he intended to leave the city at night and attempt to escape through the enemy's lines. The letter was entrusted to two messengers, one of whom spoke Arabic fluently. When they crossed the ditch, they fell into the hands of some Saracen soldiers, and pretended to be in the Caliph's service. But as they did not know the names of the generals or the regiments they were suspected as spies, and sent to the Caliph's tent, where they were searched and the letter was discovered.

The Caliph took every precaution to frustrate the intentions of escape which the intercepted letter disclosed. Troops of cavalry sat all night in full armour on their horses watching the gates. But it was easier to hinder escape than to take the city. The breadth of the ditch and the height of the walls rendered it difficult to operate effectively with siege-engines, and the usual devices of raising the ballistae on platforms and filling up the ditch were tried without success. But the breach in the wall was gradually widening, and the Greek officer to whom that section of the defence was entrusted despaired of being able to hold out. The Arabic historian, to whom we owe our information concerning the details of the siege, states-what seems almost incredible-that Aetius refused to furnish additional forces for the defence of the dangerous spot, on the ground that it was the business of each captain and of no one else to provide for the safety of his own allotted section. But he saw that there was little hope, and he sent an embassy to Mutasim, offering to capitulate on condition that the inhabitants should be allowed to depart in safety. The envoys were the bishop of Amorion and three officers, of whom one was the captain of the weak section of the walls. His name was Boiditzes. The Caliph required unconditional surrender, and the ambassadors returned to the city. But Boiditzes went back to Mutasim's tent by himself and offered to betray the breach. The interview was protracted, and in the meantime the Saracens gradually advanced towards the wall, till they were close to the breach. The defenders, in obedience to the strict orders of their officer to abstain from hostilities till his return, did not shoot or attempt to oppose them, but only made signs that they should come no farther. At this juncture, Mutasim and Boiditzes issued from the pavilion, and at the same moment, at a signal from one of Mutasim's officers, the Saracens rushed into Amorion. The Greek traitor, dismayed at this perfidious practice, clutching his beard, upbraided the Caliph for his breach of faith, but the Caliph reassured him that all he wished would be his.

A part of the unfortunate population sought refuge in a large church, in which after an obstinate resistance they perished by fire. The walls were razed to the ground and the place left desolate; and the Caliph, finding that the Emperor was not preparing to take the field, slowly returned to his own country, with thousands of captives. The fate of these Amorians was unhappy. The land was suffering from drought; the Saracens were unable to procure water, and some of the prisoners, exhausted by thirst, refused to go farther. These were at once dispatched by the sword; but as the army advanced, and the need grew more urgent, the Caliph gave orders that only the more distinguished captives should be retained; the rest were taken aside and slaughtered. The siege of Amorion had lasted for nearly two weeks. But for the culpable neglect of the officer responsible for the integrity of the walls and the treachery which revealed the weak spot to the besiegers, the city could probably have defied all the skill and audacity of the enemy. Its fall seems to have made a deep impression on both Moslems and Christians, and popular imagination was soon busy with the treachery which had brought about the catastrophe. The name of the culprit, Boiditzes, is derived from boidion, an ox; and, according to one story, he wrote a letter to the Saracens bidding them direct their attack close to the tower, where they saw a marble lion carved on the face and a stone ox above. The ox and the lion may have been there; but if the ox was a coincidence, the lion furnished a motive to myth. Boiditzes was said to be a pupil of Leo the Philosopher, and an Arabic writer calls him Leo.

A sequel of the siege of Amorion rendered it memorable in the annals of the Greek Church. Forty-two distinguished prisoners were carried off to Samarra and languished in captivity for seven years. The Caliph attempted in vain to persuade them to embrace Islam, and finally the choice was offered to them of conversion or death. According to the story, Boiditzes, who had betrayed Amorion, became a Mohammadan, and was sent at the last moment to represent to his countrymen the folly of resisting. But they stood steadfast in their faith, and on the 6th March 845 they were led to the banks of the Tigris and beheaded. Their bodies were thrown into the river, and miraculously floated on the top of the water. The renegade traitor Boiditzes shared their fate-at least in the legendary tale; for the Saracen magnates said to the Caliph: "It is not just that he should live, for if he was not true to his own faith, neither will he be true to ours". Accordingly he was beheaded, but his body sank to the bottom. This was the last great martyrdom that the Greek Church has to record. Before two years passed, it was fashioned by the pens of Greek hagiographers into the shape of an edifying legend. The deacon Ignatius, who wrote the life of the Patriarch Nicephorus, celebrated it in a canon, and the Forty-two Martyrs of Amorion, established as "stars in the holy firmament of the Church", inspired some of the latest efforts of declining Greek hymnography.

The fact that a number of distinguished captives, who had been carried from Amorion to the Tigris, were executed by Mutasim's successor admits of no doubt. But it would be rash to consider it merely an act of religious intolerance. We may rather suppose it to have been dictated by the motive of extorting large ransoms for prisoners of distinction. The Caliphs probably hoped to receive an immense sum for the release of the Amorian officers, and it was adroit policy to apply pressure by intimating that, unless they were ransomed, they could only purchase their lives by infidelity to their religion. The Emperor, immediately after the catastrophe, had indeed made an attempt to redeem the prisoners. He sent Basil, the governor of the Charsian frontier district, bearing gifts and an apologetic letter to the Caliph, in which the Emperor regretted the destruction of Zapetra, demanded the surrender of Aetius, and offered to liberate his Saracen captives. He also gave Basil a second letter of menacing tenor, to be delivered in case the terms were rejected. Mutasim, when he had read the first, demanded the surrender of Manuel the patrician, whose desertion he had not forgiven, and Nasr the apostate. The envoy replied that this was impossible, and presented the second missive. Mutasim angrily flung back the gifts.

§7. The Warfare of the years 839-867

The disastrous events of the invasion of Mutasim, along with the steady advance of the African Moslems in the island of Sicily, not to speak of the constant injuries which the Arabs of Crete inflicted on the Empire, convinced Theophilus that the Empire was unable to cope alone with the growing power of Islam in the Mediterranean, and he decided to seek the alliance and co-operation of other powers. He sent an embassy, which included a bishop and a patrician, to the Western Emperor, Lewis the Pious, asking him to send a powerful armament, perhaps to attack Syria or Egypt, in order to divert or divide the forces of the Caliph. The envoys were welcomed and honourably entertained at Ingelheim (June 17, 839), but the embassy led to no result. Equally fruitless was the attempt to induce the ruler of Spain, Abd ar-Rahman II, to cooperate with the Empire against his rival the Eastern Caliph. Spain was in such a disturbed state at this time that it was impossible for him to undertake a distant expedition beyond the seas. His good-will was unreserved, and in reply to the Imperial Embassy he sent to Constantinople his friend the poet Yahya al-Ghazzal with promises to dispatch a fleet as soon as internal troubles permitted him. But those troubles continued, and the fleet never sailed.

Meanwhile the fall of Amorion had led to no new permanent encroachment on Roman territory. The Emir of Syria raided the Empire more than once with little success, and in A.D. 841 the Imperial forces took Adata and Marash, and occupied part of the territory of Melitene. It was perhaps in the previous year that a Roman fleet appeared off the coast of Syria and pillaged the port of Antioch. These successes inclined Mutasim to be gracious, when Theophilus again proposed an exchange of captives, and he displayed insolent generosity. "We", he said, "cannot compare the values of Moslems and Christians, for God esteems those more than these. But if you restore me the Saracens without asking for anything in return, we can give you twice as many Romans and thus surpass you in everything". Aetius and his fellows were not included in the exchange, but a truce was concluded (A.D. 841).

It was only a truce, for Mutasim cherished the illusory hope of subjugating the Empire. He revived the ambitious designs of the Omayyad Caliphs, and resolved to attack Constantinople. The naval establishment had been suffered to decay under the Abbasids, and, as a powerful fleet was indispensable for any enterprise against the city of the Bosphorus, some years were required for preparation. The armament was not ready to sail till the year 842, when 400 dromonds sailed from the ports of Syria. Mutasim, who died in the same month as Theophilus, did not live to witness the disaster which befell his fleet. It was wrecked on the dangerous Chelidonian islets off the south-eastern cape of the coast; only seven vessels escaped destruction.

Mutasim's unpopular successor, Wathik, was throughout his short reign (842-847) so embarrassed by domestic troubles-religious strife, risings in Damascus and Arabia, discontent in Baghdad-that he was unable to prosecute the Holy War. The two powers exchanged their prisoners, and, though no regular peace was made, they desisted from hostilities for several years.

The exchange of prisoners from time to time was such a characteristic feature of the warfare between the Empire and the Caliphate, that the formal procedure by which such exchanges were conducted is not without interest. A full account has been preserved of the redemption of captives in the year 845. In response to an embassy which the Roman government sent to Baghdad, a plenipotentiary arrived at Constantinople in order to obtain exact information as to the number of the Mohammadans who were detained in captivity. They were estimated as 3000 men, and 500 women and children; according to another account, they were 4362 in all. The Greek prisoners in the Saracen prisons were found to be less numerous, and in order to equalise the numbers, the Caliph bought up Greek slaves in Baghdad, and even added some females who were employed in the service of his palace. The place usually chosen for the interchange of prisoners of war was on the banks of the river Lamos, about a day's march from Tarsus and close to Seleucia. Here the Greeks and the Saracens met on September 16. The two Greek officers who were entrusted with the negotiation were alarmed to see that the other party was attended by a force of 4000 soldiers. They refused to begin business till the Saracens consented to an armistice of forty days, an interval which would permit the redeemed prisoners to return to their homes without the risk of being recaptured. There were preliminary disputes as to the method of exchange. The Romans declined to accept children or aged persons for able-bodied men, and some days were wasted before it was agreed to purchase man with man. The bridges were thrown across the river, and at the same moment at which a Christian passed over one, a Mohammadan traversed the other in the opposite direction. But the unfortunate Mohammadans were subjected to a religious test. The Caliph had appointed a commission to examine the theological opinions of the captives. Himself an adherent, like Mamun and Mutasim, of the pseudo-rationalistic school which denied the eternity of the Koran and the visible epiphany of Allah in a future life, he commanded that only those should be redeemed who denounced or renounced these doctrines. Many refused to sacrifice their convictions, and the application of the test was probably not very strict. The exchange was carried out in four days, and more than 4000 Saracens were redeemed, including women and children, as well as Zimmi, that is, Christian or Jewish subjects of the Caliph.

Between the religious bigotry of rulers of Islam like Wathik and Mutawakkil and that of Christian sovrans like Theophilus and Theodora there was little to choose. For the persecution of the Paulicians, which must be regarded as one of the greatest political disasters of the ninth century, Theophilus as well as Theodora was responsible, though the crime, or rather the glory, is commonly ascribed entirely to her. This sect, widely diffused throughout Asia Minor, from Phrygia and Lycaonia to Armenia, had lived in peace under the wise and sympathetic iconoclasts of the eighth century. They have been described as "the left wing of the iconoclasts"; their doctrines-they rejected images, pictures, crosses, as idolatrous-had undoubtedly a great influence on the generation of the iconoclastic movement; it has even been supposed that Constantine V was at heart a Paulician. We saw how they had been favoured by Nicephorus, and how Michael I was stirred up by the ecclesiastics to institute a persecution. Michael committed the execution of his decree in Phrygia and Lycaonia to Leo the Armenian, as strategos of the Anatolic Theme; while the suppression of the heresy in Cappadocia and Pontus was enjoined on two ecclesiastics, the exarch or visitor of the Patriarchal monasteries in those parts, and the bishop of Neo-Caesarea. The evidence leaves us in doubt whether Leo, when he came to the throne, pursued the policy of which he had been the instrument. Did the reviver of iconoclasm so far desert the principles of his exemplar, Constantine V, as to pursue the Paulicians? It is not incredible that he may have adopted this course, if it were only to dissociate himself from a sect which the Church maliciously or ignorantly branded as Manichaean; for it is certain that the Paulicians were persecuted by Theophilus. It was either in the reign of Theophilus or during the earlier persecution that Karbeas, a Paulician who held an office under the general of the Anatolic Theme, led 5000 men of his faith to the region beyond Cappadocia, and placed himself under the protection of the Emir of Melitene. He is said to have been moved to this flight by the news that his father had been hanged. It is probable that there were already Paulicians in the districts north and west of Melitene; new fugitives continually arrived; and in their three principal cities, Argaus, Tephrike, and Amara, these martial heretics proved a formidable enemy to the State of which their hardy valour had hitherto been a valuable defence.

Seeing that even iconoclasts sought to suppress a religion with which they had important points in common, the Paulicians could expect little mercy after the triumph of image-worship. It was a foregone conclusion that Theodora, under the influence of orthodox ecclesiastical advisers, would pursue her husband's policy with more insistent zeal, and endeavour to extirpate the "Manichaean" abomination. A fiat went forth that the Paulicians should abandon their errors or be abolished from the earth which they defiled. An expedition was sent under several commanders to carry out this decree, and a wholesale massacre was enacted. Victims were slain by the sword, crucified, and drowned in thousands; those who escaped sought shelter across the frontier. The property of the Paulicians was appropriated by the State—a poor compensation for the loss of such a firm bulwark as the persecuted communities had approved themselves.

It is just after the fall of the Empress Theodora from power that we find the Paulicians effectively cooperating with the enemies of the Empire. Her brother Petronas, who was then strategos of the Thrakesian Theme, was entrusted with the supreme command of the army, and in the late summer (A.D. 856), having made successful raids into the districts of Samosata and Amida, he proceeded against Tephrike, the headquarters of Karbeas, who had been actively helping the Emir of Melitene and the governor of Tarsus to waste the Roman borders. In this year begins a short period of incessant hostility, marked on one hand by the constant incursions of the commanders of Melitene and Tarsus, in cooperation with Karbeas, and on the other by the appearance in the field of the Emperor Michael himself, as well as his uncles Bardas and Petronas. The first expedition of Michael, who had now reached the age of twenty years, was directed against Samosata, under the guidance of Bardas. His army was at first successful, and the town was besieged. But the garrison made a sudden sally on a Sunday, choosing the hour at which the Emperor was engaged in the ceremonies of his religion. He escaped with difficulty, and the whole camp fell into the hands of the Saracens (A.D. 859). It was said that Karbeas performed prodigies of valour and captured a large number of Greek officers.

In the ensuing winter negotiations were opened for the exchange of captives, and the Saracen envoy, Nasr, came to Constantinople. He wrote an interesting account of his mission. As soon as he arrived, he presented himself at the Palace, in a black dress and wearing a turban and a sword. Petronas (but it is not improbable that Bardas is meant) informed him that he could not appear in the Emperor's presence with a sword or dressed in black. "Then", said Nasr, "I will go away". But before he had gone far he was recalled, and as soon as the Emperor, who was then receiving a Bulgarian embassy, was disengaged, he was admitted to the hall of audience. Michael sat on a throne which was raised on another throne, and his patricians were standing around him. When Nasr had paid his respects, he took his place on a large chair which had been set for him, and the gifts which he had brought from the Caliph-silk robes, about a thousand bottles of musk, saffron, and jewels-were presented. Three interpreters came forward, and Nasr charged them to add nothing to what he said. The Emperor accepted the gifts, and Nasr noticed that he did not bestow any of them on the interpreters. Then he desired that the envoy should approach, graciously caressed him, and gave orders that a lodging should be found for him in or near the Palace. But the business on which Nasr had come did not progress rapidly. He mentions that a message arrived from the garrison of Lulon, which consisted of Mohammadan Slavs, signifying their desire to embrace Christianity and sending two hostages. It will be remembered that this important fortress had been captured by Mamun in A.D. 832, and the opportunity for recovering it was welcome. For four months Nasr was detained at Constantinople. Then new tidings arrived from Lulon, which prompted Michael to settle the question of the captives without delay. He had sent a patrician, who promised the garrison a handsome largess; but they repented of their treachery, and handed over both the place and the patrician to a Saracen captain. The patrician was carried into captivity and threatened with death if he did not renounce his religion. It would seem that the Emperor was seriously concerned for his fate, for, as soon as the news came, the exchange of captives was promptly arranged with Nasr. It was agreed that both sides should surrender all the prisoners who were in their hands. Nasr and Michael's uncle confirmed the agreement by oath in the Imperial presence. Then Nasr said: "O Emperor, your uncle has sworn. Is the oath binding for you?". He inclined his head in token of assent. And, adds the envoy, "I did not hear a single word from his lips from the time of my arrival till my departure. The interpreter alone spoke, and the Emperor listened and expressed his assent or dissent by motions of his head. His uncle managed all his affairs". The Emperor received 1000 Greek captives in return for 2000 subjects of the Caliph, but the balance was redressed by the release of the patrician whom he was so anxious to recover.

Not many weeks later, committing the charge and defence of his capital to Ooryphas, the Prefect, Michael again set forth to invade the Caliph's dominions. But even, as it would seem, before he reached the frontier, he was recalled (in June) by the alarming news that the Russians had attacked Constantinople. When the danger had passed, he started again for the East, to encounter Omar, the Emir of Melitene, who had in the meantime taken the field. Michael marched along the great high-road which leads to the Upper Euphrates by Ancyra and Sebastea. Having passed Gaziura, he encamped in the plain of Dazimon, where Afshin had inflicted on his father an overwhelming defeat. Here he awaited the approach of the Emir, who was near at hand, advancing, as we may with certainty assume, from Sebastea.

An enemy marching by this road, against Amasea, had the choice of two ways. He might proceed northward to Dazimon and then westward by Gaziura; or he might turn westward at Verisa (Bolous) and reach Amasea by Sebastopolis (Sulu-serai) and Zela. On this occasion the first route was barred by the Roman army, which lay near the strong fortress of Dazimon, and could not be advantageously attacked on this side. It would have been possible for Omar, following the second route, to have reached Gaziura from Zela, and entered the plain of Dazimon from the west. But he preferred a bolder course, which surprised the Greeks, who acknowledged his strategic ability. Leaving the Zela road, a little to the west of Verisa, he led his forces northward across the hills (Ak-Dagh), and descending into the Dazimon plain occupied a favourable position at Chonarion, not far from the Greek camp. The battle which ensued resulted in a rout of the Imperial army, and Michael sought a refuge on the summit of the same steep hill of Anzeu which marked the scene of his father's defeat. Here he was besieged for some hours, but want of water and pasture induced the Emir to withdraw his forces.

It is possible that the victorious general followed up his success by advancing as far as Sinope. But three years later, Omar revisited the same regions, devastated the Armeniac Theme, and reached the coast of the Euxine (A.D. 863). His plan seems to have been to march right across the centre of Asia Minor and return to Saracen territory by the Pass of the Cilician Gates. He took and sacked the city of Amisus (Samsun), and the impression which the unaccustomed appearance of an enemy on that coast made upon the inhabitants was reflected in the resuscitation of an ancient legend. Omar, furious that the sea set a bound to his northern advance, was said, like Xerxes, to have scourged the waves. The Emperor appointed his uncle Petronas, who was still strategos of the Thrakesian Theme, to the supreme command of the army; and not only all the troops of Asia, but the armies of Thrace and Macedonia, and the Tagmatic regiments, were placed at his disposal. When Omar heard at Amisus of the preparations which were afoot, he was advised by his officers to retire by the way he had come. But he determined to carry out his original plan, and setting out from Amisus in August, he chose a route which would lead him by the west bank of the Halys to Tyana and Podandos. The object of Petronas was now to intercept him. Though the obscure localities named in the chronicles have not been identified, the general data suggest the conclusion that it was between Lake Tatta and the Halys that he decided to surround the foe. The troops of the Armeniac, Bukellarian, Paphlagonian, and Kolonean Themes converged upon the north, after Omar had passed Ancyra. The Anatolic, Opsikian, and Cappadocian armies, reinforced by the troops of Seleucia and Charsianon, gathered on the south and south-east; while Petronas himself, with the Tagmata, the Thracians, and Macedonians, as well as his own Thrakesians, appeared on the west of the enemy's line of march. A hill separated Petronas from the Saracen camp, and he was successful in a struggle to occupy the height. Omar was caught in a trap. Finding it impossible to escape to the north or to the south, he attacked Petronas, who held his ground. Then the generals of the northern and southern armies closed in, and the Saracen forces were almost annihilated. Omar himself fell. His son escaped across the Halys, but was caught by the turmarch of Charsianon. The victory of Poson (such was the name of the place), and the death of one of the ablest Moslem generals were a compensation for the defeat of Chonarion. Petronas was rewarded by receiving the high post of the Domestic of the Schools, and the order of magister. Strains of triumph at a victory so signal resounded in the Hippodrome, and a special chant celebrated the death of the Emir on the field of battle, a rare occurrence in the annals of the warfare with the Moslems.

It would appear that this success was immediately followed up by an invasion of Northern Mesopotamia. We know not whether the Greek army was led by Petronas, but another victory was won, somewhere in the neighbourhood of Martyropolis, and this battlefield was likewise marked by the fall of a Saracen commander who, year after year, had raided Roman territory-Ali ibn Yahya.

These victories are the last events worthy of record in the Eastern war during the reign of Michael III. While the young Emperor was sole Augustus, and Bardas was the virtual ruler, the defence of the Empire in the east was steadily maintained. Michael had himself marched to the front, and the Saracens had won no important successes while his uncle was at the helm. It was probably after the death of Bardas that an incident occurred which has stamped Michael as supremely indifferent to the safety of his Empire. One evening as he was preparing in his private hippodrome in the Palace of St. Mamas to display his skill as a charioteer, before a favoured company, the spectators were alarmed and distracted by seeing a blaze illuminated in the Pharos of the Great Palace, which announced tidings flashed from Cappadocia, that the Saracens were abroad within the Roman borders. The spectacle was not discontinued, but the attention of the onlookers languished, and the Emperor, determined that such interruptions should not again occur, commanded that the beacon signals in the neighborhood of Constantinople should be kindled no more. It might be thought that the signal system had been abandoned for some serious reason, connected perhaps with the loss of Lulon, and that this anecdote, illustrating the Emperor's frivolity, had been invented to account for it. But the very moderation of the story may be held to show that it had a basis of fact. For it does not suggest that the beacon messages were discontinued; on the contrary, it expressly states that the lighting of the beacons in or close to Constantinople, that is at the Pharos and on Mt. Auxentios, was forbidden. This Imperial order, though dictated by a frivolous motive, need not have caused a very serious delay in the arrival of the news at Constantinople, nor can it be alleged that Michael endangered thereby the safety of the provinces.

On the whole, the frontiers between the two powers in Asia Minor had changed little under the rule of the Amorian dynasty. The Moslems had won a few more fortresses; and what was more serious, in Cappadocia east of the Halys their position was strengthened by the invaluable support of the Paulician rebels. The Amorians bequeathed to their successor the same task which had lain before them and which they had failed to achieve, the expulsion of the enemy from Cappadocia; but the difficulty of that task was aggravated by the disastrous policy of the Paulician persecution for which Theophilus and Theodora were responsible.

In the last years of the reign of Michael the Caliphate was troubled by domestic anarchy, and offered a good mark for the attack of a strenuous foe. The Caliph Mustain writhed under the yoke of the powerful Turkish party, and he desired to return from Samarra to the old capital of Baghdad. But he was compelled to abdicate in favour of Mutazz, whom the Turks set up against him (January 866). The best days of the Abbasid dynasty were past, and the Caliphate had begun to decline, just as the Empire was about to enter on a new period of power and expansion.

Chapter IX
The Saracen Conquest of Crete and Sicily

§1. The Saracen Conquest of Crete

Since the remote ages which we associate with the uncertain name of Minos, when it was the home of a brilliant civilization and the seat of an Aegean power, the island of Crete played but a small part in Greek and Roman history. In the scheme of administration which was systematized in the eighth century, it formed, along with some neighbouring islands, a distinct theme; but its name rarely occurs in our chronicles until its happy obscurity is suddenly disturbed in the reign of Michael II by an event which rendered it, for long years to come, one of the principal embarrassments and concerns of the Imperial Government. The fate of Crete was determined by events in a distant Western land, whose revolutions, it might have seemed, concerned the Cretans as little as those of any country in the world.

The Omayyads in Spain no less than the Abbasids in the East, Cordova no less than Baghdad, were troubled by outbreaks of discontent and insurrection, in which the rationalistic school of theology also played its part. The Emir Al-Hakam dyed his hands in the blood of insurgents, and finally when the inhabitants of one of the quarters of Cordova rose against him, he commanded those who escaped the edge of his sword to leave Spain with their families in three days (A.D. 814). Ten thousand men, as well as women and children, sailed to Egypt, and, placing themselves under the protection of a powerful Beduin family, settled in the outskirts of Alexandria. Soon they felt strong enough to act for themselves, and under the leadership of Abu Hafs they seized the city (A.D. 818-819).

At this time the governor of Egypt had availed himself of the revolts with which the Caliph Mamun had to cope in the eastern provinces of his dominion to declare himself independent. The Spanish fugitives held Alexandria for six years before Mamun had his hands free to deal with Egypt. At length (A.D. 825) he sent Abdallah ibn Tahir to compel the submission both of the rebellious governor and of the Andalusian intruders. The governor was overthrown by one of his officers before Abdallah arrived, and the Spaniards readily submitted to the representative of the Caliph and obtained permission to leave Egypt and win a settlement within the borders of the Empire. In the previous year they had made a descent on the island of Crete, and their ships had returned laden with captives and booty; and they now chose Crete as their place of permanent habitation. They sailed in forty ships, with Abu Hafs as their leader, and anchored probably in the best harbour of the island, in the bay of Suda. Abu Hafs commanded his followers to plunder the island and return to the port in twelve days, retaining twenty men to guard each ship. It would appear that no serious resistance was offered by the islanders, who perhaps had little love for the Imperial government, which, besides being oppressive, had in recent years been heretical. It is related that when the Spaniards returned to the port, they were dismayed to find that their ships had disappeared. They had been burned by the orders of Abu Hafs. To their loud and mutinous complaints that they were now irrevocably severed from their wives and children whom they had left in Egypt, he replied by bidding them marry the women of the island whom they had taken captive. We may question the truth of the story, but it seems to point to the fact that there was a considerable fusion by marriage between the invaders and the natives.

The modern capital of Crete was founded by Abu Hafs. He chose, to be the seat of his dominion, a site on the northern shore of the island, not far from the hill of Knossos, the ancient stronghold of Minos. The new town was central; it looked towards the isles of the Aegean which the conquerors of Crete hoped to plunder; but it had the disadvantage of having no harbour or natural shelter for ships. It was surrounded by a deep moat (handak), from which it derived its name Chandax or Candia. Twenty-nine towns were taken and their inhabitants reduced to slavery. One alone was excepted from this general fate by a special capitulation, and in it the Christians were permitted freely to celebrate the rites of their religion.

The Emperor Michael and his successors did not underestimate the danger with which Crete in the possession of the Moslems menaced the Empire. Michael appointed Photeinos, the governor of the Anatolic Theme, to be strategos of Crete, and not many months after the Saracen occupation this general arrived at the island. But he found that his forces were unequal to his task, and at his request Damianos, Count of the Stable, was sent with reinforcements. The Saracens routed the Greek army, Damianos was wounded, and Photeinos escaped to the little island of Dios which faces Candia. A second expedition was sent soon afterwards, under Krateros, in command of a fleet of seventy ships. A battle was fought where the troops landed, and the Greeks were victorious, but instead of following up their success they celebrated it by a night of carousal, and in their sleep they were attacked and almost annihilated by the enemy. Krateros escaped and was pursued by the Arabs to Cos, where they caught him and hanged him on a cross.

It was not only for the recovery of Crete, but also for the protection of the islands of the Aegean that the Imperial government was concerned. A third armament which Michael despatched under the command of Ooryphas cleared the enemy out of a number of small islands which they had occupied, but it is not recorded that he renewed the attempt to recover Crete. The Arabs did not confine their attacks to the islands in the immediate vicinity of Crete; they extended far and wide, on both sides of the Aegean, depredations of which only stray notices have been preserved by chance. We know that Aegina was cruelly and repeatedly devastated; we know that, some two generations later, Paros was a waste country, which attracted only the hunter of the wildgoat. Just after the death of the Emperor Michael, an expedition from Crete pillaged the coasts of Caria and Ionia, and despoiled the monastery of Mt. Latros. Constantine Kontomytes, the strategos of the Thrakesian Deme, surrounded the depredators with a superior force and cut them to pieces. But about the same time a Roman fleet was completely destroyed in a battle at Thasos, and the Cretans for some years seem to have worked their will unhindered in the Aegean Sea. Their attacks on Mt. Athos compelled the monks to abandon their cells.

If the story is true that the original fleet of the Cretan Arabs was burnt, it is clear that they had, however, speedily furnished themselves with a considerable naval establishment. At the same time, Sicily was in great danger. The Moslems of Spain had hardly conquered Crete before the Moslems of Africa descended upon the western island and set themselves to accomplish a conquest which would give them a unique position for winning the maritime lordship of the Mediterranean. To rescue Sicily, to recover Crete, and to defend the islands and coast which were exposed to the depredations of a piratical enemy to the very precincts of the capital itself, a far stronger naval equipment was necessary than that which the Empire possessed. The navy which had saved Asia Minor and the Aegean under the successors of Heraclius from the Saracens in the first tide of their conquests, had been allowed to decline, and the Amorian Emperors reaped the fruits of this neglect. The naval question suddenly became the most pressing interest of Imperial policy; and, as we have seen, the revival of the navy was begun by the efforts of the Amorian dynasty. No further attempt, however, to recover Crete seems to have been made in the reign of Theophilus, who may have thought, perhaps justly, that it would be better to employ all his available strength upon curbing the advance of the Arabs in the island of Sicily. But after his death, Theoktistos organized a great Cretan expedition which sailed in March (A.D. 843) under his own command. It seems to have been far more powerful than those which had been despatched by Michael II., and when it appeared the Saracens were in consternation. But they found a means of playing upon the general's fears for his own influence at the court of Theodora. They bribed some of his officers to spread the rumour, or to insinuate to Theoktistos, that the Empress had raised one of his rivals to be the colleague of herself and her son. The general, deeply alarmed, hastened to Constantinople, leaving his army to do nothing, if not to meet with disaster.

Abu Hafs and his successors were virtually independent, but they may have found it expedient to acknowledge the overlordship of the Caliph, and to consider Crete as in some sense affiliated to the province of Egypt. In any case they continued to maintain relations with Egypt and to receive supplies from Alexandria. It was probably in view of this connexion that the government of Theodora decided on an expedition beyond the usual range of the warfare of this period. Three fleets, numbering in all nearly three hundred ships, were equipped. The destination of two of these armaments is unknown; perhaps they were to operate in the Aegean or off the coast of Syria. But the third, consisting of eighty-five vessels and carrying 5000 men, under an admiral whose true name is concealed under Ibn Katuna, the corruption of an Arabic chronicler, sailed to the coast of Egypt and appeared before Damietta (May 22, A.D. 853).

In the ninth century Damietta was closer to the sea than the later town which the Sultan Bibars founded in the thirteenth. The city lies on the eastern channel of the Nile about seven miles from the mouth; and less than a mile to the east is Lake Menzale, which a narrow belt of sand severs from the sea. When the Greek fleet arrived, the garrison was absent at Fustat, attending a feast to which it had been summoned by the governor Anbas, the last ruler of Arabic descent. The inhabitants hastily deserted the undefended city, which the Greeks plundered and burned. They captured six hundred Arab and Coptic women, and discovered a store of arms which was destined for the ruler of Crete. The spoiling of Damietta detained them only two days, and they sailed eastward to the island of Tinnis; but fearing sandbanks, they did not pass farther, and proceeded to the fortress of Ushtum, a strongly walled place with iron gates. Burning the war-engines which he found there, Ibn Katuna returned home from an expedition which fortune had singularly favoured.

If the conquests of Crete and Sicily taught the Romans the necessity of a strong navy, the burning of Damietta was a lesson which was not lost upon the Saracens of Egypt. An Arabic writer observes that from this time they began to show serious concern for the fleet, and this became an affair of the first importance in Egypt. Warships were built, and the pay of marines was equalized with that of soldiers who served on land. Only intelligent and experienced men were admitted to the service. Thus, as has been remarked, the Greek descent on Damietta led to the establishment of the Egyptian navy, which, a century later, was so powerful under the dynasty of the Fatimids.

In the later years of Michael III the Cretan Arabs pursued their quests of plunder and destruction in the Aegean. We learn that Lesbos was laid waste, and that monks were carried away from their cells in the hills of Athos. The last military effort of Michael and Bardas was to organize a great Cretan expedition, which was to sail from the shores of the Thrakesian Theme, a central gathering-place for the various provincial fleets, and for those regiments of the Asiatic themes which were to take part in the campaign. We saw how this enterprise was frustrated by the enemies of the Caesar. Another generation was to pass before the attempt to recover Crete and secure tranquillity for the Aegean was renewed.

§2. The Invasion of Sicily

In the two great westward expansions of the Semite, in the two struggles between European and Semitic powers for the waters, islands, and coasts of the Mediterranean, Sicily played a conspicuous part, which was determined by her geographical position. The ancient history of the island, when Greeks and Phoenicians contended for the mastery, seems to be repeated when, after a long age of peace under the mighty rule of Rome, it was the scene of a new armed debate between Greeks and Arabs. In both cases, the Asiatic strangers were ultimately driven out, not by their Greek rivals, but by another people descending from Italy. The Normans were to expel the Saracens, as the Romans had expelled the Phoenicians. The great difference was that the worshippers of Baal and Moloch had never won the whole island, while the sway of the servants of Allah was to be complete, extending from Panormos to Syracuse, from Messina to Lilybaeum

A fruitful land and a desirable possession in itself, Sicily's central position between the two basins of the Mediterranean rendered it an object of supreme importance to any Eastern sea-power which was commercially or politically aggressive; while for an ambitious ruler in Africa it was the stepping-stone to Italy and the gates of the Hadriatic. As soon as the Saracens created a navy in the ports of Syria and Egypt, it was inevitable that Sicily should be exposed to their attacks, and the date of their first descent is only twenty years after the death of Mohammad. But no serious attempt to win a permanent footing in the island was made till a century later. The expeditions from Syria and Egypt were raids for spoil and captives, not for conquest. The establishment of the Saracen power in Africa and in Spain changed the situation, and history might have taught the Roman Emperors that a mortal struggle in Sicily could not be avoided. It was, however, postponed. The island had to sustain several attacks during the first half of the eighth century, but they came to little; and the design of Abd ar-Rahman, governor of Africa, who (A.D. 752) made great preparations to conquer both Sicily and Sardinia, was frustrated by the outbreak of domestic troubles. There was no further danger for many years, and in the reign of Nicephorus there might have seemed to be little cause for alarm concerning the safety of the Sicilian Theme. Ibrahim, the first ruler of the Aghlabid dynasty, concluded (A.D. 805) a ten years' peace with Constantine the governor of Sicily. Just after this, Tunis and Tripoli cast off their allegiance to Ibrahim and formed a separate state under the Idrisids. This division of Africa between Idrisids and Aghlabids must have been a welcome event to the Imperial government; it afforded a probable presumption that it would be less easy in the future to concentrate the forces of the African Moslems against the tempting island which faced them. In the meantime, commerce was freely carried on between the island and the continent; and in A.D. 813 Abul-Abbas, the son and successor of Ibrahim, made a treaty with Gregory, the governor of Sicily, by which peace was secured for ten years and provision was made for the safety of merchants.

It was after the expiration of this ten years' peace that the temptation to conquer Sicily was pressed upon the African ruler by an invitation from Sicily itself. The distance of the island from Constantinople had once and again seduced ambitious subjects into the paths of rebellion. The governor, Sergius, had set up an Emperor in the reign of Leo III., and more recently, under Irene, Elpidios had incurred the suspicion of disloyalty and had fled to Africa, where the Saracens welcome him as Roman Emperor and placed a crownon his head. He does not appear to have had a following in the island; nor is there evidence that the inhabitants were actively discontented at this period against the government of Constantinople. The rebellion of Thomas the Slavonian may have awakened hopes in the breasts of some to detach Sicily from the Empire, but there is nothing to show that there was any widespread disaffection when, in the year A.D. 826, an insurrection was organized which was destined to lead to calamitous consequences.

A certain Euphemios was the leader of this movement. Having distinguished himself by bravery, probably in maritime warfare, he was appointed to an important command, when an incident in his private life furnished an excuse for his disgrace, and this, a reason for his rebellion. Smitten with passion for a maiden who had taken the vows of a nun, he persuaded or compelled her to marry him; and the indignant brothers of Homoniza repaired to Constantinople and preferred a complaint to the Emperor. Although the example of Michael's own marriage with Euphrosyne might have been pleaded in favour of Euphemios, Michael despatched a letter to the new strategos of Sicily, Photeinos, bidding him to investigate the case and, if the charge were found to be true, to cut off the nose of the culprit who had caused a nun to renounce her vow.

Photeinos, whom we have already met as the leader of a disastrous expedition to Crete, had only recently arrived in Sicily (perhaps in the spring of A.D. 826). He had already appointed Euphemios commander of the fleet, with the official title of turmarch, and Euphemios had sailed on a plundering expedition to the coasts of Tripoli or Tunis. He returned laden with spoil, but to find that an order had gone out for his arrest. He decided to defy the authority of the strategos, and, sailing to the harbour of Syracuse, he occupied that city. His fleet was devoted to him, and he gained etfter adherents to his cause, including some military commanders who were turmarchs like himself. Photeinos marched to drive the rebel from Syracuse, but he suffered a defeat and returned to Catana. The superior forces of Euphemios and his confederates compelled him to leave that refuge, and he was captured and put to death.

Compromised irretrievably by this flagrant act of rebellion, Euphemios, even if he had been reluctant, had no alternative but to assume the Imperial title and power. He was proclaimed Emperor, but he was almost immediately deserted by one of his most powerful supporters. This man, whom he invested with the government of a district, is designated by the Arabic historians as Palata —a corrupt name which may denote some palatine dignity at the Court of the usurper. Palata and his cousin Michael, who was the military commander of Panormos, repudiated the cause of Euphemios and declared for the legitimate Emperor. At the head of a large army they defeated the tyrant and gained possession of Syracuse.

Too weak to resist the forces which were arrayed in support of legitimacy, and knowing that submission would mean death, Euphemios determined to invoke the aid of the natural enemy of the Empire. His resolve brought upon Sicily the same consequences which the resolve of Count Julian had brought upon Spain. It may be considered that it was the inevitable fate of Spain and of Sicily to fall a prey to Saracen invaders from Africa, but it is certain that the fate of each was accelerated by the passion and interests of a single unscrupulous native.

Euphemios crossed over to Africa and made overtures to Ziadat Allah, the Aghlabid Emir. He asked him to send an army over to Sicily, and undertook to pay a tribute when his own power was established in the island. The proposal was debated in Council at Kairawan. The members of the Council were not of one mind. Those who were opposed to granting the request of Euphemios urged the duty of observing the treaty which the Greeks, so far as was ascertained, had not violated. But the influence of the Cadi Asad, who appealed to texts of the Koran, of which he was acknowledged to be an authoritative interpreter, stirred the religious fanaticism of his hearers and decided them in favour of war. Ziadat named Asad to the command of the expedition, and he was allowed to retain the office of Cadi, although the union of military and judicial functions was irregular.

The fleet of Euphemios waited in the bay of Susa till the African armament was ready, and on the 14th day of June, A.D. 827, the allied squadrons sailed forth together, on an enterprise which was to prove the beginning of a new epoch in Sicilian history. The forces of the Moslems are said to have consisted of ten thousand foot soldiers, seven hundred cavalry, and seventy or a hundred ships. In three days they reached Mazara, where they were expected by the partisans of Euphemios. When Asad disembarked his forces, he remained inactive for some days. A skirmish between some Greek soldiers who were on the side of Euphemios, and Arabs who mistook them for enemies, was an evil omen for the harmony of this unnatural alliance. It was desired that the friends of Euphemios should wear a twig in their headgear to avert the repetition of such a dangerous error; but Asad declared that he did not need the help of his confederate, that Euphemios and his men should take no part in the military operations, and that thus further accidents would be avoided. The intention of the Moslem commander to take the whole conduct of the campaign in his own hands and to use the Greek usurper as a puppet, was thus shown with little disguise.

It was not long before the general, whom in ignorance of his true name we are compelled to distinguish as Palata, appeared in the neighbourhood with forces considerably superior to those of the invaders. Mazara, now Mazzara del Vallo, lies at the mouth of a like-named stream, to the southeast of Lilybaeum. South-eastward from Mazara itself, a coast plain stretches to the ruins of Selinus, and this was perhaps the scene of the first battle-shock in the struggle between Christendom and Islam for the possession of Sicily. Asad marched forth from Mazara, and when he came in sight of the Greeks and marshalled his army, he recited some verses of the Koran in front of the host and led it to victory. Palata fled to the strong fort of Castrogiovanni, and thence to Calabria, where he died.

The first object of the victors was the capture of Syracuse. Leaving a garrison in Mazara, they advanced eastward along the south coast. At a place which their historians call Kalat-al-Kurrat, and which is perhaps the ancient Acrae, a strong fort in the hills, between Gela and Syracuse, an embassy from Syracuse met them, offering to submit and pay tribute, on condition that they should not advance farther. Asad halted for some days; we do not know why he delayed, but the interval was advantageous to the Greeks, whose overtures were perhaps no more than a device to gain time to strengthen the defences and bring provisions and valuable property into the city. In the meantime Euphemios had repented of what he had done. He had discovered too late that he had loosed a wind which he could not bind. What he had desired from the ruler of Africa was a force which he could himself direct and control. He found himself a puppet in the hands of a fanatical Mohammadan, whose designs and interests did not coincide with his own, and who, as he could already surmise, aimed not at establishing his own authority but at making a new conquest for Islam. We are not told whether he accompanied Asad in the march across the island, but he entered into negotiations with the Imperialists and urged them to resist the foes whom he had himself invoked against them. Seeing that further delay would only serve the Greeks, Asad advanced on Syracuse, where he was joined by his fleet. He burned the vessels of the Greeks and closed the greater and the lesser Harbours with his own ships. The fortifications were too strong to be assaulted without siege engines, with which the Arab's were not provided, and Asad could only blockade the town, while he waited for reinforcements from Africa. He encamped among the quarries, south of Achradina.

As all the provisions had been conveyed into the city from the surrounding country, the Saracen army suffered from want of food, and the discontent waxed so great that a certain Ibn Kadim advised the general to break up his camp and sail back to Africa; "The life of one Musulman", he said, "is more valuable than all the goods of Christendom". Asad sternly replied, "I am not one of those who allow Moslems, when they go forth to a Holy War, to return home when they have still such hopes of victory". He quenched the mutiny by threatening to burn the ships and punishing with stripes the audacious Ibn Kadim. Presently reinforcements, and probably supplies, arrived from Africa.

Meanwhile the Emperor had taken measures to recall Sicily to its allegiance. The story was told that when the tidings of the rebellion of Euphemios reached him, he summoned the magister Irenaeus and said, "We may congratulate ourselves, Magister, on the revolt of Sicily". "This, sir", replied Irenaeus, is no matter for congratulation, "and turning to one of the magnates who were present, he solemnly repeated the lines : —

Dire woes will fall upon the world, what time
The Babylonian dragon 'gins to reign,
Greedy of gold and inarticulate.

The anecdote may be apocryphal, invented in the light of subsequent disasters, as a reflexion on the ruler in whose reign such grave losses had befallen the Empire. But if Michael, who sent fleet after fleet to regain Crete, and was even then perhaps engaged in organizing a new expedition, jested at the news from Sicily, the jest was bitter. The pressing concern for Crete and the Aegean islands hindered him from sending any large armament to the west. The naval establishment was inadequate to the defence of the Empire; this had been the consequence of its neglect since the days of Leo the Isaurian. The loss of Crete and the jeopardy of Sicily were to bring home to the Imperial government the importance of sea-power, and the strengthening of the navy was one of the chief tasks which successors of Michael II would be forced to take in hand.

Some troops were sent to Sicily, but the Emperor at this crisis looked for help from a western dependency, whose own interests were undoubtedly involved in not suffering the Moslem to gain a footing on Sicilian soil. The proximity of such a foe to the waters of the Hadriatic sea would be a constant distress and anxiety to the city of Venice. It was therefore a fair and reasonable demand, on the part of the Emperor, that Venice should send a squadron to cope with the invaders of Sicily, and it is not improbable that she was bound by definite agreement to cooperate in such a case. The Duke, Justinianus, sent some warships, but it does not appear that they achieved much for the relief of the Syracusans.

The besiegers had in the meantime entrenched themselves, surrounding their camp with a ditch, and digging in front of it holes which served as pitfalls for the cavalry of the Greeks. The besieged, finding themselves hard pressed, sought to parley, but their proposals were rejected, and the siege was protracted through the winter, till the invaders were confronted with a more deadly adversary than the Greeks. Pestilence broke out in their camp, and Asad, their indomitable leader, was one of its victims (A.D. 828). The army itself elected a new commander, a certain Mohammad, but fortune had deserted the Arabs; the epidemic raged among them as it had raged among the Carthaginians of Hamilcar who had sought to master Syracuse twelve hundred years before. The new reinforcements came from Constantinople, and a second squadron was expected from Venice. The besiegers despaired and decided to return to Africa. They weighed anchor, but found that they were shut in by the ships of the enemy. They disembarked, set fire to their ships, and, laden with many sick, began a weary march in the direction of Mineo.

Euphemios served them as a guide. He had not parted from his foreign friends, though he had, for a time at least, secretly worked against them. But now that they were chastened by ill-success and no longer led by the masterful Asad, he expected to be able to use them for his own purpose. The town of Mineo surrendered, and when the army recovered from the effects of the plague, it divided into two parts, of which one marched westward and captured Agrigentum. The other, accompanied by Euphemios, laid siege to the impregnable fortress which stands in the very centre of the island, the massive rock of Henna, which was called in the ninth century, as it is today, Castrogiovanni.

The garrison of Castrogiovanni opened negotiations with Euphemios, offering to recognise him as Emperor and to cast in their lot with him and his Arab confederates. But these overtures were only an artifice; the men of Castrogiovanni were loyal to the Emperor Michael. Euphemios fell into the trap. At an appointed hour and place, he met a deputation of the townsmen. While some fell down before him, as their sovran, and kissed the ground, others at the same moment stabbed him from behind.

With the disappearance of Euphemios from the scene, the warfare in Sicily was simplified to the plain and single issue of a contest between Moslem and Christian for the lordship of the island. It was a slow and tedious contest, protracted for two generations; and although the advance of the Moslems was steady, it was so slow that an observer might have forecast its result as an eventual division between the two races, a repetition of the old division between Greeks and Phoenicians. But history did not repeat itself thus. The Greek states in the days of Gelon and of Dionysios were of different metal from the provincials who were under the protection of the Eastern Emperors. The Arabs were to do what the Phoenicians had failed to do, and make the whole island a portion of Asia in Europe.

The record, which has come down to us, of the incidents of the warfare chronicles the gradual reduction of town after town, fort after fort, but is so meagre that it offers little instruction or interest We may note the most important stages in the conquest and observe the efforts made by the Imperial government to drive out the invaders. The forces which had been sent by the Emperor Michael to the relief of Syracuse were commanded by Theodotos, a patrician who was not without military talent. He followed the enemy to Castrogiovanni, where he was defeated and driven to take refuge in the fortress, which the Arabs, after the death of Euphemios continued to besiege. But Theodotos soon had his revenge. Sallying forth and gaining a victory, he surrounded and besieged the camp of the besiegers. They tried to escape at night, but the Greek general, foreseeing such an attempt, had secretly abandoned his own camp, and laid an ambush. Those who escaped from his trap made their way to Mineo, where he blockaded them so effectively that they were reduced to eating the flesh of dogs.

The Arab garrison in Agrigentum, seeing that the tide had turned, withdrew to Mazara; and in the summer of A.D. 829 only Mazara and Mineo, far distant from each other, were held by the invaders. At this moment a powerful armament from Constantinople might have been decisive. But no reinforcements were sent. The successes of Theodotos were probably taken to show that he would be able to complete his task alone, and then the death of Michael intervened. But if the government reckoned thus, it reckoned without Africa and Spain. Two hostile fleets sailed to the Sicilian shores. Ziadat Allah sent a new armament and a Spanish squadron came to join in the warfare, for the sake of plunder, not of conquest, under Asbag ibn Wakil. The African Moslems, hard pressed at Mineo, proposed common action to the Spanish adventurers, and the Spaniards agreed on condition that Asbag should be the commander-in-chief and that the Africans should provide horses. But the confederates carried on their operations separately. Asbag and his men marched first to Mineo, which, still blockaded by Theodotos, must have been suffering the last distresses of hunger. They defeated the besiegers and Theodotos fell in the battle. Asbag burned Mineo, but his career was almost immediately cut short. A pestilence broke out among his troops while he was besieging another stronghold, and, like Asad, he fell a victim to the infection. His followers returned to Spain.

Meanwhile the Africans had laid siege to Panormos. This city held out for a year, but it seems to have been an easier place to besiege than Syracuse or Castrogiovanni. In the autumn of A.D. 831 the commander of the garrison surrendered, having bargained for the safety of himself, his family, and his property. The inhabitants were treated as prisoners of war. The bishop of Panormos escaped to Constantinople, bearing the news of the calamity. The anxiety of the Emperor Theophilus to come to terms with the Caliph Mamun, points to his desire to concentrate the forces of the Empire on the defence of Sicily. But though he failed to secure peace in the East, we should expect to find that he made some extraordinary effort on the news of the fall of Panormos. There is, however, no record of the despatch of any new armament or relief to the western island at this time.

The winning of such an important basis and naval station marks the completion of the first stage in the Moslem conquest. If the operations hitherto had been somewhat of the nature of an experiment, the African Emir was now confirmed in his ambitious policy of annexing Sicily, and Panormos was the nucleus of a new province over which he appointed Abu Fihr as governor. It is probable that during the next few years progress was made in reducing the western districts of the island, but for nine years no capture of an important town or fortress marked the advance of the invaders. Abu Fihr and his successors won some battles, and directed their arms against Castrogiovanni, which on one occasion almost fell into their hands. Kephaloedion, on the north coast, now called Cefalu, was attacked in A.D. 838, but timely help arriving from Constantinople forced the enemy to raise the siege. It is probable that the success of the Greeks in stemming the tide of conquest was due to the ability of the Caesar Alexios Musele, who was entrusted with the command of the Sicilian forces. He returned to Constantinople (perhaps in A.D. 839) accused of ambitious designs against the throne, and after his departure the enemy made a notable advance by reducing the fortresses of Corleone, Platani, and Caltabellotta-the ancient Sican fortress of Kamikos (A.D. 840). Two or three years later, Al-Fald achieved the second great step in the conquest, the capture of Messina. Aided by Naples, which had allied itself to the new power in Sicily, he besieged the town by land and sea, and after all his assaults had been repelled, took it by an artifice. Secretly sending a part of his forces into the mountains which rise behind the city, he opened a vigorous attack from the sea-side. When all the efforts of the garrison were concentrated in repelling it, the concealed troops descended from the hills and scaled the deserted walls on the landward side. The town was compelled to capitulate.

The invaders had now established themselves in two of the most important sites in Sicily; they were dominant in the west and they held the principal city in the north-east. In a few years the captures of Motyke and its neighbour Ragusa gave them a footing for the conquest of the southeast. An army which the Empress Theodora sent to the island, where a temporary respite from the hostilities of the Eastern Saracens had been secured, was defeated with great loss; and soon afterwards the warrior who had subdued Messina captured Leontini. When Al-Fald laid siege to it, the Greek strategos marched to its relief, having arranged with the garrison to light a beacon on a neighbouring hill to prepare them for his approach. Al-Fald discovered that this signal had been concerted, and immediately lit a fire on three successive days. On the fourth day, when the relieving army ought to have appeared, the besieged issued from the gates, confident of victory. The enemy, by a feigned flight, led them into an ambush, and the city, meanwhile, was almost undefended and fell an easy prey.

The irregularity in the rate of progress of the conquest may probably be explained, at least in part, by the fact that the Moslems were engaged at the same time in operations in Southern Italy, which will presently claim our attention. For more than ten years after the fall of Leontini, the energy of the invaders appears to have flagged or expended itself on smaller enterprises; and then a new period of active success begins with the surrender of Kephaloedion (A.D. 857-858). A year or so later, the mighty fortress of the Sicels and now the great bulwark of the Greeks in the centre of the island, Castrogiovanni, was at last subdued. The capture of this impregnable citadel was, as we might expect, compassed with the aid of a traitor. A Greek prisoner purchased his life from the Arab governor, Abbas, by undertaking to lead him into the stronghold by a secret way. With two thousand horsemen Abbas proceeded to Castrogiovanni, and on a dark night some of them penetrated into the place through a watercourse which their guide pointed out. The garrison had no suspicion that they were about to be attacked; the gate was thrown open, and the citadel was taken (Jan. 24, A.D. 859). It was a success which ranked in importance with the captures of Panormos and Messina, and the victors marked their satisfaction by sending some of the captives as a gift to the Caliph Mutawakkil.

The fall of Castrogiovanni excited the Imperial government to a new effort. A fleet of three hundred warships arrived at Syracuse in the late autumn under the command of Constantine Kontomytes. The army landed, but was utterly defeated by Abbas, who marched from Panormos. The coming of the Greek fleet incited some of the towns in the west to rebel against their Arab lords, but they were speedily subdued, and Abbas won a second victory over the Greek forces near Cefalu. This was the last effort of the Amorian dynasty to rescue the island of the west from the clutch of Islam. Before the death of Michael III the invaders had strengthened their power in the south-east by the captures of Noto and Scicli, and in the north-east the heights of Tauromenium had fallen into their hands. Syracuse was still safe, but its fall, which was to complete the conquest of Sicily, was only reserved for the reign of Michael's successor.

§3. The Invasion of Southern Italy

As a result of the Italian conquests of Charles the Great, two sovran powers divided the dominion of Italy between them. The Eastern Empire retained Venice, a large part of Campania, and the two southern extremities; all the rest of the peninsula was subject to the new Emperor of the West. But this simple formula is far from expressing the actual situation. On one hand, the nominal allegiance to Charles which the Lombard Duchy of Beneventum pretended to acknowledge, did not affect its autonomy or hinder its Dukes from pursuing their own independent policy in which the Frankish power did not count; on the other hand, the cities of the Campanian coast, while they respected the formal authority of the Emperor at Constantinople, virtually, like Venice, managed their own affairs, and were left to protect their own interests. The actual power of Charles did not reach south of the Pontifical State and the Duchy of Spoleto; the direct government of Nicephorus extended only over the southern parts of Calabria and Apulia. These relatively inconsiderable Byzantine districts were now an appendage to Sicily; they were administered by an official entitled the Duke of Calabria; but he was dependent on the Sicilian strategos. In Calabria-the ancient Bruttii-the northern boundary of his province was south of Cosenza and Bisignano, which were Lombard; in Apulia, the chief cities were Otranto and Gallipoli. These two districts were cut asunder by the Lombards, who were lords of Tarentum; so that the communications among the three territories which formed the western outpost of the Eastern Empire-Sicily, Calabria, and Apulia-were entirely maritime.

In the eighth century the city of Naples was loyally devoted to Constantinople, and the Emperors not only appointed the consular dukes who governed her, but exercised a real control over her through the strategoi of Sicily. It seemed probable that under this Byzantine influence, Naples would, like Sicily and Calabria, become Graecised, and her attitude was signally hostile to Rome. But in the reign of Irene, a duke named Stephen played a decisive role in the history of the city and averted such a development. He aimed at loosening, without cutting, the bonds which attached Naples to Constantinople, and founding a native dynasty. His regime is marked by a reaction in favour of Latin; he is determined that the Neapolitan clergy shall inherit the traditions of Latin and not of Greek Christendom. And if he is careful to avoid any rupture with the Empire and to secure the Imperial assent to the succession of his son Stephen II, the head of the Emperor soon disappears from the bronze coinage of Naples and is replaced by that of Januarius, the patron saint of the city. This assertion of independence was followed by years of trouble and struggles among competitors for the ducal power, which lasted for a generation, and once in that period the authority reverted briefly to representatives of the Imperial government. Weary of anarchy, the Neapolitans invited the Sicilian governor to nominate a duke, and for three years the city was subject to Byzantine officials. Then (in A.D. 821) the people drove out the protospatharios Theodore, and elected a descendant of Stephen. But twenty years more elapsed before the period of anarchy was finally terminated by the strong arm of Sergius of Cumae, who was elected in A.D. 840.

Gaeta and Amalfi belonged nominally to the Duchy of Naples, and, like Naples, to the Eastern Empire. But they were virtually independent city states. Gaeta lay isolated in the north. For Terracina belonged to the Pope, and Minturnae, as well as Capua, with the mouths of the Liris and Vulturnus, belonged to the Lombard lords of Beneventum. The great object of the Lombards was to crush the cities of the Campanian coast, and the struggle to hold her own against their aggression was the principal preoccupation of Naples at this period. In this strife Naples displayed wonderful resourcefulness, but the Lombards had all the advantages. The Duchy of Beneventum comprised Samnium, the greater part of Apulia, Lucania, and the north of Calabria; moreover it came down to the coasts of Campania, so that Naples and Amalfi were isolated between Capua and Salerno. If the Beneventan power had remained as strong and consolidated as it had been in the days of Arichis, there can be small doubt that Naples and her fellows must have been absorbed in the Lombard state. They were delivered from the danger by the outbreak of internal struggles in the Beneventan Duchy.

The Lombards had never had a navy; but Arichis, the great Prince who dominated southern Italy in the reign of Constantine V. and Irene (A.D. 758-787), seems to have conceived the plan of creating a sea-power, and he made a second capital of his Principality at Salerno, where he often resided. The descent of Charles the Great into Italy, and the need of furnishing no pretext to that sovran for interfering in South-Italian affairs, prevented Arichis from pursuing the designs which he probably entertained against Naples and the Campanian cities. He hoped to find at Constantinople support against the Franks and the Roman See which regarded him with suspicion and dislike; and this policy necessarily involved peace with the Italian cities which were under the Imperial sovranty. Shortly before his death, he sent an embassy to the Empress Irene, requesting her to confer on him the title of Patrician and offering to acknowledge her supremacy. Her answer was favourable, but the Prince was dead when the ensigns of the Patriciate arrived. In connexion with this Greek policy of Arichis, we may note the fact that Byzantine civilisation was exercising a considerable influence on the Lombard court at this period.

Though the son of Arichis was compelled to accept the suzerainty of Charles the Great, his Principality remained actually autonomous. But his death (in A.D. 806) marked the beginning of a decline, which may be imputed to the growing power of the aristocracy. Insisting on their rights of election, the nobles would not recognise a hereditary right to the office of Prince, and the struggles of aspirants to power ended in the disruption of the state. The most important Princes of this period were Sicon and Sicard, and their hands were heavy against the Campanian cities. Amalfi was pillaged and reduced for some years to be a dependency of Salerno. Naples was compelled to avert the perils and miseries of a siege by paying tribute; she sought repeatedly, but in vain, the succour of the western Emperor; at length she turned to another quarter.

It was less than ten years after the Moslems of Africa began the conquest of Sicily, that the Moslems of Sicily were tempted to begin the conquest of southern Italy; and here, as in the case of Sicily, their appearance on the scene was provoked by an invitation. Naples, besieged by Sicard, sought aid from the Saracen governor of Panormos. A Saracen fleet was promptly despatched, and Sicard was compelled to raise the siege and conclude a treaty. The alliance thus begun between Naples and Panormos was soon followed by active aggression of the Moslems against the enemy of their Christian allies. Brundusium was the first sacrifice. The Moslems suddenly surprised it; Sicard marched to expel them; but they dug covered pits in front of the walls, and drawing the Lombard cavalry into the snare gained a complete victory. Sicard prepared for a new attempt, and the Arabs, feeling that they were not strong enough to hold out, burned the city and returned to Sicily.

The assassination of Sicard shortly after this event was followed by a struggle between two rivals, Sikenolf his brother and Radelchis. The Principality was rent into two parts; Salernum was ranged against Beneventum; and the contest lasting for ten years (A.D. 839-849) furnished the Moslems with most favourable opportunities and facilities for laying the foundations of a Mohammadan state in southern Italy. Tarentum fell into their hands, and this led to the interposition of the Emperor Theophilus, whose possessions in Italy were now immediately threatened. He did not send forces himself, but he requested or required his vassal, Venice, to deliver Tarentum. He could indeed appeal to Venetian interests. The affair of Brundusium may have brought home to Venice that the danger of Saracen fleets in the Hadriatic waters, of Saracen descents on the Hadriatic coasts, could no longer be ignored. In response to the pressure of the Emperor, a Venetian armament of sixty ships sailed to the Gulf of Tarentum (A.D. 840), where it encountered the powerful fleet of the Arabs who had lately captured the city. The Venetians were utterly defeated, and a few months lates (April, A.D. 841), the first expedition of the enemy up the Hadriatic proved that the Mohammadan peril was no idle word, but might soon reach the gates of St. Mark's city. The town of Ossero on the isle of Cherson off the Dalmatian coast, and on the Italian shore the town of Ancona, were burned; and the fleet advanced as far as the mouth of the Po. A year later the Arabs renewed their depredations in the gulf of Quarnero, and won a complete victory over a Venetian squadron at the island of Sansego.

The strife of two rivals for the principality of Beneventum furnished the Moslems with the opportunity of seizing Bari. The governor of that city in order to aid his master Radelchis, had hired a band of Saracens. One dark night they fell upon the sleeping town, and, killing the governor, took it for themselves. The capture of Bari (in A.D. 841) was as important a success for the advance of the Mohammadans in Italy as that of Panormos for the conquest of Sicily. But their aggression in Italy was not as yet organized. It is carried out by various bands-African or Spanish, —who act independently and sometimes take opposite side in the struggles of the Lombard princes. The Saracens of Bari, who had wrested that place from Radelchis, become his allies; but the chief of Tarentum supports his enemy, Sikenolf. Another Saracen leader, Massar, is employed by Radelchis to defend Beneventum against Sikenolf's Lombards of Salerno.

If the civil war in the Lombard Principality was favourable to the designs of the Saracens, it was advantageous to Naples and her neighbours. No sooner did the struggles break out than Amalfi recovered her independence; and Naples, relieved from the pressure of Lombard aggression was able to change her policy and renounce the alliance with the Moslems with whom she had not scrupled to cooperate. She had helped them to take Messina, but she realised in time that such a friendship would lead to her own ruin. Duke Sergius saw clearly that the Saracens, who were occupying the Archipelago of Ponza and were active on the coast south of Salerno, were an imminent danger to the Campanian cities. Through his exertions, an alliance was formed by Naples with Surrentum, Amalfi, and Gaeta to assist the aggression of the power which they now recognized as a common enemy (A.D. 845). The confederate fleet won a victory over a Sicilian squadron near Cape Licosa. Rome too seems to have been aware that the unbelievers might at any moment sail against the great city of Christendom. Pope Gregory IV had built a fort at Ostia and strengthened the town by a wall and foss. Not long after his death, they took Ostia and Porto and appeared before the walls of Rome (August A.D. 846). It is probable that their quest was only booty and that they had not come with the thought of besieging the city. They were driven off by the Margrave of Spoleto, but not till they had sacked the churches of St. Peter and St. Paul outside the walls A large body encamped before Gaeta (September), where a battle was fought, but the arrival of Caesarius, son of Duke Sergius, with a fleet forced them to retreat to Africa.

Three years later the Romans were disturbed by the alarming news that the enemy had equipped a great fleet to make another attack upon their city. Pope Leo IV concluded an agreement with the league of Gaeta, Amalfi, and Naples, for the defence of Rome. The naval forces of the four powers gathered at Ostia, and the leaders of the confederates swore solemnly in the Lateran palace to be true to the cause. But their task proved unexpectedly easy, for the forces of the elements charged themselves with the defence of the city of the Popes. The hostile fleet arrived and the battle began, but a storm suddenly arose and scattered the Arab ships. The Italians had little to do but to pick up captives from the waters. This success must have contributed much to establish the power and authority of Duke Sergius at Naples.

In the same year (A.D. 849) the domestic dissensions in the Lombard state were terminated by a treaty of partition. It was divided into two independent States, the Principality of Beneventum, and the Principality of Salerno. The latter included, along with Lucania and the north of Calabria, Capua and the greater part of Lombard Campania. But the Counts of Capua refused to acknowledge the authority of the Prince of Salerno, and thus three independent States arose from the disruption of the old Principality of Beneventum.

The Western Emperors, Lewis the Pious and Lothar, much occupied with other parts of their wide dominions, had hitherto kept aloof from South Italian affairs. But the danger which threatened Rome at the hands of the infidels moved Lothar to an intervention which appeals from Naples for help against the Lombards, or from one Lombard power for support against another, or from the Eastern Emperor for common action against the Saracens, had failed to bring about. Towards the end of A.D. 846 he decided to send an expedition against the Moslems. It was led by his son Lewis, who appeared with an army, chiefly recruited from Gaul, and was active within the Lombard borders during the following years (A.D. 847-849). At the same time he doubtless helped to arrange the agreement between the Lombard rivals. He was bent upon making his authority real, making South Italy a part of his Italian kingdom in the fullest sense, and he was bent upon driving the Saracens out. He expelled them from Beneventum, but this was only the beginning of his task. The Saracens of Bari, whose leader took the title of Sultan, dominated Apulia, in which he was master of twenty-four fortresses and from which he ravaged the adjacent regions. Bari was strongly fortified, and Lewis was beaten back from its walls (A.D. 852). For fourteen years he seems to have been able to make no further effort to cope with the invaders. North Italian affairs, and especially his struggle with Pope Nicolas I., claimed his attention, and it was as much as he could do to maintain authority over his Lombard vassals. During this time the Saracens were the terror of the South; but the confederate fleet of Naples and her maritime allies appears to have secured to those cities immunity from attack.

As against the Saracens, the interests of the Eastern and the Western Empires were bound together, and, when Lewis once more set himself earnestly to the task of recovering Apulia, he invoked the cooperation of Constantinople. How he succeeded, and how his success turned out to the profit of his Greek allies, is a story which lies beyond our present limits.

Chapter X
Relations with the Western Empire. Venice

When Nicephorus I ascended the throne, he was confronted on the western borders of his dominion by the great Western State which was founded by the genius of Charles the Great. It included the whole extent of the mainland of western Europe, with the exception of Spain and the small territories in Italy which still belonged to the lord of Constantinople. It was far larger in area than the Eastern Empire, and to Charles it might well have seemed the business of a few short years to drive the Byzantine power from Venetia, from the southern extremities of Italy, and from Sicily itself. He had annexed Istria; he had threatened Croatia; and his power had advanced in the direction of the Middle Danube. But his Empire, though to himself and his friends it might appear as a resurrection of the mighty empire of Augustus or Constantine, was not built up by the slow and sure methods which the Roman republic had employed to extend its sway over the world. Though it was pillared by the spiritual influence and prestige of Rome, it was an ill-consolidated fabric which could not be strengthened and preserved save by a succession of rulers as highly gifted as Charles himself. A few years after his death the disintegration of his Empire began; it had been a menace, it never became a serious danger, to the monarchs of Constantinople.

A treaty had been concluded between Charles and Irene in A.D. 798, by which the Empress recognised the lordship of the King in Istria and Beneventum, while he probably acknowledged her rights in Croatia. Soon afterwards, induced perhaps by overtures from a disloyal party in island, Charles seems to have formed a design upon Sicily, and in A.D. 800 it was known at Constantinople that he intended to attack the island; but his unexpected coronation led him to abandon his design.

Unexpected; when the diadem was placed on his head in St. Peter's on Christmas Day, and he was acclaimed Imperator by the Romans, he was not only taken by surprise, but even vexed. The Pope, who performed the coronation, was merely in the secret; he consented to, but he did not initiate, a scheme, which was far from being obviously conducive to the interests of pontifical policy. It has been shown that the scheme was conceived and carried through by friends and counsellors of the king, who were enthusiastic admirers of their master as a conqueror and a statesman. In poems and letters, these men-Alcuin, Theodulf, Angilbert, Paulinus, Arno —ventilated, as we may say, the Imperial idea, not formulating it in direct phrases, but allusively suggesting it. Thus Angilbert wrote:

Rex Karolus, caput orbis, amor populique decusque,
Europae venerandus apex, pater optimus, heros,
Augustus.

It was not enough for the authors of the scheme to assure themselves of the cooperation of Pope Leo, for they were sufficiently versed in the Imperial theory to know that the constitutional legitimacy of a Roman Emperor depended not on his coronation but on his election. It was essential to observe the constitutional form: the Emperor must be acclaimed by the Roman Senate, and army, and people. There was no Senate in the old sense, but the term senatus was applied to the Roman nobles, and this sufficed for the purpose. There were soldiers and there was a populace. It was necessary to prepare the Romans for an exercise of sovran authority, which had long ceased to be familiar to them. When they assembled in the Church of St. Peter to celebrate mass on Christmas Day, there was perhaps no one in the great concourse except Charles himself, who was unaware of the imminent event. When the Pope placed the crown on the head of the King, who was kneeling in prayer, the congregation-the Senate, and the Roman people-acclaimed him three times, "Life and victory to Charles, Augustus, crowned by God, great and pacific Emperor of the Romans". The Pope, who had simply fulfilled the same function as a Patriarch of Constantinople in a similar case, fell down and adored him as a subject.

If the first emotions of the new Emperor, who had thus been taken unawares, were mixed with anxiety and disquiet, one of the chief causes of his misgiving was probably the ambiguous attitude which he now occupied in regard to Constantinople. The legitimacy of the Emperors who ruled in the East as the successors of Constantine had never been questioned in Europe; it had been acknowledged by Charles himself; it was above all cavil or dispute. The election of Charles-it mattered not whether at Rome or elsewhere-without the consent of the sovran at Constantinople was formally a usurpation. It was all very well to disguise or justify the usurpation by the theory that the Imperial throne had been vacant since the deposition of Constantine VI., because a woman was incapable of exercising the Imperial sovranty; but such an argument would not be accepted in Byzantium, and would perhaps carry little weight anywhere. Nor would Irene reign for ever; she would be succeeded by a man, whose Imperial title would be indisputable. Charles saw that, elected though he was by the Romans and crowned by the Pope, his own title as Roman Imperator and Augustus could only become perfectly valid if he were recognised as a colleague by the autocrat of Constantinople. There are many "empires" in the world today; but in those days men could only conceive of one, the Roman imperium, which was single and indivisible; two Roman Empires were unimaginable. There might be more than the one Emperor; but these others could only be legitimate and constitutional if they stood to him in a collegial relation. If, then, the lord of Constantinople, whose Imperial title was above contention, refused to acknowledge the lord of Rome as an Imperial colleague, the claim of Charles was logically condemned as illegitimate.

That Charles felt the ambiguity of his position keenly is proved by his acts. To conciliate Constantinople, and obtain recognition there, became a principal object of his policy. He began by relinquishing the expedition which he had planned against Sicily. A year later (very early in A.D. 802) he received at Aachen envoys from Irene. The message which they bore is unknown, but when they returned home they were accompanied by ambassadors from Charles, who were instructed to lay before the Empress a proposal of marriage. It is said that Irene was herself disposed to entertain the offer favorably, and to acquiesce in the idea of a union between the two realms, which would have restored the Empire to something like its ancient limits. The scheme was a menace to the independence of the East, and Irene's ministers must have regarded it with profound distrust. They had no mind to submit to the rule of a German, who would inevitably have attempted to impose upon Byzantium one of his sons as successor. The influence of the patrician Aetius hindered Irene from assenting, and before the Frankish ambassadors left the city they witnessed her fall. This catastrophe put an end to a plan which, even if it had led to a merely nominal union of the two States, would have immensely strengthened the position of Charles by legalising, in a signal way, his Imperial election. It was, however, a plan which was in any case doomed to failure; the Greeks would never have suffered its accomplishment.

Nicephorus, soon after his accession, sent an embassy with some proposals to Charles. We do not know what the points at issue were, but Charles agreed, and at the same time wrote a letter to the Emperor. This letter is not preserved, but we may conjecture, with high probability, that its purport was to induce Nicephorus to recognise the Imperial dignity of the writer. Nicephorus did not deign to reply, and peace between the two powers was again suspended (A.D. 803). Active hostilities soon broke out, of which Venetia was the cause and the scene.

We are accustomed, by a convenient anticipation, to use the name Venice or Venetia in speaking of the chief city of the lagoons long before it was thus restricted. For it was not till the thirteenth century that Venice came to be specially applied to the islands of the Rialto, nor was it till the ninth century that the Rialto became the political capital. Venetia meant the whole territory of the lagoon state from the Brenta to the Isonzo. Till the middle of the eighth century the centre of government had been Heracliana on the Piave, which had taken the place of Oderzo when that city (c. 640) was captured by the Lombards. No traces remain today of the place of Heracliana, which sank beneath the marshes, even as its flourishing neighbour Jesolo, which was also peopled by fugitives from Oderzo and Altino, has been covered over by the sands. In A.D. 742 —an epoch in the history of Venice the direct government of the

Venetian province by Masters of Soldiers was exchanged for the government of locally elected Dukes, and at the same time the seat of office was transferred from Heracliana to the island of Malamocco. The noble families of Heracliana and Jesolo followed the governor, in such numbers that Malamocco could not hold them, and the overflow streamed into the islands known as Rivus Altus-the Rialto. The first consequence of this movement was the foundation of a bishopric in the northern island, the see of Olivolo, which has been signalized as the first act in the foundation of the city of Venice.

But Malamocco, the seat of government and the residence of the prominent families, was not the centre of commerce or the seat of ecclesiastical power. The northern lagoon-city of Grado, originally built as a port for Aquileia, was the residence of the Patriarch, and doubtless surpassed in the luxuries of civilization, as it certainly excelled in artistic splendour, the secular capitals Heracliana and Malamocco. For the superabundance of wealth at this time was in the coffers of the Church.

The centre of trade was Torcello, well protected in the northern corner of the lagoons, and it did not surrender to the Rialto its position as the great Venetian market-place till the tenth or eleventh century. The home products which the Venetians exported consisted chiefly in salt and fish, and their only native industry seems to have been basket-work. The commercial importance of Venice in these early ages lay in its serving as a market-place between the East and the West; and its possession had for Constantinople a similar value to that of Cherson in the Euxine. Greek merchants brought to Torcello the rich products of the East-silk, purple, and linen-peacocks, wines, articles of luxury; and Venetian traders distributed these in Italy, Gaul, and Germany. The Greek exports were paid for by wood, and metals, and slaves. The traffic in slaves, with Greeks and Saracens, was actively prosecuted by the merchants notwithstanding the prohibitions of the Dukes.

The Dukes remained unswervingly loyal to the Empire throughout the eighth century. In A.D. 778 the Duke Maurice introduced into the Dukedom the principle of co-regency, similar to that which was customary in the Imperial office itself; he appointed his son as a colleague, and this was a step towards hereditary succession. This innovation must have received the Emperor's sanction; Maurice was invested with the dignities of stratelates and hypatos, and his official title ran, magister militum, consul et imperialis dux Venetiarum provinciae.

The Italian conquest of Charles the Great and his advance to the north of the Hadriatic threatened to interrupt the peaceful development of Venice and to rob the Empire of a valuable possession. The bishops of Istria were subject to the Patriarch of Grado. When Charles conquered Istria (A.D. 787-788), he transferred them to the See of Aquileia; he had already promised the Pope to submit to his spiritual dominion both Istria and Venetia (A.D. 774). At Grado he won an adherent in the Patriarch himself, who, however, paid the penalty for his treason to the Empire. The young Duke Maurice sailed to Grado and hurled the Patriarch from the pinnacle of a tower (c. 802). This act of violence did not help the government; it gave a pretext to the disaffected. Fortunatus, a friend of Charles the Great, was elected Patriarch (A.D. 803), and with some Venetians, who were opposed to the government, he seceded to Treviso, and then went by himself to Charles, with whom he discussed plans for overthrowing the Imperial Dukes. The disloyal party at Treviso elected a certain Obelierius to the Dukedom; the loyal Dukes fled; and Obelierius with his adopted brother took unhindered possession of the government in Malamocco.

This revolution (A.D. 804) was a rebellion against Constantinople, and the new Dukes signalized their hostility to the Empire by a maritime attack on the Imperial province of Dalmatia. At first they seem to have contemplated the design of making their State independent both of the Frank and of the Greek, for they refused to allow Fortunatus, the confidential friend of Charles, to return to Grado. But they soon abandoned this idea as impracticable; they submitted unreservedly to the Western potentate and visited him at his Court (Christmas, A.D. 805). He conferred upon them the Duchy of Venetia as a fief, and when he divided the Empire prospectively among his sons (Feb. A.D. 806) he assigned Venetia, Istria, and Dalmatia to Pippin.

It is not improbable that in making this submission Venice hoped to induce Charles to remove the embargo which he had placed upon her trade in A.D. 787, but if she counted on this, she was disappointed. It may be that Charles himself did not calculate on the permanent retention of Venetia, and it belonged to his Empire for little more than a year. In the spring of A.D. 807 the Emperor Nicephorus dispatched a fleet to recall the rebellious dependency to its allegiance. The patrician Nicetas, who was in command, encountered no resistance; the Dukes submitted; Obelierius was confirmed in his office and created a spathar; his brother was carried as a hostage to Constantinople along with the bishop of Olivolo. Fortunatus, who had been reinstated at Grado, fled to Charles.

Thus Venice was recovered without bloodshed. Pippin, who, with the title of King, was ruling Italy, was unable to interfere because he was powerless at sea, and he concluded a truce with the Byzantine admiral till August A.D. 808. But the trial of strength between the Western and the Eastern powers was only postponed. Another Greek fleet arrived, under the patrician Paulus, strategos of Kephallenia, wintered in Venice, and in spring (A.D. 809) attacked Comacchio, the chief market of the Po trade. The attack was repelled, and Taulus treated with Pippin, but the negotiations were frustrated by the intrigues of the Dukes, who perhaps saw in the continuance of hostilities a means for establishing their own independence between the two rival powers. Paulus departed, and in the autumn Pippin descended upon Venetia in force. He attacked it from the north and from the south, both by land and by sea. His operation's lasted through the winter. In the north he took Heracliana, in the south the fort of Brondolo on the Brenta; then Chioggia, Palestrina, and Albiola; finally Malamocco. The Dukes seem to have fallen into his hands, and a yearly tribute was imposed (A.D. 810). Paulus again appeared on the scene, but all he could do was to save Dalmatia from an attack of Pippin's fleet.

The news quickly reached Constantinople, and Nicephorus sent Arsaphios, an officer of spathar rank, to negotiate with Pippin. When he arrived, the King was dead (July A.D. 810), and he proceeded to Aachen (October).

Charles was now in a better position to bargain for his recognition as Imperator than seven years before. He had now a valuable consideration to offer to the monarch of Constantinople, and he proved, by what he was ready to pay, how deeply he desired the recognition of his title. He agreed to restore to Nicephorus Venetia, Istria, Liburnia, and the cities of Dalmatia which were in his possession. He entrusted to Arsaphios a letter to the Emperor, and handed over to him the Duke Obelierius to be dealt with by his rightful lord. Arsaphios, who was evidently empowered to make a provisional settlement at Venice, returned thither, deposed the Dukes, and caused the Venetians to elect Agnellus Parteciacus, who had proved his devotion and loyalty to the Empire (Spring A.D. 811).

In consequence of the death of Nicephorus in the same year, the conclusion of peace devolved upon Michael I. He agreed to the proposals, his ambassadors saluted Charles as Emperor-Basileus-at Aachen (A.D. 812), and Charles, who had at last attained the desire of his heart, signed the treaty. The other copy was signed by the successor of Michael and received by the successor of Charles (A.D. 814). This transaction rendered valid retrospectively the Imperial election of 800 at Rome, and, interpreted strictly and logically, it involved the formal union of the two sovran realms. For the recognition of Charles as Basileus meant that he was the colleague of the Emperor at Constantinople; they were both Roman Emperors, but there could be, in theory, only one Roman Empire. In other words, the Act of 812 revived, in theory, the position of the fifth century. Michael I. and Charles, Leo V. and Lewis the Pious, stood to one another as Arcadius to Honorius, as Valentinian III to Theodosius II; the imperium Romanum stretched from the borders of Armenia to the shores of the Atlantic. The union, of course, was nominal, and glaringly unreal, and this has disguised its theoretical significance. The bases of the civilizations in east and west were now so different, the interests of the monarchs were so divergent, that there could be no question of even a formal cooperation-of issuing laws, for instance, in their joint names. And even if closer intimacy had been possible, there was no goodwill on the part of Constantinople in conceding the Imperial dignity, for which a substantial price had been paid. Nor did the Eastern Emperors consider that the concession was permanent. It became hereafter a principle of their policy to decline to accord the title of Basileus to the Western Emperor, unless they required his assistance or had some particular object to gain. Thus in diplomatic negotiations they had the advantage of possessing a consideration cheap to themselves, but valuable to the other party.

To return to Venice, the treaty between the two sovran powers contained provisions which were of high importance for the subject state. The limits of its territory were probably defined; the embargo on its trade in the empire of Charles was at last removed; and its continental possessions, in the borders of Prankish Italy, were restored to it, on the condition of paying a yearly tribute of about £1550 to the Italian king. Commercially, this treaty marks the beginning of a new period for Venice ; it laid the foundations of her mercantile prosperity.

Not so politically; the state of things which had existed before the Frankish intervention was restored. The Venetians gladly acquiesced in the rule of Constantinople. They had felt the conquest of Pippin as a profound humiliation; their historians afterwards cast a veil over it. Their long and obstinate defence of Malamocco showed their repugnance to the Franks. A Greek writer tells us that, when Pippin called upon them to yield, they replied, "We will be the subjects of the Emperor of the Romans, not of thee". This, at all events, expresses their feeling at the time. There are signs that during the following years the Imperial government manifested a closer and more constant interest in Venetian affairs and perhaps drew the reins tighter. Two yearly tribunes were appointed to control the Duke. On the accessions of Leo V. and Michael II., Agnellus sent his son and his grandson to Constantinople to offer homage. The Venetians were also called upon to render active aid to the Imperial fleets against the pirates of Dalmatia who infested the Hadriatic and against the Saracens in Sicilian waters.

The Frankish occupation was followed by a change which created modern Venice. The Duke Agnellus moved the seat of government from Malamocco to the Rivus Altus (A.D. 811), and in these islands a city rapidly grew which was to take the place of Torcello as a centre of commerce, and to overshadow Grado in riches and art. The official house of Agnellus stood on the site of the Palace of the Doges, and hard by, occupying part of the left side of the later Church of St. Mark, arose the Chapel of St. Theodore, built by a wealthy Greek. The Emperor Leo V. himself took an interest in the growth of the Rialto; he founded at his own expense, and sent Greek masons to build, the nunnery of S. Zaccaria, which stands further to the east. Soon afterwards St. Mark, perhaps replacing St. Theodore, became the patron saint of Venice. Leo V. had issued an edict forbidding the merchants of his empire to approach the ports of the infidels in Syria and Egypt. This command was enforced by the Dukes; but notwithstanding, about A.D. 828, some Venetian traders put in at Alexandria, and stole what they supposed to be the corpse of Mark the Evangelist. When the precious remains, which Aquileia vainly claimed to possess, reached the Rialto, they were hidden in a secret place in the Duke" house until a fitting shrine should be prepared to receive them. The Duke Justinian bequeathed money for the building, and before seven years had passed, the first Church of St. Mark had been reared between the Chapel of St. Theodore and the ducal palace, by Greek workmen, a purely Byzantine edifice. The Cathedral of S. Piero in the south-eastern extremity of Castello was erected in these years, which also witnessed the building of S. Ilario, on the mainland due north of Rialto, a basilica with three apses, of which the ground plan was excavated not long ago.

A conspiracy (A.D. 836) terminated the rule of the Parteciaci. The last duke was relegated to a monastery at Grado, and he was succeeded by Peter Trandenicus, an illiterate, energetic man, under whose memorable government Venice made a long leap in her upward progress. For she now practically asserted, though she did not ostentatiously proclaim, a virtual independence. There was no revolution; there was no open renunciation of the authority of the Eastern Empire; the Venetians still remained for generations nominally Imperial subjects. But the bonds were weakened, the reins were relaxed, and Venice actually conducted herself as a sovran state. Her independence was promoted by the duty which fell upon her of struggling against the Croatian pirates; the fleet of the Empire, occupied with the war in Sicily, could not police the upper waters of the Hadriatic. Hitherto Venice had used the same craft for war and trade; Peter Trandenicus built her first warships-chelandia of the Greek type. Theophilus created him a spathar; he styled himself Duke and Spathar, but he did not, like his predecessors, describe himself as "submissive" (humilis); presently he assumed the epithet of "glorious". It is significant that in the dates of public documents anni Domini begin to replace the regnal years of the Emperor. But the most important mark of the new era is that Venice takes upon herself to conclude, on her own account, agreements with foreign powers. The earliest of these is the contract with the Emperor Lothar (Feb. 22, A.D. 840), which among other provisions ensured reciprocal freedom of commerce by land and sea, and bound the Venetians to render help in protecting the eastern coasts of Frankish Italy against the Croatian pirates. This, the oldest monument, as it has been called, of independent Venetian diplomacy, may be said to mark the inauguration of the independence of Venice.

If Venice was thus allowed to slide from under the controlling hand of the Emperors, without scandal or ill-feeling, she retained her supreme importance for Byzantine commerce, and for the next two centuries she was probably as valuable to the Empire, of which she was still nominally a part, as if she had remained in her earlier state of strict subordination.

The conquest of Istria by the Franks affected not only the history of Venetia, but also that of Dalmatia. The realm of Charles the Great was now adjacent to the province of Dalmatia, which included the Roman cities and islands of the coast, from Tarsatica in Liburnia to Cattaro, and also to the Slavs of the "hinterland" who were in a loose subjection to the government of Constantinople. In the treaty of A.D. 798, the Franks acknowledged the Imperial rights over the Slavs; but in the following years both the heads or zupans of these Slavs, and even the Roman communities of the coast, seem to have discerned, like the Venetians, in the rivalry between the two Imperial powers an opportunity for winning independence. The duke and the bishop of Zara went to the court of Charles, along with the duke of Venice, in 806, and paid him homage. About the same time some of the more northern Slavonic tribes submitted to him, a submission which was nominal and involved no obligations. But this, like the corresponding political change in Venice, was only transient. By the treaty of A.D. 812 the old order was formally restored and the Franks undertook not to molest or invade the Dalmatian communities. Some particular questions concerning the boundaries in the north were settled in the reign of Leo V., and no further attempts were made by the Western Empire to seduce Dalmatia from its allegiance. But this allegiance was unstable and wavering. The Slavonic zupans acknowledged no lord in the reign of Michael III or perhaps at an earlier date. The Roman communities of the coast, which were under their own magistrates, subject to an Imperial governor or archon, are said to have asserted their autonomy in the time of Michael II.—and this may well have happened when he was engaged in the struggle with Thomas. But the control of Constantinople was soon reimposed, and Dalmatia continued to be a province or Theme, under an archon, though the cities enjoyed, as before, a measure of self-government, which resembled that of Cherson.

The settlement of another question in the reign of Michael II tended to pacify the relations between the two empires. The Istrian bishops who were subjects of the Western Emperor had been permitted by the Peace of A.D. 812 to remain under the Patriarch of Grado, who was a subject of the Eastern Emperor. This was an awkward arrangement, which probably would not have been allowed to continue if the Patriarch Fortunatus had not proved himself a good friend of the Franks. But it was satisfactory to both Emperors to transfer the Istrian churches from the See of Grado to that of Aquileia, so that the ecclesiastical jurisdictions were coincident with the boundaries between the two realms. This settlement was effected in A.D. 827 by a synod held at Mantua.

The letter which the Emperor, Michael II., addressed to Lewis the Pious has already demanded our attention, in connexion with the iconoclastic controversy. Although his recognition of the Imperial title of Lewis was grudging and ambiguous, Lewis, who consistently pursued the policy of keeping on good terms with Constantinople, did not take offence. Under

Theophilus the relations between the two great powers continued to be friendly. The situation in the Mediterranean demanded an active cooperation against the Saracens, who were a common enemy; Theophilus pressed for the assistance of the Franks; but the Western Empire was distracted by the conflicts between Lewis and his sons. In the last year of his life, Theophilus proposed a marriage between Lewis, the eldest son of Lothar, and one of his own daughters (perhaps Thecla), and Lothar agreed. But after the Emperor's death the project was allowed to drop, nor can we say whether Theodora had any reason to feel resentment that the bridegroom designate never came to claim her daughter. There seems to have ensued a complete cessation of diplomatic intercourse during the reign of Michael III., and it is probable that there may have been some friction in Italy. But, as we have already seen, the struggle between Photius and the Pope led to an approximation between the Byzantine court and the recreant bridegroom, who was proclaimed Basileus in Constantinople (A.D. 867). During the following years, the cooperation against the Saracens, for which Theophilus had hoped, was to be brought about; the Emperor Lewis was to work hand in hand with the generals of Basil in southern Italy.

Chapter XI
Bulgaria

§1. The Bulgarian Kingdom

The hill-ridge of Shumla, which stretches from north-west to south-east, divides the plain of Aboba from the plain of Preslav, and these two plains are intimately associated with the early period of Bulgarian history. It must have been soon after the invaders established their dominion over Moesia, from the Danube to the Balkans, that they transferred their capital and the seat of their princes from a marshy fortress in the Dobrudzha to a more central place. Their choice fell upon Pliska. It is situated north-east of Shumla, in the plain of Aboba, and near the modern village of that name. Travellers had long since recognized the site as an ancient settlement, but it was taken for granted that the antiquities which the ground evidently concealed were of Roman origin, and it has only recently been discovered by excavation that here were the great entrenched camp and the royal palace of the early khans of Bulgaria.

The camp or town formed a large irregular quadrilateral, and some idea of its size may be conveyed, if it is said that its greatest length from north to south was four miles, and that its width varied from two miles and a half to about one mile and three-quarters. It was enclosed by a fortification, consisting of a ditch outside a rampart of earth, the crown of which appears to have been surmounted by a wooden fence. Although early destruction and later cultivation have done what they could to level and obliterate the work, the lines can be clearly traced, and it has been shown that the town could be entered by eleven gates. Near the centre of the enclosure was an inner stronghold, and within this again was the palace of the Khans. The stronghold, shaped like a trapezium, was surrounded by thick walls, which were demolished at an ancient date, and now present the appearance of a rampart about ten feet high. Four circular bastions protected the four angles, and two double rectangular bastions guarded each of the four gates, one of which pierced each of the four walls. The walls were further strengthened by eight other pentagonal bastions. The main entrance was on the eastern side.

Within this fortress stood a group of buildings, which is undoubtedly to be identified as the palatial residence of the Khans. The principal edifice, which may be distinguished as the Throne-palace, was curiously constructed. A large room in the basement, to which there seems to have been no entrance from without, except perhaps a narrow issue underneath a staircase, points to the fact that the ground-floor was only a substructure for an upper storey. This storey consisted of a prodomos or entrance-hall on the south side, to which the chief staircase ascended, and a hall of audience. The hall was nearly square, and was divided by rows of columns into three parts, resembling the nave and aisles of a church. The throne stood in a round apse, in the centre of the northern wail. Not far from this building stood a rectangular temple, which in the days of Krum and Omurtag was devoted to the heathen cult of the Bulgarians, but was converted, after the adoption of Christianity, into a church.

The fortress and the palace, which seem to have been built much about the same time, certainly belong to no later period than the first half of the ninth century. The architecture of the Throne-palace bears the impress of Byzantine influence, and has a certain resemblance to the Trikonchos of Theophilus, as well as to the Magnaura. It was doubtless constructed by Greek masons. The columns may have been imported from Constantinople; it is recorded that Krum, when he attacked that city, carried off works of art from the suburban buildings.

The title of the rulers of Bulgaria was Kanas uvegé, "sublime khan", but even while they were still heathen, they did not scruple to have themselves described sometimes in their official monuments as "rulers by the will of God". Of the political constitution of the kingdom little can be ascertained. The social fabric of the ruling race was based on the clan system, and the head of each clan was perhaps known as a zupan. From early ages the monarchy had been hereditary in the clan of Dulo, but in the middle of the eighth century, Kormisos, who belonged to another family, ascended the throne, and after his death Bulgaria was distracted for some years by struggles for the royal power. We may probably see in these events a revolt of the clans against the hereditary principle and an attempt to make the monarchy elective. There were two ranks of nobility, the boilads and the bagains, and among the boilads there were six or perhaps twelve who had a conspicuous position at the court. When a Bulgarian ambassador arrived at Constantinople, etiquette required that the foreign minister should make particular inquiry first for "the six great boilads", and then for the other boilads, "the inner and the outer". There were thus three grades in this order. We do not know whether the high military offices of tarkan and kaukhan were confined to the boilads. The khan himself had a following or retinue of his own men, which seems to have resembled the German comitatus. The kingdom was divided into ten administrative divisions, governed by officers whose title we know only under the equivalent of count.

The Bulgarians used the Greek language for their official documents, and like the ancient Greeks recorded their public acts by inscriptions on stones. Mutilated texts of treaties and records of important events have been discovered. They are composed in colloquial and halting Greek, not in the diplomatic style of the chancery of Byzantium, and we may guess that they were written by Bulgarians or Slavs who had acquired a smattering of the Greek tongue. Among these monuments are several stones inscribed by the khans in memory of valued officers who died in their service. One of them, for instance, met his death in the waters of the Dnieper, another was drowned in the Theiss. This use of the Greek language for their records is the most striking sign of the influence which was exercised on the Bulgarians by the civilization of Constantinople. We can trace this influence also in their buildings, and we know that they enlisted in their service Greek engineers, and learned the use of those military engines which the Greeks and Romans had invented for besieging towns. Notwithstanding the constant warfare in which they were engaged against the Empire, they looked to Constantinople much as the ancient Germans looked to Rome. Tervel had been created a Caesar by the gratitude of Justinian II, and two of his successors found an honourable refuge in the Imperial city when they were driven by rivals from their own kingdom. Tserig fled to the court of Leo IV. (A.D. 777), accepted baptism and the title of Patrician, and was honoured by the hand of an Imperial princess. It might be expected that the Bulgarians would have found it convenient to adopt the Roman system of marking chronology by indictions or even to use the Roman era of the Creation of the world, and we actually find them employing both these methods of indicating time in their official records. But they had also a chronological system of their own. They reckoned time by cycles of sixty lunar years, starting from the year A.D. 659, memorable in their history as that in which they had crossed the Danube and made their first permanent settlement in Moesia. For historical purposes, this system involved the same disadvantage as that of Indictions, though to a much smaller degree; for instance, when an event was dated by the year shegor alem or 48, it was necessary also to know to what cycle the year referred. But for practical purposes there was no inconvenience, and even in historical records little ambiguity would have been caused until the Bulgarian annals had been extended by the passage of time into a larger series. It is possible that the Bulgarian lunar years corresponded to the years of the Hijra, and if so, this would be a remarkable indication of Mohammadan influence, which there are other reasons for suspecting. We know that in the ninth century there must have been some Bulgarians who were acquainted with Arabic literature.

But the Bulgarians had other neighbours and foes besides the Romans, and political interests in other directions than in that of Constantinople. It is recorded that the same prince who crossed the Danube and inaugurated a new period in Bulgarian history, also drove the Avars westward, and the record expresses the important fact that in the seventh century the Bulgarians succeeded to the overlordship which the Avar khans had exercised over Dacia in the reigns of Maurice and Heraclius. This influence extended to the Theiss or beyond. Eastward, their lordship was bounded by the Empire of the Khazars, but it is impossible to define the precise limit of its extent. There can be no doubt that in the seventh and eighth centuries Bulgaria included the countries known in later times as Walachia and Bessarabia, and the authority of the khans may have been recognised even beyond the Dniester. At all events it appears to be certain that in this period Bulgarian tribes were in occupation of the coastlands from that river wellnigh to the Don, and this Bulgarian continuity was not cleft in twain till the ninth century. The more easterly portion of the people were known as the Inner Bulgarians, and they were probably considered to belong to the Empire of the Khazars. But we cannot decide whether it was at the Dniester or rather at the Dnieper that the authority of the Khazars ended and the claims of the Great Bulgarians of Moesia began.

South of the Danube, the kingdom extended to the Timok, which marked the Servian frontier.The Bulgarians lived on terms of unbroken friendship with the Servians, and this may perhaps be explained by the fact that between their territories the Empire still possessed an important stronghold in the city of Sardica.

For the greater security of their country the Bulgarians reinforced and supplemented the natural defences of mountain and river by elaborate systems of fortification and entrenchment. Their kingdom, almost girt about by an artificial circumvallation, might be compared to an entrenched camp, and the stages in its territorial expansion are marked by successive ramparts. Beyond the Danube, a ditch and earthen wall connected the Pruth with the Dniester in northern Bessarabia, and a similar fence protected the angle between the mouths of the Sereth, the Danube, and the Pruth. The early settlement of Isperikh at Little Preslav, near the mouth of the Danube, was fortified by a rampart across the Dobrudzha, following the line of older Roman walls of earth and stone, but turned to confront a foe advancing from the south, while the Roman defences had been designed against barbarians descending from the north. When the royal residence was moved to Pliska, a line of fortifications was constructed along the heights of Haemus; and a trench and rampart from the mountains to the Danube marked the western frontier. When their successes at the expense of the Empire enabled the conquerors to bestride the mountains, a new fence, traversing Thrace, marked the third position in their southward advance. The westward expansion is similarly separated by two more entrenchments connecting the Haemus with the Danube, while the right bank of that river was defended by a series of fortresses and entrenchments from Little Preslav to the neighbourhood of Nicopolis.

The main road from Constantinople to the capital of the Bulgarian kings crossed the frontier, east of the Tundzha, near the conspicuous heights of Meleona, which, still covered with the remains of Bulgarian fortifications, marked an important station on the frontier, since they commanded the road. To the north-west of Meleona, the Bulgarians held Diampolis, which preserves its old name as Jambol, situated on the Tundzha. The direct road to Pliska did not go by Diampolis, but ran northward in a direct course to the fortress of Marcellae, which is the modern Karnobad. This stronghold possessed a high strategic importance in the early period of Bulgarian history, guarding the southern end of the pass of Veregava, which led to the gates of the Bulgarian king. Not far to the west of Veregava is the pass of Verbits, through which the road lay from Pliska to Diampolis. The whole route from Marcellae to Pliska was flanked by a succession of fortresses of earth and stone.

§2. Krum and Nicephorus I.

In the wars during the reign of Irene and Constantine VI, the Bulgarians had the upper hand; king Kardam repeatedly routed Roman armies, and in the end the Empress submitted to the humiliation of paying an annual tribute to the lord of Pliska. A period of peace ensued, lasting for about ten years (A.D. 797-807). We may surmise that the attention of the Bulgarian king was at this time preoccupied by the political situation which had arisen in the regions adjacent to the Middle Danube by the advance of the Frank power and the overthrow of the Avars. On the other hand, Nicephorus who, soon after his accession, was embroiled in war with the Saracens, may have taken some pains to avoid hostilities on his northern frontier. It is at all events significant that he did not become involved in war with Bulgaria until the tide of the eastern war had abated. We do not know what cause of provocation was given, but so far as our record goes, it was the Roman Emperor who began hostilities. Kardam had in the meantime been succeeded by Krum, a strong, crafty, and ambitious barbarian, whose short reign is memorable in the annals of his country.

It was in A.D. 807 that Nicephorus set forth at the head of an army to invade Bulgaria. But when he reached Hadrianople a mutiny broke out, and he was compelled to abandon his expedition. The next hostile movement of which we hear-we cannot say which occurred-was the appearance of a Bulgarian army in Macedonia, in the regions of the Strymon, towards the close of the following year. Many regiments of the garrison of the province, with the strategos himself and the officers, were cut to pieces, and the treasury of the khan was enriched by the capture of 1100 lbs. of gold which had been destined to pay the soldiers. It would seem that the Romans had not expected an attack so late in the year; but the presence of a considerable force in the Strymon regions points to the fact that the Bulgarians had already betrayed their designs against Macedonia. In the ensuing spring (A.D. 809) Krum followed up his success on the Strymon by an attack on the town of Sardica, which seems at this time to have been the most northerly outpost of the Empire towards the Danube. He captured it not by violence, but by wily words, and put to death a garrison of six thousand soldiers and (it is said) the population of the place. It does not appear that he had conceived the idea of annexing the plain of Sardica to his realm. He dismantled the fortifications and perhaps burned the town, which was one day to be the capital of the Bulgarian name. When the tidings of the calamity arrived, Nicephorus left Constantinople in haste on the Tuesday before Easter (April 3). Although the monk, who has related these events, says nothing of his route, we can have no doubt that he marched straight to the mountains by Meleona and Marcellae, and descended on Pliska from the Veregava Pass. For he dispatched to the city an Imperial letter in which he mentioned that he spent Easter day in the palace of the Bulgarian king. The plunder of Pliska was a reprisal for the sack of Sardica, to which Nicephorus then proceeded for the purpose of rebuilding it. We are not told what road he took, but he avoided meeting the victorious army of the enemy. It is said that some officers who had escaped the massacre asked Nicephorus in vain for a promise that he would not punish them, and were forced to desert to the Bulgarians.

The Emperor desired to rebuild Sardica as speedily and as cheaply as possible, and, fearing that the soldiers would be unwilling to submit to a labour which they might say was not a soldier's business, he prompted the generals and officers to induce the soldiers to address a spontaneous request to the Emperor that the city might be rebuilt. But the men saw through this stratagem, and were filled with indignation. They tore down the tents of their superiors, and, standing in front of the Emperor's pavilion, cried that they would endure his rapacity no more. It was the hour of noon and Nicephorus was dining. He directed two patricians to attempt to tranquillise the army; the noise abated; the soldiers formed a company on a hillock hard by, and, forgetting the matter in hand, kept crying, "Lord, have mercy!". This unorganized mutiny was soon quelled by Imperial promises, and the officers were all on the Emperor's side. Punishment, however, was afterwards inflicted on the ringleaders.

Nicephorus viewed with anxiety the western provinces of his Empire in Macedonia and Thessaly. The Slavs, on whose fidelity no reliance could be placed, were predominant there, and it was the aim of the Bulgarians to bring the Macedonian Slavs under their dominion. To meet the dangers in this quarter the Emperor determined to translate a large number of his subjects from other parts of the Empire and establish them as Roman colonists in what was virtually a Slavonic land. They could keep the Slavs in check and help in repulsing Bulgarian aggression. The transmigration began in September 809 and continued until Easter 810. It seems to have been an unpopular measure. Men did not like to leave the homes to which they were attached, to sell their property, and say farewell to the tombs of their fathers. The poor cling far more to places than the rich and educated, and it was to the poor agriculturists that this measure exclusively applied. Some, we are told, were driven to desperation and committed suicide rather than go into a strange and distant land; and their richer brethren sympathized with them; in fact, the act was described as nothing short of "a captivity". But though it may have been hard on individuals, it was a measure of sound policy; and those who on other grounds were ill-disposed to the government exaggerated the odium which it aroused. Nicephorus, who, as we are told, prided himself greatly on this act, seems to have realised the danger that the Slavonic settlements in Macedonia and Greece might eventually be gathered into a Bulgarian empire; and these new colonies were designed to obviate such a possibility.

Meanwhile the Emperor was preparing a formidable expedition against Bulgaria, to requite Krum for his cruelties and successes. In May A.D. 811 the preparations were complete, and Nicephorus marched through Thrace at the head of a large army. The troops of the Asiatic Themes had been transported from beyond the Bosphorus; Romanus, general of the Anatolics, and Leo, general of the Armeniacs, were summoned to attack the Bulgarians, as their presence was no longer required in Asia to repel the Saracen. When he reached Marcellae, at the foot of the mountains, where he united the various contingents of his host, ambassadors arrived from Krum, who was daunted by the numbers of the Romans. But the Augustus at the head of his legions had no thought of abandoning his enterprise, and he rejected all pleadings for peace. He knew well that a humiliating treaty would be violated by the enemy as soon as his own army had been disbanded; yet nothing less than a signal humiliation could atone for the massacres of Sardica and the Strymon. The march, difficult for a great army, through the pass of Veregava, occupied some time, and on the 20th of July the Romans approached the capital of Krum. Some temporary consternation was caused by the disappearance of a trusted servant of the Emperor, who deserted to the enemy with the Imperial apparel and 100 lbs. of gold.

No opposition was offered to the invaders, and the Roman swords did not spare the inhabitants. Arriving at Pliska, Nicephorus found that the king had fled; he set under lock and key, and sealed with the Imperial seal, the royal treasures, as his own spoil; and burned the palace. Then Krum said, "Lo, thou hast conquered; take all thou pleasest, and go in peace". But the victor disdained to listen. Perhaps it was his hope to recover Moesia and completely to subdue the Bulgarian power. But if this was his design it was not to be realised; Nicephorus was not to do the work which was reserved for Tzimiskes and Basil Bulgaroktonos. He allowed himself to be drawn back into the mountain where Krum and his army awaited him. It is generally supposed that an obvious precaution had been neglected and that the Romans had not taken care to guard their retreat by leaving soldiers to protect the mountain pass behind them. But it seems probable that the pass of Veregava was not the scene of the disaster which followed, and the imprudence of Nicephorus did not consist in neglecting to secure the road of return. So far as we can divine, he permitted the enemy to lure him into the contiguous pass of Verbits, where a narrow defile was blocked by wooden fortifications which small garrisons could defend against multitudes. Here, perhaps, in what is called today the Greek Hollow, where tradition declares that many Greeks once met their death, the army found itself enclosed as in a trap, and the Emperor exclaimed, "Our destruction is certain; if we had wings, we could not escape". The Bulgarians could conceal themselves in the mountains and abide their time until their enemies were pressed by want of supplies; and as the numbers of the Roman army were so great, they would not have to wait long. But the catastrophe was accelerated by a successful night attack. The defiles had been fortified on Thursday and Friday, and on Sunday morning just before dawn the tent in which Nicephorus and the chief patricians were reposing was assailed by the heathen. The details of the attack are not recorded; perhaps they were never clearly known; but we must suppose that there was some extraordinary carelessness in the arrangements of the Roman camp. The Roman soldiers, taken unawares, seem to have been paralysed and to have allowed themselves to be massacred without resistance. Nicephorus himself was slain, and almost all the generals and great officers who were with him, among the rest the general of Thrace and the general of the Anatolics.

This disaster befell on the 26th of July. It seemed more shameful than any reverse that had happened throughout the invasions of the Huns and the Avars, worse than any defeat since the fatal day of Hadrianople. After the death of Valens in that great triumph of the Visigoths, no Roman Augustus had fallen a victim to barbarians. During the fifth and sixth centuries the Emperors were not used to fight, but since the valour of Heraclius set a new example, most of the Roman sovrans had led armies to battle, and if they were not always victorious, they always succeeded in escaping. The slaughter of Nicephorus was then an event to which no parallel could be found for four centuries back, and it was a shock to the Roman world.

Krum exposed the head of the Emperor on a lance for a certain number of days. He then caused the skull to be hollowed out in the form of a large drinking bowl, and lined with silver, and at great banquets he used to drink in it to the health of his Slavonic boliads with the Slavonic formula "zdravitsa".

A memorial of this disaster survived till late times at Eskibaba in Thrace, where a Servian patriarch of the seventeenth century saw the tomb of a certain Nicolas, a warrior who had accompanied the fatal expedition of Nicephorus and seen a strange warning dream. The Turks had shrouded the head of the corpse with a turban.

§3. Krum and Michael I.

Sated with their brilliant victory, the Bulgarians did not pursue the son and son-in-law of the Emperor, who escaped from the slaughter, and they allowed the Romans ample time to arrange the succession to the throne, which, as we have seen, was attended by serious complications. But Michael I had not been many months established in the seat of Empire, when he received tidings that the enemy had invaded Thrace (A.D: 812). The city which Krum first attacked was near the frontier. On an inner curve of the bays, on whose northern and southern horns Anchialus and Apollonia faced each other, lay the town of Develtos. It might pride itself on its dignity as an episcopal seat, or on its strength as a fortified city. But its fortifications did not now avail it, nor yet its bishop. Krum reduced the place, and transported inhabitants and bishop beyond the mountains to Bulgaria. The Emperor meanwhile prepared to oppose the invader. On the 7th day of June he left the capital, and the Empress Procopia accompanied him as far as Tzurulon, a place which still preserves its name as Chorlu, on the direct road from Selymbria to Hadrianople.

It does not seem that Michael advanced farther than to Tzurulon. The news of the fate of Develtos came, and a mutiny broke out in the army. It was thought that the Emperor had shown incompetence or had followed injudicious advice. While we can well understand that little confidence could be felt in this weak and inexperienced commander, we must also remember that there was in the army a large iconoclastic section hostile to the government. The Opsikian and Thrakesian Themes played the most prominent parts in the rioting. A conspiracy in favour of the blind brothers of Constantine V. followed upon this mutiny, and Michael returned to the City. The field was thus left to the Bulgarians, who prevailed in both Thrace and Macedonia. But the alarm felt by the inhabitants caused perhaps more confusion than the actual operations of the invaders. It does not indeed appear that the Bulgarians committed in this year any striking atrocities or won any further success of great moment. But the fate of the Roman Emperor in the previous year had worked its full effect. The dwellers in Thrace were thoroughly frightened, and when they saw no Roman army in the field they had not the heart to defend their towns. The taking of Develtos brought the fear home to neighbouring Anchialus on the sea. Anchialus had always been one of the firmest and strongest defences against the barbarians-against the Avars in olden days and against the Bulgarians more recently. Fifty years ago the inhabitants had seen the Bulgarian forces defeated in the neighbouring plain by the armies of the Fifth Constantine. But Michael was not like Constantine, as the men of Anchialus well knew; and now, although the defences of their, city had recently been restored and strengthened by Irene, they fled from the place though none pursued. Other cities, not only smaller places like Nicaea and Probaton, but even such as Beroe and the great city of Western Thrace, Philippopolis, did likewise. The Thracian Nicaea is little known to history; it seems to have been situated to the south-east of Hadrianople. Probaton or Sheep-fort, which is to be sought at the modern Provadia, north-east of Hadrianople, had seen Roman and Bulgarian armies face to face in a campaign of Constantine VI. (A.D. 791). Stara Zagora is believed to mark the site of Beroe, at the crossing of the Roman roads, which led from Philippopolis to Anchialus and from Hadrianople to Nicopolis on the Danube. It was in this neighbourhood that the Emperor Decius was defeated by the Goths. The town had been restored by the Empress Irene, who honoured it by calling it Irenopolis; but the old name persisted, as in the more illustrious cases of Antioch and Jerusalem. Macedonian Philippi behaved like Thracian Philippopolis, and those reluctant colonists whom Nicephorus had settled in the district of the Strymon seized the opportunity to return to their original dwellings in Asia Minor.

Later in the same year (A.D. 812) Krum sent an embassy to the Roman Emperor to treat for peace. The ambassador whom he chose was a Slav, as his name Dargamer proves. The Bulgarians wished to renew an old commercial treaty which seems to have been made about half a century before between king Kormisos and Constantine V; and Krum threatened that he would attack Mesembria if his proposals were not immediately accepted. The treaty in question

(1) had defined the frontier by the hills of Meleona; (2) had secured for the Bulgarian monarch a gift of apparel and red dyed skins to the value of £1350; (3) had arranged that deserters should be sent back; and (4) stipulated for the free intercourse of merchants between the two states in case they were provided with seals and passports; the property of those who had no passport was to be forfeited to the treasury.

After some discussion the proposal for the renewal of this treaty was rejected, chiefly on account of the clause relating to refugees. True to his threat, Krum immediately set his forces in motion against Mesembria and laid siege to it about the middle of October (A.D. 812). Farther out on the bay of Anchialus than Anchialus itself, where the coast resumes its northward direction, stood this important city, on a peninsula hanging to the mainland by a low and narrow isthmus, about five hundred yards in length, which is often overflowed by tempestuous seas. It was famous for its salubrious waters; it was also famous for its massive fortifications. Here had lived the parents of the great Leo, the founder of the Isaurian Dynasty. Hither had fled for refuge a Bulgarian king, driven from his country by a sedition, in the days of Constantine V. Krum was aided by the skill of an Arab engineer, who, formerly in the service of Nicephorus, had been dissatisfied with that Emperor's parsimony and had fled to Bulgaria. No relief came, and Mesembria fell in a fortnight or three weeks. Meanwhile the promptness of Krum in attacking had induced Michael to reconsider his decision. The Patriarch was strongly in favour of the proposed peace; but he was opposed by Theodore, the abbot of Studion, who was intimate with Theoktistos, the Emperor's chief adviser. The discussion which was held on this occasion (November 1) illustrates how the theological atmosphere of the time was not excluded from such debates. The war party said, "We must not accept peace at the risk of subverting the divine command; for the Lord said, Him who cometh unto me I will in no wise cast out", referring to the clause concerning the surrender of refugees. The peace party, on their side, submitted that in the first place there were, as a matter of fact, no refugees, and secondly, even if there were, the safety of a large number was more acceptable to God than the safety of a few; they suggested, moreover, that the real motive of those who rejected the peace was a short-sighted parsimony, and that they were more desirous of saving the 30 lbs. worth of skins than concerned for the safety of deserters; these disputants were also able to retort upon their opponents passages of Scripture in favour of peace. The war party prevailed.

Four days later the news came that Mesembria was taken. The barbarians had found it well stocked with the comforts of life, full of gold and silver; and among other things they discovered a considerable quantity of Roman Fire, and thirty-six engines (large tubes) for hurling that deadly substance. But they did not occupy the place; they left it, like Sardica, dismantled and ruined. It would seem that, not possessing a navy, they judged that Mesembria would prove an embarrassing rather than a valuable acquisition.

All thoughts of peace were now put away, and the Emperor made preparations to lead another expedition against Bulgaria in the following year. In February (A.D. 813) two Christians who had escaped from the hands of Krum announced that he was preparing to harry Thrace. The Emperor immediately set out and Krum was obliged to retreat, not without some losses. In May all the preparations were ready. The Asiatic forces had been assembled in Thrace, and even the garrisons which protected the kleisurai leading into Syria had been withdrawn to fight against a foe who was at this moment more formidable than the Caliph. Lycaonians, Isaurians, Cilicians, Cappadocians, and Galatians were compelled to march northwards, much against their will, and the Armeniacs and Cappadocians were noticed as louder than the others in their murmurs. As Michael and his generals issued from the city they were accompanied by all the inhabitants, as far as the Aqueduct. Gifts and keepsakes showered upon the officers, and the Empress Procopia herself was there, exhorting the Imperial staff to take good care of Michael and to fight bravely for the Christians.

Michael, if he had some experience of warfare, had no ability as a general, and he was more ready to listen to the advice of the ministers who had gained influence over him in the palace than to consult the opinion of two really competent military men who accompanied the expedition. These were Leo, general of the Anatolics, whom, as we have already seen, he had recalled from exile, and John Aplakes, the general of Macedonia. During the month of May the army moved about Thrace, and was little less burdensome to the inhabitants than the presence of an enemy. It was specially remarked by contemporaries that no attempt was made to recover Mesembria. Early in June Krum entered Roman territory and both armies encamped near Versinicia, a place not far from Hadrianople. At Versinicia, nearly twenty years before, another Emperor had met another Khan. Then Kardam had skulked in a wood, and had not ventured to face Constantine. Krum, however, was bolder than his predecessor, and, contrary to Bulgarian habit, did not shrink from a pitched battle. For fifteen days they stood over against one another, neither side venturing to attack, and the heat of summer rendered this incessant watching a trying ordeal both for men and for horses. At last John Aplakes, who commanded one wing, composed of the Macedonian and Thracian troops, lost his patience and sent a decisive message to the Emperor: "How long are we to stand here and perish? I will strike first in the name of God, and then do ye follow up bravely, and we can conquer. We are ten times more numerous than they". The Bulgarians, who stood on lower ground in the valley, fell before the charge of Aplakes and his soldiers who descended on them from a slight elevation; but the brave strategos of Macedonia was not supported by the centre and the other wing. There was a general flight without any apparent cause, and the Anatolics were conspicuous among the fugitives. Aplakes, left with his own men, far too few to hold their ground, fell fighting. The enemy were surprised and alarmed at this inexplicable behaviour of an army so far superior in numbers, so famous for its discipline. Suspecting some ambush or stratagem the Bulgarians hesitated to move. But they soon found out that the flight was genuine, and they followed in pursuit. The Romans threw away their weapons, and did not arrest their flight until they reached the gates of the capital

Such was the strange battle which was fought between Hadrianople and Versinicia on June 22, A.D. 813. It has an interest as one of the few engagements in which an army chiefly consisting of Slavs seems to have voluntarily opposed a Roman host on open ground. As a rule the Slavs and Bulgarians avoided pitched battles in the plain and only engaged in mountainous country, where their habits and their equipment secured them the advantage. But Krum seems to have been elated by his career of success, and to have conceived for his opponents a contempt which prompted him to desert the traditions of Bulgarian warfare. His audacity was rewarded, but the victory was not due to any superiority on his side in strategy or tactics. Historians have failed to realise the difficulties which beset the battle of Versinicia, or to explain the extraordinary spectacle of a Roman army, in all its force, routed in an open plain by a far smaller army of Slavs and Bulgarians. It was a commonplace that although the Bulgarians were nearly sure to have the upper hand in mountainous defiles they could not cope in the plain with a Roman army, even much smaller than their own. The soldiers knew this well themselves, and it is impossible to believe that the Anatolic troops, disciplined by warfare against the far more formidable Saracens, were afraid of the enemy whom they met in Thrace.

The only reasonable explanation of the matter is treachery, and treachery was the cause assigned by contemporary report. The Anatolic troops feigned cowardice and fled; their flight produced a panic and the rest fled too. Others may have been in the plot besides the Anatolics, but the soldiers of Leo, the Armenian, were certainly the prime movers. The political consequences of the battle show the intention of the Asiatic troops in courting this defeat. The Emperor Michael lost credit and was succeeded by Leo. This was what the Asiatic soldiers desired. The religious side of Michael's rule was highly unpopular in Phrygia and the districts of Mount Taurus, and Michael himself was, probably, a Thracian or Macedonian. The rivalry between the Asiatic and European nobles, which played an important part at a later period of history, was perhaps already beginning; and it is noteworthy that the Thracians and Macedonians under Aplakes were the only troops who did not flee. Reviewing all the circumstances, so far as we know them, we cannot escape the conclusion that the account is right which represents the regiments of Leo, if not Leo himself, as guilty of intentional cowardice on the field of Versinicia. It was planned to discredit Michael and elevate Leo in his stead, and the plan completely succeeded.

§4. The Bulgarian Siege of Constantinople (A.D. 813)

After his victory over the army of Michael, the king of the Bulgarians resolved to attempt the siege of two great cities at the same time. He had good reason to be elated by his recent successes against the Roman Empire; he might well dream of winning greater successes still. He had achieved what few enemies of the Empire in past time could boast that they had done. He had caused the death of two Emperors and the downfall of a third; for he might attribute the deposition of Michael to his own victory; and within two years he had annihilated one Roman army and signally defeated another. In point of fact, these successes were due rather to luck than to merit; the Bulgarian king had shown craft but no conspicuous ability in generalship; the battles had not been won by superiority in tactics or by signal courage. But the facts could not be ignored; the head of a Roman Emperor was a drinking-cup in the palace of Pliska, and a large Roman army had been routed near Hadrianople.

It was an ambition of Leo the Armenian, as has been already noticed, to emulate the great Isaurian Emperors of the previous century; and fortune gave him, at his very accession, an opportunity of showing how far he could approach in military prowess the Fifth Constantine, whom the Bulgarians had found so formidable. Krum left his brother to blockade the city of Hadrian, and advanced himself to lay siege to the city of Constantine. He appeared before it six days after the accession of the new Emperor. In front of the walls he made a display of his power, and in the park outside the Golden Gate he prepared sacrifices of men and animals. The Romans could see from the walls how this "new Sennacherib" laved his feet on the margin of the sea and sprinkled his soldiers; they could hear the acclamations of the barbarians, and witness the procession of the monarch through a line of his concubines, worshipping and glorifying their lord. He then asked the Emperor to allow him to fix his lance on the Golden Gate as an emblem of victory; and when the proposal was refused he retired to his tent. Having produced no impression by his heathen parade, and having failed to daunt New Rome, he threw up a rampart and plundered the neighbourhood for several days. But there was no prospect of taking the queen of cities where so many, greater than he, had failed before, and he soon offered terms of peace, demanding as the price a large treasure of gold and raiment, and a certain number of chosen damsels. The new Emperor Leo saw in the overtures of the enemy a good opportunity to carry out a design, which in the present age public opinion would brand as an infamous act of treachery, but which the most pious of contemporary monks, men by no means disposed to be lenient to Leo, regarded as laudable. The chronicler Theophanes, whom Leo afterwards persecuted, said that the failure of the plot was due to our sins.

The Emperor sent a message to Krum: "Come down to the shore, with a few unarmed men, and we also unarmed will proceed by boat to meet you. We can then talk together and arrange terms". The place convened was on the Golden Horn, just north of the seawall; and at night three armed men were concealed in a house outside the Gate of Blachern, with directions to issue forth and slay Krum when a certain sign was given by one of Leo's attendants.

Next day the Bulgarian king duly rode down to the shore, with three companions, namely his treasurer, a Greek deserter, Constantine Patzikos, who had married Krum's sister, and the son of this Constantine. Krum dismounted and sat on the ground; his nephew held his horse ready, "saddled and bridled". Leo and his party soon arrived in the Imperial barge, and while they conversed, Hexabulios, who was with Leo, suddenly covered his face with his hands. The motion offended the sensitive pride of the barbarian; highly offended he started to his feet and leaped upon his horse. Nor was he too soon; for the gesture was the concerted sign, and the armed ambush rushed out from the place of hiding. The attendants of Krum pressed on either side of him as he rode away, trying to defend him or escape with him; but, as they were on foot, the Greeks were able to capture them. Those who watched the scene from the walls, and saw, as they thought, the discomfiture of the pagan imminent, cried out, "The cross has conquered"; the darts of the armed soldiers were discharged after the retreating horseman; but though they hit him he received no mortal wound, and escaped, now more formidable than ever, as his ferocity was quickened by the thirst of vengeance. His treasurer was slain; his brother-in-law and nephew were taken alive.

On the next day the wrath of the deceived Bulgarian blazed forth in literal fire. The inhabitants of the city, looking across the Golden Horn, witnessed the conflagration of the opposite suburbs, churches, convents, and palaces, which the enemy plundered and destroyed. They did not stay their course of destruction at the mouth of the Golden Horn. They burned the Imperial Palace of St. Mamas, which was situated opposite to Scutari, at the modern Beshik-tash, to the south of Orta Keui. They pulled down the ornamental columns, and carried away, to deck the residence of their king, the sculptured images of animals which they found in the hippodrome of the palace and packed in waggons. All living things were butchered. Their ravages were extended northwards along the shores of the Bosphorus, and in the inland region behind. But this was only the beginning of the terrible vengeance. The suburbs outside the Golden Gate, straggling as far as Rhegion, were consigned to the flames, and we cannot suppose that their energy of destruction spared the palace of Hebdomon. The fort of Athyras and a bridge of remarkable size and strength over the river of the same name, which flows into the Propontis, were destroyed. Along the western highroad the avenger advanced till he reached Selymbria, where he destroyed the churches and rased the citadel. The fort of Daonin was levelled, and the first obstacle in the path of destruction was the strong wall of Heraclea which had once defied Philip of Macedon. Unable to enter it the Bulgarians burned the suburbs and the houses of the harbour. Continuing their course, they razed the fort of Rhaedestos and the castle of Apros. Having spent ten days there, they marched southward to the hills of Ganos, whither men and beasts had fled for concealment. The fugitives were easily dislodged from their hiding-places by the practised mountaineers; the men were slain; the women, children, and animals were sent to Bulgaria. After a visit of depredation to the shore of the Hellespont, the desolater returned slowly, capturing forts as he went, to Hadrianople, which his brother had not yet succeeded in reducing by blockade. Poliorcetic Engines were now applied; hunger was already doing its work; no relief was forthcoming; and the city perforce surrendered. All the inhabitants, including the archbishop Manuel, were transported to Bulgaria beyond the Danube, where they were permitted to live in a settlement, governed by one of themselves and known as Macedonia.

It was now the turn of the Imperial government to make overtures for peace, and of the victorious and offended Bulgarian to reject them. Leo then took the field himself, and by a stratagem, successfully executed, he inflicted an overwhelming defeat on the army of the enemy, or a portion of it which was still active in the neighbourhood of Mesembria. Entrenching himself near that city and not far from the Bulgarian camp, he waited for some days. The Roman troops had command of abundant supplies, but he soon heard that the Bulgarians were hard pressed for food. Confiding his plan only to one officer, Leo left the camp by night with a company of experienced warriors, and lay in ambush on an adjacent hill. Day dawned, and the Romans, discovering that the Emperor was not in the camp, imagined that he had fled. The tidings reached the camp of the enemy before evening, and the barbarians thought that their adversaries were now delivered an easy prey into their hands. Intending to attack the Roman camp on the morrow, and meanwhile secure, they left aside the burden of their arms and yielded to the ease of sleep. Then Leo and his men descended in the darkness of the night and wrought great slaughter. The Roman camp had been advised of the stratagem just in time to admit of their cooperation, and not soon enough to give a deserter the opportunity of perfidy. The Bulgarians were annihilated; not a firebearer, to use the Persian proverb, escaped. This success was followed up by an incursion into Bulgaria; and Leo's policy was to spare those who were of riper years, while he destroyed their children by dashing them against stones.

Henceforward the hill on which Leo had lain in ambush was named the hill of Leo, and the Bulgarians, whenever they pass that way, shake the head and point with the finger, unable to forget that great disaster.

The ensuing winter was so mild, and the rivers so low, that an army of 30,000 Bulgarians crossed the frontier and advanced to Arcadiopolis. They passed the river Erginus and made many captives. But when they returned to the river, they found that a week's rain had rendered it impassable, and they were obliged to wait for two weeks on the banks. The waters gradually subsided, a bridge was made, and 50,000 captives were led back to Bulgaria, while the plunder was carried in waggons, loaded with rich Armenian carpets, blankets and coverlets, raiment of all kinds, and bronze utensils. His censorious critics alleged that the Emperor was remiss in not seizing the opportunity to attack the invaders during the enforced delay.

Shortly after this incursion, tidings reached Constantinople that it was destined soon to be the object of a grand Bulgarian expedition. Krum was himself engaged in collecting a great host; "all the Slavonias" were contributing soldiers; and, from his Empire beyond the Danube, Avars as well as Slavs were summoned to take part in despoiling the greatest city in the world. Poliorcetic machines of all the various kinds which New Rome herself could dispose of were being prepared for the service of Bulgaria. The varieties of these engines, of which a list is recorded, must be left to curious students of the poliorcetic art to investigate. There were three-throwers and four-throwers, tortoises, fire-hurlers and stone-hurlers, rams, little scorpions, and dart-stands, besides a large supply of balls, slings, long ladders, levers, and ropes, and the inevitable city-takers. In the stables of the king fed a thousand oxen destined to draw the engines, and five thousand iron-bound cars were prepared. The attempt which had been made on his life still rankled in Krum's memory, and he determined to direct his chief efforts against Blachernae, the quarter where the arrow had wounded him.

Leo had taken measures for the defence of the city. He employed a large number of workmen to build a new wall outside that of Heraclius, and he caused a wide moat to be dug. But, as it turned out, these precautions proved unnecessary; and, indeed, the work was not completed when the death of Krum changed the situation. The most formidable of the Bulgarian monarchs with whom the Empire had yet to deal died suddenly through the bursting of a bloodvessel on the 14th of April A.D. 814, and his plan perished with him.

§5. The Reign of Omurtag

After the death of Krum, Bulgaria was engaged and distracted by a struggle for the throne. Of this political crisis we have no clear knowledge, but it appears that it ended by the triumph of a certain Tsok over one, if not two, rivals. The rule of Tsok is described as inhumane. He is said to have required all the Christian captives, both clerical and lay, to renounce their religion, and when they refused, to have put them to death. But his reign was brief. It was possibly before the end of the year (A.D. 814) that he was slain, and succeeded by Omurtag, the son of Krum. The first important act of the sublime Khan Omurtag was to conclude a formal treaty of peace with the Roman Empire (A.D. 815-816). It is probable that a truce or preliminary agreement had been arranged immediately after Krum's death, but when Krum's son ascended the throne negotiations were opened which led to a permanent peace. The contracting parties agreed that the treaty should continue in force for thirty years, with a qualification perhaps that it should be confirmed anew at the expiration of each decennium. A fortunate chance has preserved a portion of what appears to be an official abstract of the instrument, inscribed on a marble column and set up in the precincts of his residence at Pliska by order of the Bulgarian king. Provision was made for the interchange and ransom of captives, and the question of the surrender of deserters, on which the negotiations between Krum and Michael I had fallen through, was settled in a manner satisfactory to Omurtag. All the Slavs who had been undoubtedly subject to the Bulgarians in the period before the war, and had deserted to the Empire, were to be sent back to their various districts. The most important articles concerned the delimitation of the frontier which divided Thrace between the two sovrans. The new boundary ran westward from Develtos to Makrolivada, a fortress situated between Hadrianople and Philippopolis, close to the junction of the Hebrus with its tributary the Arzus. At Makrolivada the frontier-line turned northward and proceeded to Mt. Haemus. The Bulgarians, who put their faith in earthworks and circumvallations, proposed to protect the boundary, and give it a visible form, by a rampart and trench. The Imperial government, without whose consent the execution of such a work would have been impossible, agreed to withdraw the garrisons from the forts in the neighbourhood of the frontier during the construction of the fortification, in order to avoid the possibility of hostile collisions.

The remains of the Great Fence, which marked the southern boundary of the Bulgarian kingdom in the ninth and tenth centuries, can be traced across Thrace, and are locally known as the Erkesiia. Some parts of it are visible to the eye of the inexperienced traveller, while in others the line has disappeared or has to be investigated by the diligent attention of the antiquarian. Its eastern extremity is near the ruins of Develtos, on that inlet of the Black Sea whose horns were guarded by the cities of Anchialus and Apollonia. It can be followed easily in its westward course, past Busokastro, as far as the river Tundzha, for about forty miles; beyond that river it is more difficult to trace, but its western extremity seems to have been discovered at Makrolivada, near the modern village of Trnovo-Seimen. The line roughly corresponds to the modern boundary between Turkey and Bulgaria. The rampart was on the north, the ditch on the south, showing that it was designed as a security against the Empire; the rampart was probably surmounted, like the wall of Pliska, by timber palisades, and the Bulgarians maintained a constant watch and ward along their boundary fences. In the eastern section, near the heights of Meleona, the line of defence was strengthened by a second entrenchment to the south, extending for about half a mile in the form of a bow, and locally known as the Gipsy Erkesiia, but we do not know the origin or date of this fortification. It would seem that the Bulgarians contented themselves with this fence, for no signs have been discovered of a similar construction on the western frontier, between Makrolivada and the mountains.

Sanctity was imparted to the contract by the solemn rites of superstition. Omurtag consented to pledge his faith according to the Christian formalities, while Leo, on his part, showing a religious toleration only worthy of a pagan, did not scruple to conform to the heathen customs of the barbarians. Great was the scandal caused to pious members of the Church when the Roman

Emperor, "peer of the Apostles", poured on the earth a libation of water, swore upon a sword, sacrificed dogs, and performed other unholy rites. Greater, if possible, was their indignation, when the heathen envoys were invited to pollute by their touch a copy of the Holy Gospels; and to these impieties earthquakes and plagues, which happened subsequently, were attributed.

This peace, which the Bulgarians considered satisfactory for many years to come, enabled Omurtag to throw his energy into the defence of his western dominions against the great German Empire, which had begun to threaten his influence even in regions south of the Danube. The Slavonic peoples were restless under the severe yoke of the sublime Khan, and they were tempted by the proximity of the Franks, whose power had extended into Croatia, to turn to the Emperor Lewis for protection. The Slavs of the river Timok, on the borders of Servia, who were under Bulgarian lordship, had recently left their abodes and sought a refuge within the dominion of Lewis. Their ambassadors presented themselves at his court in A.D. 818, but nothing came of the embassy, for the Timocians were induced to throw in their lot with Liudewit, the Croatian zupan, who had defied the Franks and was endeavouring to establish Croatian independence. It seemed for a moment that the Croatian leader might succeed in creating a Slavonic realm corresponding to the old Diocese of Illyricum, and threatening Italy and Bavaria; but the star of Liudewit rose and declined rapidly; he was unable to cope with the superior forces of Lewis, and his flight was soon followed by his death (A.D. 823). The Franks established their ascendency in Croatia, and soon afterwards Bulgarian ambassadors appeared in Germany and sought an audience of the Emperor (A.D. 824). It was the first time that a Frank monarch had received an embassy from a Bulgarian khan. The ambassadors bore a letter from Omurtag, who seems to have proposed a pacific regulation of the boundaries between the German and Bulgarian dominions. Their empires touched at Singidunum, which was now a Croatian town, under its new Slavonic name of Belgrade, the "white city", and the Bulgarian ruler probably claimed that his lordship extended, northward from Belgrade, as far perhaps as Pest, to the banks of the Danube. The Emperor Lewis cautiously determined to learn more of Bulgaria and its king before he committed himself to an answer, and he sent the embassy back along with an envoy of his own. They returned to Bavaria at the end of the year. In the meantime an embassy arrived from a Slavonic people, whose denomination the German chroniclers disguised under the name Praedenecenti. They were also known, or were a branch of a people known, as the Abodrites, and must be carefully distinguished from the northern Abodrites, whose homes were on the Lower Elbe. This tribe, who seem to have lived on the northern bank of the Danube, to the east of Belgrade, suffered, like the Timoeians, under the oppressive exactions of the Bulgarians, and, like them, looked to the advance of the Pranks as an opportunity for deliverance. Lewis, whom they had approached on previous occasions, received their envoys in audience, and kept the Bulgarians waiting for nearly six months. Finally he received them at Aachen, and dismissed them with an ambiguous letter to their master.

It is clear that Lewis deemed it premature to commit his policy to a definite regulation of the boundaries of the southeastern mark, or to give any formal acknowledgment to the Bulgarian claims on the confines of Pannonia and Croatia; but he hesitated to decline definitely the proposals of the Khan. Omurtag, impatient of a delay which encouraged the rebellious spirit of his Slavonic dependencies, indited another letter, which he dispatched by the same officer who had been the bearer of his first missive (A.D. 826). He requested the Emperor to consent to an immediate regulation of the frontier; and if this proposal were not acceptable, he asked that, without any formal treaty, each power should keep within his own borders. The terms of this message show that the principal object of Omurtag was an agreement which should restrain the Franks from intervening in his relations to his Slavonic subjects. Lewis found a pretext for a new postponement. A report reached him that the Khan had been slain or dethroned by one of his nobles, and he sent an emissary to the Eastern Mark to discover if the news were true. As no certain information could be gained, he dismissed the envoy without a letter.

The sublime Khan would wait no longer on the Emperor's pleasure. Policy as well as resentment urged him to take the offensive, for, if he displayed a timid respect towards the Franks, his prestige among the Slavs beyond the Danube was endangered. The power of Bulgaria was asserted by an invasion of Pannonia (A.D. 827). A fleet of boats sailed from the Danube up the Drave, carrying a host of Bulgarians who devastated with fire and sword the Slavs and Avars of Eastern Pannonia. The chiefs of the Slavonic tribes were expelled and Bulgarian governors were set over them. Throughout the ninth century the Bulgarians were neighbours of the Franks in these regions, and seem to have held both Sirmium and Singidunum. We may be sure that Omurtag did not fail to lay a heavy hand on the disloyal Slavs of Dacia.

The operations of Omurtag in this quarter of his empire are slightly illustrated by an incidental memorial, in a stone recording the death of Onegavon. This officer, who was one of the king's "men" and held the post of tarkan, was on his way to the Bulgarian camp and was drowned in crossing the river Theiss.

A similar memorial, in honour of Okorses, who in proceeding to a scene of war was drowned in the Dnieper, shows that the arms of Omurtag were also active in the East. The situation in the Pontic regions, where the dominion of the Bulgarians confronted the empire of the Khazars, is at this time veiled in obscurity. The tents of the Magyars extended over the region between the Don and the Dnieper. The country to the west was exposed to their raids, and not many years later we shall find their bands in the neighbourhood of the Danube. The effect of the Magyar movement would ultimately be to press back the frontier of Great Bulgaria to the Danube, but they were already pressing the Inner Bulgarians into a small territory north of the Sea of Azov, and thus dividing by an alien and hostile wedge the continuous Bulgarian fringe which had extended along the northern coast of the Euxine. Although the process of the Magyar advance is buried in oblivion, it is not likely that it was not opposed by the resistance of the lords of Pliska, and it is tempting to surmise that the military camp to which the unlucky Okorses was bound when the waters of the Dnieper overwhelmed him was connected with operations against the Magyars.

From the scanty and incidental notices of Omurtag which occur in the Greek and Latin chronicles, we should not have been able to guess the position which his reign takes in the internal history of Bulgaria. Bub the accidents of time and devastation have spared some of his own records, which reveal him as a great builder. He constructed two new palaces, or palatial fortresses, one on the bank of the Danube, the other at the gates of the Balkans, and both possessed strategic significance. Tutrakan, the ancient Transmarisca (to the east of Rustchuk), marks a point where the Danube, divided here by an island amid-stream, offers a conspicuously convenient passage for an army. Here the Emperor Valens built a bridge of boats, and in the past century the Russians have frequently chosen this place to throw their armies across the river. The remains of a Bulgarian fortress of stone and earth, at the neighbouring Kadykei, probably represent the stronghold which Omurtag built to command the passage of Transmarisca. On an inscribed column, which we may still read in one of the churches of Tyrnovo, whither the pagan monument was transported to serve an architectural use, it is recorded that "the sublime Khan Omurtag, living in his old house (at Pliska), made a house of high renown on the Danube". But the purpose of this inscription is not to celebrate the building of this residence, but to chronicle the construction of a sepulchre which Omurtag raised half-way between his "two glorious houses" and probably destined for his own resting-place. The measurements, which are carefully noted in the inscription, have enabled modern investigators to identify Omurtag's tomb with a large conical mound or kurgan close to the village of Mumdzhilar. The memorial concludes with a moralising reflexion: "Man dies, even if he live well, and another is born, and let the latest born, considering this writing, remember him who made it. The name of the ruler is Omurtag, Kanas Ubege. God grant that he may live a hundred years".

If the glorious house on the Danube was a defence, in the event of an attack of Slavs or other enemies coming from the north, Omurtag, although he lived at peace with the Roman Empire, thought it well to strengthen himself against his southern neighbours also, in view of future contingencies. The assassination of Leo and the elevation of Michael II, whose policy he could not foresee, may have been a determining motive. At all events it was in the year following this change of dynasty that Omurtag built a new royal residence and fortress in the mountains, on the river Tutsa, commanding the pass of Veregava, by which Roman armies had been wont to descend upon Pliska, as well as the adjacent pass of Verbits. We do not know how the new town which the King erected in front of the mountain defiles was called in his own tongue, but the Slavs called it Preslav, "the glorious", a name which seems originally to have been applied to all the palaces of the Bulgarian kings. It is not probable that Omurtag intended to transfer his principal residence from the plain to the hills, but his new foundation was destined, as Great Preslav, to become within a hundred years the capital of Bulgaria.

The foundation of the city is recorded on a large limestone column which was dug out of the earth a few years ago at Chatalar, about four miles from the ruins of Preslav. "The sublime Khan Omurtag is divine ruler in the land where he was born. Abiding in the Plain of Pliska, he made a palace (aule) on the Tutsa and displayed his power to the Greeks and Slavs. And he constructed with skill a bridge over the Tutsa. And he set up in his fortress four columns, and between the columns he set two bronze lions. May God grant that the divine ruler may press down the Emperor with his foot so long as the Tutsa flows, that he may procure many captives for the Bulgarians, and that subduing his foes he may, in joy and happiness, live for a hundred years". The date of the foundation was the Bulgarian year shegor alem, or the fifteenth indiction of the Greeks (A.D. 821-822). In this valuable record of the foundation of Preslav, we may note with interest the hostile reference to the Roman Emperor as the chief and permanent enemy of Bulgaria, although at this time Bulgaria and the Empire were at peace. It was probably a standing formula which had originally been adopted in the reign of some former king, when the two powers were at war.

It has been already related how Omurtag intervened in the civil war between Michael and Thomas, how he defeated the rebel on the field of Keduktos, and returned laden with spoils (A.D. 823). This was his only expedition into Roman territory: the Thirty Years' Peace was preserved inviolate throughout his reign. The date of his death is uncertain.

§6. The Reigns of Malamir and Boris

Omurtag was succeeded by his youngest son Presiam, though one at least of his elder sons was still living. Presiam is generally known as Malamir, a Slavonic name which he assumed, perhaps toward the end of his reign. The adoption of this name is a landmark in the gradual process of the assertion of Slavonic influence in the Bulgarian realm. We may surmise that it corresponds to a political situation in which the Khan was driven to rely on the support of his Slavonic subjects against the Bulgarian nobles.

We have some official records of the sublime Khan Malamir, though not so many or so important as the records of his father. We have a memorial column of Tsepa, a boilad and king's liegeman who died of illness. From another stone we learn that Isbules, the kaukhan, who was one of the king's old boilads, built an aqueduct for Malamir at his own expense. This aqueduct was probably to supply one of the royal palaces. Malamir celebrated the occasion by giving a feast to the Bulgarians, and bestowing many gifts upon the boilads and bagains.

There was some risk that the treaty with the Empire might be denounced during the reign of Theophilus.

The Thracian and Macedonian captives who had been transported by Krum to regions beyond the Danube formed a plan to return to their homes. This colony of exiles, who are said to have numbered 12,000 not counting females, were permitted to choose one of their own number as a governor, and Kordyles, who exercised this function, contrived to make his way secretly to Constantinople and persuaded Theophilus to send ships to rescue the exiles and bring them home. This act was evidently a violation of the Thirty Years' Peace, and at the same moment the Bulgarian ruler was engaged in a hostile action against the Empire by advancing to Thessalonica. It can hardly be an accident that the date to which our evidence for their transaction points (c. 836) coincides with the termination of the second decade of the Peace, and if it was a condition that the Treaty should be renewed at the end of each decade, it was a natural moment for either ruler to choose for attempting to compass an end to which the other would not agree. We cannot determine precisely the order of events, or understand the particular circumstances in which the captives effected their escape. We are told that the whole population began to cross over a river, in order to reach the place where the Imperial ships awaited them. The Bulgarian Count of the district crossed over to their side to prevent them, and being defeated with great loss, sought the help of the Magyars, who were now masters of the north coast of the Euxine as far as the Bulgarian frontier. Meanwhile the Greeks crossed, and were about to embark when a host of Magyars appeared and commanded them to surrender all their property. The Greeks defied the predatory foe, defeated them in two engagements, and sailed to Constantinople, where they were welcomed by the Emperor and dismissed to their various homes.

We have no evidence as to the object of the expedition to Thessalonica, but it has been conjectured that the Macedonian Slavs, infected by rebellious movements of the Slavs in Greece, were in a disturbed state, and that the Bulgarian monarch seized the opportunity to annex to his own kingdom by peaceful means these subjects of the Empire. In support of this guess it may be pointed out that not many years later his power seems to have extended as far west as Ochrida, and there is no record of a conquest of these regions by arms. And a movement in this direction might also explain the war which broke out between Bulgaria and Servia in the last years of Theophilus.

About this time the Servians, who had hitherto lived in a loose group of independent tribes, acknowledging the nominal lordship of the Emperor, were united under the rule of Vlastimir into the semblance of a state. If it is true that the extension of Bulgarian authority over the Slavs to the south of Servia was effected at this epoch, we can understand the union of the Servian tribes as due to the instinct of self-defence. Hitherto they had always lived as good neighbours of the Bulgarians, but the annexation of western Macedonia changed the political situation. Vlastimir's policy of consolidating Servia may have been a sufficient motive with Malamir to lose no time in crushing a power which might become a formidable rival, and he determined to subjugate it. But it is not unlikely that the Emperor also played a hand in the game. Disabled from interfering actively by the necessities of the war against the Moslems, he may have reverted to diplomacy and stirred up the Servians, who were nominally his clients, to avert a peril which menaced themselves, by driving the Bulgarians from western Macedonia. The prospect of common action between the Empire and the Servians would explain satisfactorily Malamir's aggression against Servia. The war lasted three years, and ended in failure and disaster for the Bulgarians.

These speculations concerning the political situation in the Balkan peninsula in the last years of Theophilus depend on the hypothesis, which cannot be proved, that the Bulgarians had succeeded in annexing the Slavonic tribes to the west of Thessalonica. In any case, whatever may have occurred, the Thirty Years' Peace had been confirmed, and remained inviolate till its due termination in 845-846. It was not renewed, and soon afterwards a Bulgarian army under the general Isbules seems to have invaded Macedonia and operated in the regions of the Strymon and the Nestos; while the Imperial government retaliated by reinforcing the garrisons of the frontier forts of Thrace in order to carry out a systematic devastation of Thracian Bulgaria. This plan released Macedonia from the enemy; Isbules was recalled to defend his country. The absence of the Thracian and Macedonian troops, which these events imply, is explained, if they were at this time engaged in reducing the Slavs of the Peloponnesus.

These hostilities seem to have been followed by a truce, and soon afterwards Malamir was succeeded by his nephew Boris (c. 852). This king, whose reign marks an important epoch in the development of Bulgaria, was soon involved in war with the Servians and with the Croatians. He hoped to avenge the defeats which his uncle had suffered in Servia. But the Servians again proved themselves superior and captured Vladimir, the son of Boris, along with the twelve great boliads. The Bulgarian king was compelled to submit to terms of peace in order to save the prisoners, and fearing that he might be waylaid on his homeward march he asked for a safe-conduct. He was conducted by two Servian princes to the frontier at Rasa, where he repaid their services by ample gifts, and received from them, as a pledge of friendship, two slaves, two falcons, two hounds, and ninety skins. This friendship bore political fruits. The two princes were sons of Muntimir, one of three brothers, who, soon after the Bulgarian invasion, engaged in a struggle for supreme power, and when Muntimir gained the upper hand he sent his rivals to Bulgaria to be detained in the custody of Boris.

During the reign of Boris peace was maintained, notwithstanding occasional menaces, between Bulgaria and the Empire; and before the end of the reign of Michael III. the two powers were drawn into a new relation, when the king accepted Christian baptism. But the circumstances of this event, which is closely connected with larger issues of European politics, must be reserved for another chapter.

Chapter XII
The Conversion of the Slavs and the Bulgarians

§1. The Slavs in Greece

The ninth century was a critical period in the history of the Slavonic world. If in the year A.D. 800 a political prophet had possessed a map of Europe, such as we can now construct, he might have been tempted to predict that the whole eastern half of the continent, from the Danish peninsula to the Peloponnesus, was destined to form a Slavonic empire, or at least a solid group of Slavonic kingdoms. From the mouth of the Elbe to the Ionian Sea there was a continuous line of Slavonic peoples-the Abodrites, the Wilzi, the Sorbs, the Lusatians, the Bohemians, the Slovenes, the Croatians, and the Slavonic settlements in Macedonia and Greece. Behind them were the Lechs of Poland, the kingdom of Great Moravia, Servia, and the strongly organized kingdom of Bulgaria; while farther in the background were all the tribes which were to form the nucleus of unborn Russia. Thus a vertical line from Denmark to the Adriatic seemed to mark the limit of the Teutonic world, beyond which it might have been deemed impossible that German arms would make any permanent impression on the serried array of Slavs; while in the Balkan peninsula it might have appeared not improbable that the Bulgarian power, which had hitherto proved a formidable antagonist to Byzantium, would expand over Illyricum and Greece, and ultimately drive the Greeks from Constantinople. Such was the horoscope of nations which might plausibly have been drawn from a European chart, and which the history of the next two hundred years was destined to falsify. At the beginning of the eleventh century the Western Empire of the Germans had extended its power far and irretrievably beyond the Elbe, while the Eastern Empire of the Greeks had trampled the Bulgarian power under foot. And in the meantime the Hungarians had inserted themselves like a wedge between the Slavs of the north and the Slavs of the south. On the other hand, two things had happened which were of great moment for the future of the Slavonic race: the religion of the Greeks and the Teutons had spread among the Slavs, and the kingdom of Russia had been created. The beginnings of both these movements, which were slow and gradual, fall in the period when the Amorian dynasty reigned at New Rome.

It was under the auspices of Michael III that the unruly Slavonic tribes in the Peloponnesus were finally brought under the control of the government, and the credit of their subjugation is probably to be imputed to Theodora and her fellow-regents. The Slavs were diffused all over the peninsula, but the evidence of place-names indicates that their settlements were thickest in Arcadia and Elis, Messenia, Laconia, and Achaia. In the plains of Elis, on the slopes of Taygetos, and in the great marshlands of the lower Eurotas, they seem almost entirely to have replaced the ancient inhabitants. Somewhere between Sparta and Megalopolis was the great Slavonic town Veligosti, of which no traces remain. Of the tribes we know only the names of the Milings and the Ezerites. The Milings had settled in the secure fastnesses of Taygetos; the Ezerites, or Lake-men, abode in the neighboring Helos or marshland, from which they took their name. Living independently under their own zupans, they seized every favourable opportunity of robbery and plunder. In the reign of Nicephorus (A.D. 807) they formed a conspiracy with the Saracens of Africa to attack the rich city of Patrae. The strategos of the province whose residence was at Corinth, delayed in sending troops to relieve the besieged town, and the citizens suffered from want of food and water. The story of their deliverance is inextricably bound up with a legend of supernatural aid, vouchsafed to them by their patron saint. A scout was sent to a hill, east of the town, anxiously to scan the coast road from Corinth, and if he saw the approach of the troops, to signal to the inhabitants, when he came within sight of the walls, by lowering a flag; while if he kept the flag erect, it would be known that there was no sign of the help which was so impatiently expected. He returned disappointed, with his flag erect, but his horse slipped and the flag was lowered in the rider's fall. The incident was afterwards imputed to the direct interposition of the Deity, who had been moved to resort to this artifice by the intercessions of St. Andrew, the guardian of Patrae. The citizens, meanwhile, seeing the flag fall, and supposing that succour was at hand, immediately opened the gates and fell upon the Saracens and the Slavs. Conspicuous in their ranks rode a great horseman, whose more than human appearance terrified the barbarians. Aided by this champion, who was no other than St. Andrew himself, the Greeks routed the enemy and won great booty and many captives. Two days later the strategos arrived, and sent a full report of all the miraculous circumstances to the Emperor, who issued a charter for the Church of St. Andrew, ordaining that the defeated Slavs, their families, and all their belongings should become the property of the Church inasmuch as the triumph and the victory were the work of the apostle. A particular duty was imposed upon these Slavs, a duty which hitherto had probably been a burden upon the town. They were obliged to provide and defray the board and entertainment of all Imperial officials who visited Patrae, and also of all foreign ambassadors who halted there on their way to and from Italy and Constantinople. For this purpose they had to maintain in the city a staff of servants and cooks. The Emperor also made the bishopric of Patrae a Metropolis, and submitted to its control the sees of Methone, Lacedaemon, and Korone. It is possible that he sent military colonists from other parts of the Empire to the Peloponnesus, as well as to the regions of the Strymon and other Slavonic territories, and if so, these may have been the Mardaites, whom we find at a later period of the ninth century playing an important part among the naval contingents of the Empire. We may also conjecture with some probability that this settlement was immediately followed by the separation of the Peloponnesus from Hellas as a separate Theme.

It would be too much to infer from this narrative that the Slavonic communities of Achaia and Elis, which were doubtless concerned in the attack on Patrae, were permanently reduced to submission and orderly life on this occasion, and that the later devastations which vexed the peninsula in the reigns of Theophilus and Michael III were wrought by the Slavs of Laconia and Arcadia. It is more probable that the attack on Patrae was not confined to the inhabitants of a particular district; and that all the Slavs in the peninsula united in another effort to assert their independence before the death of Theophilus. Their rebellion, which meant the resumption of their predatory habits, was not put down till the reign of his son, and we do not know how soon. We may, however, conjecture that it was the Empress Theodora who appointed Theoktistos Bryennios-the first recorded member of a family which was long afterwards to play a notable part in history-to be strategos of the Peloponnesian Theme, and placed under his command large detachments from the Themes of Thrace and Macedonia, to put an end to the rapine and brigandage of the barbarians. Theoktistos performed efficiently the work which was entrusted to him. He thoroughly subjugated the Slavs throughout the length and breadth of the land, and reduced them to the condition of provincial subjects. There were only two tribes with whom he deemed it convenient to make special and extraordinary terms. These were the Milings, perched in places difficult of access on the slopes of Mount Taygetos, and the Ezerites in the south of Laconia. On these he was content to impose a tribute, of 6 0 nomismata on the Milings, and 300 on the Ezerites. They paid these annual dues so long at least as Theoktistos was in charge of the province, but afterwards they defied the governors, and a hundred years later their independence was a public scandal.

The reduction of the Peloponnesian Slavs in the reign of Michael prepared the way for their conversion to Christianity and their hellenization. The process of civilization and blending required for its completion four or five centuries, and the rate of progress varied in different parts of the peninsula. The Milings maintained their separate identity longest, perhaps till the eve of the Ottoman conquest; but even in the thirteenth century Slavonic tribes still lived apart from the Greeks and preserved their old customs in the region of Skorta in the mountainous districts of Elis and Arcadia. We may say that by the fifteenth century the Slavs had ceased to be a distinct nationality; they had become part of a new mixed Greek-speaking race, destined to be still further regenerated or corrupted under Turkish rule by the absorption of the Albanians who began to pour into the Peloponnesus in the fourteenth century. That the blending of Slavonic with Greek blood had begun in the ninth century is suggested by the anecdote related of a Peloponnesian magnate, Nicetas Kentakios, whose daughter had the honour of marrying a son of the Emperor Romanus I. He was fond of boasting of his noble Hellenic descent, and drew upon himself the sharp tongue of a distinguished grammarian, who satirized in iambics his Slavonic cast of features. But the process of hellenization was slow, and in the tenth century the Peloponnesus and northern Greece were still regarded, like Macedonia, as mainly Slavonic.

We can designate one part of the Peloponnesus into which the Slavonic element did not penetrate, the border-region between Laconia and Argolis. Here the old population seems to have continued unchanged, and the ancient Doric tongue developed into the Tzakonian dialect, which is still spoken in the modern province of Kynuria.

It is interesting to note that on the promontory of Taenaron in Laconia a small Hellenic community survived, little touched by the political and social changes which had transformed the Hellenistic into the Byzantine world. Surrounded by Slavs, these Hellenes lived in the fortress of Maina, and in the days of Theophilus and his son still worshipped the old gods of Greece. But the days of this pagan immunity were numbered; the Olympians were soon to be driven from their last recess. Before the end of the century the Mainotes were baptized.

§2. The Conversion of Bulgaria

Christianity had made some progress within the Bulgarian kingdom before the accession of Boris. It is not likely that the Roman natives of Moesia, who had become the subjects of the Bulgarian kings, did much to propagate their faith; but we can hardly doubt that some of the Slavs had been converted, and Christian prisoners of war seem to have improved the season of their captivity by attempting to proselytize their masters. The introduction of Christianity by captives is a phenomenon which meets us in other cases, and we are not surprised to learn that some of the numerous prisoners who were carried away by Krum made efforts to spread their religion among the Bulgarians, not without success. Omurtag was deeply displeased and alarmed when he was informed of these proceedings, and when threats failed to recall the perverts to their ancestral cult, he persecuted both those who had fallen away and those who had corrupted them. Amongst the martyrs was Manuel, the archbishop of Hadrianople. The most illustrious proselyte is said to have been the eldest son of Omurtag himself, who on account of his perversion was put to death by his brother Malamir.

The adoption of Christianity by pagan rulers has generally been prompted by political considerations, and has invariably a political aspect. This was eminently the case in the conversion of Bulgaria. She was entangled in the complexities of a political situation, in which the interests of both the Western and the Eastern Empire were involved. The disturbing fact was the policy of the Franks, which aimed at the extension of their power over the Slavonic states on their south-eastern frontier. Their collision with Bulgaria on the Middle Danube in the reign of Omurtag had been followed by years of peace, and a treaty of alliance was concluded in A.D. 845. The efforts of King Lewis the German were at this time directed to destroying the independence of the Slavonic kingdom of Great Moravia, north of the Carpathians. Prince Rostislav was making a successful stand against the encroachments of his Teutonic neighbours, but he wanted allies sorely and he turned to Bulgaria. He succeeded in engaging the cooperation of Boris, who, though he sent an embassy to Lewis just after his accession, formed an offensive alliance with Rostislav in the following year (A.D. 853). The allies conducted a joint campaign and were defeated. The considerations which impelled Boris to this change of policy are unknown; but it was only temporary. Nine years later he changed front. When Karlmann, who had become governor of the East Mark, revolted against his father Lewis, he was supported by Rostislav, but Boris sided with Lewis, and a new treaty of alliance was negotiated between the German and Bulgarian kings (A.D. 862).

Moravia had need of help against the combination of Bulgaria with her German foe, and Rostislav sent an embassy to the court of Byzantium. It must have been the purpose of the ambassadors to convince the Emperor of the dangers with which the whole Illyrian peninsula was menaced by the Bulgaro-German alliance, and to induce him to attack Bulgaria. The Byzantine government must have known much more than we of the nature of the negotiations between Boris and Lewis. In particular, we have no information as to the price which the German offered the Bulgarian for his active assistance in suppressing the rebellion. But we have clear evidence that the question of the conversion of Bulgaria to Christianity was touched upon in the negotiations. As a means of increasing his political influence at the Bulgarian court, this matter was of great importance to Lewis, and Boris did not decline to entertain the proposition. The interests of the Eastern Empire were directly involved. Bulgaria was a standing danger; but that danger would be seriously enhanced if she passed under the ecclesiastical supremacy of Rome and threw in her lot with Latin Christianity. It was a matter of supreme urgency to detach Boris from his connexion with Lewis, and the representatives of Rostislav may have helped Michael and his advisers to realize the full gravity of the situation. It was decided to coerce the Bulgarians, and in the summer of A.D. 863 Michael marched into their territory at the head of his army, while his fleet appeared off their coast on the Black Sea. The moment was favourable. Bulgarian forces were absent, taking part in the campaign against Karlmann, and the country was suffering from a cruel famine. In these circumstances, the Emperor accomplished his purpose without striking a blow; the demonstration of his power sufficed to induce Boris to submit to his conditions. It was arranged that Bulgaria should receive Christianity from the Greeks and become ecclesiastically dependent on Constantinople; that Boris should withdraw from the offensive alliance with Lewis and only conclude a treaty of peace. In return for this alteration of his policy, the Emperor agreed to some territorial concessions. He surrendered to Bulgaria a district which was uninhabited and formed a march between the two realms, extending from the Iron Gate, a pass in the Stranja-Dagh, northward to Develtos. It has been supposed that at the same time the frontier in the far west was also regulated, and that the results of the Bulgarian advance towards the Hadriatic were formally recognized.

The brilliant victory which was gained over the Saracens in the autumn of the same year at Poson was calculated to confirm the Bulgarians in their change of policy, and in the course of the winter the details of the treaty were arranged. The envoys whom Boris sent to Constantinople were baptized there; this was a pledge of the loyal intentions of their master. When the peace was finally concluded (A.D. 864-5), the king himself received baptism. The Emperor acted as his sponsor, and the royal proselyte adopted the name of Michael. The infant Church of Bulgaria was included in the see of Constantinople.

Popular and ecclesiastical interest turned rather to the personal side of the conversion of the Bulgarian monarch than to its political aspects, and the opportunity was not lost of inventing edifying tales. According to one story, Boris became acquainted with the elements of Christian doctrine by conversations with a captive monk, Theodore Kupharas. The Empress Theodora offered him a ransom for this monk, and then restored to him his sister who had been led captive by the Greeks and honourably detained in the Imperial palace at Constantinople, where she had embraced the Christian faith. When she returned to her country she laboured incessantly to convert her brother. He remained loyal to his own religion until Bulgaria was visited by a terrible famine, and then he was moved to appeal to the God whom Theodore Kupharas and his own sister had urged him to worship. There are two points of interest in this tale. It reflects the element of feminine influence, which is said to have played a part in the conversions of many barbarian chiefs, and which, for all we know, may have co-operated in shaping the decision of Boris; and it represents the famine, which prevailed in Bulgaria at the time of Michael's invasion, as a divine visitation designed to lead that country to the true religion. Another tale, which bears on the face of it a monkish origin, is of a more sensational kind. Boris was passionately addicted to hunting, and he desired to feast his eyes upon the scenes of the chase during those nocturnal hours of leisure in which he could not indulge in his favourite pursuit. He sent for a Greek monk, Methodius by name, who practised the art of painting, but instead of commanding him to execute pictures of hunting as he had intended, the king was suddenly moved by a divine impulse to give him different directions. "I do not want you to depict", he said, "the slaughter of men in battle, or of animals in the hunting-field; paint anything you like that will strike terror into the hearts of those that gaze upon it". Methodius could imagine nothing more terrible than the second coming of God, and he painted a scene of the Last Judgment, exhibiting the righteous receiving their rewards, and the wicked ignominiously dismissed to their everlasting punishment. In consequence of the terror produced by this spectacle, Boris received instruction in Christian doctrine and was secretly baptized at night.

In changing his superstition, Boris had to reckon with his people, and the situation tested his strength as a king. He forced his subjects to submit to the rite of baptism, and his policy led to a rebellion. The nobles, incensed at his apostasy, stirred up the people to slay him, and all the Bulgarians of the ten districts of the kingdom gathered round his palace, perhaps at Pliska. We cannot tell how he succeeded in suppressing this formidable revolt, for the rest of the story, as it reached the ears of Bishop Hincmar of Reims, is of a miraculous nature. Boris had only forty-eight devoted followers, who like himself were Christians. Invoking the name of Christ, he issued from his palace against the menacing multitude, and as the gates opened seven clergy, each with a lighted taper in his hand, suddenly appeared and walked in front of the royal procession. Then the rebellious crowd was affected with a strange illusion. They fancied that the palace was on fire and was about to fall on their heads, and that the horses of the king and his followers were walking erect on their hind feet and kicking them with their fore feet. Subdued by mortal terror, they could neither flee nor prepare to strike; they fell prostrate on the ground. When we are told that the king put to death fifty-two nobles, who were the active leaders of the insurrection, and spared all the rest, we are back in the region of sober facts. But Boris not only put to death the magnates who had conspired against his life; he also destroyed all their children. This precaution against future conspiracies of sons thirsting to avenge their fathers has also a political significance as a blow struck at the dominant race, and must be taken in connexion with the gradual transformation of the Bulgarian into a Slavonic kingdom.

Greek clergy now poured into Bulgaria to baptize and teach the people and to organize the Church. The Patriarch Photius indited a long letter to his "illustrious and well-beloved son", Michael, the Archon of Bulgaria, whom he calls the "fair jewel of his labours". In the polished style which could only be appreciated and perhaps understood by the well-trained ears of those who had enjoyed the privilege of higher education, the Patriarch sets forth the foundations of the Christian faith. Having cited the text of the creed of Nicaea and Constantinople, he proceeds to give a brief, but too long, history of the Seven Ecumenical Councils, in order to secure his new convert against the various pitfalls of heresy which lie so close to the narrow path of orthodox belief. The second part of the letter is devoted to ethical precepts and admonitions. Having attempted to deduce the universal principles of morality from the two commandments, to love God and thy neighbour as thyself, Photius traces the portrait of the ideal prince. Isocrates had delineated a similar portrait for the instruction of Nicocles, prince of Cyprus, and Photius has blended the judicious counsels of the Athenian teacher with the wisdom of Solomon's Proverbs and Jesus the son of Sirach. The philosophical reader observes with interest that it is not Christian but pre-Christian works to which the Patriarch resorts for his practical morality. Seldom has such a lecture been addressed to the patient ears of a barbarian convert, and we should be curious to know what ideas it conveyed to the Bulgarian king, when it was interpreted in Bulgarian or Slavonic. The theological essay of the Patriarch can hardly have simplified for the minds of Boris and his subjects those abstruse metaphysical tenets of faith which the Christian is required to profess, and the lofty ideal of conduct, which he delineated, assuredly did not help them to solve the practical difficulties of adjusting their native customs to the demands of their new religion.

Not only Greek priests, but Armenians and others, busied themselves in spreading their faith, and the natives were puzzled by the discrepancies of their teaching. A grave scandal was caused when it was discovered that a Greek who baptized many was not really a priest, and the unfortunate man was condemned by the indignant barbarians to lose his ears and nose, to be beaten with cruel stripes, and driven from the country which he had deceived. A year's experience of the missionaries by whom his dominion was inundated may probably have disappointed Boris. Perhaps he would not have broken with Byzantium if it had not become evident that the Patriarch was determined to keep the new Church in close dependence on himself, and was reluctant to appoint a bishop for Bulgaria. But it is evident that Boris felt at the moment able to defy the Imperial government. The strained relations which existed between Rome and Constantinople suggested the probability that the Pope might easily be induced to interfere, and that under his authority the Bulgarian Church might be organized in a manner more agreeable to the king's views. Accordingly he despatched ambassadors to Rome who appeared before Pope Nicolas (August 866), asked him to send a bishop and priests to their country, and submitted to him one hundred and six questions as to the social and religious obligations which their new faith imposed upon their countrymen. They also presented to him, along with other gifts, the arms which the king had worn when he triumphed over his unbelieving adversaries. Boris at the same time sent an embassy to King Lewis, begging him to send a bishop and priests. The Pope selected Paul, bishop of Populonia, and Formosus, bishop of Porto, as his legates, to introduce the Roman rites in Bulgaria, and add a new province to his spiritual empire. He provided them with the necessary ecclesiastical books and paraphernalia, and he sent by their hands a full reply in writing to the numerous questions, trivial or important, on which the Bulgarians had consulted him.

This papal document is marked by the caution and moderation which have generally characterized the policy of the ablest Popes when they have not been quite sure of their ground. It is evident that Nicolas was anxious not to lay too heavy a yoke upon the converts, and it is interesting to notice what he permits and what he forbids. He insists on the observance of the fasts of the Church, on abstinence from work on holy days, on the prohibition of marriages within the forbidden degrees. Besides these taboos, he lays down that it is unlawful to enter a church with a turban on the head, and that no food may be tasted before nine o'clock in the morning. On the other hand, he discountenances some taboos which the Greek priests had sought to impose, that it is unlawful to bathe on Wednesdays and Fridays, and to eat the flesh of an animal that has been killed by a eunuch. But he rules that it is not allowable to taste an animal which has been hunted by a Christian if it has been killed by a pagan, or killed by a Christian if it has been hunted by a pagan. The Bulgarians had inquired whether they should adopt the habit of wearing drawers; he replied that it was a matter of no importance. It was the custom for their king to eat in solitary grandeur, not even his wife was permitted to sit beside him. The Pope observes that this is bad manners and that Jesus Christ did not disdain to eat with publicans and sinners, but candidly affirms that it is not wrong nor irreligious. He bids them substitute the cross for the horse's tail which was their military standard. He strictly prohibits the practice of pagan superstitions, the use of healing charms, and swearing by the sword. He commands them to discontinue the singing of songs and taking of auguries before battle, and exhorts them to prepare for combat by reciting prayers, opening prisons, liberating slaves, and bestowing alms. He condemns the superstition of sortes biblicae to which the Greeks resorted.

A pleasing feature of the Pope's Responses is his solicitude to humanize the Bulgarians by advising them to mitigate their punishments in dealing with offenders. He sternly denounces, and supports his denunciation by the argument of common sense, the use of torture for extracting confessions from accused persons. He condemns the measures which had been taken to destroy the rebels and their families as severe and unjust, and censures the punishment which had been inflicted on the Greek who had masqueraded as a priest. He enjoins the right of asylum in churches, and lays down that even parricides and fratricides who seek the refuge of the sanctuary should be treated with mildness. But in the eyes of the medieval Christian, murder, which the unenlightened sense of antiquity regarded as the gravest criminal offence, was a more pardonable transgression than the monstrous sin of possessing two wives. "The crime of homicide", the Pope asserts, "the crime of Cain against Abel, could be wiped out in the ninth generation by the flood; but the heinous sin of adultery perpetrated by Lamech could not be atoned for till the seventy-seventh generation by the blood of Christ". The Bulgarians are commanded, not indeed, as we might expect, to put the bigamist to death, but to compel him to repudiate the unfortunate woman who had the later claim upon his protection and to perform the penance imposed by the priest.

The treatment of unbelievers was one of the more pressing questions which Nicolas was asked to decide, and his ruling on this point has some interest for the theory of religious persecution. A distinction is drawn between the case of pagans who worship idols and refuse to accept the new faith, and the case of apostates who have embraced or promised to embrace it, but have fallen back into infidelity. No personal violence is to be offered to the former, no direct compulsion is to be applied, because conversion must be voluntary; but they are to be excluded from the society of Christians. In the case of a backslider, persuasive means should first be employed to recall him to the faith; but if the attempts of the Church fail to reform him, it is the duty of the secular power to crush him. "For if Christian governments did not exert themselves against persons of this kind, how could they render to God an account of their rule; for it is the function of Christian kings to preserve the Church their mother in peace and undiminished. We read that King Nebuchadnezzar decreed, when the three children were delivered from the flames, 'Whosoever shall blaspheme the God of Shadrach, Meshach, and Abednego, shall perish, and their houses shall be destroyed'. If a barbarian king could be so wroth at blasphemy against the God of Israel because he could deliver three children from temporal fire, how much greater wrath should be felt by Christian kings at the denial and mockery of Christ who can deliver the whole world, with the kings themselves, from everlasting fire. Those who are convicted of lying or infidelity to kings are seldom if ever allowed to escape alive; how great should be the royal anger when men deny, and do not keep their promised faith to, Christ, the King of Kings and Lord of Lords. Be zealous with the zeal of God". Thus was the principle of the Inquisition laid down by Rome for the benefit of Bulgaria.

In the eyes of Boris the most important question submitted to the Pope was the appointment of a Patriarch. On this point Nicolas declined to commit himself. He said that he could not decide until he had heard the report of his legates; but he promised that in any case Bulgaria should have a bishop, and when a certain number of churches had been built, an archbishop, if not a Patriarch. The prospect of an archbishopric seems to have satisfied the king. He welcomed the papal legates and, expelling all other missionaries from the kingdom, committed to them exclusively the task of preaching and baptizing. Formosus succeeded so well in ingratiating himself, that Boris destined him for the future archbishopric; but the Pope declined to spare him from his Italian see, and sent out other bishops and priests, promising to consecrate as archbishop whichever of them the king should select.

The Latin ecclesiastics worked for more than a year (A.D. 866-867) in the land which the Pope hoped he had annexed to the spiritual dominion of Rome. Bulgaria, however, was not destined to belong to the Latin Church; her fate was linked in the religious as in the political sphere to Constantinople. But the defeat of papal hopes and the triumph of Byzantine diplomacy transcend the limits of the present volume.

§3. The Slavonic Apostles

The Slavonic land of Moravia, which extended into the modern Hungary as far eastward as the river Gran, was split into small principalities, the rivalries of whose lords invited the interference of the Franks. The margraves of the East Mark looked on the country as a client state; the archbishops of Passau considered it as within their spiritual jurisdiction; and German ecclesiastics worked here and there in the land, though Christian theology had penetrated but little into the wilds, and only by an abuse of terms could Moravia be described as Christian. The Moravian Slavs chafed under a dependency which their own divisions had helped to bring about, and we have seen how Rostislav, a prince who owed his ascendancy in the land to the support of King Lewis the German, sent an embassy to Constantinople.

Ecclesiastical tradition affirms that his envoys, who arrived at the court of Michael III. in A.D. 862-863,requested the Emperor to send to Moravia a teacher who knew Slavonic and could instruct the inhabitants in the Christian faith and explain the Scriptures. "Christian teachers have been amongst us already, from Italy, Greece, and Germany, teaching us contradictory doctrines; but we are simple Slavs and we want someone to teach us the whole truth".

We may confidently reject this account of the matter as a legend. The truth probably is that, when the Moravian embassy arrived, the Patriarch Photius saw an opportunity of extending the influence of the Greek Church among the Slavs, and incidentally of counteracting, in a new field, the forms of Western Christianity which he so ardently detested. The suggestion may have come to him from his friend Constantine the Philosopher, a man of Thessalonica, who had a remarkable gift for languages and was a master of that Slavonic tongue which was spoken in the regions around his birthplace.

There is not the least reason to suppose that the family of Constantine (more familiarly known under his later name of Cyril) was not Greek. His elder brother, Methodius, had entered the public service, had held the post of governor of some region where there were Slavonic settlements, and had then retired to a monastery on Mt. Olympus in Bithynia. Constantine (born about A.D. 827) had been devoted to learning from his youth. Legend says that at the age of seven years he had chosen, in a dream, Wisdom as his bride. The promise of his boyhood excited the interest of the statesman Theoktistos, who fetched him to Constantinople to complete his education. He pursued his studies under two eminent men of learning, Leo and Photius. But he disappointed the hopes of his patron, who destined him for a secular career and offered him the hand of his god-daughter, a wealthy heiress. He took orders and acted for some time as librarian of the Patriarch's library, a post which, when Photius was Patriarch, could not have been filled by one who was not exceptionally proficient in learning. But Constantine soon buried himself in a cloister, which he was with difficulty persuaded to leave, in order to occupy what may be described as an official chair of philosophy at Constantinople. His biographer says that he was chosen by the Emperor to hold a disputation with Saracen theologians on the doctrine of the Trinity. Subsequently he retired to live with his brother on Mount Olympus. He was in this retreat when envoys from the Chagan of the Khazars arrived at Constantinople and asked the Emperor to send him a learned man to explain the tenets of Christianity, so that the Khazars might judge between it and two other faiths, Judaism and Mohammadanism, which were competing for their acceptance. Michael, by the advice of Photius, entrusted the mission to Constantine, who, accompanied by Imperial envoys, travelled to Cherson with the embassy of the Khazars. At Cherson he remained some months to learn the Khazar language, and to seek for the body of St. Clement, the first bishop of Rome, who had suffered martyrdom in the neighbourhood. But St. Clement was a name almost forgotten by the natives, or rather the strangers, who inhabited Cherson; the church near which his coffin had been placed on the seashore was fallen into decay; and the coffin itself had disappeared in the waves. But it was revealed to the Philosopher where he should search, and under miraculous guidance, accompanied by the metropolitan and clergy of Cherson, he sailed to an island, where diligent excavation was at length rewarded by the appearance of a human rib "shining like a star". The skull and then all the other parts of what they took to be the martyr's sacred body were gradually dug out, and the very anchor with which he had been flung into the sea was discovered. Constantine wrote a short history of the finding of the relics, in which he modestly minimized his own share in the discovery; and to celebrate the memory of the martyr he composed a hymn and a panegyrical discourse. Of his missionary work among the Khazars nothing more is stated than that he converted a small number and found much favour with the Chagan, who showed his satisfaction by releasing two hundred Christian captives.

In this account of Constantine's career the actual facts have been transmuted and distorted, partly by legendary instinct, partly by deliberate invention. We need not hesitate to accept as authentic some of the incidents which have no direct bearing on his titles to fame, and which the following generation had no interest in misrepresenting. The date of his birth, for instance, the patronage accorded to him by the Logothete (Theoktistos), the circumstances that he taught philosophy and acted as librarian of the Patriarch, there is no reason to doubt. His visit to the Khazars for missionary purposes is an undoubted fact, and even the panegyrical tradition does not veil its failure, though it contrives to preserve his credit; but the assertion that he was sent in response to a request of the Chagan is of one piece with the similar assertion in regard to his subsequent mission to Moravia. His discovery of the body of St. Clement is a myth, but underlying it is the fact that he brought back to Constantinople from Cherson what he and all the world supposed to be relics of the Roman saint.

The visit to the Khazars may probably be placed in the neighbourhood of A.D. 860, and it was not long after Constantine's return to Constantinople that the arrival of the Moravian envoys suggested the idea of a new sphere of activity. We are quite in the dark as to how the arrangements were made, but it was at all events decided that Constantine and his brother Methodius should undertake the task of propagating Christianity in Moravia. They set out not later than in the summer of A.D. 864.

According to the naive story, which, as we have seen, represents Rostislav as begging for teachers, Constantine accomplished, in the short interval between the embassy and his departure, what was no less than a miracle. He invented a new script and translated one of the Gospels or compiled a Lectionary in the Slavonic tongue. If we consider what this means we shall hardly be prepared to believe it. The alphabet of the early Slavonic books that were used by Constantine and his brother in Moravia was a difficult script, derived from Greek minuscule characters, so modified that the origin can only be detected by careful study. It would have been impossible to invent, and compose books in, this Glagolitic writing, as it is called, in a year. It has been suggested that the Macedonian Slavs already possessed an alphabet which they employed for the needs of daily life, and that what Constantine did was to revise this script and complete it, for the more accurate rendering of the sounds of Slavonic speech, by some additional symbols which he adapted from Hebrew or Samaritan. His work would then have been similar to that of Wulfilas, who adapted the Runic alphabet already in use among the Goths and augmented it by new signs for his literary purpose. But we have no evidence of earlier Slavonic writing; and the Glagolitic forms give the impression that they were not the result of an evolution, but were an artificial invention, for which the artist took Greek minuscules as his guide, but deliberately set himself to disguise the origin of the new characters.

It must have been obvious to Constantine that the Greek signs themselves without any change, supplemented by a few additional symbols, were an incomparably more convenient and practical instrument. And, as a matter of fact, his name is popularly associated with the script which ultimately superseded the Glagolitic. The Cyrillic script, used to this day by the Bulgarians, Servians, and Russians, is simply the Greek uncial alphabet, absolutely undisguised, expanded by some necessary additions. That tradition is wrong in connecting it with Cyril, it is impossible to affirm or deny; it is certain only that he used Glagolitic for the purpose of his mission to Moravia and that for a century after his death Glagolitic remained in possession. To expend labour in manufacturing such symbols as the Glagolitic and to use them for the purpose of educating a barbarous folk, when the simple Greek forms were ready to his hand, argues a perversity which would be incredible if it had not some powerful motive. It has been pointed out that such a motive existed. In order to obtain a footing in Moravia, it was necessary to proceed with the utmost caution. There could be no question there, in the existing situation, of an open conflict with Rome or of falling foul of the German priests who were already in the country. Rostislav would never have acquiesced in an ecclesiastical quarrel which would have increased the difficulties of his own position. The object of Photius and Constantine, to win Moravia ultimately from Rome and attach her to Byzantium, could only be accomplished by a gradual process of insinuation. It would be fatal to the success of the enterprise to alarm the Latin Church at the outset, and nothing would have alarmed it more than the introduction of books written in the Greek alphabet. Glagolitic solved the problem. It could profess to be a purely Slavonic script, and could defy the most suspicious eye of a Latin bishop to detect anything Greek in its features. It had the further advantage of attracting the Slavs, as a proper and peculiar alphabet of their own.

But the important fact remains that the invention of Glagolitic and the compilation of Glagolitic books required a longer time than the short interval between the Moravian embassy and the departure of the two apostles. There is no ground for supposing, and it is in itself highly improbable, that the idea of a mission to that distant country had been conceived before the arrival of Rostislav's envoys. Moreover, if the alphabet and books had been expressly designed for Moravian use, it is hard to understand why Constantine should have decided to offer his converts a literature written in a different speech from their own. He translated the Scripture into the dialect of Macedonian Slavonic, which was entirely different from the Slovak tongue spoken in Moravia. It is true that the Macedonian was the only dialect which he knew, and it was comparatively easy for the Moravians to learn its peculiarities; but if it was the needs of the Moravian mission that provoked Constantine's literary services to Slavonic, the natural procedure for a missionary was to learn the speech of the people whom he undertook to teach, and then prepare books for them in their own language.

The logical conclusion from these considerations is that the Glagolitic characters were devised, and a Slavonic ecclesiastical literature begun, not for the sake of Moravia, but for a people much nearer to Byzantium. The Christianization of Bulgaria was an idea which must have been present to Emperors and Patriarchs for years before it was carried out, and Constantine must have entertained the conviction that the reception of his religion by the Bulgarian Slavs would be facilitated by procuring for them Scripture and Liturgy in their own tongue and in an alphabet which was not Greek. That he had some reason for this belief is shown by the resistance which Glagolitic offered in Bulgaria to the Greek (Cyrillic) alphabet in the tenth century. The Slavs of Bulgaria spoke the same tongue as the Slavs of Macedonia, and it was for them, in the first instance, that the new literature was intended. The Moravian opportunity unexpectedly intervened, and what was intended for the Slavs of the south was tried upon the Slavs beyond the Carpathians —experimentum in corpore vili.

If Constantine had been really concerned for the interests of the Moravians themselves, he would have written for them in their own language, not in that of Salonika, and in the Latin, not in an artificially barbarous or Greek, alphabet. But he was playing the game of ecclesiastical policy; Photius was behind him; and the interest of the Moravian adventure was to hoodwink and outmanoeuvre Rome.

The adventure was a failure so far as Moravia itself was concerned. It brought no triumph or prestige to the Church of Constantinople, and the famous names of Constantine and Methodius do not even once occur in the annals of the Greek historians.

The two apostles taught together for more than three years in Moravia, and seem to have been well treated by the prince. But probably before the end of A.D. 867 they returned to Constantinople, and in the following year proceeded to Rome, Pope Nicolas, hearing of their activity in Moravia, and deeming it imperative to inquire into the matter, had addressed to them an apostolic letter, couched in friendly terms and summoning them to Rome. They had doubtless discovered for themselves that their position would be soon impossible unless they came to terms with the Pope. The accession of Basil and the deposition of Photius changed the situation. A Patriarch who was under obligations to the Roman See was now enthroned, and Constantine and Methodius, coming from Constantinople and bearing as a gift the relics of St. Clement, could be sure of a favourable reception. They found that a new Pope had succeeded to the pontifical chair. Hadrian II., attended by all the Roman clergy, went forth at the head, of the people to welcome the bearers of the martyr's relics, which, it is superfluous to observe, worked many miracles and cures.

The Pope seems to have approved generally of the work which Constantine had inaugurated. Methodius and three of the Moravian disciples were ordained priests; but Moravia was not made a bishopric and still remained formally dependent on the See of Passau. Hadrian seems also to have expressed a qualified approval of the Slavonic books. The opponents of the Greek brethren urged that there were only three sacred tongues, Latin, Greek, and Hebrew, appealing to the superscription on the Cross. The Pope is said to have rejected this "Pilatic" dogma in its extreme form, and to have authorized preaching and the reading of the Scriptures in Slavonic; but he certainly did not, as was afterwards alleged, license the singing of the service of the Mass in the strange tongue, even though it were also chanted in Latin, nor did he cause the Slavonic liturgy to be recited in the principal churches of Rome.

At this time, the most learned man at Rome was the librarian Anastasius, who knew Greek, kept himself in contact with the Greek world, and translated into Latin the Chronicle of Theophanes. He made the acquaintance of Constantine, of whose character and learning he entertained a profound admiration. Writing at a later time to the Western Emperor, Anastasius mentions that Constantine knew by heart the works of Dionysios the Areopagite and recommended them as a powerful weapon for combating heresies. But the days of Constantine the Philosopher were numbered. He fell ill and was tonsured as a monk, assuming the name of Cyril. He died on February 14, A.D. 869, and his body was entombed near the altar in the church which had been newly erected in honour of St. Clement.

The subsequent career of Methodius in Moravia and Pannonia lies outside our subject. He was in an untenable position, and the forces against him were strong. He was determined to celebrate mass in Slavonic, yet he depended on the goodwill of the Roman See. His disciples, soon after their master's death, were compelled to leave the country, and they found a more promising field of work in Bulgaria, the land for which, as we have seen reason to think, Cyril's literary labours were originally intended.

Chapter XIII
The Empire of the Khazars and the Peoples of the North

§1. The Khazars

At the beginning of the ninth century the Eastern Empire had two dependencies, remote and isolated, which lived outside the provincial organization, and were governed by their own magistrates, Venice and Cherson. We have seen how Venice, in the reign of Theophilus, virtually became independent of Constantinople; under the same Emperor, the condition of Cherson was also changed, but in a very different sense-it was incorporated in the provincial system. The chief value of both cities to the Empire was commercial; Venice was an intermediary for Byzantine trade with the West, while Cherson was the great centre for the commerce of the North. And both cities lay at the gates of other empires, which were both an influence and a menace. If the people of the lagoons had to defend themselves against the Franks, the Chersonites had as good reason to fear the Khazars.

In the period with which we are concerned, it is probable that the Khan of the Khazars was of little less importance in the view of the Imperial foreign policy than Charles the Great and his successors. The marriage of an Emperor to the daughter of a Khazar king had signalised in the eighth century that Byzantium had interests of grave moment in this quarter of the globe, where the Khazars had formed a powerful and organized state, exercising control or influence over the barbarous peoples which surrounded them.

Their realm extended from the Caucasus northward to the Volga and far up the lower reaches of that river; it included the basin of the Don, it reached westward to the banks of the Dnieper, and extended into the Tauric Chersonese. In this empire were included peoples of various race-the Inner Bulgarians, the Magyars, the Burdas, and the Goths of the Crimea; while the Slavonic state of Kiev paid a tribute to the Chagan. The Caucasian range divided the Khazars from Iberia and the dependencies of the Caliphate; towards the Black Sea their neighbours were the Alans and the Abasgi; the Dnieper bounded their realm on the side of Great Bulgaria; in the north their neighbours were the Bulgarians of the Volga, and in the east the Patzinaks. All these folks came within the view of Byzantine diplomacy; some of them were to play an important part in the destinies of the Eastern Empire.

The capital of the ruling people was situated on the Caspian Sea, at the mouths of the Volga, and was generally known as Itil. It was a double town built of wood. The western town was named Saryg-shar, or Yellow City, in which the Chagan resided during the winter; over against it was the eastern town of Chamlich or Khazaran, in which were the quarters of the Mohammadan and the Scandinavian merchants. Chamlich seems to have lain on the eastern bank of the eastern branch of the river, while Saryg-shar was built on the island and on the western shore of the western mouth, the two portions being connected by a bridge of boats; so that Itil is sometimes described as consisting of three towns. The island was covered with the fields and vineyards and gardens of the Chagan.

Three other important towns or fortresses of the Khazars lay between Itil and the Caspian gates. Semender was situated at the mouth of the Terek stream at Kizliar. It was a place rich in vineyards, with a considerable Mohammadan population, who lived in wooden houses with convex roofs. The fortress of Belenjer, which lay on the lower course of the Sulek, on the road which leads southward from Kizliar to Petrovsk, seems to have played some part in the earlier wars between the Khazars and the Saracens. Further south still was the town of Tarku, on the road to Kaiakend and the Caspian gates.

The Arabic writers to whom we owe much of our knowledge of Khazaria suggest a picture of agricultural and pastoral prosperity. The Khazars were extensive sheep-farmers; their towns were surrounded by gardens and vineyards; they were rich in honey and wax; and had abundance of fish. The richest pastures and most productive lands in their country were known as the Nine Regions, and probably lay in the modern districts of Kuban and Ter. The king and his court wintered in Itil, but in the spring they went forth and encamped in the plains. According to one report, the Chagan had twenty-five wives, each the daughter of a king, and sixty concubines eminent for their beauty. Each of them had a house of her own, a qubba covered with teakwood, surrounded by a large pavilion, and each was jealously guarded by a eunuch who kept her from being seen. But at a later period a Chagan boasts of his queen, her maidens, and eunuchs, and we are left to wonder whether polygamy had been renounced or was deliberately concealed.

The Chagan himself seems to have taken no direct share in the administration of the state or the conduct of war. His sacred person was almost inaccessible; when he rode abroad, all those who saw him prostrated themselves on the ground and did not rise till he had passed out of sight. On his death, a great sepulchre was built with twenty chambers, suspended over a stream, so I hat neither devils nor men nor worms might be able to penetrate it. The mausoleum was called paradise, and those who deposited his body in one of its recesses were put to death, that the exact spot in which he was laid might never be revealed. A rider who passed it by dismounted, and did not remount until the tomb could be no longer seen. When a new Chagan ascended the throne, a silk cord was bound tightly round his neck and he was required to declare how long he wished to reign; when the period which he mentioned had elapsed, he was put to death. But it is uncertain how far we can believe the curious stories of the Arabic travellers, from whom these details are derived.

We have no information at what time the active authority of the Chagan was exchanged for this divine nullity, or why he was exalted to a position, resembling that of the Emperor of Japan, in which his existence, and not his government, was considered essential to the prosperity of the State. The labours of government were fulfilled by a Beg or viceroy, who commanded the army, regulated the tribute, and presided over the administration. He appeared in the presence of the Chagan with naked feet, and lit a torch; when the torch had burnt out he was permitted to take his seat at the right hand of the monarch. When evil times befell, the people held the Chagan responsible and called upon the Beg to put him to death; the Beg sometimes complied with their demand. The commander of an army who suffered defeat was cruelly treated: his wife, children, and property were sold before his eyes, and he was either executed or degraded to menial rank.

The most remarkable fact in the civilisation of this Turkish people was the conversion of the Chagan and the upper rank of society to Judaism. The religion of the Hebrews had exercised a profound influence on the creed of Islam, and it had been a basis of Christianity; it had won scattered proselytes; but the conversion of the Khazars to the undiluted religion of Jehovah is unique in history. The date of this event has been disputed, and the evidence variously assigns it to the first half of the eighth century or to the beginning of the ninth. There can be no question that the ruler was actuated by political motives in adopting Judaism. To embrace Mohammadanism would have made him the spiritual dependent of the Caliphs, who attempted to press their faith on the Khazars, and in Christianity lay the danger of his becoming an ecclesiastical vassal of the Eoman Empire. Judaism was a reputable religion with sacred books which both Christian and Mohammadan respected; it elevated him above the heathen barbarians, and secured him against the interference of Caliph or Emperor. But he did not adopt, along with circumcision, the intolerance of the Jewish cult. He allowed the mass of his people to abide in their heathendom and worship their idols.

The circumstances of the conversion are as uncertain as the date. Joseph, the Chagan whose Hebrew letter to the Rabbi Chisdai of Cordova in the tenth century is preserved, states that the Roman Emperor and the Caliph, whom he respectively styles the King of Edom and the King of the Ishmaelites, sent embassies laden with rich gifts and accompanied by theological sages, to induce his ancestor to embrace their civilisations. The prince found a learned Israelite and set him to dispute with the foreign theologians. When he saw that they could not agree on a single point, he said, "Go to your tents and return on the third day". On the morrow, the Chagan sent for the Christian and asked him, "Which is the better faith, that of Israel or that of Islam?" and he replied, "There is no law in the world like that of Israel". On the second day the Chagan sent for the learned Mohammadan and said, "Tell me the truth, which law seems to you the better, that of Israel or that of the Christians?" And the Mohammadan replied, "Assuredly that of Israel". Then on the third day the Chagan called them all together and said, "You have proved to me by your own mouths that the law of Israel is the best and purest of the three, and I have chosen it".

The truth underlying this tradition-which embodies the actual relation of Judaism to the two other religions-seems to be that endeavours were made to convert the Chagans both to Christianity and to Islam. And, as a matter of fact, in the reign of Leo III the Caliph Mar wan attempted to force the faith of Mohammad upon the Khazars, and perhaps succeeded for a moment. He invaded their land in A.D. 737, and marching by Belenjer and Semender, advanced to Itil. The Chagan was at his mercy, and obtained peace only by consenting to embrace Islam. As Irene, who married the Emperor Constantine V, must have been the daughter or sister of this Chagan, it is clear that in this period there were circumstances tending to draw the Khazars in the opposite directions of Christ and Mohammad. And this is precisely the period to which the evidence of the Letter of Joseph seems to assign the conversion to Judaism. We may indeed suspect that Judaism was first in possession —a conclusion which the traditional story unintentionally suggests. The Jewish influence in Khazaria was due to the encouragement given by the Chagans to Hebrew merchants. Of the Jewish port of Tamatarkha more will be said presently; and we may notice the Jewish population at Jundar, a town in the Caucasus, which was governed in the ninth century by a relation of the Chagan, who is said to have prayed impartially with the Moslems on Friday, with the Jews on Saturday, and with the Christians on Sunday.

Somewhat later in the eighth century a princess of the Khazars married the Saracen governor of Armenia, and there was peace on the southern frontier till the reign of Harun al-Rashid. In A.D. 798 another marriage alliance was arranged between a daughter of the Chagan and one of the powerful family of the Barmecides. The lady died in Albania on the way to her bridal, and the officers who were in charge of her reported to her father their suspicion that she had been poisoned. The suggestion infuriated the Chagan, and in the following year the Khazars invaded Armenia, by the Gates of Derbend, and returned with an immense booty in captives. Then Harun's son, Mamun, carried his arms victoriously into the land of the Khazars.

§2. The Subjects and Neighbours of the Khazars

The Khazars had never succeeded in extending their lordship over their neighbours the Alans, whose territory extended from the Caucasus to the banks of the river Kuban and was bounded on the west by the Euxine. The Alans, who have survived to the present day under the name of the Ossetians, were a mainly pastoral people; their army consisted in cavalry; and they had a fortress, which was virtually impregnable, at the so-called Alan-gate of the Caucasus or Pass of Dariel. We are told that the habitations of the people were so close together that when a cock crowed in one place he was answered by all the cocks in the rest of the kingdom. At some time before the tenth century the king adopted Christianity, but the mass of his subjects remained heathen. He received his Christianity from Constantinople, and the Emperors appropriated to him the special title of exusiastes. Between the Alans and the Khazars were the habitations of the Sarirs, a heathen people whose name does not come into the annals of Byzantium.

North of the Alans, between the rivers Kuban and Don, the territory of the Khazars extended to the shores of the Maeotic lake, and at the mouth of that water they possessed the important town of Tamatarkha, the modern Taman, which had arisen close to the ancient Phanagoria, over against the city of Bosporos on the other side of the straits. The commercial importance of Tamatarkha, which had a large Jewish population, will claim our attention presently. Bosporos itself, the ancient Pantikapaion, was under the control of the Khazars, and the Tetraxite Goths, who occupied the greater part of the Crimea, were subject to their sway. The Gothic capital, Doras, had been taken by the Khazars before A.D. 787, and in the following years the Goths, under the leadership of their bishop, had made an attempt to throw off the yoke of their powerful neighbours.

North of the Don and extending to the banks of the Dnieper were the tents and hunting-grounds of the Magyars or Hungarians. The continuous history of this Finnish people, who lived by hunting and fishing, begins in the ninth century, and if we think we can recognise it under other names in the days of Attila and the early migrations, our conclusions are more or less speculative. It is, however, highly probable that the Magyars had lived or wandered for centuries in the regions of the Volga, had bowed to the sway of the great Hun, and had been affected by the manners of their Turkish neighbours. They spoke a tongue closely akin to those of the Finns, the Ostyaks, the Voguls, and the Samoyeds, but it is likely that even before the ninth century it had been modified, in its vocabulary, by Turkish influence. A branch of the people penetrated in the eighth century south of the Caucasus, and settled on the river Cyrus, east of Tiflis and west of Partav, where they were known to the Armenians by the name of Sevordik or "Black children". These Black Hungarians, in the ninth century, destroyed the town of Shamkor, and the governor of Armenia repeopled it with Khazars who had been converted to Islam (A.D. 854-855).

On the northern shore of the Sea of Azov, and extending towards the Dnieper, was the land of the Inner or Black Bulgarians, which thus lay between the Magyars and the Goths. The lower Dnieper seems to have formed the western boundary of the Khazar Empire, but their influence extended up that river, over some of the Eastern Slavs. The Slavs round Kiev paid at one time tribute to the Chagan, who perhaps ensured them against the depredations of the Magyars.

On the central Volga was the extensive territory of the Burdas, who were subject to the Khazars, and formed a barrier against the Outer Bulgarians, their northern neighbours, whose dominion lay on the Volga and its tributary the Kama, including the modern province of Kasan.

If the Burdas served the Khazars as a barrier against the northern Bulgarians, they were also useful in helping to hold the Patzinaks in check. This savage people possessed a wide dominion between the Volga and the Ural; their neighbours were, to the north-west the Burdas, to the north the Kipchaks, to the east the Uzes, to the south-west the Khazars. It would seem that some of their hordes pressed early in the ninth century, west of the Volga, into the basin of the Don, and became the formidable neighbours of the most easterly Slavonic tribes.

§3. The Russians and their Commerce

Such, in the early part of the ninth century, was the general chart of the Turkish Empire of the Khazars, their clients, and their neighbours. Before we consider the import of this primitive world for the foreign policy of the Roman Empire, it is necessary to glance at yet another people, which was destined in the future to form the dominant state in the region of the Euxine and which, though its home still lay beyond the horizon of Constantinople and Itil, was already known to those cities by the ways of commerce. The Russians or Rus were Scandinavians of Eastern Sweden who, crossing the Baltic and sailing into the Gulf of Finland, had settled on Lake Ilmen, where they founded the island town, known as Novgorod, the Holmgard of Icelandic Saga, at the point where the river Volkhov issues from the northern waters of the lake. They were active traders, and they monopolized all the traffic of north-eastern Europe with the great capitals of the south, Constantinople, Baghdad, and Itil. Their chief wares were the skins of the castor and the black fox, swords, and men. The Slavs were their natural prey; they used to plunder them in river expeditions, and often carry them off, to be transported and sold in southern lands. Many of the Slavs used to purchase immunity by entering into their service. The Russians did not till the soil, and consequently had no property in land; when a son was born, his father, with a drawn sword in his hand, addressed the infant: "I leave thee no inheritance; thou shalt have only what thou winnest by this sword". They were, in fact, a settlement of military merchants-it is said their numbers were 100,000 — living by plunder and trade. They had a chief who received a tithe from the merchants.

The Russian traders carried their wares to the south by two river routes, the Dnieper and the Volga. The voyage down the Dnieper was beset by some difficulties and dangers. The boats of the Russians were canoes, and were renewed every year. They rowed down as far as Kiev in the boats of the last season, and here they were met by Slavs, who, during the winter had cut down trees in the mountains and made new boats, which they brought down to the Dnieper and sold to the merchants. The gear and merchandise were transhipped, and in the month of June they sailed down to the fort of Vytitshev, where they waited till the whole flotilla was assembled. South of the modern Ekaterinoslav the Dnieper forces its way for some sixty miles through high walls of granite rock, and descends in a succession of waterfalls which offer a tedious obstacle to navigation. The Slavs had their own names for these falls, which the Russians rendered into Norse. For instance, Vlnyi-prag was translated literally by Baru-fors, both names meaning "billowy waterfall", and this "force" is still called Volnyi, "the billowy". In some cases the navigators, having unloaded the boats, could guide them through the fall; in others it was necessary to transport them, as well as their freights, for a considerable distance. This passage could not safely be made except in a formidable company; a small body could have fallen a prey to predatory nomads like the Hungarians and the Patzinaks. On reaching the Black Sea, they could coast westwards to Varna and Mesembria, but their usual route was to Cherson. There they supplied the demands of the Greek merchants, and then rounding the south of the peninsula, reached the Khazar town of Tamatarkha, where they could dispose of the rest of their merchandise to the Jewish traders, who in their turn could transport it to Itil, or perhaps to Armenia and Baghdad. But the Russians could also trade directly with Itil and Baghdad. The Volga carried them to Itil, where they lodged in the eastern town; then they embarked on the Caspian Sea and sailed to various ports within the Saracen dominion; sometimes from Jurjan they made the journey with camels to Baghdad, where Slavonic eunuchs served as their interpreters.

This commerce was of high importance both to the Emperor and to the Chagan, not only in itself, but because the Emperor levied a tithe at Cherson on all the wares which passed through to Tamatarkha, and the Chagan exacted the same duty on all that passed through Chamlieh to the dominion of the Saracens. The identity of the amount of the duties, ten per cent, was the natural result of the conditions

§4. Imperial Policy. The Russian Danger

The first principle of Imperial policy in this quarter of the world was the maintenance of peace with the Khazars. This was the immediate consequence of the geographical position of the Khazar Empire, lying as it did between the Dnieper and the Caucasus, and thus approaching the frontiers of the two powers which were most formidable to Byzantium, the Bulgarians and the Saracens. From the seventh century, when Heraclius had sought the help of the Khazars against Persia, to the tenth, in which the power of Itil declined, this was the constant policy of the Emperors. The Byzantines and the Khazars, moreover, had a common interest in the development of commerce with Northern Europe ; it was to the advantage of the Empire that the Chagan should exercise an effective control over his barbarian neighbours, that his influence should be felt in the basin of the Dnieper, and that this route should be kept free for the trade of the north. It is not improbable that attempts had been made to convert the Khazars to Christianity, for no means would have been more efficacious for securing Byzantine influence at Itil. The Chagans were not impressed by the religion of Christ; but it was at least a matter for satisfaction at Byzantium that they remained equally indifferent to the religion of Mohammad.

While the relations of Constantinople and Itil were generally peaceful, there were, however, possibilities of war. The two powers were neighbours in the Crimea. We have seen how the sway of the Khazars extended over the Crimean Goths and the city of Bosporos or Kerch, and it was their natural ambition to extend it over the whole peninsula, and annex Cherson. The loss of Cherson, the great commercial port and market-place in the north-east, would have been a sensible blow to the Empire. There were other forts in the peninsula, in the somewhat mysterious Roman territory or frontier which was known as the Klimata or Regions. The business of defence was left entirely to the Chersonites; there was no Imperial officer or Imperial troops to repel the Khazars, who appear to have made raids from time to time. But Imperial diplomacy, in accordance with the system which had been elaborated by Justinian, discovered another method of checking the hostilities of the Khazars. The plan was to cultivate the friendship of the Alans, whose geographical position enabled them to harass the march of a Khazar army to the Crimea and to make reprisals by plundering the most fertile parts of the Khazar country. Thus in the calculations of Byzantine diplomacy the Alans stood for a check on the Khazars.

The situation at Cherson and the movements in the surrounding countries must have constantly engaged the attention of the Imperial government, but till the reign of Theophilus no important event is recorded. This Emperor received (c. 833) an embassy from the Chagan and the Beg or chief minister of the Khazars, requesting him to build a fort for them close to the mouth of the Don, and perhaps this fort was only to be the most important part of a long line of defence extending up that river and connected by a fosse with the Volga. Theophilus agreed to the Chagan's proposal. He entrusted the execution of the work to an officer of spatharo-candidate rank, Petronas Kamateros, who sailed for Cherson with an armament of ships of the Imperial fleet, where he met another contingent of vessels supplied by the Katepano or governor of Paphlagonia. The troops were re-embarked in ships of burden, which bore them through the straits of Bosporos to the spot on the lower Don where this stronghold was to be built. As there was no stone in the place, kilns were constructed and bricks were prepared by embedding pebbles from the river in a sort of asbestos. The fort was called in the Khazar tongue Sarkel, or White House, and it was guarded by yearly relays of three hundred men.

When Petronas returned to Constantinople he laid a report of the situation before the Emperor and expressed his opinion that there was grave danger of losing Cherson, and that the best means of ensuring its safety would be to supersede the local magistrates and commit the authority to a military governor. The advice of Petronas was adopted, and he was himself appointed the first governor, with the title of "Strategos of the Klimata". The magistrates of Cherson were not deposed, but were subordinated to the strategos.

In attempting to discover the meaning and motives of these transactions we must not lose sight of the close chronological connection between the service rendered by the Greeks to the

Khazars, in building Sarkel, and the institution of the strategos of Cherson. The latter was due to the danger of losing the city, but we are not told from what quarter the city was threatened. It is evident that the Khazars at the same moment felt the need of defence against some new and special peril. The fortification cannot have been simply designed against their neighbours the Magyars and the Patzinaks; for the Magyars and Patzinaks had been their neighbours long. We can hardly go wrong in supposing that the Khazars and the Chersonites were menaced by the same danger, and that its gravity had been brought home both to the Emperor and to the Khazar ruler by some recent occurrence. The jeopardy which was impending over the Euxine lands must be sought at Novgorod.

It was not likely that the predatory Scandinavians would be content with the gains which they earned as peaceful merchants in the south. The riches of the Greek towns on the Euxine tempted their cupidity, and in the reign of Theophilus, if not before, they seem to have descended as pirates into the waters of that sea, to have plundered the coasts, perhaps venturing into the Bosphorus, and especially to have attacked the wealthy and well-walled city of Amastris, which was said to have been saved by a miracle. We also hear of an expedition against the Chersonese, the despoiling of Cherson, and the miraculous escape of Sugdaia. Such hostings of Russian marauders, a stalwart and savage race, provide a complete explanation of the mission of Petronas to Cherson, of the institution of a strategos there, and of the cooperation of the Greeks with the Khazars in building Sarkel. In view of the Russian attack on Amastris, it is significant that the governor of Paphlagonia assisted Petronas; and we may conjecture with some probability that the need of defending the Pontic coasts against a new enemy was the motive which led to the elevation of this official from the rank of katepano to the higher status of a strategos.

The timely measures adopted by Theophilus were efficacious for the safety of Cherson. That outpost of Greek life was ultimately to fall into the hands of the Russians, but it remained Imperial for another century and a half; and when it passed from the possession of Byzantium, the sacrifice was not too dear a price for perpetual peace and friendship with the Russian state, then becoming a great power.

Some years after the appointment of the strategos of Cherson, Russian envoys arrived at the court of Theophilus (A.D. 838-839). Their business is not recorded; perhaps they came to offer excuses for the recent hostilities against the Empire. But they seem to have dreaded the dangers of the homeward journey by the way they had come. The Emperor was dispatching an embassy to the court of Lewis the Pious. He committed the Russians to the care of the ambassadors, and in his letter to Lewis requested that sovran to facilitate their return to their own country through Germany.

In their settlement at Novgorod, near the Baltic, the Russians were far away from the Black Sea, to the shores of which their traders journeyed laboriously year by year. But they were soon to form a new settlement on the Dnieper, which brought them within easy reach of the Euxine and the Danube. The occupation of Kiev is one of the decisive events in Russian history, and the old native chronicle assigns it to the year A.D. 862. If this date is right, the capture of Kiev was preceded by one of the boldest marauding expeditions that the Russian adventurers ever undertook.

In the month of June, A.D. 860, the Emperor, with all his forces, was marching against the Saracens. He had probably gone far when he received amazing tidings, which recalled him with all speed to Constantinople. A Russian host had sailed across the Euxine in two hundred boats, entered the Bosphorus, plundered the monasteries and suburbs on its banks, and overrun the Islands of the Princes. The inhabitants of the city were utterly demoralised by the sudden horror of the danger and their own impotence. The troops (Tagmata) which were usually stationed in the neighbourhood of the city were far away with the Emperor and his uncle; and the fleet was absent. Having wrought wreck and ruin in the suburbs, the barbarians prepared to attack the city. At this crisis it was perhaps not the Prefect and the ministers entrusted with the guardianship of the city in the Emperor's absence who did most to meet the emergency. The learned Patriarch, Photius, rose to the occasion; he undertook the task of restoring the moral courage of his fellow-citizens. If the sermons which he preached in St. Sophia were delivered as they were written, we may suspect that they can only have been appreciated by the most educated of his congregation. His copious rhetoric touches all sides of the situation, and no priest could have made better use of the opportunity to inculcate the obvious lesson that this peril was a punishment for sin, and to urge repentance. He expressed the general feeling when he dwelt on the incongruity that the Imperial city, "queen of almost all the world", should be mocked by a band of slaves, a mean and barbarous crowd. But the populace was perhaps more impressed and consoled when he resorted to the ecclesiastical magic which had been used efficaciously at previous sieges. The precious garment of the Virgin Mother was borne in procession round the walls of the city; and it was believed that it was dipped in the waters of the sea for the purpose of raising a storm of wind. No storm arose, but soon afterwards the Russians began to retreat, and perhaps there were not many among the joyful citizens who did not impute their relief to the direct intervention of the queen of heaven. Photius preached a sermon of thanksgiving as the enemy were departing; the miraculous deliverance was an inspiring motive for his eloquence.

It would be interesting to know whether Photius regarded the ceremony which he had conducted as a powerful means of propitiation, or rather valued it as an efficacious sedative of the public excitement. He and all who were not blinded by superstition knew well that the cause which led to the sudden retreat of the enemy was simple, and would have sufficed without any supernatural intervention. It is evident that the Russians became aware that the Emperor and his army were at hand, and that their only safety lay in flight. But they had delayed too long. Michael and Bardas had hurried to the scene, doubtless by forced marches, and they must have intercepted the barbarians and their spoils in the Bosphorus. There was a battle and a rout; it is possible that high winds aided in the work of destruction.

The Russians had chosen the moment for their surprise astutely. They must have known beforehand that the Emperor had made preparations for a campaign in full force against the Saracens. But what about the fleet? Modern historians have made this episode a text for the reproach that the navy had been allowed to fall into utter decay. We have seen, on the contrary, that the Amorians had revived the navy, and the impunity which the barbarians enjoyed until the arrival of the Emperor must be explained by the absence of the Imperial fleet. And, as a matter of fact, it was absent in the west. The Sicilian fortress of Castrogiovanni had been captured by the Moslems in the previous year, and a fleet of 300 ships had been sent to Sicily. The possibility of an attack from the north did not enter into the calculations of the government. It is clear that the Russians must have been informed of the absence of the fleet, for otherwise they would never have ventured in their small boats into the jaws of certain death.

The episode was followed by an unexpected triumph for Byzantium, less important in its immediate results than as an augury for the future. The Northmen sent ambassadors to Constantinople, and-this is the Byzantine way of putting it-besought the Emperor for Christian baptism. We cannot say which, or how many, of the Russian settlements were represented by this embassy, but the object must have been to offer amends for the recent raid, perhaps to procure the deliverance of prisoners. It is certain that some of the Russians agreed to adopt Christianity, and the Patriarch Photius could boast (in A.D. 866) that a bishop had been sent to teach the race which in cruelty and deeds of blood left all other peoples far behind. But the seed did not fall on very fertile ground. For upwards of a hundred years we hear no more of the Christianity of the Russians. The treaty, however, which was concluded between 860 and 866, led probably to other consequences. We may surmise that it led to the admission of Norse mercenaries into the Imperial fleet —a notable event, because it was the beginning of the famous Varangian service at Constantinople, which was ultimately to include the Norsemen of Scandinavia as well as of Russia, and even Englishmen.

It has been already observed that the attack upon Constantinople happened just before the traditional date of a far more important event in the history of Russia-the foundation of the principality of Kiev. According to the old Russian chronicle, Rurik was at this time the ruler of all the Scandinavian settlements, and exercised sway over the northern Slavs and some of the Finns. Two of his men, Oskold and Dir, set out with their families for Constantinople, and, coming to the Dnieper, they saw a castle on a mountain. On enquiry they learned that it was Kiev, and that its inhabitants paid tribute to the Khazars. They settled in the place, gathered many Norsemen to them, and ruled over the neighbouring Slavs, even as Rurik ruled at Novgorod. Some twenty years later Rurik's son Oleg came down and put Oskold and Dir to death, and annexed Kiev to his sway. It soon overshadowed Novgorod in importance, and became the capital of the Russian state. It has been doubted whether this story of the founding of Kiev is historical, but the date of the foundation, in chronological proximity to 860, is probably correct.

§5. The Magyars

The Russian peril had proved a new bond of common interest between the Empire and the Khazars, and during the reign of Michael (before A.D. 862), as we have seen, a Greek missionary, Constantine the Philosopher, made a vain attempt to convert them to Christianity.

About this time a displacement occurred in the Khazar Empire which was destined to led to grave consequences not only for the countries of the Euxine but for the history of Europe. At the time of Constantine's visit to the Khazars, the home of the Magyars was still in the country between the Dnieper and the Don, for either in the Crimea itself or on his journey to Itil, which was probably by way of the Don, his party was attacked by a band of Magyars. A year or two later the Magyar people crossed the Dnieper.

The cause of this migration was the advance of the Patzinaks from the Volga. We may guess that they were pressed westward by their Eastern neighbours, the Uzes; we are told that they made war upon the Khazars and were defeated, and were therefore compelled to leave their own land and occupy that of the Magyars. The truth may be that they made an unsuccessful attempt to settle in Khazaria, and then turned their arms against the Magyar people, whom they drove beyond the Dnieper. The Patzinaks thus rose above the horizon of the Empire and introduced a new element into the political situation. They had no king; they were organized in eight tribes, with tribal chiefs, and each tribe was subdivided into five portions under subordinate leaders. When a chief died he was succeeded by a first cousin or a first cousin's son; brothers and sons were excluded, so that the chieftainship should be not confined to one branch of the family.

The Magyars now took possession of the territory lying between the Dnieper and the lower reaches of the Pruth and the Seret —a country which had hitherto belonged to the dominion of the Khans of Bulgaria. They were thus close to the Danube, but the first use they made of their new position was not against Bulgaria. In A.D. 862 they showed how far they could strike by invading territories in central Europe which acknowledged the dominion of Lewis the German, the first of that terrible series of invasions which were to continue throughout a hundred years, until Otto the Great won his crushing victory at Augsburg. If we can trust the accounts of their enemies, the Magyars appear to have been a more terrible scourge than the Huns. It was their practice to put all males to the sword, for they believed that warriors whom they slew would be their slaves in heaven; they put the old women to death; and dragged the young women with them, like animals, to serve their lusts. Western writers depict the Hungarians of this period as grotesquely ugly, but, on the other hand, Arabic authors describe them as handsome. We may reconcile the contradiction by the assumption that there were two types, the consequence of blending with other races. The original Finnish physiognomy had been modified by mixture with Iranian races in the course of many generations, during which the Magyars, in the Caucasian regions, had pursued their practice of women-lifting.

Up to the time of their migration the Magyars, like the Patzinaks, had no common chieftain, but among the leaders of their seven tribes one seems to have had a certain preeminence. His name was Lebedias, and he had married a noble Khazar lady, by whom he had no children. Soon after the crossing of the Dnieper, the Chagan of the Khazars, who still claimed the rights of suzerainty over them, proposed to the Magyars to create Lebedias ruler over the whole people. The story is that Lebedias met the Chagan-but we must interpret this to mean the Beg-at Kalancha in the gulf of Perekop, and refused the offer for himself, but suggested Salmutzes, another tribal chief, or his son Arpad. The Magyars declared in favour of Arpad, and he was elevated on a shield, according to the custom of the Khazars, and recognized as king. In this way the Khazars instituted kingship among the Magyars. But while this account may be true so far as it goes, it furnishes no reason for such an important innovation, and it is difficult to see why the Khazar government should have taken the initiative. We shall probably be right in connecting the change with another fact, which had a decisive influence on Magyar history. Among the Turks who composed the Khazar people, there was a tribe — or tribes-known as the Kabars, who were remarkable for their strength and bravery. About this time they rose against the Chagan; the revolt was crushed; and those who escaped death fled across the Dnieper and were received and adopted by the Magyars, to whose seven tribes they were added as an eighth. Their bravery and skill in war enabled them to take a leading part in the counsels of the nation. We are told that they taught the Magyars the Turkish language, and in the tenth century both Magyar and Turkish were spoken in Hungary. The result of this double tongue is the mixed character of the modern Hungarian language, which has supplied specious argument for the two opposite opinions as to the ethnical affinities of the Magyars. We may suspect that the idea of introducing kingship was due to the Kabars, and it has even been conjectured that Arpad belonged to this Turkish people which was now permanently incorporated in the Hungarian nation.

Chapter XIV
Art, Learning and Education. The Amorian Period

Throughout the Middle Ages, till its collapse at the beginning of the thirteenth century, the Eastern Roman Empire was superior to all the states of Europe in the efficiency of its civil and military organization, in systematic diplomacy, in wealth, in the refinements of material civilization, and in intellectual culture. It was the heir of antiquity, and it prized its inheritance-its political legacy from Rome, and its spiritual legacy from Hellas. These traditions, no less than the tradition of the Church, which was valued most of all, may be said to have weighed with crushing force upon the Byzantine world; conservatism was the leading note of the Byzantine spirit. Yet though the political and social fabric always rested on the same foundations, and though the authority of tradition was unusually strong and persistent, the proverbial conservatism of Byzantium is commonly exaggerated or misinterpreted. The great upheaval of society in the seventh century, due to the successive shocks of perilous crises which threatened the state with extinction, had led to a complete reform of the military organization, to the creation of a navy, to extensive innovations in the machinery of the civil and financial government, to important changes in the conditions of the agricultural population and land-tenure; and it is a matter of no small difficulty to trace the organization of the eighth and ninth centuries from that of the age of Justinian. But even after this thoroughgoing transformation, the process of change did not halt. The Emperors were continually adjusting and readjusting the machinery of government to satisfy new needs and meet changing circumstances. The principles and the framework remained the same; there was no revolution; but there was constant adaptation here and there. It will be found, for instance, that the administrative arrangements in the twelfth century differ in endless details from those of the ninth. To this elasticity, which historians have failed to emphasize, the Empire owed its longevity. Byzantium was conservative; but Byzantine uniformity is a legend.

The history of the period described in this volume exhibits the vitality of the Empire. It experienced losses and reverses, but there are no such symptoms of decline as may be detected in the constitution of its rival, the Caliphate, and no tendencies to disintegration, like those which in the same period were at work in the Carolingian realm. The Amorian age, however, is apt to be regarded as an inglorious interval between the rule of the Isaurians who renovated the strength of the Empire and the brilliant expansion under Basil I and his successors. The losses of Crete and Sicily have been taken as a proof of decline; the character and the regime of Theophilus have been viewed with antipathy or contempt; and the worthlessness of Michael III has prejudiced posterity against the generation which tolerated such a sovran. This unfavourable opinion is not confined to the learned slaves of the Papacy, who are unable to regard with impartial eyes the age of Theophilus the enemy of icons, and of Photius the enemy of the Pope. The deepest cause of the prevalent view has been the deliberate and malignant detraction with which the sovrans and servile chroniclers of the Basilian period pursued the memory and blackened the repute of the Amorian administration; for modern historians have not emancipated themselves completely from the bias of those prejudiced sources.

In the foregoing pages we have seen that while even detraction has not ventured to accuse the Amorian rulers of exceptional rigour in taxing their subjects, the Empire was wealthy and prosperous. We have seen that it maintained itself, with alternations of defeat and victory, but without losing ground, against the Caliphate, that peace was preserved on the Bulgarian frontier, and that the reduction of the Slavs in Greece was completed. Oversea dominions were lost, but against this we have to set the fact that the Amorian monarchs, by taking in hand the reconstruction of the naval establishment, which the Isaurians had neglected, prepared the way for the successes of Basil I in Italy. We have still to see what services they rendered to art, education, and learning. In these spheres we shall find a. new pulse of movement, endeavour, revival, distinguishing the ninth century from the two hundred years which preceded it. We may indeed say that our period established the most fully developed and most pardonably self-complacent phase of Byzantinism.

It is a striking fact, and may possibly be relevant in this connexion, that the Armenian element, which had long been an ethnical constituent of the Empire, comes conspicuously forward in the ninth century. Before now, Hellenized Armenians had often occupied high posts, once even the throne; but now they begin to rise in numbers into social and political prominence. The pretender Bardanes, Leo V, Basil would not be significant if they stood alone. But the gifted family of the Empress Theodora was of Armenian stock; it included Manuel, Bardas, and Petronas. Through his mother, Photius the Patriarch; John the Grammarian and his brother (who held a high dignity), were also of Armenian descent; and Alexius Musele and Constantine Babutzikos are two other eminent examples of the Armenians who rose to high rank and office in the Imperial service. All these men were thorough Byzantines, saturated with the traditions of their environment; but their energy and ability, proved by their success, suggest the conjecture that they represented a renovating force which did much to maintain the vitality of the State.

§1. Art

It is commonly supposed that the iconoclastic movement was a calamity for art, and the dearth of artistic works dating from the period in which religious pictures were discouraged, proscribed, or destroyed, seems, at first sight, to bear out this opinion. If, however, we examine the facts more closely, we shall find that the iconoclastic age was far from being inartistic, and that it witnessed the insurrection of new ideas and tendencies which exercised a potent and valuable influence upon the religious art of the succeeding period. One immediate effect, indeed, which may be considered a loss and a calamity, the doctrine of the image-breakers produced. It exterminated a whole branch of art, it abolished sculpture. The polemic against images had carried weight with orthodox opinion so far that sculptured representations of holy persons or sacred scenes were discontinued by common consent. It was a partial victory for the iconoclasts, an illogical concession of the image-worshippers. No formal prohibition was enacted by Church or State; the rejection of plastic images was a tacit but authoritative decree of public opinion.

The iconoclastic sovrans were not unfriends of pictorial art as such. Two of the most illustrious and uncompromising, Constantine V and Theophilus, who desired to abolish entirely religious pictures of a monumental kind, sought a substitute in secular painting for the decoration of both sacred and profane buildings. The antique traditions of profane art had never disappeared in the Byzantine world, but they had become inconspicuous and uninfluential through the domination of religious art, with its fixed iconographic types, which had ascended to its highest plane of excellence in the sixth century. Under the auspices of the iconoclasts, profane art revived. Constantine V caused the church of Blachernae to be decorated with landscapes, trees, and birds and animals; Theophilus followed his example. This was not really a novelty; it was a return to the primitive decoration of early Christian churches, which had been gradually abandoned. Scenes de genre, pictures of the chase, scenes in the hippodrome, were demanded from the artists who adorned the halls of the Imperial Palace. Of such frescoes and mosaics we know only what chroniclers tell us, but some ivory coffers which were carved in the ninth century illustrate the revival of profane art under the iconoclasts. One of them may be seen in London, exhibiting scenes of pagan mythology, such as the rape of Europa and the sacrifice of Iphigeneia.

The taste for rich ornament also characterized this period, and did not expire with the defeat of iconoclasm. It is apparent in the description of the sumptuously decorated buildings of Theophilus; and Basil I., in the new palaces which he erected, did not fall behind the splendour of the impious. Amorian. This taste displayed itself also in the illumination of books, of which brilliant specimens are preserved dating from the tenth and eleventh centuries.

Even under the iconoclastic dispensation, artists who desired to represent religious subjects had an outlet for the expression of their ideas in the illustration of manuscripts. A psalter is preserved at Moscow which is supposed to have been written in the early part of the ninth century in the monastery of Studion. It is simply and elegantly illustrated by coloured vignettes in the margins, animated and realistic, free from the solemnity which we associate with Byzantine art. The proud who "set their mouth against the heavens and their tongue walketh through the earth" are portrayed by two bearded men with long tongues touching the ground, and upper lips, like beaks, which touch a bowl, surmounted by a cross, representing the sky.

The iconoclastic controversy itself supplied the monastic artists with motives to point the moral and adorn the text of sacred writ. In another psalter which must have been written in the generation succeeding the triumph of orthodoxy, the congregation of the wicked is exemplified by a picture of the Synod of 815. We see Leo the Amorian on a throne, the Patriarch Theodotos seated by his side, and two men defacing with long spears the icon of Christ. The assembling of the righteous is depicted as the Council of 843, where Jannes is trampled under foot by the orthodox Patriarch who holds the image of Christ in his hand, while above we see the Biblical sorcerer Simon hurled down by St. Peter. In another book of the same period, designed for popular instruction, the Physiologus, some of the illustrations are allusive to the recent controversy and inspired by monastic spite; but this manuscript exhibits at the same time the influence of the profane art which the iconoclasts had revived, in the realism of its pictures and in the pagan subjects, such as sirens, nymphs, and centaurs.

The employment of art in the service of controversy, or as an outlet for controversial spite, seems to be characteristic of the age. The archbishop Gregory Asbestas, the friend and supporter of Photius, had some skill in painting, and he illustrated a copy of the Acts of the synod which condemned Ignatius with realistic and somewhat scurrilous caricatures. At the beginning of the first Act he depicted the flogging of the Patriarch, above whose head was inscribed "the Devil". The second picture showed the bystanders spitting upon him as he was haled to prison; the third represented him, "the son of perdition", suffering dethronement; the fourth, bound in chains and going into exile. In the fifth his neck was in a collar; and in the sixth he was condemned to death. Each vignette had an insulting legend; and in the seventh, and last, the head of "Antichrist" was severed from his body. This manuscript, in a rich cover of purple silk, was found among the books of Photius, and was burned, with others, at the Eighth Ecumenical Council.

Enough has been said to indicate the significance of the iconoclastic movement for the history of art. A ban was placed on certain forms of pictorial work; but whatever temporary disadvantages this may be thought to have entailed, they were far outweighed by the revival of other styles which were in danger of complete extinction. If there had been no iconoclastic movement, the dead religious art of the seventh-century decadence might have continued, without reanimation, to the end. Under the Isaurian and Amorian dynasties profane art revived; there was a renaissance of the old picturesque decorative style which, originating in Alexandria, had spread over the world, and profoundly influenced the development of the art of the early Church. Alexandrine decoration, with its landscapes, idyllic scenes, mythological themes, still life, and realistic portraits, came to life again in the iconoclastic period; a school of secular artists, who worked for the Emperors and the Court, arose; and the spirit of their work, with its antique inspiration, did not fail to awaken religious painters from their torpor. For the second great period of her art, which coincided with the Macedonian dynasty, Byzantium was chiefly indebted to the iconoclastic sovrans. Or rather we should say that art revived under the Amorians, religious art under their successors.

Wealth was a condition of this artistic revival, of which a chief characteristic was rich and costly decoration. In the work of the age of Justinian the richness of the material had been conspicuous; in the subsequent period, when all the resources of the State were strained in a life and death struggle with formidable enemies, there were no funds for the luxuries of art. By the ninth century the financial prosperity of the Empire had revived; the Imperial coffers were well filled; and the Emperors could indulge their taste or their pride in artistic magnificence. In the flourishing condition of the minor arts of the jeweller and the enameller, from the ninth to the twelfth century, we may also see an indication of the wealth of Constantinople. Here, too, we may probably suspect oriental influence. The jewellers did not abandon repoussé work, but they devoted themselves more and more to the colour effects of enamel decoration; the richest altars and chalices, crosses and the caskets which contained crosses or relics, the gold and silver cups and vessels in the houses of the rich, gold-embroidered robes, the bindings of books, all shone with cloisonné enamels. The cloisonné technique was invented in the East, probably in Persia, and though it seems to have been known at Byzantium in the sixth century, we may ascribe its domestication and the definite abandonment of the old champ-levé method to the oriental influences of the ninth. Portable objects with enamel designs, as well as embroidered fabrics, easily travelled, and were frequently offered by the Emperors to foreign potentates; they must have performed an appreciable part in diffusing in Western Europe the influence of the motives and styles of Byzantine art.

§2. Education and Learning

Among the traditions which the Empire inherited from antiquity, one of the most conspicuous, but not perhaps duly estimated in its importance as a social fact, was higher education. The children of the well-to-do class, from which the superior administrative officials of the State were mainly drawn, were taught ancient Greek, and gained some acquaintance at least with some of the works of the great classical writers. Illiterateness was a reproach among reputable people; and the possession of literary education by laymen generally and women was a deep-reaching distinction between Byzantine civilisation and the barbarous West, where the field of letters was monopolized by ecclesiastics. It constituted one of the most indisputable claims of Byzantium to superiority, and it had an important social result. In the West the cleavage between the ecclesiastical and lay classes was widened and deepened by the fact that the distinction between them coincided with the distinction between learned and ignorant. In the East there were as many learned laymen as learned monks and priests; and even in divinity the layman was not helplessly at the mercy of the priest, for his education included some smattering of theology. The Patriarchs Tarasius and Nicephorus must have acquired, before they were suddenly moved into the spiritual order, no contemptible knowledge of theology; and Photius, as a layman, was a theological expert. Thus layman and cleric of the better classes met on common ground; there was no pregnant significance in the word clerk; and ecclesiastics never obtained the influence, or played the part, in administration and politics which their virtually exclusive possession of letters procured for them in Western Europe.

The circumstance, however it may be explained, that the period from the Saracen invasion in the reign of Heraclius to the beginning of the ninth century is sterile in literary productions, must not be suffered to obscure the fact that the traditions of literary education were not interrupted. There rose no men of eminent secular learning; the Emperors did not encourage it; but Homer did not cease to be read. The ninth century witnessed a remarkable revival of learning and philosophy, and it is highly probable that at Constantinople this intellectual movement stimulated general education, improved its standards, and heightened its value in public opinion. It is to be noticed that our oldest Byzantine manuscripts of classical writers date from this century, the age of Photius, who stands out, not only above all his contemporaries, but above all the Greeks of the Middle Ages, as a scholar of encyclopaedic erudition.

It is, however, in the field of philosophy and science, more definitely than in that of literature and rhetoric, that we can speak of a revival of learning at this period. During the reign of Michael III there were three eminent teachers of philosophy at Constantinople-Photius himself, Constantine who became the apostle of the Slavs, and Leo the mathematician. Both Leo and Constantine were official professors, endowed by the State, and the interest taken by the Court in science and learning is perhaps the greatest title of the Amorian dynasty to importance in the history of Byzantine civilisation. Since the age of Theophilus and Bardas, although some generations were not as fruitful as others, there was no interruption, no dark period, in the literary activity of the Greeks, till the final fall of Constantinople.

Theophilus was a man of culture, and is said to have been taught by John, whom he afterwards raised to the patriarchal throne, and who possessed considerable attainments in science and philosophy. His intimacy with the learned Methodius is also a sign of his interest in speculation. He seems to have realized what had not occurred to his predecessors, that it behoved a proud centre of civilisation like Byzantium to assert and maintain preeminence in the intellectual as well as in other spheres. Hitherto it had been taken for granted that all the learning of the world was contained within the boundaries of the Empire, and that the Greeks and Romans alone possessed the vessel of knowledge. Nobody thought of asking, Have we any great savants among us, or is learning on the decline? But the strenuous cultivation of scientific studies at Baghdad under the auspices of Harun and Mamun, and the repute which the Caliphs were winning as patrons of learning and literature, awakened a feeling at the Byzantine court that the Greeks must not surrender their preeminence in intellectual culture, the more so as it was from the old Greek masters that in many branches of science the Saracens were learning. If the reports of the magnificence of the palaces of Baghdad stimulated Theophilus to the construction of wonderful buildings in a new style at Constantinople, we may believe that Mamu's example brought home to him the idea that it was a ruler's duty to foster learning. We need not accept the story of the career of Leo, the philosopher and mathematician, as literally exact in all its details, but it probably embodies, in the form of an anecdote, the truth that the influence of suggestion was exercised by the court of Baghdad upon that of Byzantium.

Leo was a cousin of John the Patriarch. He had studied grammar and poetry at Constantinople, but it was in the island of Andros that he discovered a learned teacher who made him proficient in philosophy and mathematics. Having visited many monastic libraries, for the purpose of consulting and purchasing books, he returned to Constantinople, where he lived poorly in a cheap lodging, supporting himself by teaching. His pupils were generally successful. One, to whom he had taught geometry, was employed as a secretary by a strategos, whom he accompanied in a campaign in the East. He was taken prisoner and became the slave of a Saracen, who must have been a man of some importance at Baghdad and treated him well. One day his master's conversation turned on the Caliph, and he mentioned Mamun's interest in geometry. "I should like", said the Greek youth, "to hear him and his masters discourse on the subject". The presence in Baghdad of a Greek slave who professed to understand geometry came to the ears of Mamun, who eagerly summoned him to the Palace. He was confronted with the Saracen geometers. They described squares and triangles; they displayed a most accurate acquaintance with the nomenclature of Euclid; but they showed no comprehension of geometrical reasoning. At their request, he gave them a demonstration, and they inquired in amazement how many savants of such a quality Constantinople possessed. "Many disciples like myself" was the reply, "but not masters". "Is your master still alive?" they asked. "Yes, but he lives in poverty and obscurity". Then Mamun wrote a letter to Leo, inviting him to come to Baghdad, offering him rich rewards, and promising that the Saracens would bow their heads to his learning. The youth, to whom gifts and honours and permission to return to his country were promised if he succeeded in his mission, was dispatched as ambassador to Leo. The philosopher discreetly showed the Caliph's letter to Theoktistos, the Logothete of the Course, who communicated the matter to the Emperor. By this means Leo was discovered, and his value was appreciated. Theophilus gave him a salary and established him as a public teacher, at the Church of the Forty Martyrs, between the Augusteon and the Forum of Constantine.

Mamun is said to have afterwards corresponded with Leo, submitting to him a number of geometrical and astronomical problems. The solutions which he received rendered the Caliph more anxious than ever to welcome the eminent mathematician at his court, and he wrote to Theophilus begging him to send Leo to Baghdad for a short time, as an act of friendship, and offering in return eternal peace and 2000 pounds of gold. But the Emperor, treating science as if it were a secret to be guarded like the manufacture of Greek fire, and deeming it bad policy to enlighten barbarians, declined. He valued Leo the more, and afterwards arranged his election as archbishop of Thessalonica (c. 840). The interest of Mamun in science and learning is an undoubted fact. He founded a library and an observatory at Baghdad; and under him and his successors many mathematical, medical, and philosophical works of the ancient Greeks appeared in Arabic translations. The charge that the Arabic geometers were unable to comprehend the demonstrations of Euclid is the calumny of a jealous Greek, but making every allowance for the embellishments with which a story-teller would seek to enhance the interest of his tale, we may accept it as evidence for the stimulating influence of Baghdad upon Byzantium and emulation between these two seats of culture. And in this connexion it is not insignificant that two other distinguished luminaries of learning in this age had relations with the Caliphate. We have seen how John the Patriarch and Photius were sent on missions to the East. Constantine the Philosopher is said to have been selected to conduct a dispute with learned Mohammadans on the doctrine of the Trinity, which was held by the Caliph's request. The evidence for this dispute is unconvincing, yet the tradition embodies the truth that there was in the ninth century a lively intellectual interest among the Christians and the Mohammadans in the comparative merits of their doctrines. It is not impossible that there were cases of proselytism due not to motives of expediency but to conviction. The controversial interest is strongly marked in the version of the Acts of the Amorian Martyrs composed by Euodios, but the great monument the concern which the creed of Islam caused to the Greeks is the Refutation of Mohammad by Nicetas of Byzantium, a contemporary of Photius. The fanaticism of the two creeds did not exclude mutual respect. We have an interesting instance in the friendship of Photius with an Emir of Crete. The Patriarch, says one of his pupils, writing to the Emir's son and successor, "knew well that though difference in religion is a barrier, yet wisdom, kindness, and the other qualities which adorn and dignify human nature attract the affection of those who love fair things; and therefore, notwithstanding the difference of creeds, he loved your father, who was endowed with those qualities".

When Leo, as an iconoclast, was deposed from his see, he resumed the profession of teaching, and during the regency of Theodora there were three eminent masters at Constantinople-Leo, Photius, and Constantine. It was to Theoktistos that Constantine owed the official chair of philosophy which he was induced to accept; but Leo and Photius belonged to the circle of Bardas, who seems to have had a deeper and sincerer interest in intellectual things than either Theophilus or Theoktistos. To Bardas belongs the credit-and his enemies freely acknowledge it-of having systematically undertaken the task of establishing a school of learning. In fact, he revived, on new lines and apparently on a smaller scale, the university of Constantinople, which had been instituted by Theodosius II., and allowed to decay and disappear under the Heraclian and Isaurian dynasties. Leo was the head of this school of advanced studies, which was known as the School of Magnaura, for rooms in the palace of Magnaura were assigned for the purpose. His pupils Theodore, Theodegios, and Kometas became the professors of geometry, astronomy, and philology.

The intensity of this revival of profane studies, and the new prestige which they enjoyed, might be illustrated by the suspicious attitude of a monk like the Patriarch Ignatius towards secular learning. But the suspicion which prevailed in certain ecclesiastical or monastic circles is violently expressed in a venomous attack upon Leo the Philosopher after his death by one Constantine, a former pupil, who had discovered the wickedness of Hellenic culture. The attack is couched in elegiacs, and he confesses that he owed his ability to write them to the instruction of Leo:

I, Constantine, these verses wrought with skill,
Who drained the milk of thy dear Muse's rill.
The secrets of thy mind I searched and learned,
And now, at last, their sinfulness discerned.

He accuses his master of apostasy to Hellenism, of rejecting Christ, of worshipping the ancient gods of Greece:

Teacher of countless arts, in worldly lore
The peer of all the proud wise men of yore,
Thy soul was lost, when in the unhallowed sea
Thou drankest of its salt impiety.
he shining glory of the Christian rite
With its fair lustrous waters, the awful might
Of the great sacrifice, the saintly writ, —
Of all these wonders recking not one whit,
Into the vast and many-monster'd deep
Of heathen Greece did thy fair spirit leap,
The prey of soul-devouring beasts to be.
Who would not pity and make moan for thee?

Then a chorus of good Christians is invited to address the apostate who had made Zeus his divinity, in the following strain:

Go to the house of gloom, yea down to hell,
Laden with all thine impious lore, to dwell
Beside the stream of Pyriphlegethon,
In the fell plain of Tartarus, all undone.
There thy Chrysippus shalt thou haply spy,
And Socrates and Epicure descry,
Plato and Aristotle, Euclid dear,
Proclus, and Ptolemy the Astronomer,
Aratus, Hesiod, and Homer too
Whose Muse is queen, in sooth, of all that crew.

The satire was circulated, and evoked severe criticism. The author was sharply attacked for impiety towards his master, and some alleged that he was instigated by Leo's enemies to calumniate the memory of the philosopher. Constantine replied to these reproaches in an iambic effusion. He does not retract or mitigate his harsh judgment on Leo, but complacently describes himself as "the parricide of an impious master-even if the pagans (Hellenes) should burst with spite". His apology consists in appealing to Christ, as the sole fountain of truth, and imprecating curses on all heretics and unbelievers. The spirit of the verses directed against Hellenists may be rendered thus:

Foul fare they, who the gods adore
Worshipped by Grecian folk of yore!
Amorous gods, to passions prone,
Gods as adulterers well known,
Gods who were lame, and gods who felt
The wound that some mean mortal dealt;
And goddesses, a crowd obscene,
Among them many a harlot queen;
Some wedded clownish herds, I trow,
Some squinted hideously enow.

The sentiment is quite in the vein of the early Fathers of the Church; but it would not have displeased Xenophanes or Plato, and the most enthusiastic Hellenist could afford to smile at a display of such blunt weapons. The interest of the episode lies in the illustration which it furnishes of the vitality of secular learning in the ninth century. Though the charges which the fanatic brings against Leo may be exaggerations, they establish the fact that he was entirely preoccupied by science and philosophy and unconcerned about Christian dogma. The appearance of a man of this type is in itself significant. If. we consider that the study of the Greek classics was a permanent feature of the Byzantine world and was not generally held to clash with orthodox piety, the circumstance that in this period the apprehensions of fanatical or narrow-minded people were excited against the dangers of profane studies confirms in a striking way our other evidence that there was a genuine revival of higher education and a new birth of enthusiasm for secular knowledge. Would that it were possible to speak of any real danger, from science and learning, to the prevailing superstitions! Danger there was none. Photius, not Leo, was the typical Byzantine savant, uniting ardent devotion to learning with no less ardent zeal for the orthodox faith.

Another sign of the revival of secular studies is the impression which some of their chief exponents made on the popular imagination-preserved in the stories that were told of Leo, of John the Patriarch, and of Photius. It was said that when Leo was archbishop of Thessalonica the crops failed and there was a distressing dearth. Leo told the people not to be discouraged.

By making an astronomical calculation he discovered at what time benignant and sympathetic influences would descend from the sky to the earth, and directed the husbandmen to sow their seed accordingly. They were amazed and gratified by the plenteousness of the ensuing harvest. If the chronicler, who tells the tale, perfunctorily observes that the result was due to prayer and not vain science of the archbishop, it is clear that he was not unimpressed.

But Leo the astrologer escaped more easily than his kinsman John the Grammarian-the iconoclast Patriarch-who was believed to be a wicked and powerful magician. His brother, the patrician Arsaber, had a suburban house on the Bosphorus, near its issue from the Euxine, a large and rich mansion, with porticoes, baths, and cisterns. Here the Patriarch used constantly to stay, and he constructed a subterranean chamber accessible by a small door and a long staircase. In this "cave of Trophonius" he pursued his nefarious practices, necromancy, inspection of livers, and other methods of sorcery. Nuns were his accomplices, perhaps his "mediums" in this den, and scandal said that time was spared for indulgence in forbidden pleasures as well as for the pursuit of forbidden knowledge. An interesting legend concerning his black magic is related. An enemy, under three redoubtable leaders, was molesting and harassing the Empire. Theophilus, unable to repel them, was in despair, when John came to the rescue by his magic art. A three-headed statue was made under his direction and. placed among the statues of bronze which adorned the euripos in the Hippodrome. Three men of immense physical strength, furnished with huge iron hammers, were stationed by the statue in the dark hours of the night, and instructed, at a given sign, simultaneously to raise their hammers and smite off the heads. John, concealing his identity under the disguise of a layman, recited a magical incantation which translated the vital strength of the three foemen into the statue, and then ordered the men to strike. They struck; two heads fell to the ground; but the third blow was less forceful, and bent the head without severing it. The event corresponded to the performance of the rite. The hostile leaders fell out among themselves; two were slain by the third, who was wounded, but survived; and the enemy retreated from the Roman borders.

That John practised arts of divination, in which all the world believed, we need no more doubt than that Leo used his astronomical knowledge for the purpose of reading the secrets of the future in the stars. It was the medieval habit to associate scientific learning with supernatural powers and perilous knowledge, and in every man of science to see a magician. But the vulgar mind had some reason for this opinion, as it is probable that the greater number of the few men who devoted themselves to scientific research did not disdain to study occult lore and the arts of prognostication. In the case of John, his practices, encouraged perhaps by the Emperor's curiosity, furnished a welcome ground of calumny to the image-worshippers who detested him. The learning of Photius also gave rise to legends which were even more damaging and had a far more slender foundation. It related that in his youth he met a Jew who said, "What will you give me, young man, if I make you excel all men in Grecian learning?". "My father", said Photius, "will gladly give you half his estate". "I need not money", was the tempter's reply, "and your father must hear nought of this. Come hither with me and deny the sign of the cross on which we nailed Jesus; and I will give you a strange charm, and all your life will be lived in wealth and wisdom and joy". Photius gladly consented, and from that time forth he devoted himself assiduously to the study of forbidden things, astrology and divination. Here the Patriarch appears as one of the forerunners of Faustus, and we may confidently set down the invention of a compact with the Evil One to the superstition and malignancy of a monk. For in another story the monastic origin is unconcealed. John the Solitary, who had been conversing with two friends touching the iniquities of the Patriarch, dreamed a dream. A hideous negro appeared to him and gripped his throat. The monk made the sign of the cross and cried, "Who are you? who sent you?". The apparition replied, "My name is Lebuphas; I am the master of Beliar and the familiar of Photius; I am the helper of sorcerers, the guide of robbers and adulterers, the friend of pagans and of my secret servant Photius. He sent me to punish you for what was said against him yesterday, but you have defeated me by the weapon of the cross".

Thus the learning of Photius was honoured by popular fancy like the science of Gerbert; legend represented them both as sorcerers and friends of the devil.

The encyclopaedic learning of Photius, his indefatigable interest in philosophy and theology, history and grammar, are shown by his writings and the contents of his library. He collected ancient and modern books on every subject, including many works which must have been rarities in his own time and have since entirely disappeared. We know some of his possessions through his Bibliotheca, and the circumstances which suggested the composition of this work throw light on a side of Byzantine life of which we are seldom permitted to gain a glimpse. A select circle of friends seems to have been in the habit of assembling at the house of Photius for the purpose of reading aloud literature of all kinds, secular and religious, pagan and Christian. His library was thus at the service of friends who were qualified to appreciate it. His brother Tarasius was a member of this reading-club, and when Photius was sent on a mission to the East, Tarasius, who had been unable to attend a number of the gatherings, asked him to write synopses of those books which had been read in his absence. Photius complied with this request, and probably began the task, though he cannot have completed it, before his return to Constantinople.

He enumerates more than 270 volumes, and describes their contents sometimes very briefly, sometimes at considerable length. As some of these works are long, and as many other books must have been read when Tarasius was present, the reading stances must have continued for several years. The range of reading was wide. History was represented by authors from the earliest to the latest period; for instance, Herodotus, Ktesias, Theopompus, Dionysius of Halicarnassus, Appian, Josephus, Arrian, Plutarch, Diodorus, Dion Cassius, Herodian, Procopius, to name some of the most familiar names. Geographers, physiologists, writers on medicine and agriculture, grammarians, as well as orators and rhetoricians, furnished entertainment to this omnivorous society. All or almost all the works of the ten Attic orators were recited, with the exception of Lycurgus, whose speeches, we are expressly told, there was no time to read. We may note also Lucian, the life of Apollonius the Wonderworker by Philostratus, the lives of Pythagoras and Isidore, and a work on Persian magic. Fiction was not disdained. The romances of Iamblichus, Achilles Tatius, and Antonius Diogenes were read, as well as the Aethiopica of Heliodorus, which Photius highly appreciated. The theological and ecclesiastical items in the list largely preponderate; but it may gratify us to note that their proportion to the number of pagan and secular works is not more than double; and we may even suspect that if we could estimate not by the tale of volumes but by the number of words or pages, we should find that the hours devoted to Hellenic literature and learning were not vastly fewer than those which were occupied with the edifying works of the Fathers and controversial theologians. We are ourselves under a considerable debt to Photius for his notices of books which are no longer in existence. His long analysis of the histories of Ktesias, his full descriptions of the novel of Iamblichus and the romance of Thule by Antonius Diogenes, his ample summary of part of the treatise of Agatharchides on the Red Sea, may specially be mentioned. But it is a matter for our regret, and perhaps for wonder, that he seems to have taken no interest in the Greek poets. The Bibliotheca is occupied exclusively with writers of prose.

Photius gave an impulse to classical learning, which ensured its cultivation among the Greeks till the fall of Constantinople. His influence is undoubtedly responsible for the literary studies of Arethas, who was born at Patrae towards the close of our period, and became, early in the tenth century, archbishop of Caesarea. Arethas collected books.

In A.D. 888 we find him purchasing a copy of Euclid; and seven years later the famous manuscript of Plato, formerly at Patmos, and now one of the treasures of the Bodleian Library, was written expressly for him. Students of early Christianity owe him a particular debt for preserving apologetic writings which would otherwise have been lost.

It is notorious that the Byzantine world, which produced many men of wide and varied learning, or of subtle intellect, such as Photius, Psellos, and Eustathios-to name three of the best-known names,—never gave birth to an original and creative genius. Its science can boast of no new discovery, its philosophy of no novel system or explanation of the universe. Age after age, innumerable pens moved, lakes of ink were exhausted, but no literary work remains which can claim a place among the memorable books of the world. To the mass of mankind Byzantine literature is a dead thing; it has not left a single immortal book to instruct and delight posterity.

While the unquestioned authority of religious dogma, and the tyranny of orthodoxy, confined the mind by invisible fetters which repressed the instinct of speculation and intellectual adventure, there was another authority no less fatal to that freedom which is an indispensable condition of literary excellence as of scientific progress, the authority of the ancients. We have seen the superiority of the Eastern Empire to the contemporary European states in the higher education which it provided. In this educational system, which enabled and encouraged studious youths to become acquainted with the great pagan writers of Greece, we might have looked to find an outlet of escape from the theories of the universe and the views of life dogmatically imposed by religion, or at least a stimulus to seek in the broad field of human nature material for literary art. But the influence of the great Greek thinkers proved powerless to unchain willing skies, who studied the letter and did not understand the meaning. And so the effect of this education was to submit the mind to another yoke, the literary authority of the ancients. Classical tradition was an incubus rather than a stimulant; classical literature was an idol, not an inspiration. The higher education was civilizing, but not quickening; it was liberal, but it did not liberate.

The later Greeks wrote in a style and manner which appealed to the highly educated among their own contemporaries, and the taste of such readers appreciated and demanded an artificial and laboured style, indirect, periphrastic, and often allusive, which to us is excessively tedious and frigid. The vocabulary and grammar of this literature were different from the vocabulary and grammar of everyday life, and had painfully to be acquired at school. Written thus in a language which was purely conventional, and preserving the tradition of rhetoric which had descended from the Hellenistic age, the literature of Byzantium was tied hand and foot by unnatural restraints. It was much as if the Italians had always used Latin as their literary medium, and were unable to emancipate themselves from the control of Cicero, Livy, and Seneca. The power of this stylistic tradition is one of the traits of the conservative spirit of Byzantine society.

These facts bear upon the failure of Byzantine men of letters to produce anything that makes an universal appeal. Yet if the literature of the world is not indebted to the Byzantines for contributions of enduring value, we owe to them and to their tenacity of educational traditions an inestimable debt for preserving the monuments of Greek literature which we possess today. We take our inheritance for granted, and seldom stop to remember that the manuscripts of the great poets and prose-writers of ancient Greece were not written for the sake of a remote and unknown posterity, but to supply the demand of contemporary readers.

www.ingramcontent.com/pod-product-compliance
Ingram Content Group UK Ltd.
Pitfield, Milton Keynes, MK11 3LW, UK
UKHW021908190726
13853UKWH00002B/567